Applied Human Resource Management

Strategic Issues and Experiential Exercises

Kenneth M. York
Oakland University

SAGE
Los Angeles • London • New Delhi • Singapore • Washington DC

For information:

SAGE Publications, Inc.
2455 Teller Road
Thousand Oaks, California 91320
E-mail: order@sagepub.com

SAGE Publications Ltd.
1 Oliver's Yard
55 City Road
London EC1Y 1SP
United Kingdom

SAGE Publications India Pvt. Ltd.
B 1/I 1 Mohan Cooperative Industrial Area
Mathura Road, New Delhi 110 044
India

SAGE Publications Asia-Pacific Pte. Ltd.
33 Pekin Street #02-01
Far East Square
Singapore 048763

Printed in the United States of America

Library of Congress Cataloging-in-Publication Data

York, Kenneth M.
Applied human resource management: strategic issues and experiential exercises/Kenneth M. York.
p. cm.
Includes bibliographical references and index.
ISBN 978-1-4129-5491-4 (cloth)
ISBN 978-1-4129-5492-1 (pbk.)
1. Personnel management. I. Title.

HF5549.Y58 2009
658.3—dc22 2008036880

This book is printed on acid-free paper.

09 10 11 12 13 10 9 8 7 6 5 4 3 2 1

Acquisitions Editor: Lisa Cuevas Shaw
Editorial Assistant: MaryAnn Vail
Production Editor: Catherine M. Chilton
Copy Editor: Youn-Joo Park
Typesetter: C&M Digitals (P) Ltd.
Proofreader: Doris Hus
Indexer: Hyde Park Publishing Services LLC
Cover Designer: Candice Harman
Marketing Manager: Jennifer Reed Banando

Contents

Human Resource Certification Institute Body of Knowledge		
Body of Knowledge	*Chapter*	*Exercise*
Strategic Management	Chapter 1: Introduction to the Management of Human Resources	• Strategic Issues in HRM: HRM as a Partner in Strategic Planning • Strategic Issues in HRM: What Everyone Knows Is True About HRM (and isn't) • Strategic Issues in HRM: The Cost of Efficiency • Strategic Issues in HRM: The HR Scorecard
	Chapter 2: Equal Employment Opportunity	• Strategic Issues in HRM: The Unavoidable Lawsuit? • Strategic Issues in HRM: Sexual Harassment in the Workplace • Strategic Issues in HRM: Age Discrimination, Retirement, and Bridge Employment • Strategic Issues in HRM: Checking References and Giving References
	Chapter 3: Job Analysis	• Strategic Issues in HRM: Essential and Nonessential Job Functions • Strategic Issues in HRM: Job Descriptions in Team-Based Organizations • Strategic Issues in HRM: Personality Traits as a Position Requirement • Strategic Issues in HRM: Selecting for the Job or the Organization
	Chapter 4: Recruitment and Socialization	• Strategic Issues in HRM: Recruiting for Executive Positions • Strategic Issues in HRM: Volunteer Employees • Strategic Issues in HRM: Recruitment and Turnover • Strategic Issues in HRM: On-Boarding
	Chapter 5: Selection	• Strategic Issues in HRM: Equal Employment Opportunity Postures • Strategic Issues in HRM: Adverse Impact in Mortgage Lending • Strategic Issues in HRM: What Is a Fair Selection Test? • Strategic Issues in HRM: When Is an Applicant Really an Applicant? • Strategic Issues in HRM: Honesty Testing • Strategic Issues in HRM: Predictive and Concurrent Validation Studies

Body of Knowledge	*Chapter*	*Exercise*
	Chapter 6: Performance Appraisal	• Strategic Issues in HRM: Reward, Develop, Promote • Strategic Issues in HRM: Graphic Rating Scales Versus BARS • Strategic Issues in HRM: Rater Error Training Versus Rater Accuracy Training • Strategic Issues in HRM: Sex Discrimination in Performance Appraisal
	Chapter 7: Training and Developing Employees	• Strategic Issues in HRM: Employee Development and Turnover • Strategic Issues in HRM: Ways to Manage • Strategic Issues in HRM: The Role of the Manager • Strategic Issues in HRM: Systems Thinking
	Chapter 8: Compensation and Benefits	• Strategic Issues in HRM: A Fair Day's Work for a Fair Day's Pay • Strategic Issues in HRM: Pay Secrecy • Strategic Issues in HRM: Sharing Salary Information and Antitrust • Strategic Issues in HRM: Equal Pay and Comparable Worth
	Chapter 9: Occupational Safety and Health	• Strategic Issues in HRM: Selecting Safe Employees • Strategic Issues in HRM: Repetitive Strain Injury • Strategic Issues in HRM: Drug Testing • Strategic Issues in HRM: Biorhythms and Accidents
	Chapter 10: Employee Relations and Labor/ Management Relations	• Strategic Issues in HRM: Interest-Based Bargaining • Strategic Issues in HRM: Graduate Student Unions • Strategic Issues in HRM: Unions, Wages, and Financial Performance • Strategic Issues in HRM: Unionized Professionals
	Chapter 11: Organizational Change and Development	• Strategic Issues in HRM: Professional Employer Organizations • Strategic Issues in HRM: Entropy in Organizations

(Continued)

(Continued)

Body of Knowledge	*Chapter*	*Exercise*
		• Strategic Issues in HRM: Technology-Driven Change • Strategic Issues in HRM: Downsizing
	Chapter 12: International HRM	• Strategic Issues in HRM: Global Recruiting on the Internet • Strategic Issues in HRM: Global Compensation • Strategic Issues in HRM: Global Virtual Teams • Strategic Issues in HRM: Adapting to Life in the United States • Application: International Business Literacy
Workforce Planning and Employment	Chapter 2: Equal Employment Opportunity	• Application: Completing the EEO-1 Report • Application: Determining the Adverse Impact of a Selection Procedure • Experiential Exercise: Identifying Barriers to Access in the Workplace • Experiential Exercise: Internet Applications and Illegal Pre-employment Inquiries • Creative Exercise: Making Reasonable Accommodations Under the Americans With Disabilities Act • Creative Exercise: Creating a Sexual Harassment Prevention Program
	Chapter 3: Job Analysis	• Application: Matching Job Titles and Job Descriptions • Application: A TQM Approach to Writing Job Descriptions • Experiential Exercise: Mission to Mars • Experiential Exercise: Job Analysis Interview of a College or University Professor • Creative Exercise: Writing Job Descriptions • Creative Exercise: Job Analysis
	Chapter 4: Recruitment and Socialization	• Application: Job Hunting • Application: Applicant Pools for Part-Time Workers • Experiential Exercise: Realistic Job Previews • Experiential Exercise: Writing an Effective Radio Advertisement • Creative Exercise: Socialization of Newcomers • Creative Exercise: Measuring the Effectiveness of Recruitment

Body of Knowledge	*Chapter*	*Exercise*
	Chapter 5: Selection	• Application: Using the Mental Measurement Yearbook to Choose a Selection Test • Application: Measuring the Reliability of a Selection Test • Application: Measuring the Validity of a Selection Test • Application: Determining Whether a Selection Test Has Adverse Impact • Application: Evaluating Whether to Upgrade to a New Test • Application: Using an Affirmative Action Plan • Application: Expanded Protection for Workers in State Equal Employment Opportunity Laws • Experiential Exercise: Test Validation • Experiential Exercise: Creating and Using a Structured Interview Guide • Creative Exercise: Developing an In-Basket • Creative Exercise: Creating an Assessment Center
	Chapter 12: International HRM	• Experiential Exercise: Expatriate Selection • Experiential Exercise: Expatriate Socialization • Creative Exercise: Training Employees for an International Assignment • Creative Exercise: Returning to Headquarters
Human Resource Development	Chapter 6: Performance Appraisal	• Application: Developing Performance Dimensions • Application: Rating Errors in Performance Appraisal • Experiential Exercise: Selecting Players for the All-Star Game • Experiential Exercise: Using a Graphic Rating Scale • Creative Exercise: Developing a Graphic Rating Scale • Creative Exercise: Creating a Faculty Evaluation Form
	Chapter 7: Training and Developing Employees	• Application: Calculating the Utility of a Training Program • Application: My Dream Job • Experiential Exercise: Conducting a Training Needs Assessment

(Continued)

(Continued)

Body of Knowledge	*Chapter*	*Exercise*
		• Experiential Exercise: Assessment Center for Management Development • Experiential Exercise: Dealing With a Plateaued Employee • Creative Exercise: Developing Management Talent • Creative Exercise: Creating Team-Building Exercises
	Chapter 11: Organizational Change and Development	• Application: Cross-Functional Organizational Development • Application: Re-engineer This • Experiential Exercise: The New Manager • Experiential Exercise: The Value of a College Education • Creative Exercise: Managing Change • Creative Exercise: Developing a Valuing Diversity Program
Total Rewards	Chapter 8: Compensation and Benefits	• Application: Federal and State Minimum Wage Laws • Application: Evaluation of Exempt Versus Nonexempt Jobs • Experiential Exercise: Choose the Investments for Your 401(k) Plan • Experiential Exercise: Gender Bias in Wage Rates • Creative Exercise: Developing a Merit Pay Plan for Teams • Creative Exercise: Job Evaluation for University Professors
Employee and Labor Relations	Chapter 10: Employee Relations and Labor-Management Relations	• Application: National Labor Relations Board Cases • Application: Family-Friendly Workplaces • Experiential Exercise: Assessment of Employee Opinions • Experiential Exercise: Indie Phenom Makes Jump to Big Bucks Pic • Creative Exercise: Redesigning a Job Creative Exercise: Dancing Is Life
Risk Management	Chapter 9: Occupational Safety and Health	• Application: What Are the Most Hazardous Occupations? • Application: Calculating Incidence Rates • Experiential Exercise: OSHA Compliance

Body of Knowledge	*Chapter*	*Exercise*
		• Experiential Exercise: Drug Testing • Creative Exercise: Stress and Burnout • Creative Exercise: Reducing the Risks of High-Risk Employees
	Chapter 12: International HRM	• Application: Host Country Employment Laws

SOURCE: Human Resource Certification Institute, 2008.

Preface

Human Resources Management is only important for organizations that have people in them.

The organization of this book is designed to give instructors flexibility in how they teach their students human resource management concepts. Within each chapter, there are 10 different topics in 4 different types of exercises. Instructors can choose the topics and exercises that best meet their objectives for what and how they want their students to learn. Each exercise is followed by a list of resources, which go beyond the material presented in the exercise, for further exploration of the topic.

Strategic Issues in Human Resource Management describe issues that organizations must deal with to effectively manage their human resources. Each strategic issue includes a set of related questions for students to answer. These questions might be used as the basis of a class discussion, homework assignments, topics for group presentations, or as essay test questions.

Applications are brief projects in which some HRM concept is applied to a practical HRM situation. Each application gives students an opportunity to apply what they have learned in a realistic situation. These exercises could be given as homework assignments; instructor illustrations and demonstrations; or done in class by students, individually or in teams.

Experiential Exercises are more extensive hands-on interactive learning experiences in which students learn by doing. The experiential exercises provide a realistic context for learning about HRM. These exercises are designed to be in-class exercises.

Creative Exercises are open-ended projects with specific deliverables, but with multiple possible solutions. The creative exercises are designed to go beyond the typical experiential exercise; they are "weak situations" in which each student or team may develop a different solution to the problem, and students learn both from their solution to the problem and the different solutions of others.

Introduction to the Management of Human Resources 1

Strategic Objective

The purpose of human resource management (HRM) is to manage the people who run the organization. Just as organizations must effectively manage their physical, capital, and information resources, they must also effectively manage their human resources—the people who run the organization. Organizations must recruit, select, and retain qualified people to perform important tasks, motivate them, and train them to maintain and improve their job skills. Organizations must forecast their human resources needs by accurately predicting how many people with specific job skills will be needed in the near future and in the long term. Policies must be established specifying how much each employee in a specific job will be paid, what percentage of the pay will be based on job performance, and whether workers in that job will be paid incentives or commission or salary. Policies must also be established to provide workers with legally required benefits such as family and medical leave and provide other benefits that can be used to attract qualified applicants and retain productive employees. The organization must establish methods to appraise the job performance of workers, discipline and grievance procedures to resolve conflicts between supervisors and workers, and programs to protect workers' health and safety. And the organization must monitor its compliance with laws protecting applicants and employees from discrimination and unfair labor practices.

The human resources of an organization are different from the physical, capital, and information resources. Physical, capital, and information resources are typically treated as investments, with decisions about investments made based on costs and benefits, risks, and returns. An investment in a piece of machinery may improve productivity enough to justify its cost, but the value of physical assets such as tools and machinery typically declines over time. Conversely, employees gain knowledge and experience over time, so their value appreciates rather than depreciates. Despite this, organizations have two significant disincentives to investments in human resources. First, employees are not a physical asset like a piece of machinery that is owned. An investment in an employee to improve the employee's individual capability may justify the cost of training by making the employee more productive, but also carries the risk that the employee will leave the organization, because the employee's increased capability has made the employee a more valuable resource to another organization. Second, investments in human resources are not reflected in the balance sheet; they lower accounting earnings by the full amount in the year in which they are incurred (Becker, Huselid, Pickus, & Spratt, 1997), although the return on these investments may continue for years.

HISTORICAL OVERVIEW OF HRM

The ancient world. The management of human resources in organizations today has a long history of different approaches that reflect the social conditions of the time. Prior to the industrial revolution, a number of different approaches to managing human resources were taken. In ancient Egypt, everything belonged to the pharaoh, which meant that everyone worked for the pharaoh. Some of the workers on large construction projects were slaves captured in wars, and their work motivation was quite different from that of the peasants or artists providing for "God on Earth." The skills of the Egyptians in managing human resources can be seen in the remains of their public works projects: the pyramids at Giza, the burial chambers in the Valley of the Kings, and the temples at Luxor.

Feudalism. In a feudal society, a new type of employer-employee relationship was invented. In the depressed economies of the Middle Ages, there was a shortage of currency, and wealth was contained in land. A landowner would grant his vassal some income-producing property (typically a parcel of land to use to grow food) and collect from the vassal a promise to work a certain number of days on the landowner's land and to provide military service for a specified period of time. In the late Middle Ages, as currency became less scarce, this military service was often replaced by a monetary payment, which the landowner would use to purchase military service from mercenaries. To describe the feudal system in modern terms, the landowner was the employer, and the vassal and the knight were contract workers.

Industrial revolution. Prior to the industrial revolution, economies were primarily agricultural, and manufacturing typically consisted of small groups of craftsmen working in their homes. Apprentices would work for and be trained in a craft by a master craftsman until, as experienced journeymen, they produced their masterpiece. Then they would take on apprentices of their own and pass on their knowledge and skills. During the industrial revolution, more and more workers left the farms and shops for jobs in factories. Adam Smith (1776/1976) described how a factory could produce more goods more cheaply than could be made by hand by a craftsman, because each worker did one part of the production process and could become more skilled and efficient at that task. The basis of the industrial revolution was division of labor and specialization of function. Greater efficiency in production translated into lower costs and greater profitability. Although Eli Whitney is best known for the invention of the cotton gin, he made his fortune by mass-producing guns to sell to the government (Burke, 1978). Before mass production techniques were applied, guns were individually crafted and each of the parts would fit only one gun; with mass production, parts became interchangeable. The skills of the craftsman were built into machine tools, and craftsmanship was replaced by monitoring the machines that made the products. Management of factory workers monitoring machines was focused on maximizing the number of hours the machines were producing goods.

Scientific Management. At the turn of the 20th century, the focus of HRM shifted from machines to people, with the advent of Frederick Winslow Taylor's (1911) ideas on Scientific Management. Taylor's insight was that to maximize productivity, the interaction between the machine and the worker must be carefully analyzed. The job of managers was to find the one most efficient way of performing the operations required by the job and then make sure that the workers did the job that way. Time-and-motion studies were used to make the job as simple as possible to learn and to do, minimizing training costs and maximizing productivity. If a worker is shoveling coal, Taylor observed, there is an optimal number of pounds of coal per shovel to maximize the total amount of coal shoveled in a workday. If the number of pounds is too small, more shovelfuls will be required to move a given weight of coal. If the number of pounds is too large, fatigue will reduce the total amount of coal that is moved. As a result of Scientific Management ideas, organizations became divided into those who determined the optimal way to perform the work and those who did the work. This division between managers and workers can still be seen in many workplaces today, where managers are considered to be sources of value and the people who do the work are assumed not to have any sound ideas about increasing productivity or quality.

Human Relations. During the early part of the 20th century, HRM ideas shifted in focus to the interactions among workers. A series of studies carried out in the 1930s established that the social environment of work had a strong influence on the productivity of the organization (Roethlisberger & Dickson, 1934). In a group working under a piecework system during the Great Depression, few workers exceeded the quota set by management to collect the productivity bonus. Interviews revealed that the workers had a deep distrust of management and were afraid that if many of them got the bonus, the bonus level would then become the daily production quota and they would have to work at what was formerly the bonus level just to make the daily production target. Observations of workers on the job revealed that if a worker was working "too hard," coworkers would exert social pressure on the worker to reduce his or her output. In a series of studies to determine the effect of illumination levels on productivity, productivity increased when illumination levels were raised, when they were lowered, and when old light bulbs were replaced with new light bulbs of identical wattage. Throughout the experiment, daily production rates were posted; feedback was a key factor that motivated workers to increase their productivity (Parsons, 1974).

Total Quality Management (TQM). TQM represents another fundamental shift in HRM to focusing on the moving target of quality. Focusing on quality means that all employees in the organization take responsibility for examining individual and group work processes to find ways to improve them. TQM transforms the traditional workplace with a hierarchical structure of managers who plan the work and the workers who do the work, to a workplace where the focus is on satisfying internal and external customers, improving work processes, and ensuring that workers are committed to achieving a clearly stated mission. Organizations with better strategies for meeting the wants and needs of current and potential future customers will have a higher level of organizational effectiveness. The Malcolm Baldrige National Quality Award is a competitive prize given to companies that have achieved excellence in TQM.

THE FUNCTIONS AND ROLES OF HRM

There are four basic functions of HRM: recruitment and selection, employee training and development, motivation, and employee health and safety. Recruitment and selection means human resource planning so that the organization knows how many workers with what specific knowledge and skills are needed now and into the future; recruiting, attracting potential applicants to apply for jobs in the organization and retaining them; and selection, deciding which applicants to hire from the pool of qualified applicants, and using fair selection processes so that the organization is not discriminating on the basis of race, color, religion, sex, national origin, age, or disability. Employee training and development involves orienting and socializing employees to the organization and the organization's way of doing things, improving employee knowledge and skills, and assisting with their career planning, to prepare them for their next job. Motivation means designing or redesigning jobs to be motivating and satisfying for the people doing them, evaluating employees' job performance, providing performance incentives or rewards, determining how much different employees in specific jobs should be paid, and developing compensation plans to keep salaries fair and competitive with what other organizations are paying for similar jobs. Employee health and safety includes building a positive organizational climate, effectively communicating with workers, and promoting worker health and safety.

These HRM functions also interact with each other, based on the strategic decisions that the organization has made. For some jobs, the organization will be highly selective, looking for someone who has all of the necessary knowledge, skills, and experience to do the job. For other jobs, the organization will be less selective and invest in developing the employee's knowledge and skills. If an organization makes a strategic decision to pay less than what the market is paying for similar jobs, then it will have a harder time attracting applicants and retaining employees, because the employees can get paid more for the same work at another organization. If an employee's job performance is unsatisfactory because he or she lacks knowledge or skills needed in the job, the employee can be given training or development opportunities to improve his or her job performance. Similarly, when an employee's career plan identifies a higher level job that he or she would like to have, the organization can help the employee identify training and development opportunities so that the employee can become qualified for that job.

HRM has four roles and four deliverables (Ulrich, 1997). The first role is Administrative Expert, and the deliverable is the design and delivery of efficient processes for staffing, training, appraising, rewarding, promoting, and otherwise managing the flow of employees through the organization. The second role is Employee Champion, and the deliverable is dealing with the day-to-day problems, concerns, and needs of employees, which links employee contributions to the organization's success. This role is especially important in companies where intellectual capital is a critical source of the firm's value. The third role is Change Agent, and the deliverable is effectively managing transformation and change, acting as cultural guardians and cultural catalysts. The fourth role is Strategic Partner, and the deliverable is aligning HRM strategies and practices with the organization's strategy, helping to ensure the success of those strategies.

HRM plays an important role in the formulation of strategy by identifying the people resources required to support strategic plans, by helping to develop the necessary capabilities to enact the strategy, and playing a role in strategy implementation and change management (Lawler & Mohrman, 2003). To perform effectively as a strategic partner in the organization, the HRM function needs to be staffed by people who understand the business and change management, are valued members of management teams because they contribute to business strategy and operations decision making, have high levels of competency in designing human resource systems and managing their implementation, and effectively use information technologies to support the development of individual competencies and organizational capabilities (Mohrman & Lawler, 1997).

Brockbank (1999) has identified two modes of acting in the HRM function. In strategically reactive mode, HRM uses existing business strategy and adds value by linking HRM practices to the business strategy and by managing change. In strategically proactive mode, HRM creates competitive advantage by creating cultures of creativity and innovation and by linking internal processes and structures with changes in the marketplace. Becker and Huselid (1998) found that firms with the greatest intensity of HRM practices that reinforce performance (i.e., high performance work systems) had the highest market value per employee and that the best firms are able to achieve both operational and strategic excellence in their human resource systems and functions.

Strategic Issues in HRM

HRM AS A PARTNER IN STRATEGIC PLANNING

To be successful, an organization must effectively manage its physical, capital, and information resources, and effectively manage the people who run the business. Effective HRM means focusing on quality and meeting the customers' requirements, continuously improving productivity, actively encouraging and rewarding innovation and creativity, and promoting flexibility in the design of work processes. Yet in most organizations, HRM is not a strategic partner. HRM is expected to provide support services for recruitment and performance appraisal to other functional areas, but HRM is not always included when strategic objectives are defined. If HRM is not a strategic partner, there can be no integration of business strategies and the people who will implement the strategies. Unless HRM is a strategic partner, strategic plans are likely to fail because (a) strategic plans need to be communicated to the employees who carry them out so that they understand them; (b) both managers and employees need to have a shared vision and a common understanding of the mission of the organization so that strategies can be translated into organizational goals and objectives; and (c) strategic plans may require changes in recruitment and selection, organizational structure, compensation systems, performance evaluation methods, and training and development programs. Therefore, HRM issues and strategies should be directly linked to business issues and strategies as part of management thinking, planning, and action.

Whether the organization is newly formed or has been in existence for many years, a number of important decisions about the management of human resources must be made. How these issues are resolved defines the nature of the work environment, affects employees' quality of work life, and has an impact on the achievement of the organization's mission.

Strategic Questions

1. To attract and retain highly skilled workers, how much above the market average should an organization be willing to pay? What factors should be considered when making this decision?
2. Other than pay, what else might attract and retain highly skilled employees?
3. To select employees from the pool of qualified applicants, what level of reliability and validity should the selection procedure have?
4. More valid selection procedures usually cost more, but greater validity translates into better job performance for those selected—how much should an organization be willing to invest in selection procedure validity?
5. If a valid selection procedure has adverse impact on one or more minority groups (i.e., producing a less diverse workforce), how should adverse impact be balanced against diversity goals?
6. To keep employee skill levels high, how much training and development (in dollars and hours) should the organization be willing to pay for?
7. To what degree should employees share in the profits of the organization?
8. At what level is absenteeism and turnover too high?
9. Should an organization provide an Employee Assistance Plan for its employees?
10. Should the organization help employees plan their careers, or should employees be expected to do career planning on their own?
11. Should the organization share data on its pay structure with competitors?
12. Should information on pay levels for jobs in the organization be made available to employees, or should pay information be kept secret?
13. How often should an organization evaluate the job performance of employees?

(Continued)

(Continued)

14. If the organization can afford to offer a health club membership as a benefit to a limited number of employees, who should be given the benefit?
15. Should the organization be an at-will employer (both employer and employee can terminate the employment relationship at any time) or a just-cause employer (employees will only be terminated for poor job performance or other proper reason and have the right of due process in grievance procedures)?
16. What percentage of an employee's compensation should be linked to his or her job performance?
17. How should it be determined how much each job in the organization should be paid?
18. How can it be determined whether a training program was effective (i.e., worth more to the organization than it cost)?
19. How can an organization reduce occupational injuries?
20. Should an organization provide partner benefits?
21. How does HRM add to shareholder value?

Resources

Becker, B. E., Huselid, M. A., Pickus, P. S., & Spratt, M. R. (1997). HR as a source of shareholder value: Research and recommendations. *Human Resource Management, 36*(1), 39-47.

Buyens, D., & De Vos, A. (2001). Perception of the value of the HR function. *Human Resource Management Journal, 11*(3), 70-89.

Heritage, C. (2006). Microsoft: Innovation through HR's partnership. *Strategic HR Review,* 5(3), 24-27.

Jamrog, J. J., & Overholt, M. H. (2004). Measuring HR and organizational effectiveness. *Employment Relations Today, 31*(2), 33-45.

Lawler, E. E., III. (2005). Making strategic partnership a reality. *Strategic HR Review, 4*(3), 3.

Martell, K., & Carroll, S. J. (1995). How strategic is HRM? *Human Resource Management, 34*(2), 253-267.

WHAT EVERYONE KNOWS IS TRUE ABOUT HRM (AND ISN'T)

Employees bring to the organization certain assumptions about the management of human resources, and as with all assumptions, sometimes the assumptions are true, and sometimes they are false. Common assumptions about HRM are that (a) it is all just common sense and does not require any special training or expertise and (b) human resources are a cost to be minimized rather than a resource to be managed. It is as if a student were to survey some of the different functional areas of business and conclude as follows:

"Accounting is counting—adding, subtracting, multiplying, and dividing. Who needs a degree to do counting?"

"Production and operations management is manufacturing—the more you produce, the more you make. What's so hard about that?"

"Marketing is sales—all you have to do is just tell people what you're selling and how much it costs; and if they want it, they will buy it."

"Human resource management is managing humans. I'm a human—I can do that."

Assumptions that employees bring with them to the organization about the management of human resources cover a wide range from how to motivate others, to what makes a good leader, to how to determine whether an applicant will make a good employee. A short list of assumptions people sometimes have about HRM is as follows:

- Happy workers are productive workers
- Interviews are useful to select applicants for a job
- HRM functions are not quantifiable in dollars saved or lost
- HRM is done by HRM people
- It is best to hire the most qualified applicant
- Labor and management negotiations are naturally adversarial

Strategic Questions

1. If happy workers are productive workers, what would you do to increase productivity? What message would this send to a group of very unproductive workers?
2. How qualified does an applicant have to be to be "qualified"? Can an applicant be overqualified?
3. While the interviewer is trying to determine whether the applicant will make a good employee, what is the applicant trying to do? What are the best questions for an interviewer to ask?
4. What HRM tasks are done by all managers? Could an organization function without an HRM department?
5. If an organization spends a million dollars on a training program, how does it measure the return on its investment?
6. If an organization has twice the turnover rate of its competitors, how much is this higher rate of turnover costing it?
7. What other things do people know are true about HRM (but aren't)?

(Continued)

(Continued)

Resources

Bohren, J. (1993). Six myths of sexual harassment. *Management Review, 82*(5), 61-63.

Cutcher-Gershenfeld, J., & Kochan, T. (2004). Taking stock: Collective bargaining at the turn of the century. *Industrial & Labor Relations Review, 58*(1), 3-26.

Longenecker, C. O., & Gioia, D. A. (1991). SMR Forum: Ten myths of managing managers. *Sloan Management Review, 33*(1), 81-90.

Markham, S. K., & Aiman-Smith, L. (2001). Product champions: Truths, myths and management. *Research Technology Management, 44*(3), 44-50.

Masternak, R. L. (1993/1994). Gainsharing: Overcoming common myths and problems to achieve dramatic results. *Employment Relations Today, 20*(4), 425-436.

Silvestro, R. (2002). Dispelling the modern myth: Employee satisfaction and loyalty drive service profitability. *International Journal of Operations & Production Management, 22*(1), 30-49.

THE COST OF EFFICIENCY

To apply Frederick Winslow Taylor's (1911) ideas about Scientific Management, the job should be carefully analyzed and broken down into its smallest parts, and then put in the most efficient order, eliminating extraneous movements. For a wide variety of jobs ranging from secretarial to assembly line jobs, a time-and-motion study may determine the most efficient way to do the job. If the worker then adopts the new and improved way to do the job, and if it really is a more efficient way of doing the job, then the "cycle time" for the job will be reduced and the worker will be more productive. Although minimizing cycle times may appear to be the best way to maximize productivity, it does not take into consideration the physical limits of the human machinery doing the job, which may suffer damage due to fatigue or strain or boredom.

One of the most common occupational injuries is a kind of cumulative trauma injury (or repetitive strain) called Carpal Tunnel Syndrome (CTS). The U.S. Department of Labor has cited CTS as well as other cumulative trauma disorders, as the cause of 48% of all industrial workplace illnesses, affecting more than 5 million Americans (American Physical Therapy Association, 1997). According to the Bureau of Labor Statistics (2005e), among major disabling injuries and illnesses in 2004, median days away from work were highest for CTS. This injury results from repeated stressful movements of the wrist or from holding the hand in the same position for long periods of time, which causes a swelling of the tendons that pass through the wrist bones, accompanied by pain due to pressure on the stressed median nerve. People with CTS usually experience feelings of numbness, weakness, and tingling and burning in the fingers and hands; if they are not given proper treatment, the symptoms may escalate into acute, persistent pain, and the individual may no longer be able to work. CTS is most commonly found among jobs requiring extended periods of typing or other repetitive motions, including positions such as computer programmer, secretary, data entry clerk, and assembly line worker.

Strategic Questions

1. If the incidence of CTS among a group of assembly line workers increased after implementing the recommendations of a time-and-motion study, what might be the cause?
2. If workers are very productive when they are working but miss many workdays due to CTS, how should you measure the difference in productivity of the old versus the new time-and-motion study way of doing the job?
3. What impact on worker motivation and job satisfaction would you expect if the cycle time of a job was significantly reduced?
4. If workers in a certain job tend to have a high rate of CTS, in what ways could the job be changed?
5. If workers in a certain job tend to have a high rate of CTS, what could you do to prepare workers before they begin the job?

Resources

American Physical Therapy Association. (1997). *What you need to know about Carpal Tunnel Syndrome: A physical therapist's perspective.* http://www.apta.org/AM/Images/APTAIMAGES/ContentImages/ptandbody/carpaltunnel/Carpal.pdf

Bureau of Labor Statistics. (2005). *Lost-worktime injuries and illnesses: Characteristics and resulting time away from work, 2004.* http://www.bls.gov/iif/oshwc/osh/case/osnr0024.pdf

Chaplin, C. (Director). (1936). *Modern times* [Motion picture]. Hollywood, CA: Charles Chaplin Productions.

Cheng, A. S., & Hung, L. (2007). Randomized controlled trial of workplace-based rehabilitation for work-related rotator cuff disorder. *Journal of Occupational Rehabilitation, 17*(3), 487-503.

Hamper, B. (1991). *Rivethead: Tales from the assembly line.* New York: Warner Books.

Taylor, F. W. (1911). *The principles of scientific management.* New York: Harper & Bros.

Williamson, J. (1949). *The humanoids.* Boston: Gregg.

THE HR SCORECARD

Traditional financial performance measures worked well for the industrial era, but they are out of step with the skills and competencies that companies are trying to master today, so Kaplan and Norton (1992) developed the Balanced Scorecard. The Balanced Scorecard is "a set of measures that gives top managers a fast but comprehensive view of the business. The balanced scorecard includes financial measures that tell the results of actions already taken. And it complements the financial measures with operational measures on customer satisfaction, internal processes, and the organization's innovation and improvement activities—operational measures that are the drivers of future financial performance" (Kaplan & Norton, 1992, p. 71). The Balanced Scorecard allows managers to look at the business from four important perspectives:

- How do customers see us? (customer perspective)
- What must we excel at? (internal perspective)
- Can we continue to improve and create value? (innovation and learning perspective)
- How do we look to shareholders? (financial perspective)

Building on the idea of the Balanced Scorecard, Becker, Huselid, and Ulrich (2001) developed the HR Scorecard for the HRM function. The HR Scorecard includes four perspectives:

- Strategic: measures HRM's success in achieving five HRM strategic thrusts (talent, leadership, customer service and support, organizational integration, and HRM capability)
- Operations: measures HRM's success in three operational areas (staffing, technology, and HRM processes and transactions)
- Customer: measures how HRM is viewed by key customer segments, employee engagement, competitive capability, and links to productivity
- Financial: measures how HRM adds measurable financial value to the organization (return on investment in training, technology, staffing, risk management, and cost of service delivery)

Strategic Questions

1. What is the benefit to the organization of using an HR scorecard? What is the benefit to the HRM department?
2. What is the difference between what HRM can contribute to the success of the organization and what it is contributing to the success of the organization?
3. Are human resources a cost to be minimized or an asset to be managed? In what ways do organizations tend to view HRM activities as costs rather than investments?
4. How does HRM help an organization achieve its strategic objectives?

5. Are its human resources an organization's greatest asset?
6. Compared to a "typical" organization, for what type of organization would its human resources be less important? More important?

Resources

Beatty, R. W., Huselid, M. A., & Schneier, C. E. (2003). New HR metrics: Scoring on the Business Scorecard. *Organizational Dynamics, 32*(2), 107-121.

Becker, B. E., Huselid, M. A., & Ulrich, D. (2001). *The HR Scorecard: Linking people, strategy and performance.* Boston: Harvard Business School Press.

Kaplan, R. S., & Norton, D. P. (1992). The Balanced Scorecard—measures that drive performance. *Harvard Business Review, 70*(1), 71-79.

Walker, G., & MacDonald, J. R. (2001). Designing and implementing an HR scorecard. *Human Resource Management, 40*(4), 365-377.

Applications

HRM IN MOTION PICTURES

When rocket scientists watch a science fiction movie such as "Star Wars," they find that many of the laws of physics they deal with on a daily basis are bent or completely violated. For example, according to Einstein's equations, when an object approaches the speed of light, its mass increases toward infinity, so spaceships cannot travel faster than the speed of light. When HRM tasks are presented in a motion picture or television show, how do HRM professionals view them?

To Do

Write a short paper describing how HRM tasks are presented in motion pictures or television shows. Use this format and headings for the paper: In the "HRM Scenes" section, describe the scene or scenes where some HRM task is being done and the movie or TV show it is taken from. In the "Links" section, make four links between something in the HRM Scenes and something you have learned about HRM. If the scene shows an employment interview and the interviewer asks whether the applicant is married or single, a link could be made to what you learned about inappropriate pre-employment inquiries. Explain why each scene shows a good or bad example of effective HRM.

For example, in the television show "American Idol," contestants are given an opportunity to sing a song for a panel of judges, a kind of work sample. The panel of judges does a performance appraisal on each contestant's performance, although it is not always clear that the judges are using the same set of performance dimensions. The judges often disagree on a contestant's

(Continued)

(Continued)

performance; one judge seems to have a leniency bias and another seems to have a severity bias. Sometimes the contestants are sent to a trainer (mentor) as a developmental experience to improve their skills. Although the sample size is too small for a validation study, the contestants that have been chosen as the winners of the annual contest have sometimes gone on to succeed in the music industry (true positives), and some nonwinners have also become successful (false negatives).

Resources

Champoux, J. (2007). *Our feature presentation: Human Resource Management.* Mason, OH: Southwestern.

Darnell, E. (Director). (1998). *Antz.* [Motion picture]. Glendale, CA: Dreamworks Animation.

Dent, E. B. (2001). Seinfeld, professor of organizational behavior: The psychological contract and systems thinking. *Journal of Management Education, 25*(6), 648-659.

Hunt, C. S. (2001). Must see TV: The timelessness of television as a teaching tool. *Journal of Management Education, 25*(6), 631-647.

Pierson, K. (1997). Would you fire Jerry Maguire? *HR Focus, 74*(11), 1-2.

Stone, O. (Director, Screenwriter). (1987). *Wall Street* [Motion picture]. Century City, CA: 20th Century Fox.

Universal Studios. (Producer). (2005). *The office* [Television series]. Universal City, CA: Author.

KEY SUPREME COURT CASES AND IMPLICATIONS FOR HRM

The legal environment of business affects HRM as well as other functional areas. Legal protections to employees and applicants include the Civil Rights Act of 1964 and 1991, the Age Discrimination in Employment Act, and the Americans with Disabilities Act. Often, Supreme Court cases affect HRM practices, changing the way that HRM is done. In the landmark case of *Griggs v. Duke Power* (1971), the ruling of the Supreme Court was that the tests and high school diploma requirement for promotion used by Duke Power was illegal because they disqualified Black employees at a much higher rate than White employees and there was no demonstrable relationship to successful performance on the job. Selection procedures that are neutral on their face or in their intent may freeze the status quo of past discrimination, and the Civil Rights Act proscribes both overt discrimination and practices that are fair in form but discriminatory in operation.

To Do

Each of the Supreme Court cases listed below illustrates a key fair employment practice. Use Findlaw.com to get the text of the case. News stories and law reviews might also be useful resources to gain a better understanding of the Supreme Court ruling and the implications for the practice of HRM.

Analyze one of the cases below and report:

1. The facts of the case
2. The ruling of the Supreme Court
3. The relevant law or guideline illustrated by the case
4. The application of the case to the effective and legal management of human resources

General Dynamics Land Systems v. Cline, 540 U.S. 581 (Supreme Court of the United States, 2004).
Grutter v. Bollinger, 539 U.S. 982 (Supreme Court of the United States, 2003).
International Union, United Autoworkers v. Johnson Controls, 499 U.S. 187 (Supreme Court of the United States, 1991).
Johnson v. Transportation Agency, 480 U.S. 616 (Supreme Court of the United States, 1987).
McDonnell Douglas Corp. v. Green, 411 U.S. 792 (Supreme Court of the United States, 1973)
Meritor Savings. Bank v. Vinson, 477 U.S. 57 (Supreme Court of the United States, 1986).
O'Connor v. Consolidated Coin Caterers Corp., 517 U.S. 308 (Supreme Court of the United States, 1996).
Oncale v. Sundowner Offshore Services, 523 U.S. 75 (Supreme Court of the United States, 1998).
PGA Tour, Inc. v. Martin, 532 U.S. 661 (Supreme Court of the United States, 2001).
Price Waterhouse v. Hopkins, 485 U.S. 933 (Supreme Court of the United States, 1988).
Regents of University of California. v. Bakke, 438 U.S. 265 (Supreme Court of the United States, 1978).
Toyota Motor Manufacturing, Kentucky. v. Williams, 534 U.S. 184 (Supreme Court of the United States, 2002).
United Steelworkers v. Weber, 443 U.S. 193 (Supreme Court of the United States, 1979).

Resources

Findlaw.com, U.S. Supreme Court Opinions. http://www.findlaw.com/; http://www.findlaw.com/casecode/supreme.html.
Griggs v. Duke Power Co., 401 U.S. 424 (Supreme Court of the United States, 1971).

Experiential Exercises

DEVELOPING MISSION STATEMENTS

The mission of the organization defines its business purpose and the reason for its existence. The mission describes the primary products or services of the organization in a statement that is brief and to the point. A clear and effectively written mission statement will provide the basis for employee commitment to the organization and focus employee efforts on the most important tasks. Some mission statements also include a vision of the future, describing what the organization intends to become, so that strategic objectives can be created to transform the organization from what it is today into the vision of the organization tomorrow.

For example, Caribou Coffee's mission statement is "An Experience that Makes the Day Better." Their mission statement is expanded into a list of their Core Values: "Life is Short . . . Blaze new trails; Be excellent, not average; Enjoy what you do; Respect diversity; Teamwork builds success; Success and profit create opportunities; Make a difference in our community; Guests are always our priority—everything else waits." The Nike mission statement is one sentence: "To bring inspiration and innovation to every athlete in the world."

To Do

For each of the organizations described below, develop a brief mission statement that defines the business purpose of the organization and a vision of what the organization will become in the future.

American Girl: direct marketer, children's publisher, and experiential retailer. http://www.americangirl.com/

Belle Tire: tires and automotive service. http://www.belletire.com/

DHL Worldwide Express: international express and logistics. http://www.dhl.com/splash.html

Enhanced Communications Group: a telecommunications reseller offering residential and business services. http://www.ecg1.com/

ESPN: a provider of comprehensive sports coverage. http://espn.go.com/

Ferrari: a manufacturer of high-performance sports cars. http://www.ferrariworld.com/FWorld/fw/index.jsp

Frito-Lay: a manufacturer of snack foods. http://www.fritolay.com/

General Dynamics: a manufacturer of business aircraft, land and amphibious combat machines and systems. http://www.generaldynamics.com/

Land's End: casual clothing for women, men, and kids. http://www.landsend.com/

Lifetime Fitness: health and fitness clubs. http://www.lifetimefitness.com/

Music Basics: a discount and specialty retailer for violins, violas, and band instruments. http://store.musicbasics.com/

North Dakota Tourism: government agency to increase tourism within the state. http://www.ndtourism.com/

PC Gamer: a PC games magazine. http://www.pcgamer.com/

Recording Industry Association of America: the trade group that represents the U.S. recording industry. http://www.riaa.com

Star Trek 1701: a deep space exploration vessel. http://www.startrek.com/startrek/view/index.html

U.S. Customs and Border Protection: protecting the American public from terrorists. http://www.cbp.gov/

Weight Watchers: a weight loss and nutrition counseling service. http://www.weightwatchers.com/index.aspx

Resources

Business Resource Software. *Mission statement.* http://www.businessplans.org/Mission.html

Caribou Coffee. *Company information.* http://www.cariboucoffee.com/page/1/company-info.jsp

DEVELOPING STRATEGIC OBJECTIVES FROM MISSION STATEMENTS

Once an organization has defined its direction and purpose with a mission statement, the organization must develop strategic objectives that direct the work of the members of the organization toward achievement of the mission. To energize and focus the work of the members of the organization, strategic objectives must be developed from the mission statement to specify the tasks that must be done and the goals that must be met to achieve the mission. Employees at all levels can be involved in the process of defining performance goals, measuring their achievement, and then developing new goals. The clearer it is to employees what the goals are and how progress toward meeting those goals is measured, the greater the likelihood that the goals will be accomplished. Strategic HRM objectives must be developed for human resource planning, recruitment, selection, training and development, job design, compensation and benefits, quality of work life (including work motivation, job satisfaction, communication, and employee involvement), and worker health and safety.

For example, this is the vision, mission, and strategic plan for the Department of Homeland Security:

The DHS Strategic Plan—Securing Our Homeland

The National Strategy for Homeland Security and the Homeland Security Act of 2002 served to mobilize and organize our nation to secure the homeland from terrorist attacks. This exceedingly complex mission requires a focused effort from our entire society if we are to be successful. To this end, one primary reason for the establishment of the Department of Homeland Security was to provide the unifying core for the vast national network of organizations and institutions involved in efforts to secure our nation. In order to better do this and to provide guidance to the 180,000 DHS men and women who work every day on this important task, the Department developed its own high-level strategic plan. The vision and mission statements, strategic goals and objectives provide the framework guiding the actions that make up the daily operations of the department.

Vision

Preserving our freedoms, protecting America . . . we secure our homeland.

Mission

We will lead the unified national effort to secure America. We will prevent and deter terrorist attacks and protect against and respond to threats and hazards to the nation. We will ensure safe and secure borders, welcome lawful immigrants and visitors, and promote the free flow of commerce.

(Continued)

(Continued)

Strategic Goals

Awareness—Identify and understand threats, assess vulnerabilities, determine potential impacts and disseminate timely information to our homeland security partners and the American public.

Prevention—Detect, deter and mitigate threats to our homeland.

Protection—Safeguard our people and their freedoms, critical infrastructure, property and the economy of our Nation from acts of terrorism, natural disasters, or other emergencies.

Response—Lead, manage and coordinate the national response to acts of terrorism, natural disasters, or other emergencies.

Recovery—Lead national, state, local and private sector efforts to restore services and rebuild communities after acts of terrorism, natural disasters, or other emergencies.

Service—Serve the public effectively by facilitating lawful trade, travel and immigration.

Organizational Excellence—Value our most important resource, our people. Create a culture that promotes a common identity, innovation, mutual respect, accountability and teamwork to achieve efficiencies, effectiveness, and operational synergies.

SOURCE: http://www.dhs.gov/dhspublic/interapp/editorial/editorial_0413.xml.

To Do

Choose one of the mission statements listed below, and develop six to eight strategic HRM objectives to focus the work of employees toward achievement of the mission:

Levi Strauss & Co.

Our values are fundamental to our success. They are the foundation of our company, define who we are and set us apart from the competition. They underlie our vision of the future, our business strategies and our decisions, actions and behaviors. We live by them. They endure.

Four core values are at the heart of Levi Strauss & Co.: Empathy, Originality, Integrity and Courage. These four values are linked. As we look at our history, we see a story of how our core values work together and are the source of our success.

http://www.levistrauss.com/Company/ValuesAndVision.aspx

Manulife Financial

Manulife Financial's vision is to be the most professional life insurance company in the world: providing the very best financial protection and investment management services tailored to customers in every market where we do business.

With vision comes values. These values guide everything we do—from strategic planning to day-to-day decision-making, to the manner in which we treat our customers and other stakeholders. These values are described by the acronym PRIDE:

Professionalism. We will be recognized as having the highest professional standards. Our employees and agents will possess superior knowledge and skill, for the benefit of our customers.

Real Value to Customers. We are here to satisfy our customers. By providing the highest quality products, services, advice and sustainable value, we will ensure our customers receive excellent solutions to meet their individual needs.

Integrity. All of our dealings are characterized by the highest levels of honesty and fairness.

Demonstrated Financial Strength. Our customers depend on us to be here in the future to meet our financial promises. We earn this faith by maintaining uncompromised claims paying ability, a healthy earnings stream, and superior investment performance results, consistent with a prudent investment management philosophy.

Employer of Choice. Our employees will determine our future success. In order to attract and retain the best and brightest employees, we will invest in the development of our human resources and reward superior performance.

http://www.manulife.com/corporate/corporate2.nsf/Public/vision.html

Apple Computer

Apple ignited the personal computer revolution in the 1970s with the Apple II and reinvented the personal computer in the 1980s with the Macintosh. Apple is committed to bringing the best personal computing experience to students, educators, creative professionals and consumers around the world through its innovative hardware, software and Internet offerings.

http://www.corporate-ir.net/ireye/ir_site.zhtml?ticker=aapl&script=1800&layout=7#corpinfo2

Long John Silver's

To be America's best quick service restaurant chain. We will provide each guest great tasting, healthful, reasonably priced fish, seafood, and chicken in a fast, friendly manner on every visit.

http://www.ljsilvers.com/

(Continued)

(Continued)

U.S. Department of the Interior, U.S. Fish and Wildlife Service

The U.S. Fish and Wildlife Service's mission is, working with others, to conserve, protect and enhance fish, wildlife, and plants and their habitats for the continuing benefit of the American people.

http://www.fws.gov/

The Minneapolis Institute of Arts

The Minneapolis Institute of Arts is dedicated to national leadership in bringing arts and people together to discover, enjoy, and understand the world's diverse artistic heritage.

http://www.artsmia.org/index.php?section_id=7

American College of Forensic Examiners Institute of Forensic Science

The American College of Forensic Examiners Institute of Forensic Science (ACFEI) is an independent, scientific, and professional society. Multi-disciplinary in its scope, the society actively promotes the dissemination of forensic information. The association's purpose is the continued advancement of forensic examination and consultation across the many professional fields of our membership. ACFEI has elevated standards through education, basic and advanced training, and Diplomate Status.

http://www.acfei.com/

Alien Abduction Experience and Research

Alien Abduction Experience and Research (AAER) is an independent research center dedicated to providing support and research into the alien abduction experience. The AAER is a worldwide network of field and laboratory researchers and scientists. AAER is not affiliated with any UFO, New Age, subversive, political, military, university, or other organization or government group.

http://www.abduct.com/mission.php.

The Rochester Hills Public Library

The Rochester Hills Public Library provides up-to-date materials and information to people of all ages for their recreation, education, and lifelong learning. The Library emphasizes efficient, convenient access and courteous, professional service in welcoming surroundings.

http://www.rhpl.org/

Your College/University

Creative Exercises

WHAT MAKES FOR A GOOD PLACE TO WORK?

If people are asked whether they like their jobs, they give a wide variety of answers, focusing on different aspects of the job. For some people, it is their relationship with their supervisor or coworkers; for others, it is the opportunity to do challenging and important work; and for others, it is the chance to learn new skills. When an organization must compete with other organizations for workers with skills in high demand but in low supply, the quality of work life may have a large impact on the success of recruitment and retention.

To Do

In small groups, construct a worker opinion survey of "What Makes for a Good Place to Work?" You may ask any question you would like and use any questionnaire format that you think is appropriate. Administer the survey to at least 20 employees other than your classmates, either all at the same company or at a number of different companies. Analyze the data collected and report the results you obtained. Your report should include a description of the sample of people that answered the survey (age, sex, type of job, size of the organization, type of business, etc.), and indicate what kinds of things were most and least important for determining what makes for a good place to work. Some example questions and formats are given below.

How satisfied are you in your current job?

- ☐ Very satisfied
- ☐ Somewhat satisfied
- ☐ Neither satisfied nor dissatisfied
- ☐ Somewhat dissatisfied
- ☐ Very dissatisfied

To what extent are you given the opportunity to make decisions about your job?

- ☐ To a little extent
- ☐ To some extent
- ☐ To a great extent

(Continued)

(Continued)

How important are each of the following for your quality of work life? (100 = *Essential*, 0 = *Unimportant*)

_____ Quality circles or other types of employee problem-solving groups

_____ Participative work design

_____ Gainsharing or other profit-sharing plan

_____ Challenging work

_____ An opportunity to learn new skills

_____ Supervisor helps you schedule your work efficiently

Resources

Alreck, P. L., & Settle, R. B. (1995). *The survey research handbook.* Chicago: Irwin.

Rogelberg, S. G., Church, A. H., Waclawski, J., & Stanton, J. M. (2002). Organizational survey research. In S. G. Rogelberg (Ed.), *Handbook of research methods in industrial and organizational psychology* (pp. 141-160). Malden, MA: Blackwell.

Thomas, S. J. (1999). *Designing surveys that work! A step-by-step guide.* Thousand Oaks, CA: Corwin.

RUNNING AN EFFECTIVE MEETING

Despite technological advances in organizational communication such as teleconferencing, instant messaging, and groupware, face-to-face meetings are still commonly used to share information and make decisions. A study conducted by INFOCOMM (1998) found that the typical professional attends more than 60 meetings a month, and more than a third of them are rated unproductive. If all of the resources used at a meeting (people and time) are considered, most organizations spend 7% to 15% of their personnel budgets directly on meetings (Chen, 2003). A 2-hour staff meeting with 10 people each making $60,000 per year plus benefits costs about $300 per hour (Levine, 2007). If this is a weekly meeting, it costs $31,200 per year.

Meetings can be an effective way of getting buy-in and making good decisions, but they can also be poorly run or suffer from the symptoms of Groupthink (Janis, 1982). Running effective meetings is a skill that can be taught. And like other processes in the organization, by consistently following the basics of meeting planning and control, the effectiveness of meetings can be increased over time.

There are six basic principles to running effective meetings:

1. Decide whether a meeting is necessary. Consider whether there are there alternative ways to achieve the meeting objectives.

2. Clearly state the purpose of the meeting. What issues must be discussed, what decisions need to be made, what actions will be taken?
3. Write an agenda that tells the meeting participants what the purpose of the meeting is and what they need to do to prepare. During the meeting, stick to the agenda.
4. Summarize the results of the meeting so that everyone is clear on what was done and assignments for the next meeting.
5. Set the time and place for the next meeting.
6. Evaluate the meeting. What went well, and what can be improved for the next meeting? The key to continuously improving the meeting process is for the group to reflect on what happened during the meeting and identify actions that can be taken to improve the next meeting.

To Do

Apply the principles for running an effective meeting to one of the business situations described below. For the meeting, team members should be assigned the roles of team leader (the person who runs the meeting), recorder (who records the minutes of the meeting), and scribe (who uses a whiteboard or flipchart as the team works, such as during brainstorming).

Web Training Courses

1. Discuss a proposal to offer some training courses as online Web courses (where trainees would get all of the training materials on the Web) and communicate with each other and the trainer by e-mail, instant messaging, electronic bulletin boards, and so forth.
2. Decide which training courses to offer as Web courses (based on the content of the course) and list possible problems that may be encountered.
3. Determine how you would measure whether the new Web training courses were successful.

Professional Employer Organization

1. Identify a list of HRM functions that your organization will outsource to a Professional Employer Organization (PEO) and a list of local PEOs.
2. Make a decision about which PEO to partner with.
3. Determine how you would measure the success of your partnership with the PEO.

Performance Feedback System

1. Develop a proposal for a Performance Feedback System for nonexempt employees that will be linked to the merit pay raise process.

(Continued)

(Continued)

2. Decide what kinds of feedback managers should give to employees, for their current job and for their roles on cross-functional teams.
3. Determine how you would measure the success of the Performance Feedback System.

New Office Space

1. Generate a list of employees and types of office spaces needed for the new office building.
2. Decide how the space will be divided up into offices, conference rooms, common areas, and other areas.
3. Determine how you would measure the success of your plan for the new office building.

Human Resources Information System (HRIS)

1. Generate a list of vendors for an HRIS to replace the current paper-and-file-cabinet system.
2. Determine what functions your organization needs, and determine which program best meets your organization's needs.
3. Determine how you would measure whether the HRIS is meeting expectations and needs.

Assessment Center

1. Develop a list of performance dimensions for the district sales manager.
2. Determine what assessment center exercises to include in the assessment center for the district sales manager that will measure all of the performance dimensions.
3. Determine how you would measure how well the Assessment Center worked for selection.

Resources

The CEO Refresher. *Effective meetings.* http://www.refresher.com/archives33.html

Chen, M. T. (2003). Project meeting cost analysis. *AACE International Transactions,* PM.07.1.

EffectiveMeetings.com. *Six tips for more effective meetings.* http://www.effectivemeetings.com/meetingbasics/6tips.asp

INFOCOMM. (1998). *Meetings in America: A study of trends, costs and attitudes toward business travel, teleconferencing, and their impact on productivity* (MCI Conferencing White Paper). http://e-meetings.verizonbusiness.com/global/en/meetingsinamerica/uswhitepaper.php

Levine, S. R. (2007). Make meetings less dreaded. *HR Magazine, 52*(1), 107-109.

National Association of Professional Employer Organizations. *NAPEOnline.* http://www.napeo.org/

Robinson, P. (Director), Cleese, J., & Hardy, R. (Writers). (2002). *Meetings, bloody meetings* [Motion picture]. Morton Grove, IL: AIM Learning Group.

2 Equal Employment Opportunity

Strategic Objective

The Civil Rights Act of 1964 was a landmark piece of legislation; it was workers' first substantial legal protection from discrimination in the workplace. Prior to the Civil Rights Act, it was legal for employers to discriminate in hiring, promotion, pay, access to training programs, and any other employment decision. The Civil Rights Act of 1964 makes it illegal to discriminate on the basis of race, color, religion, sex, or national origin. The Equal Pay Act of 1963 requires men and women doing the same job to be paid the same, except for differences resulting from a seniority system, merit pay, or incentive programs. The Age Discrimination in Employment Act of 1967 prohibits discrimination on the basis of age for workers over 40 years old. The Pregnancy Discrimination Act of 1978 makes it illegal to discriminate on the basis of pregnancy, childbirth, or related medical conditions. The Americans with Disabilities Act of 1990 prohibits discrimination against qualified people with disabilities.

At first glance, discrimination in employment seems to make no sense. The rational employer hires applicants only based on their ability to do the job, not on their race, color, religion, sex, or national origin, all of which are unrelated to their ability to do the job. Why would there need to be a law to require employers to hire fairly, when hiring unfairly would put them at a competitive disadvantage compared to other organizations that do hire fairly? In 1946, there were no Black players in Major League Baseball (MLB), despite a substantial pool of talent in the Negro Leagues. Yet even 5 years after Jackie Robinson broke the color line in 1947, less than half of the MLB teams had been desegregated. Gwartney and Haworth (1974) tested the theory that employers who discriminate are at a competitive disadvantage compared to firms that follow a less discriminatory policy using MLB data from the 1940s and 1950s, and found that teams employing Black players did have a competitive advantage; they won more games, acquired quality players at a lower cost, and increased annual revenue from admissions.

The most recent federal equal employment opportunity law is the Americans with Disabilities Act. When the law was passed, the unemployment rate among people with disabilities was about 70% (Wells, 2001). Supporters of the law pointed out that working is a major life activity that many people with disabilities are missing, and it would benefit both people with disabilities and taxpayers generally if more people with disabilities are employed and paying taxes than unemployed and collecting welfare benefits. Unfortunately, despite the Americans with Disability Act, the unemployment rate for people with disabilities has remained at about the same level (Acemoglu & Angrist, 2001; Altman, 2005; Dutton, 2000; Kruse & Schur, 2003; Stein, 2000). Do organizations that are more willing to hire qualified applicants with disabilities have a competitive advantage?

Although equal employment opportunity laws are often referred to as compliance issues, they may also be strategic issues. Attracting qualified employees is challenging and will get more difficult. Bureau of Labor Statistics projections indicate a substantial reduction in labor force growth rates through 2020, down from 1.6% per year during 1950-2000, to 0.4% between 2010 and 2020 (Horrigan, 2004). According to a 1997 study by the Families and Work Institute, "the quality of workers' jobs and the supportiveness of their workplaces are the most powerful predictors of productivity, job satisfaction, commitment to their employers, and retention" (Bond, Galinsky, & Swanberg, 1998, p. 1). A company's reputation with consumers, current and prospective employees, and other stakeholders can have a profound effect on its ability to succeed, and employers increasingly see the need to establish inclusive policies as part of an effort to compete for employees who may choose employers based on their progressive workplace policies (Human Rights Campaign Foundation, 2004).

Strategic Issues in HRM

THE UNAVOIDABLE LAWSUIT?

In *Griggs v. Duke Power* (1971), the Duke Power company instituted a new promotion policy. To qualify for placement in a position in any other department but Labor required a passing score on the Wonderlic Personnel Test and the Bennett Mechanical Comprehension Test and a high school diploma (incumbent employees who lacked a high school education could qualify for transfer from Labor or Coal Handling to an inside job by passing the two tests). A passing score was defined as the national median for high school graduates. The Supreme Court ruled that these three tests had an adverse impact, noting in footnote 6 that "In North Carolina, 1960 census statistics show that, while 34% of white males had completed high school, only 12% of Negro males had done so. Similarly, with respect to standardized tests, the EEOC in one case found that use of a battery of tests, including the Wonderlic and Bennett tests used by the Company in the instant case, resulted in 58% of whites passing the tests, as compared with only 6% of the blacks." The Civil Rights Act of 1964 makes it illegal for an employer to use a test that disqualifies minority applicants at a substantially higher rater than White applicants (i.e., adverse impact) when these tests had not been shown to be significantly related to successful job performance (i.e., a valid test).

In *Albemarle Paper Company v. Moody* (1975), the Albemarle Paper company required applicants for positions in the skilled lines of progression to have a high school diploma and to pass two tests, the Revised Beta Examination and the Wonderlic Personnel Test. Perhaps anticipating that a high school diploma and two general cognitive skills tests might have adverse impact, just before the trial began, the company conducted a validation study. The results showed statistically significant correlations between test scores and supervisor ratings of job performance in 3 of 10 job groupings for the Beta, 7 for the Wonderlic, and 2 for the Beta and Wonderlic together. The Supreme Court ruled that the employer's testing program—as measured by the U.S. Equal Employment Opportunity Commission's (EEOC) Guidelines for employers seeking to determine, through professional validation studies, whether their employment tests were job related—was not proven to be job related.

In *University of California Regents v. Bakke* (1978), the medical school maintained two tracks for admission, regular for most applicants and special for disadvantaged applicants. Bakke applied for admission twice and was not admitted, although he had a better admission score than some applicants who were admitted under the special track. The Supreme Court ruled that the special admissions program was a racial classification (not a racial preference system) and therefore illegal, because White applicants could compete for only 84 openings whereas minority candidates could compete for all 100, and that the Court has never approved preferential classifications without evidence of past discrimination. Affirmative Action Plans are a remedy for past or current discrimination, so if the special admissions track was an Affirmative Action Plan, then there needed to be evidence of past discrimination in admissions for the Affirmative Action Plan to remedy.

In *United Steelworkers v. Weber* (1979), Kaiser Aluminum and United Steelworkers agreed to a contract with an Affirmative Action Plan to increase the number of minorities in the craft workforce. The Affirmative Action Plan set a goal to equal the percentage of Blacks in the local labor market and created a training program for unskilled production workers to become craft workers, with 50% of the openings reserved for Black employees. At Weber's plant, 13 were selected for the training program, 7 Blacks and 6 Whites. The most junior Black had less seniority than several Whites not selected, including Weber. The Supreme Court ruled that the prohibition against racial discrimination does not apply to private voluntary race-conscious Affirmative Action Plans and Kaiser's 50% plan was a legal Affirmative Action Plan to reduce or eliminate conspicuous racial imbalances in traditionally segregated jobs such as crafts (i.e., where there is evidence of past discrimination).

In *Johnson v. Transportation Agency, Santa Clara County, California* (1987), the county had developed a voluntary Affirmative Action Plan to improve performance in the hiring, training, and promotion of minorities and women throughout the agency in all major job classifications where they were underrepresented. When a vacancy for a road dispatcher (skilled craft job) was announced in 1979, 12 county employees applied and 9 were deemed qualified and interviewed. Based on the initial interview, 7 of these 9 (8 males, 1 female) were given a second interview. Paul Johnson was given an interview score of 75 (the second highest), and Diane Joyce was given 73 (fourth highest). A panel of agency supervisors unanimously recommended that Johnson be given the job. The agency director consulted with the county coordinator for Affirmative Action and made the final decision to hire Joyce. Johnson then sued, claiming that he had been denied the promotion based on gender. The Supreme Court ruled that the Agency's Plan represented a moderate, flexible, case-by-case approach to effecting a gradual improvement in the representation of minorities and women in the agency's workforce. The plan was consistent with Title VII, because the agency had voluntarily adopted an Affirmative Action Plan, which provided that within traditionally segregated job classifications in which women were significantly underrepresented, gender could be considered as one factor in judging among qualified applicants.

Moore and Hass (1990) provide additional details on the *Johnson v. Transportation Agency, Santa Clara County, California* case. The road dispatcher job was designated a skilled craft position by the agency and required candidates to have a minimum of 4 years of dispatch or road maintenance work experience for Santa Clara County. Joyce worked as a road maintenance worker for Santa Clara County from 1975 to 1979; Johnson worked as road maintenance worker for Santa Clara County from 1977 to 1979. Joyce had applied for a road dispatcher position in 1974 but was considered ineligible because she had not worked as a road maintenance worker for 4 years.

Strategic Questions

1. Both Duke Power and Albemarle Paper companies were using tests that had not been validated. Why would they use these tests when they did not know whether they predicted job performance?
2. Why did the medical school at the University of California at Davis have an Affirmative Action Plan? Was there past discrimination to remedy? Does the university have a legitimate interest in a more diverse pool of students than would be obtained by selecting top-down by admission test scores?
3. What is the difference between Kaiser Aluminum's (*United Steelworkers v. Weber*) Affirmative Action Plan and the University of California at Davis' (*University of California Regents v. Bakke*) admissions program?
4. What could Duke Power have done to win the case? What could Duke Power have done to avoid the lawsuit?
5. What could Albemarle Paper Company have done to win the case? What could Albemarle Paper Company have done to avoid the lawsuit?
6. What could the Transportation Agency, Santa Clara County, have done to avoid the lawsuit by Johnson?
7. In *Johnson v. Transportation Agency*, who got the highest score on the interview? Why wasn't this person hired for the road dispatcher job?
8. Have there been any recent Supreme Court cases with implications for the practice of HRM?

Resources

Albemarle Paper Co. v. Moody, 422 U.S. 405 (Supreme Court of the United States, 1975).
Griggs v. Duke Power, 401 U.S. 424 (Supreme Court of the United States, 1971).
Grutter v. Bollinger, 539 U.S. 306 (Supreme Court of the United States, 2003).
Johnson v. Transportation Agency, Santa Clara County, California, 480 U.S. 616 (Supreme Court of the United States, 1987).
Moore, D. P., & Hass, M. (1990). When affirmative action cloaks management bias in selection and promotion decisions. *Academy of Management Executive*, 4(1), 84-90.
Regents of University of California. v. Bakke, 438 U.S. 265 (Supreme Court of the United States, 1978).
Wonderlic Personnel Test. *Wonderlic Personnel Test.* http://www.wonderlic.com/products/selection/wpt/

SEXUAL HARASSMENT IN THE WORKPLACE

Unwelcome sexual advances, requests for sexual favors, and other verbal or physical conduct of a sexual nature constitute sexual harassment when this conduct explicitly or implicitly affects an individual's employment; unreasonably interferes with an individual's work performance; or creates an intimidating, hostile, or offensive work environment. Sexual harassment is not just male harassers and female victims. Harassers may be male or female, and victims may be male or female. According to the EEOC (2008) enforcement statistics, the total number of charge receipts filed and resolved under Title VII alleging sexual harassment discrimination as an issue in 2007 was 12,510, down from 15,889 in 1997.

There are two types of sexual harassment, distinguished by the consequences to the victim. If there are tangible employment consequences (didn't get hired, was fired, didn't get promoted, etc.) it is quid pro quo sexual harassment. In quid pro quo sexual harassment cases, the harasser is the victim's supervisor or other employee who controls the tangible employment consequences. If there are no tangible employment consequences, it is hostile work environment sexual harassment. In this type of sexual harassment, the harasser could be a supervisor, a coworker, or even a nonemployee, anyone who poisons the work environment with sexually related comments, jokes, offensive touching, offensive pictures, and so forth. Even if victims of sexual harassment are unable to prove their claims, they may still win a retaliation claim if the victim was retaliated against for having complained about sexual harassment (Wendt & Slonaker, 2002). According to Wendt and Slonaker's analysis of sexual harassment claims closed by the Ohio Civil Rights Commission, nearly half of all women who complained of sexual harassment also experienced retaliation, and in 61% of the cases, the retaliation was termination.

Sexual harassment can occur in any kind of organization, with similar outcomes for victims (Kastl & Kleiner, 2001; Munson, Hulin, & Drasgow, 2000; Richman, Flaherty, & Johnson, 1999; Schneider, Swan, & Fitzgerald, 1997). Many educational institutions have sexual harassment policies prohibiting sexual harassment of employees and students. Although some students may be employees of the university and suffer tangible employment consequences or experience a hostile work environment, students may also be sexually harassed by another student or by an instructor, with tangible educational consequences.

Employers may be reluctant to deal with or even raise the issue of sexual harassment (Frierson, 1989; Peirce, Smolinski, & Rosen, 1998). The assumption is that by sensitizing employees to the issue of sexual harassment and showing how to make a complaint if they think they have been sexually harassed, more complaints will be made to the organization or to the EEOC than if the issue is never mentioned. But this policy of ignoring sexual harassment and hoping that it will go away is shortsighted, because victims of sexual harassment are not required to exhaust or even use the organization's grievance procedure before making a sexual harassment complaint to a state equal employment opportunity agency or the EEOC. A proactive approach to sexual harassment raises the subject, trains all employees in what is acceptable and not acceptable behavior, and clearly states the organizational consequences for violation of the organization's policy on sexual harassment. It can be highly damaging to an organization's reputation to have a highly publicized case of sexual harassment in the state or federal courts, with possible long-term consequences for recruitment and retention. In highly publicized cases, Del Laboratories paid more than $1 million to settle sexual harassment complaints, Chevron paid $2.2 million to four women for corporate retaliation for filing sexual harassment complaints, and Mitsubishi agreed to pay $34 million to several hundred women over claims of sexual harassment (Peirce et al., 1998). If employees see the organization is serious about not tolerating sexual harassment in the workplace and an effective grievance procedure is in place to handle complaints, it is far more likely that incidents of possible sexual harassment can be handled internally, rather than in the courts and the media.

The Guidelines on Sexual Harassment (Code of Federal Regulations, 1980) suggest that a proactive approach to sexual harassment will be the most effective:

> Prevention is the best tool for the elimination of sexual harassment. An employer should take all steps necessary to prevent sexual harassment from occurring, such as affirmatively raising the subject, expressing strong disapproval, developing appropriate sanctions, informing employees of their right to raise and how to raise the issue of harassment under Title VII, and developing methods to sensitize all concerned. (Sec. 1604.11, f)

The key elements of a proactive approach to dealing with sexual harassment are a statement of prohibited conduct (physical assaults; unwanted sexual advances, propositions, or other sexual comments; sexual or discriminatory displays or publications; and retaliation for sexual harassment complaints); penalties for violations of the policy; procedures for making, investigating, and resolving sexual harassment and retaliation complaints; and procedures and rules for education and training (Colquitt & Kleiner, 1996; Pearson, 1997; Stringer, Remick, Salisbury, & Ginorio, 1990). All of these elements can be found in *Robinson v. Jacksonville Shipyards, Inc.* (1991).

Strategic Questions

1. What are the personal costs for a victim of sexual harassment? What are the organizational costs of sexual harassment?
2. What tangible educational consequences might there be for a college or university student who is sexually harassed by another student or by his or her instructor?

(Continued)

(Continued)

3. Sexual harassment cases are not always a male supervisor and a female subordinate; what other possible cases of sexual harassment are there?
4. In what other types of organizations (other than colleges and universities) could a member (not an employee) be sexually harassed?
5. Who are the most likely victims of sexual harassment (by sex, age, job, industry, etc.)? Why are teen employees at high risk for sexual harassment?
6. In the organization's sexual harassment policy, who should not be the contact person for making the initial complaint?
7. What is the most effective approach for an organization to deal with sexual harassment?
8. What sexual harassment training issues are there in a global organization—for international assignments that bring employees to the United States and for international assignments that send U.S. employees to other countries?

Resources

Berta, D. (2007). EEOC: Industry sued most in claims of teen harassment. *Nation's Restaurant News, 41*(6), 1, 49.

Code of Federal Regulations. (1980). *Guidelines on sexual harassment.* 29 C.F.R Part 1604.11. http://edocket.access.gpo.gov/cfr_2008/julqtr/29cfr1604.11.htm

Colquitt, B., & Kleiner, B. H. (1996). How the best companies are preventing sexual harassment in the workplace. *Equal Opportunities International, 15*(3), 12-20.

Eaton, D. E. (2004). Beyond room service: Legal consequences of sexual harassment of staff by hotel guests. *Cornell Hotel and Restaurant Administration Quarterly, 15*(4), 347-361.

Faley, R. H., Knapp, D. E., Kustis, G. A., & Dubois, C. L. Z. (1999). Estimating the organizational costs of sexual harassment: The case of the U.S. Army. *Journal of Business and Psychology, 13*(4), 461-484.

Frierson, J. G. (1989). Reduce the costs of sexual harassment. *Personnel Journal, 68*(11), 79-85.

Greenwald, J. (2006). Companies face increased risks when employing teens. *Business Insurance, 40*(46), 4-5.

Kastl, M. A., & Kleiner, B. H. (2001). New developments concerning discrimination and harassment in universities. *International Journal of Sociology and Social Policy, 21*(8-10), 156-164.

Munson, L. J., Hulin, C., & Drasgow, F. (2000). Longitudinal analysis of dispositional influences and sexual harassment: Effects on job and psychological outcomes. *Personnel Psychology, 53*(1), 21-46.

Pearson, J. I. (1997). Harassment: Risk management tools. *Risk Management, 44*(1), 25-28.

Peirce, E. R. (1999). Sexual harassment: Why brokers trade in it, and what can be done to stop it. *Business and Society Review, 104*(1), 42-52.

Peirce, E. R., Smolinski, C. A., & Rosen, B. (1998). Why sexual harassment complaints fall on deaf ears. *Academy of Management Executive, 12*(3), 41-54.

Reese, L. A., & Lindenberg, K. E. (2002). Assessing local government sexual harassment policies. *American Review of Public Administration, 32*(3), 295-311.

Richman, J. A., Flaherty, J. A., & Johnson, T. P. (1999). Sexual harassment and generalized workplace abuse among university employees: Prevalence and mental health correlates. *American Journal of Public Health, 89*(3), 358-363.

Robinson v. Jacksonville Shipyards, Inc., 760 F.Supp 1486 (U.S. District Court for the Middle District of Florida, Jacksonville Division, 1991).

Rospenda, K. M., Richman, J. A., Ehmke, J. L. Z., & Zlatoper, K. W. (2005). Is workplace harassment hazardous to your health? *Journal of Business and Psychology, 20*(1), 95-110.

Stedham, Y., & Mitchell, M. C. (1998). Sexual harassment in casinos: Effects on employee attitudes and behavior. *Journal of Gambling Studies, 14* (4), 381-400.

Stringer, D. M., Remick, H., Salisbury, J., & Ginorio, A. B. (1990). The power and reasons behind sexual harassment: An employer's guide to solutions. *Public Personnel Management, 19*(1), 43-52.

Takeyama, D., & Kleiner, B. H. (1998). How to prevent sexual harassment in the workplace. *Equal Opportunities International, 17*(6), 6-12.

U.S. Equal Employment Opportunity Commission. (1990, March). *Policy guidance on current issues of sexual harassment.* http://www.eeoc.gov/policy/docs/currentissues.html

U.S. Equal Employment Opportunity Commission (2007, May 17). *Sexual harassment.* http://www.eeoc.gov/types/sexual_harassment.html

U.S. Equal Employment Opportunity Commission. (2008). *Sexual harassment charges EEOC & FEPAs Combined: FY 1997–FY 2007.* http://www.eeoc.gov/stats/harass.html

Wendt, A. C., & Slonaker, W. M. (2002). Sexual harassment and retaliation: A double-edged sword. *S.A.M. Advanced Management Journal, 67*(4), 49-57.

York, K. M., Barclay, L. A., & Zajack, A. B. (1997). Preventing sexual harassment: The effect of multiple training methods. *Employee Responsibilities and Rights Journal, 10*(4), 277-289.

AGE DISCRIMINATION, RETIREMENT, AND BRIDGE EMPLOYMENT

The Age Discrimination in Employment Act of 1967 (ADEA) prohibits discrimination on the basis of age for workers over 40 years of age. Specifically, it is unlawful for an employer

> (1) to fail or refuse to hire or to discharge any individual or otherwise discriminate against any individual with respect to his compensation, terms, conditions, or privileges of employment, because of such individual's age . . . (2) to limit, segregate, or classify employees in any way which would deprive or tend to deprive any individual of employment opportunities or otherwise adversely affect his status as an employee, because of such individual's age . . . or (3) to reduce the wage rate of any employee in order to comply with this chapter. (Sec. 623)

Between 1997 and 2003, age discrimination in employment plaintiffs recovered more money from jury verdicts than from any other protected group (Segal, 2006).

The original ADEA law protected individuals 40 to 65 years old, but the law was amended in 1986, and the upper age limit was eliminated.

Therefore, mandatory retirement programs are illegal, with the exception of employees who for the 2-year period immediately before retirement have been employed in a bona fide executive or high policy-making position, if the executive is entitled to an immediate, nonforfeitable, annual aggregate retirement benefit of at least $44,000 from any combination of employer sponsored retirement plans. Two other exemptions to mandatory retirement had allowed universities to have mandatory retirement for tenured college and university professors, and for law enforcement officers and firefighters, but these exemptions ended in 1994. Typically, public safety officers were required to retire between age 50 and 65, regardless of their ability to perform their duties (Pynes, 1995). Based on a sample of 16,000 faculty members at 104 colleges and universities, eliminating mandatory retirement for university faculty resulted in retirement rates for faculty over 70 years old falling to rates similar to 69-year-olds, suggesting that colleges and universities will experience a rise in the number of older faculty (Ashenfelter & Card, 2002).

The average retirement age (i.e., the youngest age at which half of the population is out of the labor force), has declined significantly over time, from 74 years old in 1910, to 70 in 1950, 65 in 1970, and 62 in 1985, and has appeared to remain stable since then (Cahill, Giandrea, & Quinn, 2006). Although the average retirement age may have recently resumed its long-run decline after leveling off for 10 to 15 years, the decline has been attributed to a rise in the labor force participation rate of older workers (Gendell, 2001). There are a number of factors that might explain why the long-term decline in average retirement age has leveled off, including the end of mandatory retirement, the shift away from defined benefit pension plans toward defined contribution pension plans, improvements in health and longevity, and changes in the physical nature of jobs.

Instead of a traditional retirement, many workers are now making the transition from a full-time career job to full-time retirement by taking a bridge job, a kind of partial retirement. Based on 10 years of data in the U.S. Bureau of Labor Statistics Health and Retirement Study, about half of the people studied with full-time career jobs had taken a bridge job rather than moving directly out of the labor force (Cahill et al., 2006). For the organization, bridge employment may be a solution to staffing problems, by providing an incentive for older workers to retire early, and by employing a better trained and more readily available alternative to temporary workers (Kim & Feldman, 2000). For some workers, bridge jobs are a financial necessity; for others, it brings three benefits: continued activity and daily structure, less work and less job-related stress, and a better sense of self-worth from providing valuable information and guidance to the next generation. Bridge employment is strongly related to retirement satisfaction and overall life satisfaction (Kim & Feldman, 2000).

Another trend in the labor market is postretirement employment, especially work after early retirement. Instead of permanent retirement, some people return to work after retirement and are referred to as working retirees (Herz, 1995). According to a survey conducted by the American Association of Retired Persons (2004), 79% of baby boomers plan to work in some capacity during their retirement years. A cost-effective strategy for the organization to deal with labor shortages is to encourage bridge employment to retain older workers beyond the normal retirement age or recruit them after they retire (Rau & Adams, 2005).

Strategic Questions

1. Public safety officers were a group of workers for whom organizations could have mandatory retirement, until the ADEA exemption expired. What made these jobs different, that mandatory retirement had been allowed for them?
2. Tenured university professors were another group of workers for whom organizations could have mandatory retirement, until the ADEA exemption expired. What made this job different, that mandatory retirement had been allowed for it?
3. What benefits would an organization gain by actively working with preretirement employees to develop a career plan, including a bridge job as their transition to retirement?
4. What benefits might an employee gain by taking a bridge job?
5. How can an organization effectively recruit for bridge jobs? What aspects of bridge jobs would be attractive to workers? What aspects of the organization would be attractive to workers looking for bridge jobs?
6. For what kinds of jobs would hiring bridge employees or postretirement employees be more effective than hiring temporary employees?

Resources

Adams, G., & Rau, B. (2004). Job seeking among retirees seeking bridge employment. *Personnel Psychology, 57*(3), 719-744.

Age Discrimination in Employment Act of 1967. http://www.eeoc.gov/policy/adea.html; especially see 1625.9: Prohibition of involuntary retirement; and 1625.12: Exemption for bona fide executive or high policymaking employees, http://www.access.gpo.gov/nara/cfr/waisidx_06/29cfr1625_06.html

American Association of Retired Persons. (2004). *Baby Boomers envision retirement II: Survey of Baby Boomers' expectations for retirement.* Washington, DC: Author.

Ashenfelter, O., & Card, D. (2002). Did the elimination of mandatory retirement affect faculty retirement? *American Economic Review, 92*(4), 957-980.

Cahill, K. E., Giandrea, M. D., & Quinn, J. F. (2006). Are traditional retirements a thing of the past? New evidence on retirement patterns and bridge jobs. *Business Perspectives, 18*(2), 26-37.

(Continued)

(Continued)

Chen, Y., & Scott, J. C. (2003). Gradual retirement: An additional option in work and retirement. *North American Actuarial Journal, 7* (3), 62-74.

Feldman, D. C. (1994). The decision to retire early: A review and conceptualization. *Academy of Management Review, 19*(2), 285-311.

Feldman, D. C., & Kim, S. (2000). Bridge employment during retirement: A field study of individual and organizational experiences with post-retirement employment. *Human Resource Planning, 23*(1), 14-25.

Gendell, M. (2001). Retirement age declines again in 1990s. *Monthly Labor Review, 124*(10), 12-21.

Herz, D. E. (1995). Work after early retirement: An increasing trend among men. *Monthly Labor Review, 118*(4), 13-20.

Honig, M., & Hanoch, G. (1985). Partial retirement as a separate mode of retirement behavior. *Journal of Human Resources, 20*(1), 21-46.

Kim, S., & Feldman, D. C. (2000). Working in retirement: The antecedents of bridge employment and its consequences for quality of life in retirement. *Academy of Management Journal, 43*(6), 1195-1210.

Krashinsky, M. (1988). The case for eliminating mandatory retirement: Why economics and human rights need not conflict. *Canadian Public Policy, 14*(1), 40-51.

Lazear, E. P. (1979). Why is there mandatory retirement? *Journal of Political Economy, 87*(6), 1261-1284.

O'Connor v. Consolidated Coin Caterers Corp., 517 U.S. 308 (Supreme Court of the United States, 1996).

Pynes, J. E. (1995). The ADEA and its exemptions on the mandatory retirement provisions for firefighters. *Public Personnel Administration, 15*(2), 34-45.

Rau, B. L., & Adams, G. A. (2005). Attracting retirees to apply: Desired organizational characteristics of bridge employment. *Journal of Organizational Behavior, 26*(6), 649-660.

Ruhm, C. J. (1990). Bridge jobs and partial retirement. *Journal of Labor Economics, 8*(4), 482-501.

Saba, T., & Guerin, G. (2005). Extending employment beyond retirement age: The case of health care managers in Quebec. *Public Personnel Management, 34*(2), 195-214.

Segal, J. A. (2006). Time is on their side. *HR Magazine, 51*(2), 129-133.

Ulrich, L. B., & Brott, P. E. (2005). Older workers and bridge employment: Redefining retirement. *Journal of Employment Counseling, 42*(4), 159-170.

Weckerle, J. R., & Shultz, K. S. (1999). Influences on the bridge employment decision among older USA workers. *Journal of Occupational and Organizational Psychology, 72*(3), 317-329.

CHECKING REFERENCES AND GIVING REFERENCES

The dean of admissions at the Massachusetts Institute of Technology resigned after the school confirmed an anonymous tip that she had lied about having a bachelor's and master's degree from Rensselaer Polytechnic Institute. The dean was an outspoken advocate of reducing the stress of college admissions, because too many students were puffing up their credentials (Winstein & Golden, 2007). A city manager for 15 years was fired after he admitted that he lied about having degrees from the University of Michigan–Flint, Washtenaw Community College, and Franklin University in Columbus, Ohio (Wouk & Cardenas, 2003). Three years previously, the manager told a local university that he had a bachelor's degree, and they hired him to teach a course on ethics, using the city's code of ethics as a teaching tool, according to a student who took the class (Manolatos & Schultz, 2003).

On one hand, prospective employers want to check references to be sure that they are hiring the person they think they are hiring. Reference checking has long been part of the selection process (Best, 1977; Messmer, 2000). Employers want to verify with the applicants' previous employers the information that the applicant has provided about themselves and their work history. Claims made by applicants may be true, exaggerated, or entirely fictional; between 10% and 30% of all job applicants distort the truth or lie on their resume (Crockett, 1999). Employers have a duty to protect their employees, customers, clients, and visitors from injury caused by employees that the employer knows—or should have known—pose a risk to others (Woska, 2007). If the organization does not do an effective job of reference checking and fails to uncover an applicant's incompetence or unfitness by a diligent search of references, the organization might be sued for negligent hiring (Edwards & Kleiner, 2002; Fenton & Lawrimore, 1992), defamation, infliction of emotional distress, and interference with a contractual relationship (Tahan & Kleiner, 2001). For example, a medical center hired a registered nurse, who later confessed to killing up to 40 other patients while employed at 10 different medical centers (Roberts, 2004).

On the other hand, past employers are often reluctant to share negative information, fearing a defamation suit. This has lead to many organizations adopting a "name, rank, and serial number" policy concerning reference checks on former employees, doing no more than verifying job titles, dates of employment, and sometimes pay information (Little & Sipes, 2000; McConnell, 2000; Peck, 2007). But even this policy can fail to protect an organization from legal liability, because an employer who knowingly withholds negative information regarding the former employee may be liable for negligent referral (Cadrain, 2004; Little & Sipes, 2000; Tahan & Kleiner, 2001).

This leaves employers in a quandary: They want to provide as little information as possible on current or past employees because of the possibility of a lawsuit, but they want to obtain as much information as possible about potential hires from other employers who are following the same policy of providing as little information as possible.

Strategic Questions

1. Did the city and the universities do an inadequate job of reference checking?
2. Is "job title and dates of employment only" the best policy for an organization to take when other organizations make reference checks about current or past employees?
3. Which is the greater risk of lawsuit, for negligent hiring or for defamation? What can the organization do to reduce the risk?
4. How can an organization obtain useful information about an applicant if the former employer refuses to give information beyond "job title and dates of employment"?

(Continued)

(Continued)

5. Who should conduct reference checks on applicants? What skills, training, or experience should they have?
6. Who should respond to reference inquiries about former employees? What skills, training, or experience should they have?

Resources

Best, R. B. (1977). Don't forget those reference checks! *Public Personnel Management, 6*(6), 422-426.

Cadrain, D. (2004). HR professionals stymied by vanishing job references. *HR Magazine, 49*(11), 31, 40.

Edwards, R. M., & Kleiner, B. H. (2002). Conducting effective and legally safe background and reference checks. *Managerial Law, 44*(1-2), 136-150.

Fenton, J. W., Jr., & Lawrimore, K. W. (1992). Employment reference checking, firm size, and defamation liability. *Journal of Small Business Management, 30*(4), 88-95.

Little, B. L., & Sipes, D. (2000). Betwixt and between: The dilemma of employee references. *Employee Responsibilities and Rights Journal, 12*(1), 1-8.

Manolatos, T., & Schultz, M. (2003, October 24). Duchane also lied on application to teach; OU says he claimed degree when he taught two-credit course on ethics for $1000. *Detroit News.*

McConnell, C. R. (2000). Employment references: Walking scared between the minefield of defamation and the specter of negligent hiring. *The Health Care Manager, 19*(2), 78-90.

Messmer, M. (2000). Reference checking: A crucial step in the hiring process. *National Public Accountant, 45*(3), 28-29.

Peck, D. (2007). High-yield reference checking: Adding new value to the hiring equation. *Employment Relations Today, 33*(4), 51-57.

Pruitt v. Pavelin, 131 Ariz. 195 (Court of Appeals of Arizona, 1984).

Randi W v. Muroc Joint Unified School District, 14 Cal 4th 1066 (Supreme Court of California, 1997).

Roberts, S. (2004). Patient deaths prompt close look at hospital employment practices. *Business Insurance, 38*(3), 3-5.

Tahan, S., & Kleiner, B. H. (2001). New developments concerning giving employment references. *Management Research News, 24*(3/4), 94-96.

Weissman v. Sri Lanka Curry House, Inc., 469 N.W.2d 471 (Court of Appeals of Minnesota, 1991).

Winstein, K. J., & Golden, D. (2007, April 27). MIT admissions dean lied on resume in 1979, quits. *Wall Street Journal*, p. B1.

Woska, W. J. (2007). Legal issues for HR professionals: Reference checking/background investigations. *Public Personnel Management, 36*(1), 79-89.

Wouk, M., & Cardenas, E. L. (2003, October 14). Resume claims ensnare Duchane; Politicians demand resignation of Sterling Heights manager who cited nonexistent U-M degree. *Detroit News.*

Applications

COMPLETING THE EEO-1 REPORT

The EEOC collects workforce data from employers with more than 100 employees (lower thresholds apply to federal contractors) through the

EEO-1 Report. Employers that meet the reporting requirements are legally required to provide the data; it is not voluntary. The record-keeping requirements come from the Civil Rights Act of 1964:

> Every employer, employment agency, and labor organization subject to this title shall (1) make and keep such records relevant to the determinations of whether unlawful employment practices have been or are being committed, (2) preserve such records for such periods, and (3) make such reports therefrom as the Commission shall prescribe by regulation or order, after public hearing, as reasonable, necessary, or appropriate for the enforcement of this title or the regulations or orders thereunder.

All employers with 100 or more employees, and all federal government contractors and first-tier subcontractors with 50 or more employees and a contract amounting to $50,000 or more are required to file an EEO-1 Report by September 30 of each year. The data collected using the EEO-1 Report are used for enforcement, self-assessment by employers, and research. Although the data are confidential, aggregated data are available to the public. In 2007, the EEO-1 report was modified. The major changes involved subdividing the job category of "Officials and Managers" and revising the race and ethnic categories (EEOC, 2006a). There is a new race category of "Two or more races (Not Hispanic or Latino)," "Asian or Pacific Islander" is divided into two separate categories, and Black is renamed "Black or African American." Also, the "Officials and Managers" category has been divided into two subcategories: Executive/Senior Level Officials and Managers and First/Middle Level Officials and Managers.

The preferred method for completing the EEO-1 Survey is the EEOC's Web-based filing system. Online filing requires no special software installation, because the online form is Web based, information entered in previous years is prefilled from the previous year to speed data entry, the data are encrypted to ensure privacy, and historical data are maintained for up to 10 years.

To Do

Use the data from the EEO-1 Aggregate report for your metropolitan statistical area to complete the EEO-1 Report (EEOC, 2006a). Go to the U.S. Census Bureau Web site, and use the state-based Metropolitan and Micropolitan Statistical Areas (MSA) Maps to find your MSA. For "state-based (page size) maps of metropolitan and micropolitan statistical areas," select the most recent year; then from the list of states, select your state. Use the map to identify your MSA. Omit the "Executive/Senior-Level Officials and Managers" and "First/Middle-Level Officials and Managers" job categories.

(Continued)

(Continued)

Resources

U. S. Census Bureau. (2004, November). *State-based metropolitan and micropolitan statistical areas maps.* http://www.census.gov/geo/www/maps/stcbsa_pg/stBased_200411_nov.htm

U.S. Equal Employment Opportunity Commission. (2005). *2005 PMSA aggregate report.* http://www.eeoc.gov/stats/jobpat/2005/msa/index.html

U.S. Equal Employment Opportunity Commission. (2006a, November 7). *EEO-1 report, section D.* http://www.eeoc.gov/eeo1/eeo1_2007_d.pdf

U.S. Equal Employment Opportunity Commission. (2006b, January). *EEO-1 report, instruction booklet.* http://www.eeoc.gov/eeo1/instruction_rev_2006.pdf

U.S. Equal Employment Opportunity Commission. (2006c, December 19). EEO surveys. http://www.eeoc.gov/employers/surveys.html

U.S. Equal Employment Opportunity Commission. (2006d). *Job classification guide.* http://www.eeoc.gov/eeo1/jobclassguide.pdf

DETERMINING THE ADVERSE IMPACT OF A SELECTION PROCEDURE

Discrimination in employment is a legal judgment, made by a judge or a jury. The administrative agencies that enforce the Civil Rights Act of 1964 use an administrative term to describe evidence of discrimination. Adverse impact is "a substantially different rate of selection in hiring, promotion, or other employment decision which works to the disadvantage of members of a race, sex, or ethnic group (Uniform Guidelines on Employee Selection Procedures, Sec. 1607.16, B)." To determine whether a selection test has adverse impact, the Four-Fifths Rule is applied to applicant flow data, looking at the outcomes obtained from using the selection test for a particular job (Uniform Guidelines on Employee Selection Procedures, Sec.1607.4, D. Information on impact):

> *Adverse impact and the Four-Fifths rule.* A selection rate for any race, sex, or ethnic group that is less than four fifths (or 80%) of the rate for the group with the highest rate will generally be regarded by the federal enforcement agencies as evidence of adverse impact, whereas a greater than four fifths rate will generally not be regarded by federal enforcement agencies as evidence of adverse impact.

If the sample size is large enough, the chi-square test may be used to test for statistically significant differences in selection ratios. A statistically significant chi-square would indicate that the selection ratio for the minority group is less than the selection ratio for the majority group. The Four-Fifths Rule and the chi-square test will typically lead to the same conclusion about adverse impact. For smaller sample sizes (less than about 150 cases), the chi-square lacks sufficient statistical power and the Four-Fifths Rule should be used, but at larger sample sizes, the chi-square will detect real differences in selection ratios when the Four-Fifths Rule does not (York, 2002).

In some cases, applicant flow data are not available, either because the organization has lost the data or never collected it. However, like failing to keep required tax documentation, this puts the organization in a difficult position (Uniform Guidelines on Employee Selection Procedures, Sec. 1607.4, D):

> Where the user has not maintained data on adverse impact as required by the documentation section of applicable guidelines, the Federal enforcement agencies may draw an inference of adverse impact of the selection process from the failure of the user to maintain such data, if the user has an underutilization of a group in the job category, as compared to the group's representation in the relevant labor market or, in the case of jobs filled from within, the applicable work force.

Instead of doing an adverse impact calculation based on applicant flow data, a Labor Market Analysis (or Utilization Analysis or Hazelwood Analysis) can be done, comparing the ratio of minority to majority of employees in a particular job in the organization to the ratio of minority to majority of potential applicants in the local labor market (i.e., the Metropolitan Statistical Area as defined by the U.S. Census). Metropolitan and micropolitan statistical areas (metro and micro areas) are geographic entities defined by the U.S. Office of Management and Budget for use by federal statistical agencies in collecting, tabulating, and publishing federal statistics. A metro area contains a core urban area of 50,000 or more population, and a micro area contains an urban core of at least 10,000 (but less than 50,000) population. Each metro or micro area consists of one or more counties and includes the counties containing the core urban area, as well as any adjacent counties that have a high degree of social and economic integration (as measured by commuting to work) with the urban core. The ninth largest Metropolitan/Micropolitan Statistical Area is Code 19820: Detroit-Warren-Livonia, with a population of 4,452,557. The smallest is Code 11380: Andrews, TX with 13,004 people.

In *Hazelwood School District v. U.S.* (1977), the Supreme Court ruled that there was a significant statistical disparity between the percentage of Black teachers employed by the school district and the percentage of Black teachers in the relevant labor market. In St. Louis County and the city of St. Louis, 15.4% of the teachers were Black; but in the 1972-1973 and 1973-1974 school years, only 1.4% and 1.8%, respectively, of Hazelwood's teachers were Black.

To Do

Do a Labor Market Analysis for a hypothetical school district in the nearest Metropolitan Statistical Area to you. Assume that in this hypothetical school district, 13 out of 244 (5.3%) of the secondary school teachers are Black. Determine whether Black teachers are underutilized.

1. Go to the U.S. Census Bureau Web site, and use the state-based Metropolitan and Micropolitan Statistical Areas Maps to find the MSA that your school district is in. For "State-based (page size) maps of metropolitan and micropolitan statistical areas," select the most recent year; then from the list of states, select your state. Use the map to identify your MSA and enter your MSA in the Labor Market Analysis Table.
2. Go to the U.S. Census Bureau Web site, to use the Census 2000 EEO Data Tool. http://www.census.gov/eeo2000/index.html.
3. For "Choose the Table You Want to Display," select "Employment by Census Occupation Codes." For "Select Geography," select "Residence: Data based on where people live."
4. For "Select one of the following levels of geography," select Metropolitan Areas (MSAs, PMSAs). Click Next.
5. For "Select one or more Metro Areas," select the metropolitan area your school district is in.
6. For "Occupation Sort Order," select "Sort Alphabetically," and click "Sort." In the box "Select one or more occupation categories (or Census Occupation Codes)," scroll down to "Secondary School Teachers," and select "Secondary School Teachers." For "Select Race Categories to Display," select "Show Detailed Race/Ethnicity Categories." For "Output Options," select "Show Total of Selected Geographies and Occupations." Click "Display table."
7. Calculate the Four-Fifths Rule on the data you have collected. Enter the data you have collected into the Labor Market Analysis Table. The adverse impact ratio is the percentage of Black secondary teachers employed by the school district, divided by the percentage of Black secondary teachers in the relevant labor market. If the adverse impact ratio is less than 80%, then there is underutilization.
8. Is there underutilization of Black secondary teachers in the school district?

Labor Market Analysis		*MSA:*
	Number Employed	*Number in Labor Market*
Black	13	
Total	244	
Percentage		
Adverse Impact Ratio		

Resources

Hazelwood School District v. U.S., 433 U.S. 299 (United States Supreme Court, 1977).

Ironson, G. H., Guion, R. M., & Ostrandet, M. (1982). Adverse impact from a psychometric perspective. *Journal of Applied Psychology, 67*(4), 419-432.

Jones, G. F. (1981). Usefulness of different statistical techniques for determining adverse impact in small jurisdictions. *Review of Public Personnel Administration,* 2(1), 85-89.

U.S. Census Bureau. (2000). *2000 EEO data tool.* http://www.census.gov/eeo2000/index.html

U.S. Census Bureau. (2004, November). *State-based metropolitan and micropolitan statistical areas maps.* http://www.census.gov/geo/www/maps/stcbsa_pg/stBased_200411_nov.htm

U.S. Census Bureau. (2008, August 19). *Metropolitan and micropolitan statistical areas.* http://www.census.gov/population/www/estimates/metroarea.html

Wollack, S. (1994). Confronting adverse impact in cognitive examinations. *Public Personnel Management,* 23(2), 217-224.

York, K. M. (2002). Disparate results in adverse impact tests: The 4/5ths Rule and the chi square test. *Public Personnel Management, 31*(2), 253-262.

Experiential Exercises

IDENTIFYING BARRIERS TO ACCESS IN THE WORKPLACE

The Americans with Disabilities Act (1990) recognized that "discrimination against individuals with disabilities persists in such critical areas as employment, housing, public accommodations, education, transportation, communication, recreation, institutionalization, health services, voting, and access to public services." When the Americans with Disabilities Act was passed, it was estimated that there were 43 million Americans with a disability. The current estimate is 54 million Americans with disabilities (Rimmer, Riley, Wang, & Rauworth, 2005; Wells, 2001), and as the baby boom generation enters middle age, this number is likely to increase, because about 25% of people aged 45 to 64 have a disability (Pointer & Kleiner, 1997).

One of the purposes of the Americans with Disabilities Act was to provide a clear national mandate for the elimination of discrimination against individuals with disabilities. This includes architectural barriers to access, common in buildings and facilities constructed prior to the Americans with Disabilities Act. Entities that receive federal funds, such as hospitals, colleges, universities, and state and local governments, are required by law to complete a Self-Evaluation and Transition Plan to achieve accessibility and eliminate discriminatory practices (Hanks, 2004). Pointer and Kleiner (1997) list four common physical barriers to buildings: doorways wide enough to accommodate a wheelchair, elevator or other access to the second or third floor, accessible restroom, and accessible office space. Many buildings have access control systems, which must be accessible to people with disabilities (e.g., an entrance requiring entry of a code number must not depend only on visual or auditory cues; McPherson, 2001).

To Do

Conduct a barrier survey of the facilities of a local business in one of industries listed below. The barriers could apply to customers or employees. Identify physical obstacles or architectural barriers that limit the accessibility to the facility or to activities within the facility, for someone with a disability covered under the Americans with Disabilities Act. Consider access for someone with disabilities in hearing, vision, mobility, or any other physical disability. Then describe in detail the nature of the barrier and what needs to be done to make the facilities accessible.

Airport limo service	Library	Salon
Bank/ATM	Movie theater	Sports arena
College/University	Public transit	Travel/Guided tours company
Health club	Restaurant	Urgent care
Hotel/Motel	Retail store	

Resources

Americans with Disabilities Act. (1990). http://www.eeoc.gov/policy/ada.html

Blanck, P. D. (1996). *Communicating the Americans with Disabilities Act, transcending compliance: 1996 follow-up report on Sears, Roebuck and Co*. Iowa City, IA: Annenberg Program.

Cavinato, J. L. (1992). Transportation and tourism for the disabled: An assessment. *Transportation Journal, 31*(3), 46-53.

Code of Federal Regulations, 28 CFR, Part 35—Nondiscrimination on the basis of disability in state and local government services; especially see Section 105: *Self-evaluation*; and Section 150, *Existing facilities*, http://www.access.gpo.gov/nara/cfr/waisidx_06/28cfr35_06.html

East Bay Regional Park District. (2006, May). *ADA self-evaluation and transition plan*. http://www.ebparks.org/resources/pdf/district/EBRPD_ADA_SETP_2006.pdf

Easter Seals Project ACTION. (2004). *Toolkit for the assessment of bus stop accessibility and safety*. http://projectaction.easterseals.com/site/DocServer/06BSTK_Complete_Toolkit.pdf?docID=21443

Hanks, D. (2004). ADA compliance: It's more than 'removing barriers.' *Nursing Homes, 53*(6), 70-71.

McPherson, R. (2001). ADA integration. *Buildings, 95*(9), 26.

Pointer, T. A., & Kleiner, B. H. (1997). Developments concerning accommodation of wheelchair users within the workplace in accordance to the Americans with Disabilities Act. *Equal Opportunities International, 16*(6/7), 44-49.

Rimmer, J. H., Riley, B., Wang, E., & Rauworth, A. (2005). Accessibility of health clubs for people with mobility disabilities and visual impairments. *American Journal of Public Health, 95*(11), 2022-2028.

University of Montana–Western. (2005, June). *ADA self-evaluation and transition plan*. http://www.umwestern.edu/studentlife/disabilities/SETP.pdf

Wells, S. J. (2001). Is the ADA working? *HR Magazine, 46*(4), 38-46.

Wilson, M. (2001). ADA unclear on merchandise access. *Chain Store Age, 77*(7), 124.

INTERNET APPLICATIONS AND ILLEGAL PRE-EMPLOYMENT INQUIRIES

An applicant is any person who has indicated an interest in being considered for hiring, promotion, or other employment opportunities. This interest might be shown by completing the application form or even orally indicating an interest in a job, depending on the employer. The use of company Web sites has made recruitment one of the most successful applications of the Internet for business purposes (Cober, Brown, & Levy, 2004). In the Internet age, e-mail, Web sites such as third-party job or resume banks and employment Web pages, electronic scanning technology, applicant tracking systems, and internal databases of job seekers has broadened the definition of who is an applicant. The state of Washington, for example, uses an Internet application system for on-line application, screening, testing, and notification, processing 100,000 employment applicants each year (Bingham, Ilg, & Davidson, 2002). In this context, an individual is an applicant when (a) the employer has acted to fill a particular position, (b) the individual has followed the employer's standard procedures for submitting applications, and (c) the individual has indicated an interest in the particular position.

Employers are limited in what pre-employment inquiries they can ask applicants. Employers should not inquire about matters that may disproportionately exclude members of protected groups, unless the inquiry concerns a legitimate attribute for the job (i.e., the employer can show that the requirement is job related and consistent with business necessity). Although there are some specific exceptions, some examples of pre-employment inquiries that normally should be avoided include as follows (Bland & Stalcup, 1999; Burrington, 1982; EEOC, 2006; Frierson & Jolly, 1988; Koen, 1995; Letizia, 2004; Munchus, 1985):

- Marital status, and if married, date of marriage. Number of dependents, including the applicant.
- Have you been convicted of a crime in the past 10 years, excluding misdemeanors and summary offenses, which has not been annulled, expunged, or sealed by a court?
- State names of relatives and friends working for this organization, other than your spouse.
- What is your ancestry?
- What is your date of birth?
- What is your race?
- What are the names and relationships of those with whom you live?
- When did you graduate?
- Does your husband support your decision to work?
- Have you ever been treated by a psychiatrist or psychologist?
- Have you had any prior worker's compensation claims?

- What religion are you?
- What language do you speak at home?
- What medications are you currently taking?
- What organizations, clubs, societies, and lodges do you belong to?
- Are you a U.S. citizen?
- Are you married, divorced, or single?
- Are you pregnant? Are you planning to have children?
- Do you have any children? How old are they? What are your child care arrangements?
- What is your gender?
- Do you have any handicaps?
- What is your financial status?
- Are you a member of any union?
- Do you own a car?
- Have you filed for bankruptcy?
- What is the minimum salary you are willing to accept?

Burrington (1982) collected application forms from the central state personnel agencies of all 50 states and found that all of the application forms contained at least one inappropriate request for information, and one contained 19, with an average of 7.7 inappropriate items on each application. Camden and Wallace collected 94 application forms from companies in a large metropolitan area, from retail stores, service industries, industrial manufacturing companies, corporate headquarters for *Fortune 1000* firms, and civic institutions, and found that 73% of the forms contained one or more illegal pre-employment inquiries. Vodanovich and Lowe (1992) examined a cross-section of 88 organizations in the service industry and found that all of the organizations' application blanks contained inadvisable items, with an average of 7.4 inadvisable items per form. Wallace, Tye, and Vodanovich (2000) found at least one inadvisable question on 97.5% of Internet-based state application forms from 41 states. Fine and Schupp (2002) collected 59 employment applications from retail outlets and found that 37 (63%) of them created discriminatory legal liability for the employers using them. Kethley and Terpstra (2005) analyzed more than 300 federal court cases involving the use of the application form and found that more than 50% of the cases involved charges related to the applicant's sex and age, and another 15% were related to the applicant's race.

To Do

Search company Web pages to find online applications for five companies. The companies can be small local businesses, multinational organizations, or state, local, or federal government. Using the form here or any piece of paper, identify on each organization's application any pre-employment inquiries that should be avoided on an application.

Inappropriate Pre-employment Inquiries

Company	*Inappropriate Pre-employment Inquiries*
1.	
2.	
3.	
4.	
5.	

(Continued)

(Continued)

Resources

Bingham, B., Ilg, S., & Davidson, N. (2002). Great candidates fast: On-line job application and electronic processing. *Public Personnel Management, 31*(1), 53-64.

Bland, T. S., & Stalcup, S. S. (1999). Build a legal employment application. *HR Magazine, 44*(3), 129-133.

Burrington, D. D. (1982). A review of state government employment application forms for suspect inquiries. *Public Personnel Management Journal, 11*(1), 55-60.

Camden, C., & Wallace, B. (1983). Job application forms: A hazardous employment practice. *Personnel Administrator, 28*(3), 31-32, 64.

Cober, R. T., Brown, D. J., Blumental, D. J., Doverspike, D., &; Paul Lev, P. (2000). The quest for the qualified job surfer: It's time the public sector catches the wave. *Public Personnel Management, 29*(4), 479-496.

Cober, R. T., Brown, D. J., & Levy, P. E. (2004). Form, content, and function: An evaluative methodology for corporate employment web sites. *Human Resource Management, 43*(2/3), 201-218.

Fine, C. R., & Schupp, R. W. (2002). Liability exposure trends in recruitment: An assessment and analysis of retail employment applications. *Employee Responsibilities and Rights Journal, 14*(4), 135-143.

Fortune 500. (2007). *Annual ranking of America's largest corporations.* http://money.cnn.com/magazines/fortune/fortune500/2007/full_list/index.html

Fortune 500. (2007). *Fortune 100 Best companies to work for.* http://money.cnn.com/magazines/fortune/bestcompanies/2007/

Frierson, J. G., & Jolly, J. P. (1988). Problems in employment application forms. *Employment Relations Today, 15*(3), 205-217.

Kethley, R. B., & Terpstra, D. E. (2005). An analysis of litigation associated with the use of the application form in the selection process. *Public Personnel Management, 34*(4), 357-375.

Letizia, J. M. (2004). How to avoid a wrongful discharge suit. *Home Health Care Management & Practice, 16*(2), 138-140.

Munchus, G., III. (1985). The status of pre-employment enquiry restrictions on the employment and hiring function. *Employee Relations, 7*(3), 20-26.

U.S. Equal Employment Opportunity Commission. (2006, May 9). *Title VII/ADEA pre-employment inquiries.* http://www.eeoc.gov/foia/letters/2006/titlevii_adea_preemployment_inquiries.html

Vodanovich, S. J., & Lowe, R. H. (1992). They ought to know better: The incidence and correlates of inappropriate application blank inquiries. *Public Personnel Management, 21*(3), 363-370.

Wallace, J. C., Tye, M. G., & Vodanovich, S. J. (2000). Applying for jobs online: Examining the legality of Internet-based application forms. *Public Personnel Management, 29*(4), 497-504.

Creative Exercises

MAKING REASONABLE ACCOMMODATIONS UNDER THE AMERICANS WITH DISABILITIES ACT

The Americans with Disabilities Act of 1990 prohibits private employers, state and local governments, employment agencies, and labor unions from discriminating against qualified individuals with disabilities in job application procedures, hiring, firing, advancement, compensation, job training, and other terms, conditions, and privileges of employment. An individual with a disability is a person who

- Has a physical or mental impairment that substantially limits one or more major life activities;
- Has a record of such an impairment; or
- Is regarded as having such an impairment.

A qualified employee or applicant with a disability is an individual who, with or without reasonable accommodation, can perform the essential functions of the job in question. Reasonable accommodation may include, but is not limited to

- Making existing facilities used by employees readily accessible to and usable by persons with disabilities;
- Job restructuring, modifying work schedules, reassignment to a vacant position;
- Acquiring or modifying equipment or devices; adjusting or modifying examinations, training materials, or policies; and providing qualified readers or interpreters.

An employer is required to make a reasonable accommodation to the known disability of a qualified applicant or employee if it would not impose an "undue hardship" on the operation of the employer's business. Undue hardship is defined as an action requiring significant difficulty or expense when considered in light of factors such as an employer's size, financial resources, and the nature and structure of its operation. An employer is not required to lower quality or production standards to make an accommodation; nor is an employer obligated to provide personal use items such as glasses or hearing aids (EEOC, 2007).

There are different kinds of accommodations that an employer might make (EEOC, 1999). The employer might restructure a job by shifting responsibility to other employees for minor job tasks that an employee is unable to perform because of a disability or alter when and/or how a job task is performed. If an employee is unable to perform a minor job task because of a disability, an employer can require the employee to perform a different minor job function in its place. Some reasonable accommodations may include a modified or part-time schedule, adjusting arrival or departure times, periodic breaks, or change of time when certain job tasks are performed. Accommodations might also require purchase of equipment or revision of training material (Drach, 1992).

The U.S. General Accounting Office's (1990) study on the cost of accommodations under Americans with Disabilities Act reported that 51% cost nothing, another 30% cost less than $500, and only 8% of the workers received accommodations costing more than $2,000. Blanck's (1996) study of Americans with Disabilities Act accommodations at Sears from January 1, 1993, to December 31, 1995, found that the average cost at Sears of providing workplace accommodations to employees with disabilities was $45, and of more than 70 workplace accommodations, almost all (99%) required little or no cost.

To Do

Choose a local business (even a college or university), contact the human resources manager, and find out what accommodations have recently been made for an employee with a disability. Also, estimate the cost of the accommodations. Using the form here or your own paper, write a short report detailing your findings: job title and job description, the essential job functions for which the employee needed accommodation, a description of the accommodations that were made, and an estimate of the cost of the accommodation. For example, if a recently hired individual required that a desk be raised on blocks to allow clearance for a wheelchair, how much did the blocks and labor cost? If an employee required frequent breaks, what was the cost to the organization of making changes in the work schedule?

Disabilities Accommodation

The Job	*The Accommodation*
Job title: Job description:	Accommodations made:
Essential functions for which the employee needed accommodation:	Cost estimate:

Resources

Americans with Disabilities Act of 1990. http://www.eeoc.gov/policy/ada.html

Blanck, P. D. (1996). *Communicating the Americans with Disabilities Act, transcending compliance: 1996 follow-up report on Sears, Roebuck and Co.* Iowa City, IA: Annenberg Program.

Drach, R. L. (1992). Making reasonable accommodations under the ADA. *Employment Relations Today, 19*(2), 167-169.

Dykxhoorn, H. J., & Sinning, K. E. (1993). Complying with the Americans with Disabilities Act: Costs and tax treatment. *National Public Accountant, 38*(6), 32-37.

Harlan, S. L., & Robert, P. M. (1998). The social construction of disability in organizations: Why employers resist reasonable accommodations. *Work and Occupations, 25*(4), 397-435.

Hirschman, C. (1997). Reasonable accommodations at a reasonable cost. *HR Magazine, 42*(9), 106-114.

Hollwitz, J., Goodman, D. F., & Bolte, D. (1995). Complying with the Americans with Disabilities Act: Assessing the costs of reasonable accommodation. *Public Personnel Management, 24*(2), 149-157.

Job Accommodation Network. http://www.jan.wvu.edu/

Lerner, C. S. (2004). "Accommodations" for the learning disabled: A level playing field or Affirmative Action for elites? *Vanderbilt Law Review, 57*(3), 1041-1124.

Nelson, J., & Kleiner, B. H. (2001). How to accommodate common disabilities in organisations. *Equal Opportunities International, 20*(5-7), 146-151.

U.S. Equal Employment Opportunity Commission. (1999, March 1). *Small employers and reasonable accommodation.* http://www.eeoc.gov/facts/accommodation.html

U.S. Equal Employment Opportunity Commission. (2007, May 17). *Disability discrimination.* http://www.eeoc.gov/types/ada.html

U.S. General Accounting Office. (1990, January). *Persons with disabilities: Reports on costs of accommodations. GAO/IiRD-9044BR.* http://archive.gao.gov/d27t7/140318.pdf

CREATING A SEXUAL HARASSMENT PREVENTION PROGRAM

According to the EEOC's Guidelines on Sexual Harassment (Code of Federal Regulations, 1980, Section F):

> Prevention is the best tool for the elimination of sexual harassment. An employer should take all steps necessary to prevent sexual harassment from occurring, such as affirmatively raising the subject, expressing strong disapproval, developing appropriate sanctions, informing employees of their right to raise and how to raise the issue of harassment under Title VII, and developing methods to sensitize all concerned.

A sexual harassment prevention program, therefore, contains two key parts. The organization must develop a sexual harassment policy and make sure that all employees are made aware of the policy and how to make a complaint if they experience sexual harassment.

An effective sexual harassment policy should clearly define both sexual harassment and retaliation and explain how retaliation can take the form of subtle reprisals such as being excluded from a training lunch (Henneman, 2006). The policy should also make it clear to employees that if a lawsuit is filed against them for sexual harassment, they may be personally liable for monetary damages (Doan & Kleiner, 1999). But having an organizational policy on sexual harassment in place is not enough. When experiencing sexual harassment, only about half of women say they would report it; instead, they choose to remove themselves from the situation or ignore the harassment (Berryman-Fink, 2001). Therefore, other ways of monitoring the organizational climate and other processes for encouraging and supporting employees in using the formal reporting procedure are needed, just as a restaurant relying only on customer complaints will have an impoverished understanding of the general level of customer satisfaction and likelihood of return business.

The second key part of a sexual harassment prevention program is training to sensitize all employees to the issue of sexual harassment. This is necessary, because sometimes harassers do not believe they are sexually harassing others (Frierson, 1989). A variety of training methods have been developed, including role playing, case studies, and videos (Moore, Gatlin-Watts, & Cangelosi, 1998). Using Merit Systems Protection Board survey data from 1987 to 1994, it was found that sexual harassment training had sensitized federal employees to sexual harassment; employees were more likely to view both hostile work environment behavior and quid pro quo behavior as sexual harassment (Pickerill, Jackson, & Newman, 2006).

Sexual harassment training is required by law for employees in California, Connecticut, New Jersey, Massachusetts, and Maine (Gottwals, 2006), as well as public employees in Illinois, Tennessee, and Utah (Befus, 2006). The California law requires that all supervisory employees receive at least 2 hours of sexual harassment training every 2 years, covering sexual harassment prevention and retaliation.

To Do

Create a set of materials for a sexual harassment prevention training program. The packet of materials should include (a) the Guidelines on Sexual Harassment; (b) the organization's sexual harassment policy; (c) EEOC and state equal employment opportunity agency charge statistics for sexual harassment; (d) a set of scenarios of possible sexual harassment, including quid pro quo and hostile work environment sexual harassment; sexual harassment by a supervisor, coworker, or nonemployee; retaliation against an employee making a sexual harassment complaint; and a successfully resolved incident of sexual harassment; (e) a set of common questions and answers about sexual harassment; (f) supplemental materials, such as cases of sexual harassment in the news involving local organizations or *Fortune 500* companies, books and videos on sexual harassment, Web sites on preventing sexual harassment, and so forth.

Resources

Befus, E. F. (2006). New sexual harassment prevention measures. *National Real Estate Investor, 48*(1), 50.

Berryman-Fink, C. (2001). Women's responses to sexual harassment at work: Organizational policy versus employee practice. *Employment Relations Today, 27*(4), 57-64.

Bingham, S. G., & Sherer, L. L. (2001). The unexpected effects of a sexual harassment educational program. *Journal of Applied Behavioral Science, 37*(2), 125-153.

Burlington Northern & Santa Fe Railway v. White, 126 S.Ct. 2406 (Supreme Court of the United States, 2006).

Caro, N. (Director). (2005). *North country* [Motion picture]. United States: Warner Home Video.

Code of Federal Regulations. (1980). *Guidelines on sexual harassment.* 29 C.F.R Part 1604.11. http://edocket.access.gpo.gov/cfr_2008/julqtr/29cfr1604.11.htm

Doan, H., & Kleiner, B. H. (1999). How to conduct sexual harassment training effectively. *Equal Opportunities International, 18*(5/6), 27-31.

Frierson, J. G. (1989). Reduce the costs of sexual harassment. *Personnel Journal, 68*(11), 79-85.

Henneman, T. (2006). After high court ruling, firms may want to take long look at anti-harassment strategies. *Workforce Management, 85*(14), 33-35.

Meritor Savings Bank v. Vinson, 477 U.S. 57 (Supreme Court of the United States, 1986).

Moore, H. L, & Bradley, D. B., III. (1997). Sexual harassment in manufacturing: Seven strategies successful companies use to curb it. *Industrial Management, 39*(6), 14-18.

Moore, H. L., Gatlin-Watts, R. W., & Cangelosi, J. (1998). Eight steps to a sexual-harassment-free workplace. *Training & Development, 52*(4), 12-13.

Pickerill, J. M., Jackson, R. A., & Newman, M. A. (2006). Changing perceptions of sexual harassment in the federal workforce, 1987-1994. *Law & Policy, 28*(3), 368-394.

Reese, L. A., & Lindenberg, K. E. (2004). Employee satisfaction with sexual harassment policies: The training connection. *Public Personnel Management, 33*(1), 99-119.

Robinson v. Jacksonville Shipyards, Inc., 760 F.Supp 1486 (United States District Court for the Middle District of Florida, Jacksonville Division, 1991).

U.S. Equal Employment Opportunity Commission. *Sexual harassment charges EEOC & FEPAs Combined: FY 1997–FY 2007.* http://www.eeoc.gov/stats/harass.html

York, K. M., Barclay, L. A., & Zajack, A. B. (1997). Preventing sexual harassment: The effect of multiple training methods. *Employee Responsibilities and Rights Journal, 10*(4), 277-289.

Job Analysis 3

Strategic Objective

Job analysis is a systematic process for collecting data about a job so that a job description (job requirements) and job specification (worker requirements) can be written for that job. To write the job description, the job analyst needs to determine what are the essential and other tasks, duties, and responsibilities that comprise the job, the reporting relationships, and the working conditions. To write the job specification, the job analyst needs to determine what knowledge, skills, abilities, and experience are required for the job.

Job analysis is an essential first step for many HRM functions. To recruit for a position, potential applicants need to be told what they would be doing in the job (the job description) and what knowledge, skills, abilities, and experience is required to be qualified for the position (the job specification). Recruiters also need job analysis information so they know what to look for in applicants. When an employee's job performance is evaluated, it is evaluated against a standard of performance for quantity and quality, based on the job description. To determine how much an employee in a specific job should be paid using the compensable factors method, salary survey data (how much other companies are paying benchmark jobs) are combined with job evaluation scores (how this job differs from other jobs on the compensable factors) to balance the goals of external competitiveness and internal equity. A job analysis may be used to identify training needs for a position, by looking at the knowledge, skills, abilities, and experience that are required for the job, which may change over time. Information on the knowledge, skills, abilities, and experience requirements of a job may be used by employees in their career planning; by identifying what they need to become qualified for the position they want, employees can make a career plan to get those qualifications. The tasks that comprise a job might be examined for opportunities to enrich the job, redesigning it to make the job more productive and satisfying for the employee doing the job. The data collected during a job analysis might also be used to improve workplace safety, by looking for unsafe work behaviors or conditions. Job analysis data may also be used to support a decision that a particular job is an exempt or nonexempt position according to the Fair Labor Standards Act.

Job analysis may be done using a structured questionnaire, either developed by the organization or a commercially available questionnaire (Harvey, Friedman, Hakel, & Cornelius, 1988). The Position Analysis Questionnaire is a structured questionnaire widely used to conduct job analyses. It is highly generalizable (it can be used for many types of jobs) and allows the job analyst to collect a large amount of data on many jobs quickly. For example, Arvey and Begalla (1975) found that the jobs most similar to homemaker were patrolman, home economist, and airport maintenance chief. Job analysis data might also be used to group similar jobs together into a common pay scale, a process called broadbanding (Arnold & Scott, 2002).

The Occupational Information Network (O*Net) has replaced the Dictionary of Occupational Titles as the "primary source of occupational information, providing comprehensive information on key attributes and characteristics of workers and occupations." O*Net uses a common language to describe different jobs (Peterson et al., 2001), uses the job component validity model to identify potential employee selection tests and determine job requirement levels (Jeanneret & Strong, 2003); and can be used for career planning (Converse, Oswald, Gillespie, Field, & Bizot, 2004).

Just as organizations change over time—changing their mission, their products and services, their organizational structure—jobs within organizations change over time, so job descriptions need to be updated periodically. Technology is a common driver; technology can change how tasks are done and what tasks are done. Although teaching still entails someone with relevant expertise helping others to obtain knowledge and skills that they didn't have before, computer technology has changed the job in a number of ways. Teachers used to write notes and draw illustrations on a chalkboard; now they can create electronic slideshow presentations, work through complex problems in spreadsheets, and respond to student questions in e-mail and through electronic bulletin boards. Strategic job analysis may be used to react to, or even anticipate, changes in the environment that change the nature of jobs (Schneider & Konz, 1989). A proactive approach to job analysis may be related to organizational performance, especially for organizations with human resource information systems and where HRM is involved in strategic planning (Siddique, 2004).

Strategic Issues in HRM

ESSENTIAL AND NONESSENTIAL JOB FUNCTIONS

The Americans with Disabilities Act of 1990 prohibits discrimination on the basis of disability. Specifically, the act makes it illegal to discriminate against qualified individuals with a disability because of their disability in regard to job application procedures; the hiring, advancement, or discharge of employees; and employee compensation, job training, and other terms, conditions, and privileges of employment. According to the Americans with Disabilities Act, the key phrase "qualified individual with a disability" means an individual with a disability who, with or without reasonable accommodation, can perform the essential functions of the employment position that such individual holds or desires. An essential job function is a duty or responsibility that is fundamental to the job or a critical and basic component of that job; a nonessential function is any other job task that is relatively incidental to the job (Grant, 1997). The process of job analysis is used to identify the essential and nonessential job functions, and the job description should contain a list of the essential functions of the job. An applicant (or employee) who cannot perform, with or without accommodation, all of the essential functions of the job, is not qualified for the position.

Every job contains a number of job tasks or duties. Some of these tasks are important; they are the tasks that employees in specific jobs are to accomplish. But every job also contains other tasks that are normally part of the job, but if someone cannot carry out the tasks, he or she can still be a satisfactory performer in the job. To determine whether a function is essential, the EEOC (2005) lists three factors to consider: (a) whether the reason the position exists is to perform that function, (b) the number of other employees available to perform the function or among whom the performance of the function can be distributed, and (c) the degree of expertise or skill required to perform the function. Evidence that a function is essential for the job includes the actual work experience of present or past employees in the job, the time spent performing a function, the consequences of not requiring that an employee perform a function, and the terms of a collective bargaining agreement. Grant (1997) suggests three tests to use to determine whether a job function is essential. First, look at the relationship of the function to other tasks within the job. Second, look at how reassigning the function would affect other employees and their jobs. Third, look at the significance of the function and the conditions under which it is performed.

There are many aspects of a job that might be an essential job function. For example, in *Laurin v. Providence Hospital and Massachusetts Nurses Association* (1995), the appellate court ruled that a hospital's shift rotation requirements (one third of scheduled hours had to be on the evening or night shift) were an essential function of a nursing position. In *Durning v. Duffens Optical* (1996), the district court ruled that a salesperson who could no longer drive long distances or work long hours was not a qualified individual for the job. In *Blankenship v. Martin Marietta Energy Systems* (1996), the appellate court ruled that an employee whose required security clearance was revoked was therefore unable to perform the essential functions of her job.

Strategic Questions

1. What makes a job function an essential job function?
2. What is an essential job function for your current (or most recent) job?
3. If an employee developed heart problems and could no longer work more than 40 hours a week in a job, whereas in the past they had consistently worked 40 to 50 hours per week, could the employee be no longer qualified to do the job because it requires long work hours?
4. What are the essential functions for the job of a college or university professor?
5. If a teacher had a disability that prevented him or her from using the computer to show PowerPoint slideshows, would that make the teacher not qualified for the job?
6. If a job was redesigned to include more managerial responsibilities (i.e., job enrichment), could a job incumbent who had been a satisfactory performer become no longer qualified to do the job?
7. Could working effectively with team members on a self-managed work team be an essential job function?

Resources

Americans with Disabilities Act. (1990). http://www.eeoc.gov/policy/ada.html

Barlow, W. E., & Hane, E. Z. (1992). A practical guide to the Americans with Disabilities Act. *Personnel Journal, 71*(6), 53-60.

Blankenship v. Martin Marrietta Energy Systems, Inc., 83 F.3d 153 (U.S. Court of Appeals for the Sixth Circuit, 1996).

Devanney, J. J. (1999). Testing the limits: Shift rotation and the ADA. *Nursing Management, 30*(3), 35-37.

Durning v. Duffens Optical, 1996 U.S. Dist. LEXIS 1685 (U.S. District Court for the Eastern District of Louisiana, 1996).

Grant, P. C. (1997). Essential or marginal? Job functions and the Americans with Disabilities Act. *Business Horizons, 40*(2), 71-74.

Laurin v. Providence Hospital and Massachusetts Nurses Association, 150 F. 3d 52 (Court of Appeals for the First Circuit, 1995).

U.S. Equal Employment Opportunity Commission. (2005). *The ADA: Your responsibilities as an employer.* http://www.eeoc.gov/facts/ada17.html

JOB DESCRIPTIONS IN TEAM-BASED ORGANIZATIONS

In traditional organizations, work activities are subdivided into separate jobs (work specialization), jobs are grouped together into departments (departmentalization), workers report to specific individuals or groups (chain of command), decision-making authority is concentrated at the top of the organization (centralization), and there are rules and regulations directing workers and managers (formalization). But not all organizations are structured this way; there are other possibilities.

A Virtual Organization is a collection of geographically distributed, functionally and culturally diverse people who are linked by electronic forms of communication (Shin, 2004). In a Virtual Organization, there is a small core organization that outsources major business functions, including human resources management. In a Team Structure Organization, worker teams are used as a central coordination device; teams tend to break down departmental barriers and decentralize decision making to the level of the work team (Thoms, Pinto, Parente, & Druskat, 2002). A Boundaryless Organization tries to eliminate the chain of command, have limitless spans of control, and replace departments with empowered teams (Kerr & Ulrich, 1995).

Even the idea of a job is evolving, along with these new organizational designs. A job is a package of tasks done in repetitive situations, with narrowly defined responsibilities, so that workers don't think about what needs to be done but rather only about the tasks that comprise their job (Bridges, 1994; Caudron, 1994). In these new organizational designs, clearly defined jobs with specific job tasks for individual workers are replaced by self-directed work teams, where teams determine what needs to be done and which team members will do what. This way of working appears to result in higher productivity, better attendance, less turnover, and improvements in product quality and the quality of working life for employees (Shipper & Manz, 1992).

Strategic Questions

1. Before mass production and assembly lines, what was a job? If mass production is replaced by customized production, what is a job?
2. In a traditional organization, the list of tasks an employee is responsible for is contained in the job description. In an organization structured around teams, what tasks is an employee responsible for?
3. In a Team Structure Organization with self-managed work teams, what do managers do?

(Continued)

(Continued)

4. In which type of business environment will a traditional organization work best? In which type of business environment will a Team Structure organization work best?
5. To comply with the Americans with Disabilities Act, job descriptions must include a list of essential job functions. In an organization structured around cross-functional customer teams, which essential job functions would be common to all of the teams?

Resources

Bridges, W. (1994). The end of the job. *Fortune, 130*(6), 62-70.

Cascio, W. F. (2000). Managing a virtual workplace. *Academy of Management Executive, 14*(3), 81-90.

Caudron, S. (1994). The de-jobbing of America. *Industry Week, 243*(16), 30-36.

Harris, T. C., & Barnes-Farrell, J. L. (1997). Components of teamwork: Impact of evaluations of contributions to work team effectiveness. *Journal of Applied Social Psychology, 27*(19), 1694-1715.

Kerr, S., & Ulrich, D. (1995). Creating the boundaryless organization: The radical reconstruction of organizational capabilities. *Planning Review, 23*(5), 41-45.

Miles, R. E., & Snow, C. C. (1995). The new network firm: A spherical structure built on human investment philosophy. *Organizational Dynamics, 23*(4), 5-18.

Shin, Y. (2004). A person-environment fit model for virtual organizations. *Journal of management, 30*(5), 725-743.

Shipper, F., & Manz, C. C. (1992). Employee self-management without formally designated teams: An alternative road to empowerment. *Organizational Dynamics, 20*(3), 48-61.

Thoms, P., Pinto, J. K., Parente, D. H., & Druskat, V. U. (2002). Adaptation to self-managing work teams. *Small Group Research, 33*(1), 3-31.

PERSONALITY TRAITS AS A POSITION REQUIREMENT

What makes an applicant qualified for a position is that he or she has the knowledge, skills, and abilities to do the job. If the job requires the ability to lift 50 pounds, any applicant that can lift 50 pounds is a qualified applicant. If the job requires knowledge of and skill in Java programming, any applicant who can do Java programming is qualified for the job. Even a prior work experience requirement may be used to distinguish qualified and nonqualified applicants. For example, in *Johnson v. Transportation Agency, Santa Clara County, California* (1987), to be qualified for the job of road dispatcher, Santa Clara County required 4 years of road maintenance experience with the county.

To be competitive in a global marketplace, organizations must develop systems that enable employees to collaborate effectively. In many organizations, employees spend much of their working day in teams—product teams, customer teams, cross-functional teams, self-managed work teams, and other forms of group structures (Frankforter & Christensen, 2005; Muthusamy, Wheeler, & Simmons, 2005; Sundstrom, McIntyre, Halfhill, & Richards, 2000). Surveys have found that 79% of Fortune 1000 companies and 81% of manufacturing organizations are using self-managed work teams (Thoms et al., 2002). In these team-based work environments, working effectively in teams is an important part of the job. Part of the selection process might assess an applicant's skill in working effectively as a team member or leading a team. Organizations might select applicants based on their teamwork skills or hire based on other criteria and train for teamwork. An Internet search of companies offering teamwork training results in a large number of companies seeking to provide this service.

There may be personality characteristics that organizations could use as part of the selection criteria for some jobs. For jobs in which large amounts of money are handled, the organization might use integrity tests as part of the selection procedure, selecting on the basis of honesty (Bernardin & Cooke, 1993). There are other personality traits that may predict job success; the Big Five personality traits are Extroversion, Agreeableness, Conscientiousness, Emotional Stability, and Openness to Experience (see Barrick & Mount, 1991; Tett, Jackson, & Rothstein, 1991). Vinchur, Schippman, Switzer, and Roth (1998) found significant correlations between Potency (a subdimension of extraversion) and Achievement (a component of conscientiousness) and sales performance; and Thoresen, Bradley, Bliese, and Thoresen (2004) found that Conscientiousness and Extraversion were related to total sales for sales representatives. Salgado's (2003) meta-analysis of American and European validation studies using the Big Five personality dimensions measured by the Five-Factor Model–based inventories found statistically significant validities for Conscientiousness (.28) and Emotional Stability (.16) predicting supervisory job performance ratings. Regardless of the personality trait that might be used, employers must still make sure that the tests do not have adverse impact, or if they do, that they have a statistically significant correlation with job performance (i.e., the test is valid).

Measures of personality might also be used to predict team member performance. Neuman and Wright (1999) found that Agreeableness and Conscientiousness predicted peer ratings of team member performance beyond measures of job-specific skills and general cognitive ability, and predicted supervisory ratings of work team performance, objective measures of work team accuracy, and work completed. Neuman, Wagner, and Christiansen (1999) found that both the average level and the variability of the Big Five personality traits predicted team job performance. And teams higher in the Big Five personality factors might receive higher supervisory ratings for team performance (Barrick, Stewart, Neubert, & Mount, 1998).

Strategic Questions

1. Is working in teams effectively a trait or characteristic that can be selected for, or a behavior or skill that can be taught?
2. Is leadership a trait or characteristic that can be selected for, or a behavior or skill that can be taught?
3. What personality characteristics are most likely to predict job performance in a sales job?
4. What personality traits are most likely to predict job performance in a nursing job?
5. What personality characteristics are most likely to predict job performance for the job of college or university professor?
6. If an organization selects based on certain personality characteristics and the selection procedure is found to have adverse impact, what are some possible causes?

Resources

Barrick, M. R., & Mount, M. K. (1991). The Big Five personality dimensions and job performance: A meta-analysis. *Personnel Psychology, 44*(1), 1-26.

Barrick, M. R., Stewart, G. L., Neubert, M. J., & Mount, M. K. (1998). Relating team member ability and personality to work-team processes and team effectiveness. *Journal of Applied Psychology,* 83(3), 377-391.

Bernardin, H. J., & Cooke, D. K. (1993). Validity of an honesty test in predicting theft among convenience store employees. *Academy of Management Journal, 36*(5), 1097-1108.

Frankforter, S. A., & Christensen, S. L. (2005). Finding competitive advantage in self-managed work teams. *Business Forum, 27*(1), 20-24.

Johnson v. Transportation Agency, Santa Clara County, California, 480 U.S. 616 (Supreme Court of the United States, 1987).

Lounsbury, J. W., Bigson, L. W., & Hamrick, F. L. (2004). The development and validation of a personological measure of work drive. *Journal of Business and Psychology, 18*(4), 427-451.

Moore, D. P., & Hass, M. (1990). When Affirmative Action cloaks management bias in selection. *Academy of Management Executive, 4*(1), 84-90.

Muthusamy, S. K., Wheeler, J. V., & Simmons, B. L. (2005). Self-managing work teams: Enhancing organizational effectiveness. *Organization Development Journal, 23*(3), 53-66.

Neuman, G. A., Wagner, S. H., & Christiansen, N. D. (1999). The relationship between work-team personality composition and the job performance of teams. *Group & Organization Management, 24*(1), 28-45.

Neuman, G. A., & Wright, J. (1999). Team effectiveness: Beyond skills and cognitive ability. *Journal of Applied Psychology, 84*(3), 376-389.

Riggio, R. E., & Taylor, S. J. (2000). Personality and communication skills as predictors of hospice nurse performance. *Journal of Business and Psychology, 15*(2), 351-359.

Salgado, J. F. (2003). Predicting job performance using FFM and non-FFM personality measures. *Journal of Occupational and Organizational Psychology, 76*(3), 323-346.

Stewart, G. L., & Carson, K. P. (1997). Moving beyond the mechanistic model: An alternative to staffing for contemporary organizations. *Human Resource Management Review, 7*(2), 157-184.

Sundstrom, E., McIntyre, M., Halfhill, T., & Richards, H. (2000). Work groups: From the Hawthorne studies to work teams of the 1990s and beyond. *Group Dynamics: Theory, Research, and Practice, 4*(1), 44-67.

Tett, R. P., Jackson, D. N., & Rothstein, M. (1991). Personality measures as predictors of job performance: A meta-analytic review. *Personnel Psychology, 44*(4), 703-742.

Thoms, P., Pinto, J. K., Parente, D. H., & Druskat, V. U. (2002). Adaptation to self-managing work teams. *Small Group Research, 33*(1), 3-31.

Thoresen, C. J., Bradley, J. C., Bliese, P. D., & Thoresen, J. D. (2004). The Big Five personality traits and individual job performance growth trajectories in maintenance and transitional job stages. *Journal of Applied Psychology, 89*(5), 835-853.

Vinchur, A. J., Schippman, J. S., Switzer, F. S., III, & Roth, P. L. (1998). A meta-analytic review of predictors of job performance for salespeople. *Journal of Applied Psychology, 83*(4), 586-597.

SELECTING FOR THE JOB OR THE ORGANIZATION

The Person–Organization (P-O) Fit approach to selection is based on the idea that the organization hires a "whole" person, not just their knowledge, skills, and abilities; therefore, job requirements should include fitting in with the characteristics of the organization (Bowen, Ledford, & Nathan, 1991). For example, Shin (2004) suggests that to achieve P-O Fit in a virtual organization, individuals should value autonomy, flexibility, and diversity. Every organization has a culture, and the P-O Fit approach assumes that everyone in the organization will work more effectively together if they share the same core values and beliefs. Rather than train new hires in the organization's culture (through the orientation and socialization process), organizations should hire applicants who already fit.

Bowen et al. (1991) outline the basic steps: (a) assess the overall work environment using job analysis and organizational analysis; (b) infer the type of person required; (c) design an organizational entry process that allows both the organization and the applicant to assess P-O Fit; and (d) reinforce P-O Fit through task design, training, orientation, and organizational design.

As with any other test, the test for P-O Fit must not have adverse impact, and if it does, then it must be shown to be valid (in this case, construct validity of the P-O Fit construct). The idea of P-O Fit implicitly assumes that a certain personality will make for a more effective performer than another personality. This puts some applicants in the situation of either giving honest answers to the test measuring P-O Fit or giving answers that they think will improve their chances of getting the job (Dalen, Stanton, & Roberts, 2001; Furnham, 1990). P-O Fit is a slippery slope; it is a short distance from looking for applicants who fit the organization's culture to looking for the "right kind of person to work here," to looking for "someone just like us." Rather than expect employees to get along and work together despite their diversity, P-O Fit expects that employees can work together effectively only when they are all similar to each other.

Strategic Questions

1. When would it be better to select for applicants who fit the organization (P-O Fit) rather than socialize new employees?
2. When would it be better to socialize new employees rather than select for P-O Fit?
3. Is using a P-O Fit approach to selection incompatible with valuing diversity?
4. When using a P-O Fit approach to selection in a global company with operations in multiple countries and employees from multiple cultures, which culture (or cultures) should applicants have to fit?

Resources

Bowen, D. E., Ledford, G. E., Jr., & Nathan, B. R. (1991). Hiring for the organization, not the job. *Academy of Management Executive, 5*(4), 35-51.

Brown, D. (2003). Fit more important than skills. *Canadian HR Reporter, 16*(13), 17-18.

Carroll, G. (Producer). (1997). *Cool hand Luke* [Motion picture]. Burbank, CA: Warner Home Video.

Erickson, T. J., & Gratton, L. (2007). What it means to work here. *Harvard Business Review, 85*(3), 104-112.

Furnham, A. (1990). The fakeability of the 16-PF, Myers-Briggs and FIRO-B personality measures. *Personality and Individual Differences, 11*(7), 711-716.

Kosnik, L. K., Brown, J., & Maund, T. (2007). Learning from the aviation industry. *Nursing Management, 38*(1), 25-30.

Kristof, A. L. (1996). Person-Organization fit: An integrative review of its conceptualizations, measurement, and implications. *Personnel Psychology, 49*(1), 1-49.

Kristof-Brown, A. L., Zimmerman, R. D., & Johnson, E. C. (2005). Consequences of individual's fit at work: A meta-analysis of person-job, person-organization, person-group, and person-supervisor fit. *Personnel Psychology, 58*(2), 281-342.

Mudrack, P. E. (2004). Job involvement, obsessive-compulsive personality traits, and workaholic behavioral tendencies. *Journal of Organizational Change Management, 17*(5), 490-508.

O'Connor, G. (Director). (2004). *Miracle* [Motion picture]. Hollywood, CA: Walt Disney Video.

Shin, Y. (2004). A person-environment fit model for virtual organizations. *Journal of management, 30*(5), 725-743.

Verquer, M. L., Beehr, T. A., & Wagner, S. H. (2003). A meta-analysis of relations between person-organization fit and work attitudes. *Journal of Vocational Behavior, 63*(3), 473-489.

Applications

MATCHING JOB TITLES AND JOB DESCRIPTIONS

Organizations are made up of people doing many different jobs. Two tools that are used to manage this complexity are job titles and job descriptions. A job description is a listing of the tasks and responsibilities for a job. For example, according to O*Net, the job of payroll clerk involves compiling and posting employee time and payroll data; may include computing employees' time worked, production, and commission; may compute and post wages and deductions; and may prepare paychecks. Job titles are labels for different jobs, a kind of shorthand for distinguishing among jobs. However, organizations vary. Sometimes two organizations use the same job title, but the job descriptions do not match; sometimes two job descriptions match but have different job titles.

Hospitals are very complex organizations, with many different technical specialties. For HRM people, there are many technical terms that must be learned to better understand the different jobs and how the people interact with each other to deliver health care to patients. One way to gain an understanding of the jobs that make up an organization is to examine the job descriptions, to see what individuals in those jobs do.

To Do

Match the job titles in the list below with the job descriptions that follow. A medical dictionary may be useful to get definitions of some of the medical terms in the job descriptions.

Job Titles

Anesthesiologist
Cardiovascular technologists and technicians
Diagnostic medical sonographers
Emergency medical technicians and paramedics
Licensed practical and licensed vocational nurses
Medical records and health information technicians
Nuclear medicine technologists
Occupational therapists
Radiologic technicians
Registered nurses
Respiratory therapists
Surgical technologists

Job Descriptions

Job Title: ______________________________

Observe patients, charting and reporting changes in patients' conditions, such as adverse reactions to medication or treatment, and taking any necessary action. Administer prescribed medications or start intravenous fluids, and note times and amounts on patients' charts. Answer patients' calls and determine how to assist them. Measure and record patients' vital signs, such as height, weight, temperature, blood pressure, pulse and respiration. Provide basic patient care and treatments, such as taking temperatures or blood pressures, dressing wounds, treating bedsores, giving enemas or douches, rubbing with alcohol, massaging, or performing catheterizations. Help patients with bathing, dressing, maintaining personal hygiene, moving in bed, or standing and walking. Supervise nurses' aides and assistants. Work as part of a health care team to assess patient needs, plan and modify care and implement interventions. Record food and fluid intake and output. Evaluate nursing intervention outcomes, conferring with other health care team members as necessary.

(Continued)

(Continued)

Job Title: ______________________________

Decide which images to include, looking for differences between healthy and pathological areas. Observe screen during scan to ensure that image produced is satisfactory for diagnostic purposes, making adjustments to equipment as required. Observe and care for patients throughout examinations to ensure their safety and comfort. Provide sonogram and oral or written summary of technical findings to physician for use in medical diagnosis. Operate ultrasound equipment to produce and record images of the motion, shape and composition of blood, organs, tissues and bodily masses such as fluid accumulations. Select appropriate equipment settings and adjust patient positions to obtain the best sites and angles. Determine whether scope of exam should be extended, based on findings. Process and code film from procedures and complete appropriate documentation. Obtain and record accurate patient history, including prior test results and information from physical examinations. Prepare patient for exam by explaining procedure, transferring them to ultrasound table, scrubbing skin and applying gel, and positioning them properly.

Job Title: ______________________________

Calculate, measure and record radiation dosage or radiopharmaceuticals received, used and disposed, using computer and following physician's prescription. Detect and map radiopharmaceuticals in patients' bodies, using a camera to produce photographic or computer images. Explain test procedures and safety precautions to patients and provide them with assistance during test procedures. Administer radiopharmaceuticals or radiation to patients to detect or treat diseases, using radioisotope equipment, under direction of physician. Produce a computer-generated or film images for interpretation by a physician. Process cardiac function studies, using computer. Dispose of radioactive materials and store radiopharmaceuticals, following radiation safety procedures. Record and process results of procedures. Prepare stock radiopharmaceuticals, adhering to safety standards that minimize radiation exposure to workers and patients. Maintain and calibrate radioisotope and laboratory equipment.

Job Title: ______________________________

Administer anesthetic or sedation during medical procedures, using local, intravenous, spinal or caudal methods. Monitor patient before, during, and after anesthesia and counteract adverse reactions or complications. Provide and maintain life support and airway management, and help prepare patients for emergency surgery. Record type and amount of anesthesia and patient condition throughout procedure. Examine patient, obtain medical history and use diagnostic tests to determine risk during surgical, obstetrical, and other medical procedures. Position patient on operating table to maximize patient comfort and surgical accessibility. Decide when patients have recovered or stabilized enough to be sent to another room or ward or to be sent home following outpatient surgery. Coordinate administration of anesthetics with surgeons during operation. Confer with other medical professionals to determine type and method of anesthetic or sedation to render patient insensible to pain. Coordinate and direct work of nurses, medical technicians and other health care providers.

Job Title: ____________________

Monitor patients' blood pressure and heart rate using electrocardiogram (EKG) equipment during diagnostic and therapeutic procedures to notify the physician if something appears wrong. Monitor patients' comfort and safety during tests, alerting physicians to abnormalities or changes in patient responses. Explain testing procedures to patient to obtain cooperation and reduce anxiety. Prepare reports of diagnostic procedures for interpretation by physician. Observe gauges, recorder, and video screens of data analysis system during imaging of cardiovascular system. Conduct electrocardiogram (EKG), phonocardiogram, echocardiogram, stress testing, or other cardiovascular tests to record patients' cardiac activity, using specialized electronic test equipment, recording devices, and laboratory instruments. Prepare and position patients for testing. Obtain and record patient identification, medical history or test results. Attach electrodes to the patients' chests, arms, and legs, connect electrodes to leads from the electrocardiogram (EKG) machine, and operate the EKG machine to obtain a reading. Adjust equipment and controls according to physicians' orders or established protocol.

Job Title: ____________________

Protect the security of medical records to ensure that confidentiality is maintained. Process patient admission and discharge documents. Review records for completeness, accuracy and compliance with regulations. Compile and maintain patients' medical records to document condition and treatment and to provide data for research or cost control and care improvement efforts. Enter data, such as demographic characteristics, history and extent of disease, diagnostic procedures and treatment into computer. Release information to persons and agencies according to regulations. Plan, develop, maintain and operate a variety of health record indexes and storage and retrieval systems to collect, classify, store and analyze information. Manage the department and supervise clerical workers, directing and controlling activities of personnel in the medical records department. Transcribe medical reports. Identify, compile, abstract and code patient data, using standard classification systems.

Job Title: ____________________

Use beam-restrictive devices and patient-shielding techniques to minimize radiation exposure to patient and staff. Position X-ray equipment and adjust controls to set exposure factors, such as time and distance. Position patient on examining table and set up and adjust equipment to obtain optimum view of specific body area as requested by physician. Determine patients' X-ray needs by reading requests or instructions from physicians. Make exposures necessary for the requested procedures, rejecting and repeating work that does not meet established standards. Process exposed radiographs using film processors or computer generated methods. Explain procedures to patients to reduce anxieties and obtain cooperation. Perform procedures such as linear tomography, mammography, sonograms, joint and cyst aspirations, routine contrast studies, routine fluoroscopy and examinations of the head, trunk, and extremities under supervision of physician. Prepare and set up X-ray room for patient. Assure that sterile supplies, contrast materials, catheters, and other required equipment are present and in working order, requisitioning materials as necessary.

(Continued)

(Continued)

Job Title: ______________________

Administer first-aid treatment and life-support care to sick or injured persons in prehospital setting. Operate equipment such as electrocardiograms (EKGs), external defibrillators and bag-valve mask resuscitators in advanced life-support environments. Assess nature and extent of illness or injury to establish and prioritize medical procedures. Maintain vehicles and medical and communication equipment, and replenish first-aid equipment and supplies. Observe, record, and report to physician the patient's condition or injury, the treatment provided, and reactions to drugs and treatment. Perform emergency diagnostic and treatment procedures, such as stomach suction, airway management or heart monitoring, during ambulance ride. Administer drugs, orally or by injection, and perform intravenous procedures under a physician's direction. Comfort and reassure patients. Coordinate work with other emergency medical team members and police and fire department personnel. Communicate with dispatchers and treatment center personnel to provide information about situation, to arrange reception of victims, and to receive instructions for further treatment.

Job Title: ______________________

Count sponges, needles, and instruments before and after operation. Hand instruments and supplies to surgeons and surgeons' assistants, hold retractors and cut sutures, and perform other tasks as directed by surgeon during operation. Scrub arms and hands and assist the surgical team to scrub and put on gloves, masks, and surgical clothing. Position patients on the operating table and cover them with sterile surgical drapes to prevent exposure. Provide technical assistance to surgeons, surgical nurses and anesthesiologists. Wash and sterilize equipment using germicides and sterilizers. Prepare, care for and dispose of tissue specimens taken for laboratory analysis. Clean and restock the operating room, placing equipment and supplies and arranging instruments according to instruction. Prepare dressings or bandages and apply or assist with their application following surgery. Operate, assemble, adjust, or monitor sterilizers, lights, suction machines, and diagnostic equipment to ensure proper operation.

Job Title: ______________________

Set up and operate devices such as mechanical ventilators, therapeutic gas administration apparatus, environmental control systems, and aerosol generators, following specified parameters of treatment. Provide emergency care, including artificial respiration, external cardiac massage and assistance with cardiopulmonary resuscitation. Determine requirements for treatment, such as type, method and duration of therapy, precautions to be taken, and medication and dosages, compatible with physicians' orders. Monitor patient's physiological responses to therapy, such as vital signs, arterial blood gases, and blood chemistry changes, and consult with physician if adverse reactions occur. Read prescription, measure arterial blood gases, and review patient information to assess patient condition. Work as part of a team of physicians, nurses and other health care professionals to manage patient care. Enforce safety rules and ensure careful adherence to physicians' orders. Maintain charts that contain patients' pertinent identification and therapy information. Inspect, clean, test and maintain respiratory therapy equipment to ensure equipment is functioning safely and efficiently, ordering repairs when necessary. Educate patients and their families about their conditions and teach appropriate disease management techniques, such as breathing exercises and the use of medications and respiratory equipment.

Job Title: ______________________________

Maintain accurate, detailed reports and records. Monitor, record and report symptoms and changes in patients' conditions. Record patients' medical information and vital signs. Modify patient treatment plans as indicated by patients' responses and conditions. Consult and coordinate with health care team members to assess, plan, implement and evaluate patient care plans. Order, interpret, and evaluate diagnostic tests to identify and assess patient's condition. Monitor all aspects of patient care, including diet and physical activity. Direct and supervise less skilled nursing or health care personnel or supervise a particular unit. Prepare patients for, and assist with, examinations and treatments. Observe nurses and visit patients to ensure proper nursing care.

Job Title: ______________________________

Complete and maintain necessary records. Evaluate patients' progress and prepare reports that detail progress. Test and evaluate patients' physical and mental abilities and analyze medical data to determine realistic rehabilitation goals for patients. Select activities that will help individuals learn work and life-management skills within limits of their mental and physical capabilities. Plan, organize, and conduct occupational therapy programs in hospital, institutional, or community settings to help rehabilitate those impaired because of illness, injury or psychological or developmental problems. Recommend changes in patients' work or living environments, consistent with their needs and capabilities. Consult with rehabilitation team to select activity programs and coordinate occupational therapy with other therapeutic activities. Help clients improve decision making, abstract reasoning, memory, sequencing, coordination and perceptual skills, using computer programs. Develop and participate in health promotion programs, group activities, or discussions to promote client health, facilitate social adjustment, alleviate stress, and prevent physical or mental disability. Provide training and supervision in therapy techniques and objectives for students and nurses and other medical staff.

Resources

The Free Dictionary, Medical Dictionary. http://medical-dictionary.thefreedictionary.com/
MedicineNet.com. http://www.medicinenet.com/script/main/hp.asp
O*Net. *Occupational Information Network.* http://online.onetcenter.org/
WebMD. http://www.webmd.com/

A TQM APPROACH TO WRITING JOB DESCRIPTIONS

TQM is the integration of all functions and processes within an organization to achieve continuous improvement in the quality of goods and services and customer satisfaction (Omachonu & Ross, 1994). Organizations using TQM methods focus on three basic principles: (a) customer focus, meeting and exceeding customer needs; (b) continuous improvement, attempting to create gains in performance from incremental innovations in organizational processes; and (c) teamwork, collaborating with all organizational members, customers, and suppliers (Victor, Boynton, & Stephens-Jahng, 2000). Therefore, a key aspect of TQM is ensuring that the organization's job descriptions emphasize customer focus, continuous improvement, and teamwork.

Meng (1992) illustrates the focus on quality and teamwork in job descriptions in a case study of a paper company, as it moved to TQM methods of management. Job descriptions were developed for each position with measures of accomplishment for each end result. The job description for "Manager of Finishing and Shipping Operations" included production scheduling; teamwork with other departments; a trained and motivated crew; safety; loading and shipping of paper, maintenance of inventory; production expertise and problem solving; maintenance of supply inventory; and maintenance of records, logs, and files. Compare this to the O*Net job description for First-Line Supervisors/Managers of Production and Operating Workers, which does not specifically include tasks related to quality or teamwork: Supervise and coordinate the activities of production and operating workers, such as inspectors, precision workers, machine setters and operators, assemblers, fabricators, and plant and system operators.

To Do

For a small home theater sales and installation company, use a TQM approach to write the job descriptions for all of the jobs in the company in the form provided on the next page. The job description should include job tasks relating to customer focus, continuous improvement, and teamwork. Job summaries from O*Net are given below for each employee.

Resources

Joyce, W. (2005). What really works: HR's role in building the 4 + 2 organization and an introduction to the case studies in the HR leadership forum. *Human Resource Management, 44*(1), 67-72.

Koumoutzis, N. (1994). Make behavioral considerations your first priority in quality improvements. *Industrial Engineering, 26*(12), 63-65.

McManis, G. L. (1993). Reinventing the system. *Hospitals & Health Networks, 67*(19), 42-44.

Meng, G. J. (1992). Using job descriptions, performance and pay innovations to support quality: A paper company's experience. *National Productivity Review, 11*(2), 247-255.

Omachonu, V. K., & Ross, J. E. (1994). *Principles of total quality.* Delray Beach, FL: St. Lucie.

O*Net. *Occupational Information Network.* http://online.onetcenter.org/

Spencer, B. A. (1994). Models of organization and Total Quality Management: A comparison and critical evaluation. *Academy of Management Review, 19*(3), 446-471.

Victor, B., Boynton, A., & Stephens-Jahng, T. (2000). The effective design of work under Total Quality Management. *Organization Science, 11*(1), 102-117.

Job Descriptions for a Small Home Theater Sales and Installation Company

Position	*Job Description*
Retail salesperson. Sell merchandise, such as furniture, motor vehicles, appliances, or apparel in a retail establishment.	
Electronic home entertainment equipment installer and repairer. Repair, adjust, or install audio or television receivers, stereo systems, camcorders, video systems, or other electronic home entertainment equipment.	
Sound engineering technician. Operate machines and equipment to record, synchronize, mix, or reproduce music, voices, or sound effects in sporting arenas, theater productions, recording studios, or movie and video productions.	
Interior designer. Plan, design, and furnish interiors of residential, commercial, or industrial buildings. Formulate design which is practical, aesthetic, and conducive to intended purposes, such as raising productivity, selling merchandise, or improving lifestyle. May specialize in a particular field, style, or phase of interior design.	
Bookkeeping, accounting, and auditing clerk. Compute, classify, and record numerical data to keep financial records complete. Perform any combination of routine calculating, posting, and verifying duties to obtain primary financial data for use in maintaining accounting records. May also check the accuracy of figures, calculations, and postings pertaining to business transactions recorded by other workers.	
First-line supervisor/manager of office and administrative support worker. Supervise and coordinate the activities of clerical and administrative support workers.	

Experiential Exercises

MISSION TO MARS

The first astronauts to land on the moon and return safely to the earth were Neil Armstrong and Buzz Aldrin in 1969. Although the engineering and human resource management challenges for this mission were considerable, some people began planning the next logical step, a manned mission to Mars. The Apollo missions to the moon took only a few days, but the mission to Mars could take more than 2 years for the round trip (Zubrin, 1996, p. 79). According to NASA's Mars Exploration Study Team (Hoffman & Kaplan, 1997), humans are the most valuable mission asset for Mars exploration. The objective for humans to spend up to 600 days on the Martian surface places unprecedented requirements on the people and their supporting systems.

There are three basic sets of tasks that must be performed by the crew on the mission to Mars:

1. *Command, control, and vehicle and facility operations functions.* These functions include command, management, and routine and contingency operations (piloting and navigation, system operations, housekeeping, maintenance, and repair of systems). Maintenance must be accomplished for facility systems, human support systems (medical facilities, exercise equipment, etc.), EVA systems, and science equipment.

2. *Scientific exploration and analysis.* This area includes field and laboratory tasks in geology, geochemistry, paleontology, or other disciplines associated with answering the principal scientific questions.

3. *Habitability tasks.* These tasks include providing medical support; operating the bioregenerative life support system experiment; performing biological, botanical, agronomy, and ecology investigations; and conducting other experiments directed at the long-term viability of human settlements on Mars.

To Do

Use the O*Net job specification format to develop a list of the skills, abilities, work activities, work context, and interests needed by crew members on the Mars Exploration Mission. All crew members need to be cross-trained to do multiple tasks in each of the three sets of tasks listed above. Use the form provided here or your own paper.

Mars Exploration Mission Crew

Position: Commander	
Skills	
Abilities	
Work activities	
Work context	
Interests	
Position: Pilot	
Skills	
Abilities	
Work activities	
Interests	
Position: Mission Specialist	
Skills	
Abilities	
Work activities	
Work context	

(Continued)

(Continued)

Pilot astronauts play a key role in shuttle flights, serving as either commanders or pilots. During flights, commanders are responsible for the vehicle, the crew, mission success and safety—duties similar to those of the captain of a ship. Shuttle commanders are assisted by pilot astronauts who are second in command and whose primary responsibilities involve controlling and operating the shuttle. During flights, commanders and pilots usually assist in spacecraft deployment and retrieval operations using the Remote Manipulator System arm or other payload-unique equipment on board the shuttle (NASA, 1988). The commander is a pilot astronaut with on-board responsibility for the vehicle, crew, mission success, and the safety of the flight.

Mission specialist astronauts, working closely with the commander and pilot, are responsible for coordinating on-board operations involving crew activity planning, use and monitoring of the shuttle's consumables (fuel, water, food, etc.), and conducting experiment and payload activities. They are required to have a detailed knowledge of shuttle systems and the "operational characteristics, mission requirements and objectives and supporting systems for each of the experiments to be conducted on the assigned missions." Mission specialists perform on-board experiments, spacewalks (extravehicular activity), and payload handling functions involving the Remote Manipulator System arm (NASA, 1988).

Resources

Eichler, P., Siene, R., Khania, E., & Schön, A. (2006). Astronaut training for the European ISS contributions Columbus module and ATV. *Acta Astronautica, 59*(12), 1146-1152.

Hoffman, S. J., & Kaplan, D. I. (1997). *Human exploration of Mars: The reference mission of the NASA Mars Exploration Study Team* (NASA Special Publication 6107). ftp://nssdcftp.gsfc.nasa.gov/miscellaneous/planetary/mars_future/mars_ref_mission_sp6107.pdf, http://exploration.jsc.nasa.gov/marsref/contents.html

The Mars Society. http://www.marssociety.org/portal

Messerschmid, E, Haignere, J. P., Damian, K., & Damann, V. (2004). The European astronaut centre prepares for International Space Station operations. *Acta Astronautica, 54*(7): 527-539.

NASA. (1988). NSTS 1988 news reference manual (Vol. 2–Operations). http://science.ksc.nasa.gov/shuttle/technology/sts-newsref/stsref-toc.html

Nayfack, N. (Producer). (1999). *Forbidden planet* [Motion Picture]. Burbank, CA: Metro Goldwyn Mayer.

Zubrin, R. (1996). *The case for Mars.* New York: Free Press.

JOB ANALYSIS INTERVIEW OF A COLLEGE OR UNIVERSITY PROFESSOR

Although the Position Analysis Questionnaire is widely used for job analysis, there may be some jobs for which additional information is needed. One way to get that information is to do an interview; ask a satisfactory performer about their job, how they do it, what knowledge they apply, what tasks are done most frequently, and what tasks are most critical to successful performance on the job. For example, the job of a firefighter includes many tasks in addition to fighting fires, such as administering first aid to people injured in a fire, driving fire-fighting vehicles, maintaining firefighting equipment, and conducting community fire safety education programs. Some of these tasks might be missed with a standardized questionnaire.

To Do

Develop a set of interview questions for a job analysis of the position of college or university professor. Find a subject matter expert to interview, either a current college or university professor or a recently retired college or university professor. Use the information obtained to write a job description and job specification for the position of university professor.

The three basic sets of tasks performed by a college or university professor are research, teaching, and service. Research means scholarly work of all kinds, creative work that adds to the fund of human knowledge. This includes articles in refereed journals, books published by university and trade presses, chapters in books, textbooks, conference presentations and proceedings, book reviews in scholarly publications, written teaching cases with case notes, published computer software, or the editing of a scholarly journal or book. Teaching activities could include undergraduate and graduate courses, executive education, and continuing education courses. Service activities could include service to the university by being on a committee or performing an administrative role; student advising or mentoring; service to the community through seminars, presentations, or workshops; consulting with people in the community; and service to the profession through organizing and participating in professional workshops or educational programs, delivering seminars to professional groups, holding office, or otherwise serving professional organizations.

Resources

Hughes, G. L., & Prien, E. P. (1989). Evaluation of task and job skill linkage judgments used to develop test specifications. *Personnel Psychology, 42*(2), 283-292.

Landy, F. J., & Vasey, J. (1991). Job analysis: The composition of SME samples. *Personnel Psychology, 44*(1), 27-50.

Maurer, T. J., & Tross, S. A. (2000). SME committee vs. field job analysis ratings: Convergence, cautions, and a call. *Journal of Business and Psychology, 14*(3), 489-499.

Mueller, M., & Belcher, G. (2000). Observed divergence in the attitudes of incumbents and supervisors as subject matter experts in job analysis: A study of the fire captain rank. *Public Personnel Management, 29*(4), 529-556.

Position Analysis Questionnaire. http://www.paq.com/

Truxillo, D. M., Paronto, M. E., Collins, M., & Sulzer, J. L. (2004). Effects of subject matter expert viewpoint on job analysis results. *Public Personnel Management, 33*(1), 33-46.

Creative Exercises

WRITING JOB DESCRIPTIONS

One method of job analysis is to find a satisfactory performer and observe him or her doing the job. The job analyst looks for what the worker does, how to do the job, what equipment is used, what skills are used, the working conditions, frequency and criticality of job tasks, and reporting relationships. Observation works best for jobs with manual tasks (i.e., jobs in which the most important job tasks are easy to see and the job tasks have short, repetitive, visible cycles; e.g., bartender, ticket taker, hotel desk clerk). Observation does not work well for knowledge-based jobs (i.e., jobs in which the key aspects of the job are cognitive or otherwise difficult to observe; e.g., manager, university professor, movie critic).

Job analysis by observation would work well for the job of television sportscaster, because most of what the job requires can be seen (although much of the pregame preparation goes on backstage). A television broadcast of a major sporting event will usually have three announcers. There will be a play-by-play announcer who will describe the action in the game, what has happened earlier in the game or in previous games with these teams, and provide relevant statistics. There will also be a color announcer, typically a former player, who provides inside-the-game expertise and insights into player and coaching strategies, sometimes using cliches. Often, there is also a third announcer who conducts interviews with players and coaches before, during, and after the game (e.g., asking the coach after two periods and down three goals what adjustments he or she plans to make for the final period).

For example, Palmer (1978) rode with six different animal wardens (i.e., animal control officer or dog catcher) for about 1,000 hours as they performed their duties. Animal wardens use some job-specific equipment to do their job (pickup truck with animal cages, two-way radio, "catcher stick," and lariat). The day-to-day work of an animal warden involves three critical tasks: patrolling the city streets looking for at-large animals, street cleanup, and responding to calls that are dispatched from the shelter. Animal wardens interact with the public and the dispatcher when they return at-large animals to their owners and when they respond to homeowner complaints about stray animals in their neighborhood.

To Do

Do an observational job analysis of any job. To collect the job analysis data, observe the job being performed. Using the form provided or your own paper, keep a job analysis diary to document your observations. Record in the diary the job tasks you have observed; the equipment and tools used; and your inferences about the knowledge, skills, and abilities required to do the tasks. Based on the observational data you have collected, write the job description (tasks requirements) and job specification (knowledge, skill, and ability requirements) for the job.

Job Analysis Diary

Observational Job Analysis	
Position:	
Observations:	
Job Description:	Job Specification:

(Continued)

(Continued)

Resources

Avildsen, J. G. (Director). (1976). *Rocky* [Motion picture]. United States: MGM.

Beentjes, J. (2002). How television commentary affects children's judgments on soccer fouls. *Communication Research, 29*(1), 31-45.

Discovery Channel. (2007). *Dirty jobs, Season 1* [Television broadcast]. Silver Spring, MD: Author.

Jenkins, G. D., Nadler, D. A., Lawler, E. E., & Cammann, C. (1975). Standardized observations: An approach to measuring the nature of jobs. *Journal of Applied Psychology, 60*(2), 171-181.

Law, L. (Producer). (2005). *Deadliest catch: Crab fishing in Alaska* [Television broadcast]. Silver Spring, MD: Discovery Channel.

Markowitz, J. (1981). Four methods of job analysis. *Training & Development Journal, 35*(9), 112-118.

McDaniel-Hine, L. C. (1988). Elementary school teachers' work behavior. *Journal of Educational Research, 81*(5), 274-280.

Olivier, L. (Director, Producer). (1994). *Richard III* [Motion picture]. Irvington, NY: Voyager Company.

Scott, R. (Director). (2003). *Matchstick men* [Motion picture]. Burbank, CA: Warner Home Video.

Wanta, W., & Leggett, D. (1988). "Hitting Paydirt": Capacity theory and sports announcers' use of cliches. *Journal of Communication, 38*(4), 82-89.

JOB ANALYSIS

There are a number of methods of doing job analysis to collect the data needed to write the job description and job specification. For Observation, the job analyst finds a satisfactory performer in the job and observes the worker doing the job, looking for what knowledge is needed to do the job, what equipment is used, what skills are used, the working conditions, frequency and criticality of job tasks, and reporting relationships. Observation works best for jobs with short, repetitive, visible cycles (i.e., the key aspects of the job are observable). Observation does not work well for jobs in which the key aspects of the job are cognitive or otherwise difficult to observe (e.g., manager, university professor, movie critic). There is also the problem of reactivity while the job analyst is observing the worker; people behave differently when they know they are being watched. This can be mitigated somewhat by making a videorecording of the worker on the job. The camera is easier to get used to than a live observer, and key portions of the recording can be viewed multiple times to increase accuracy. Video-based observation is also better for hazardous work environments, such as steel mills, construction sites, and meat packing plants; being unfamiliar with the job and work environment makes the job analyst a hazard to himself or herself and to the workers being observed. For Participant Observation, the job analyst actually does the job, learning what the job entails from working in someone else's shoes. Participant Observation works best for jobs that are easily learned and does not work well for complex jobs such as that of an airline pilot or a brain surgeon.

In the Diary method of job analysis, workers are asked to record their daily activities. Although this sounds like a straightforward approach, it has some practical limitations. Keeping an accurate daily diary takes time and effort. Workers may not be sufficiently motivated to make accurate and detailed daily entries and instead catch up on the entries just before the job analyst collects the diary. The diary may then be a collection of accurate entries, confabulations, and fiction. Instead of a notebook and a pen, better results may be obtained with a combination of pagers, cell phones, and pocket-sized dictating machines.

Another approach to job analysis is collecting Critical Incidents, a kind of systematic case study. Critical Incidents are descriptions of important events that happened on the job, either critically bad or critically good. The narratives typically include what happened before the incident, why the incident was noteworthy, the outcome, and a rating to describe how good or bad the incident was. From a number of such incidents in which something went right (e.g., the worker helped a less experienced worker get started on a complicated job) and in which something went wrong (e.g., an entire run was spoiled because the machine settings were incorrect), an understanding of the job can be obtained. The primary shortcoming to the Critical Incidents approach is the focus on unusual job behaviors (i.e., the outliers) rather than typical job behaviors.

Structured questionnaires such as the Position Analysis Questionnaire or the Management Position Description Questionnaire surveys are used to systematically collect a large amount of data about a job or set of jobs. The Management Position Description Questionnaire was specifically designed for executive and management-level jobs (Tornow, 1976), but the PAQ can be used for a wide variety of jobs (Arvey & Begalla, 1975; McCormick, Jeanneret, & Mecham, 1969).

Another method of job analysis is the Interview. Typically, job incumbents or the supervisors of job incumbents are interviewed, although department directors or others with a big-picture view of the job might also be interviewed. The Interview includes questions relating to work activities, equipment and tools used, work standards, and the job context, as well as knowledge and skill requirements. A disadvantage of the Interview is that job incumbents may be suspicious of the purpose of the questions and be tempted to make their job appear more difficult than it is and require more knowledge and skills than it does, in case the compensation system might be affected by the information obtained by the job analyst.

Some of the types of data that a job analysis interview might collect are listed in Table 3.1 (Peterson et al., 2001).

Table 3.1 Job Analysis Interview Data

Experience requirements	• Past work experience • Licenses, certifications
Generalized work activities	*Information input* • Looking for and receiving job-related information • Identifying and evaluating job-relevant information *Mental processes* • Information and data processing • Reasoning and decision making *Work output* • Performing physical and manual work activities • Performing complex and technical activities *Interacting with others* • Communicating and interacting • Coordinating, developing, managing, and advising others • Administering
Organizational context	• Decision-making systems • Job characteristics • Job stability and rotation • Human resources systems and practices • Social processes and roles • Culture and organizational values • Supervisor role
Work context	• Formality of communication • Job interactions • Responsibility for others • Conflictual contact
Physical work conditions	• Work setting • Environmental conditions • Job hazards • Body positioning • Work attire
Structural job characteristics	• Criticality of position • Pace and scheduling
Occupation specific requirements	• Characteristics of a particular occupation (e.g., occupational skills and knowledge; tasks and duties; machine, tools, and equipment)
Occupation characteristics	• The nature of the industry, job opportunities, pay in the occupation
Worker characteristics: Abilities	• Cognitive abilities • Psychomotor abilities • Physical abilities • Sensory abilities

Worker characteristics: Interests	• Holland occupational classification • Occupational values
Worker characteristics: Work styles	• Achievement orientation • Social influence • Interpersonal orientation • Adjustment • Conscientiousness • Independence • Practical intelligence
Worker requirements: Basic skills	*Content skills* • Active listening • Reading comprehension • Writing • Speaking • Mathematics • Science *Process skills* • Active learning • Learning strategies • Monitoring • Critical thinking
Worker requirements: Cross-functional skills	• Problem-solving skills • Social skills • Technical skills • Systems skills • Resource management skills
Worker requirements: Knowledge	• Business and management • Manufacturing and production • Arts and humanities • Law and public safety
Worker requirements: Education	• Prior educational experience required to perform in a job

To Do

Do a job analysis of any job using the interview method. Use the O*Net-based list above and/or your own questions to create a structured interview guide. Use the guide to interview a satisfactory performer in the job. Using the job analysis data you have collected, write the job description (tasks requirements) and job specification (knowledge, skill, and ability requirements) for the job.

For example, if you interviewed a poker dealer, you should get a job description and job specification similar to that in O*Net, shown in the Summary Report.

(Continued)

(Continued)

Summary Report

Gaming Dealer (O*Net: 39-3011.00)

Operate table games. Stand or sit behind table and operate games of chance by dispensing the appropriate number of cards or blocks to players, or operating other gaming equipment. Compare the house's hand against players' hands and payoff or collect players' money or chips.

Job Description

Exchange paper currency for playing chips or coin money.

Pay winnings or collect losing bets as established by the rules and procedures of a specific game.

Deal cards to house hands, and compare these with players' hands to determine winners, as in black jack.

Conduct gambling games such as dice, roulette, cards, or keno, following all applicable rules and regulations.

Check to ensure that all players have placed bets before play begins.

Stand behind a gaming table and deal the appropriate number of cards to each player.

Inspect cards and equipment to be used in games to ensure that they are in good condition.

Start and control games and gaming equipment, and announce winning numbers or colors.

Open and close cash floats and game tables.

Compute amounts of players' wins or losses, or scan winning tickets presented by patrons to calculate the amount of money won.

Job Specification

Knowledge:

Mathematics—Knowledge of arithmetic, algebra, geometry, calculus, statistics, and their applications.

Customer and Personal Service—Knowledge of principles and processes for providing customer and personal services. This includes customer needs assessment, meeting quality standards for services, and evaluation of customer satisfaction.

Psychology—Knowledge of human behavior and performance; individual differences in ability, personality, and interests; learning and motivation; psychological research methods; and the assessment and treatment of behavioral and affective disorders.

Skills:

Mathematics—Using mathematics to solve problems.

Speaking—Talking to others to convey information effectively.

Active Listening—Giving full attention to what other people are saying, taking time to understand the points being made, asking questions as appropriate, and not interrupting at inappropriate times.

Service Orientation—Actively looking for ways to help people.

Social Perceptiveness—Being aware of others' reactions and understanding why they react as they do.

Monitoring—Monitoring/Assessing performance of yourself, other individuals, or organizations to make improvements or take corrective action.

Learning Strategies—Selecting and using training/instructional methods and procedures appropriate for the situation when learning or teaching new things.

Coordination—Adjusting actions in relation to others' actions.

Reading Comprehension—Understanding written sentences and paragraphs in work related documents.

Abilities:

Oral Expression—The ability to communicate information and ideas in speaking so others will understand.

Problem Sensitivity—The ability to tell when something is wrong or is likely to go wrong. It does not involve solving the problem, only recognizing there is a problem.

Speech Clarity—The ability to speak clearly so others can understand you.

Oral Comprehension—The ability to listen to and understand information and ideas presented through spoken words and sentences.

Speech Recognition—The ability to identify and understand the speech of another person.

Near Vision—The ability to see details at close range (within a few feet of the observer).

Manual Dexterity—The ability to quickly move your hand, your hand together with your arm, or your two hands to grasp, manipulate, or assemble objects.

Selective Attention—The ability to concentrate on a task over a period of time without being distracted.

Category Flexibility—The ability to generate or use different sets of rules for combining or grouping things in different ways.

Deductive Reasoning—The ability to apply general rules to specific problems to produce answers that make sense.

Resources

Arvey, R. D., & Begalla, M. E. (1975). Analyzing the homemaker job using the Position Analysis Questionnaire (PAQ). *Journal of Applied Psychology, 60*(4), 513-517.

Goodall, J. (1988). *In the shadow of man*. Boston: Houghton Mifflin.

McCormick, E. J. (1979). *Job analysis: Methods and applications*. New York: Amacom.

(Continued)

(Continued)

McCormick, E. J., Jeanneret, P. R., & Mecham, R. C. (1969). *The development and background of the Position Analysis Questionnaire*. Lafayette, IN: Purdue University, Occupational Research Center.

McCormick, E. J., Jeanneret, P. R., & Mecham, R. C. (1972). A study of job characteristics and job dimensions as based on the Position Analysis Questionnaire. *Journal of Applied Psychology, 56*(4), 347-368.

Peterson, N. G., Mumford, M. D., Borman, W. C., Jeanneret, P. R., Fleishman, E. A., Levin, K. Y., et al. (2001). Understanding work using the Occupational Information Network (O*NET): Implications for practice and research. *Personnel Psychology, 54*(2), 451-492.

Plimpton, G. (1966). *Paper lion*. New York: Harper & Row.

Position Analysis Questionnaire. http://www.paq.com/

Tornow, W. (1976). The development of a managerial job taxonomy—a system for describing, classifying, and evaluating executive positions. *Journal of Applied Psychology, 61*(4), 410-418.

4 Recruitment and Socialization

Strategic Objective

The process of recruitment entails seeking and attracting a pool of applicants from which qualified candidates for job vacancies can be chosen. To attract qualified applicants for desirable positions with organizations where applicants want to work, merely posting the job opening may be sufficient. For positions with knowledge and skill requirements in greater demand than the available supply, it may be difficult for organizations to attract applicants, and the organization may have to seek out qualified applicants by participating in job fairs or visiting college campuses to meet with students. A Human Resource Information System can be used for internal recruitment, to match the job specification with current employees and notify qualified employees of job openings (Barclay & Bass, 1994). Just as organizations have to compete for customers, they must also compete for employees.

The attraction stage of the recruitment process may be the most important, because it has a direct impact on the organization's ability to generate a large pool of qualified applicants. Larger applicant pools may provide more diversity and may allow an organization to be more selective in making hiring decisions. Attracting applicants is critical, because when applicants do not apply for an opening, it is functionally the same as a rejection decision (Collins & Stevens, 2002). Attracting applicants to apply for vacancies is transforming potential applicants into actual applicants.

Researchers have found many factors that affect potential applicants' decisions to become actual applicants, including recruitment messages (Avery, 2003; Herriot & Rothwell, 1981), recruiter behaviors and characteristics (Harris & Fink, 1987; Rynes & Miller, 1983), job characteristics

(Chapman, Uggerslev, Carroll, Piasentin, & Jones, 2005; Turban, Eyring, & Campion, 1993), flexible work arrangements (Maxwell, Rankine, Bell, & MacVicar, 2007; Rau & Hyland, 2002), organizational reputation (Cable & Turban, 2003; Collins & Han, 2004), corporate image (Gatewood, Gowan, & Lautenschlager, 1993; Lemmink, Schuijf, & Streukens, 2003), corporate social performance (Backhaus, Stone, & Heiner, 2002; Greening & Turban, 2000), and being "green" (Aiman-Smith, Bauer, & Cable, 2001; Bauer & Aiman-Smith, 1996).

At this early stage in the recruitment process, in which potential applicants may know little about the job or the organization, applicants can also be affected by the characteristics of the products or services of the recruiting organization. DelVecchio, Jarvis, and Klink (2001) concluded that brand equity influences job acceptance, because it increases the attractiveness of an applicant's resume for future jobs (i.e., resume building); Collins (2007) found that product awareness (i.e., the extent to which job seekers in general were familiar with a company's products or services) influenced the intention to apply.

During the socialization stage of the recruitment process, new employees become familiar with their new job and with the organization's way of doing things. An effective socialization process gives new employees a better understanding of the organization's goals, values, history, and people, and produces employees with higher levels of commitment to the organization (Klein & Weaver, 2000). For example, the Mayo Clinic was one of the first medical practice groups to hire its staff physicians as salaried employees. As newly hired physicians join this organization, their effectiveness depends on quickly learning the methods for getting things done and developing good networks with colleagues in other disciplines (Bender, DeVogel, & Blomberg, 1999).

Retention of satisfactory employees is a measure of the success of the recruitment process. If the organization can attract applicants, but soon thereafter they are working elsewhere, then the recruitment methods were not successful. Turnover can be very costly. A study conducted at a major medical center found that the annual cost of turnover was between 3.4% and 5.8% of the annual operating budget, with the largest cost driver being the loss and necessary replacement of nurses (Waldman, Kelly, Arora, & Smith, 2004). Obviously, a recruitment and selection procedure that retains satisfactory performers for 4 years costs only half as much as one which retains satisfactory performers for only 2 years.

Internet technology has revolutionized how recruitment is done in organizations (Bingham et al., 2002; Singh & Finn, 2003). More like a job fair than a local newspaper's help wanted section, job boards are where employers seeking applicants and applicants seeking jobs meet in cyberspace. A job posting on an Internet job board can cost as little as 10% of the cost of a national newspaper advertisement, making it especially attractive to small businesses (Hausdorf & Duncan, 2004). There are other advantages, including less time to prepare the posting, less lag time between job opening and job posting, and less time to fill vacancies. Internet recruiting simultaneously enables better targeting of a specific audience and more widespread distribution of postings than traditional recruitment methods. But there are disadvantages to Internet recruiting. Because it is so easy to submit a resume to a corporate Web site or post a resume to an Internet job board, organizations that use Internet recruiting must handle more applicants than ever before. Roberts (2002) reports that one organization of 16,000 employees received as many as 40,000 resumes in a year, many unsolicited.

Strategic Issues in HRM

RECRUITING FOR EXECUTIVE POSITIONS

Recruiting for any position in the organization is important, but even more important when it is an executive position. Poor recruitment and selection has a financial impact, and because executive-level positions are more highly compensated than other positions, poor recruitment and selection for executive positions will have an even greater financial impact. Applicants chosen for executive positions can also have a significant impact on the strategic focus of the organization, for better or worse.

Some organizations are able to conduct executive searches in-house, and others hire executive search firms to conduct the search for them. Using an executive search firm has become the preferred recruitment method for many organizations where top management skills are in short supply (May, 1997). Using an executive search firm has two main advantages. First, executive search consultants may provide a more impartial evaluation of job candidates compared to internal candidates and may attract applicants more discreetly. Second, executive search firms' databases of job applicants may identify applicants more effectively and efficiently than the organization could on its own (Lim & Chan, 2001). Typical recruiting methods only reach those who are actively searching for a new position, whereas executive search firms are able to locate candidates who are happily employed and not necessarily looking to change jobs (Finlay & Coverdill, 1999). The expanded outreach of an executive search firm makes it more likely that women and minorities will be included in the pool of applicants (Rush & Barclay, 1995).

Citing a survey by the Association of Executive Search Consultants, Shulman and Chiang (2007) claim that more and more companies are relying on search firms as the competition for executive talent continues to grow. Filling executive-level positions may be getting more difficult as baby boomers retire, leaving a shrinking supply of qualified candidates for leadership positions. Executive search firms provide a specialized recruitment service, contracting with an organization to seek applicants for a particular position, typically where the consequences of making a poor decision are seen as greater than the fee charged by the executive search firm or where the organization lacks the expertise to conduct searches for executive positions. An executive search firm may assess the organization's needs, identify potential applicants, evaluate candidates, do screening interviews, schedule interviews between the applicants and the organization, and run reference and background checks (Sosnin, 2007).

However, there are some disadvantages to using executive search firms. If the search firm is paid when the open position is filled, it may be more interested in getting the organization to make a hiring decision than in finding qualified candidates. Conversely, if the search firm is paid whether or not the position is filled, it will be more selective in bringing in applicants. Also, executive search firms can be expensive, with costs ranging up to a third of the compensation package of the new hire. Some organizations have determined that they can cut the costs and improve the results of executive searches by conducting them in-house (Wells, 2003).

Strategic Questions

1. When might an executive search firm have a conflict of interest because of other business relationships it already has?
2. What services should an organization expect from an executive search firm beyond that typically provided by an employment agency?
3. Why would an organization benefit from an executive search firm being discreet and conducting a "quiet" search?
4. Should an organization employing an executive search firm specify the characteristics of the candidates it wishes to select or describe the problems and issues the organization is facing and that the candidate would be dealing with?
5. Should an executive search firm be compensated for finding candidates or for finding a candidate who has accepted the job offer?
6. What recourse does an organization employing an executive search firm have, when there are conflicts between the expectations for services to be provided and services actually delivered?
7. Which candidate is more likely to be a better selection decision, someone who is actively searching for a new position or one who is not?

Resources

Association of Executive Search Consultants. (2007). *Quarter 2 Press Release.* http://www.aesc.org/aesc.php?view=article&page=pressrelease2007081401

Britton, L. C., & Ball, D. F. (1999). Trust versus opportunism: Striking the balance in executive search. *Service Industries Journal, 19*(2), 132-149.

Britton, L. C., Wright, M., & Fall, D. F. (2000). The use of co-ordination theory to improve service quality in executive search. *Service Industries Journal, 20*(4), 85-102.

Coverdill, J. E., & Finlay, W. (1998). Fit and skill in employee selection: Insights from a study of headhunters. *Qualitative Sociology, 21*(2), 105-127.

ExecuNet.com. http://www.execunet.com/

Finlay, W., & Coverdill, J. E. (1999). The search game: Organizational conflicts and the use of headhunters. *Sociological Quarterly, 40*(1), 11-30.

Lim, G., & Chan, C. (2001). Ethical values of executive search consultants. *Journal of Business Ethics, 29*(3), 213-226.

May, A. S. (1997). How the gamekeeper can make the most of his poacher. *Career Development International, 2*(5), 254-255.

Miller, E. C. (1975). Matching manager and job: An executive search consultant's approach. *Management Review, 64*(12), 12-17.

Rush, C., & Barclay, L. (1995). Executive search: Recruiting a recruiter. *Public Management, 77*(7), 20-22.

Shulman, B., & Chiang, G. (2007). When to use an executive search firm and how to get the most out of the relationship. *Employment Relations Today, 34*(1), 13-19.

Sosnin, B. (2007). Filling spots at the top. *HR Magazine, 52*(10), 71-74.

Thompson, J. (1988). Executive search: The thrill of the chase. *Management Review, 77*(5), 49-51.

Wells, S. J. (2003). Slow times for executive recruiting. *HR Magazine, 48*(4), 61-68.

VOLUNTEER EMPLOYEES

Accommodations and food services is an industry that has a consistently high turnover rate, about twice the national average of 3% (Bureau of Labor Statistics, 2007). Organizations in the food service industry typically have higher turnover rates than other industries for a variety of reasons. Many of the jobs require few skills and training, so people use these jobs to gain work experience rather than enter into a long-term career. Many of the jobs are part-time, so students find them attractive to pay their way through school, on their way to a job in their career field. Like other businesses, there are cost pressures to keep labor costs down, so the availability of better paying jobs elsewhere further contributes to turnover. High rates of turnover make it a significant HRM challenge for the accommodations and food services industries to maintain necessary staffing levels. But what other options are there?

One alternative to trying to manage a large number of permanent part-time employees is to outsource it to charitable organizations. An organization providing food services to a sporting arena (fast food, cotton candy, ice cream, specialty foods, beer) might partner with local charities to provide workers for each event, giving a percentage of the revenues of the stand to the charity supplying the workers. These workers are not employees because they are not paid; rather, they are donating their time to the charity. In exchange for the opportunity to make money for their charity, the charities commit to recruit the necessary workers from their own membership and staff events as they are scheduled. Because these workers are "working for charity," they are highly motivated and can be expected to be absent less often. Volunteer workers have been found to have lower levels of job withdrawal and work withdrawal than paid employees and slightly higher levels of organizational commitment (Laczo & Hanisch, 1999). In short, the charity functions as a kind of temporary employment agency, supplying workers as needed on a contractual basis.

Strategic Questions

1. How can local charities be recruited to partner with a sporting arena to provide volunteer workers?
2. In what ways can a sporting arena cut costs through the use of volunteer workers instead of regular employees? What other advantages are there?
3. Should employee theft or shrinkage be higher or lower with volunteer workers?
4. Are disciplinary problems more or less likely with volunteer workers?
5. Is the money paid to the charities supplying volunteer workers a charitable donation?
6. When you last attended a sporting event at a major league arena, were the food service workers regular employees, volunteer workers, or a combination of both? How can you tell?
7. What other organizations might benefit from the use of volunteer workers?

Resources

Bureau of Labor Statistics. (2007). *Job openings and labor turnover: July 2007.* http://www.bls.gov/news.release/pdf/jolts.pdf

Gaston, K., & Alexander, J. A. (2001). Effective organisation and management of public sector volunteer workers Police Special Constables. *International Journal of Public Sector Management, 14*(1), 59-74.

King, P. (2004). Joe Sims: Cincinnati GM hits a home run, covers all the bases of foodservice at the Great American Ballpark. *Nation's Restaurant News, 38*(4), 176-177.

Laczo, R. M., & Hanisch, K. A. (1999). An examination of behavioral families or organizational withdrawal in volunteer workers and paid employees. *Human Resource Management Review, 9*(4), 453-477.

Liao-Troth, M. A. (2001). Attitude differences between paid workers and volunteers. *Nonprofit Management & Leadership, 11*(4), 423-442.

Merrick, B. (2000). Recruiting and training top-notch volunteers. *Credit Union Magazine, 66*(10), 24.

Puffer, S. M., & Meindl, J. R. (1992). The congruence of motives and incentives in a voluntary organization. *Journal of Organizational Behavior, 13*(4), 425-434.

RECRUITMENT AND TURNOVER

One measure of the success of recruitment is turnover. If a large number of qualified applicants are obtained so that the organization can be highly selective when making their hiring decisions, but soon after being hired many employees leave the organization, the recruitment process was not very successful. The components of turnover include separation costs (severance pay, administrative costs, additional overtime, temporary employees), replacement costs (recruiting, testing, training), and performance costs due to productivity loss (Hansen, 2005; Joinson, 2000). Dalton, Krackhardt, and Porter (1981) have suggested that turnover can be classified according to a matrix defined by voluntary versus involuntary and avoidable versus unavoidable. Avoidable voluntary turnover happens when an employee finds a better job opportunity elsewhere; unavoidable voluntary turnover happens when the family relocates because of one member's job. Avoidable involuntary turnover happens when the employee is laid off; unavoidable involuntary turnover happens from an unusual event, such as a severe medical condition (Abelson, 1987).

Dysfunctional turnover occurs when satisfactory performers or key employees leave the organization. Functional turnover occurs when unsatisfactory performers leave. Therefore, turnover can be a problem or a solution. Theoretically, turnover may increase organizational effectiveness by bringing in new ideas to the organization, which better enables it to adapt to changing environmental conditions. Turnover is one way that innovation is moved from firm to firm (Cassels & Randall, 1958; Dalton & Todor, 1979). Turnover may also lead to cost savings, in annual bonuses not paid, open position savings, lower salary and benefit costs for new employees, and performance gains from new hires if they are more effective than the employee terminated for unsatisfactory performance (Hansen, 2005).

Reducing dysfunctional turnover means reducing the costs associated with both recruitment and selection and getting a better return on the investments the organization has made in training and development. Turnover has other costs as well. Using data from a sample of 262 fast food restaurants, Kacmar, Andrews, Van Rooy, Steilberg, and Cerrone (2006) found that turnover had a negative impact on unit-level performance in terms of both sales and profits. McElroy, Morrow, and Rude (2001) also found negative effects of voluntary, involuntary, and reduction-in-force turnover on subunit performance for a financial services company. Shaw, Gupta, and Delery (2005) found that voluntary turnover was significantly related to workforce performance levels for truck drivers at 379 trucking companies.

Turnover is a fact of life for many organizations. A career spent working for the same organization may have already become an artifact of a bygone era. The National Longitudinal Surveys show that from 1971 to 1990, young men became more likely to change jobs (Monks & Pizer, 1998). According to the Annual Employee Tenure Report, the median number of years that wage and salary workers have been with their current employer is now 4.0 years. The proportion of all wage and salary workers age 16 and over with at least 10 years' tenure with their current employer is only 26%. Older workers tend to have more years of tenure than younger workers do; median tenure for employees ages 55 to 64 was 9.3 years, compared to 2.9 years for workers ages 25 to 34 (Bureau of Labor Statistics, 2006a). People born 1957 through 1964 have held an average of 10.2 jobs from ages 18 to 38 (Bureau of Labor Statistics, 2004c).

Strategic Questions

1. When is turnover bad? Under what conditions is it bad for the organization to have an employee leave the organization?
2. When is turnover good? Under what conditions is it good for the organization to have an employee leave the organization?
3. For a typical employee, how long has he or she been with the organization? Does average length of tenure with the organization vary by age?
4. Are there differences in turnover rates by industry? Why do high-turnover industries have high turnover? Why do low-turnover industries have low turnover?
5. What is the difference between an organization with high voluntary turnover and an organization with high involuntary turnover?

Resources

Abelson, M. A. (1987). Examination of avoidable and unavoidable turnover. *Journal of Applied Psychology, 72*(3), 382-386.

Bureau of Labor Statistics. (2004, August 25). *Number of jobs held, labor market activity, and earnings growth among younger baby boomers: Recent results from a longitudinal study.* http://www.bls.gov/news.release/History/nlsoy_08252004.txt

Bureau of Labor Statistics. (2006, September 8). *Employee tenure summary.* http://www.bls.gov/news.release/tenure.nr0.htm

Cassels, L., & Randall, R. L. (1958). Analysis of worker turnover pays off: Three ideas feature new approach to old problem, point to more effective methods. *Nation's Business, 46*(1), 34-38.

Dalton, D. R., Krackhardt, D. M., & Porter, L. W. (1981). Functional turnover: An empirical assessment. *Journal of Applied Psychology, 66*(6), 716-721.

Dalton, D. R., & Todor, W. D. (1979). Turnover turned over: An expanded and positive perspective: An expanded and positive perspective. *Academy of Management Review, 4*(2), 225-235.

Goodman, E. A., & Boss, R. W. (2002). The phase model of burnout and employee turnover. *Journal of Health and Human Services Administration, 25*(1-2), 33-47.

Hansen, F. (2005). The turnover myth. *Workforce Management, 84*(6), 34-40.

Joinson, C. (2000). Capturing turnover costs. *HR Magazine, 45*(7), 107-119.

Kacmar, K. M., Andrews, M. C., Van Rooy, D. L., Steilberg, R. C., & Cerrone, S. (2006). Sure everyone can be replaced... but at what cost? Turnover as a predictor of unit-level performance. *Academy of Management Journal, 49*(1), 133-144.

McElroy, J. C., Morrow, P. C., & Rude, S. N. (2001). Turnover and organizational performance: A comparative analysis of the effects of voluntary, involuntary, and reduction-in-force turnover. *Journal of Applied Psychology, 86*(6), 1294-1299.

Monks, J., & Pizer, S. D. (1998). Trends in voluntary and involuntary job turnover. *Industrial Relations, 37*(4), 440-459.

Shaw, J. D., Gupta, N., & Delery, J. E. (2005). Alternative conceptualizations of the relationship between voluntary turnover and organizational performance. *Academy of Management Journal, 48*(1), 50-68.

ON-BOARDING

To get newly recruited and hired employees up to speed quickly, many organizations have improved and enhanced the traditional orientation program to include technical skills training, industry background, and "soft skills" training (Varma & Collins, 2007). Citing a study done by Mellon Financial Corp., Rollag, Parise, and Cross (2005) claim that lost productivity resulting from the learning curve for new hires and transfers was between 1% and 2.5% of total revenues, and the average time for new hires to achieve full productivity ranged from 8 weeks for clerical jobs, to 20 weeks for professionals, to more than 26 weeks for executives.

On-boarding is a socialization process designed to shorten the productivity curve, to help new employees reach capacity quicker, increase employee engagement, and decrease turnover by helping new employees to build stronger relationships and establish credibility earlier (Cashman & Smye, 2007). The on-boarding process enables new employees to gain access to information, tools, and materials needed to become productive in their job (Snell, 2006). If on-boarding is done effectively, it can increase effectiveness, satisfaction, and retention, and help ensure that companies realize a return on what they invest in recruiting (Reese, 2005). Some on-boarding plans include Web-based tools to give new managers access to key information on a variety of topics, such as hiring, termination, performance management, procurement policies, and business plans (Brodie, 2006).

Organizations need an effective orientation and socialization program for all new employees, but newly hired (or promoted) executives need an even more comprehensive and systematic plan to help them make the transition to their new role. An effective on-boarding plan helps the new executive get integrated into the organization by helping them align their leadership style with the organization's culture, build relationships with peers and direct reports, and gain a better understanding of the organization's decision-making process (Gierden, 2007).

Whenever new hires join the organization or employees make a transition to a new position, there can be paperwork bottlenecks in the processing of various forms. This process can be speeded up, and error rates decreased, through the use of software that collects data from employees to provide customized packets of information for each employee (Lamont, 2007).

Strategic Questions

1. Why is on-boarding an essential HRM process?
2. Should on-boarding be used only for externally recruited employees?
3. What should be included in an on-boarding plan, beyond what is part of a typical orientation?
4. Can on-boarding be done virtually?
5. In large divisionalized organizations, should on-boarding be a centralized or decentralized process?
6. What information about the business should be included in the on-boarding plan (e.g., annual revenues, market value, primary competitors, etc.)?
7. At what transitions in an employee's career should the on-boarding plan be used?

Resources

Bender, C., DeVogel, S., & Blomberg, R. (1999). The socialization of newly hired medical staff into a large health system. *Health Care Management Review, 24*(1), 95-108.

Bigliardi, B., Petroni, A., & Dormio, A. I. (2005). Organizational socialization, career aspirations and turnover intentions among design engineers. *Leadership & Organization Development Journal, 26*(5/6), 424-441.

Brodie, J. M. (2006). Getting managers on board. *HR Magazine, 51*(11), 105-108.

Cashman, K., & Smye, M. (2007). Onboarding: Get on board with it. *Leadership Excellence, 24*(4), 5.

Garavan, T. N., & Morley, M. (1997). The socialization of high-potential graduates into the organization: Initial expectations, experiences and outcomes. *Journal of Managerial Psychology, 12*(2), 118-137.

Gierden, C. (2007). Get on right track with executive onboarding. *Canadian HR Reporter, 20*(13), 14.

King, R. C., & Sethi, V. (1998). The impact of socialization on the role adjustment of information systems professionals. *Journal of Management Information Systems, 14*(4), 195-217.

Lamont, J. (2007). Employing ECM in human resources. *KM World, 16*(9), 8-9.

Mellon Corporation. (2003). *Mellon learning curve research study.* http://www.mellon.com/pressreleases/2003/pr111203.html

Reese, V. (2005). Maximizing your retention and productivity with on-boarding. *Employment Relations Today, 31*(4), 23-29.

Rollag, K., Parise, S., & Cross, R. (2005). Getting new hires up to speed quickly. *MIT Sloan Management Review, 46*(2), 35-41.

Snell, A. (2006). Researching onboarding best practice. *Strategic HR Review, 5*(6), 32-35.

Varma, S., & Collins, B. M. (2007). On ramp to success at Network Appliance. *T + D, 61*(7), 59-61.

Application

JOB HUNTING

To sell their products or services, organizations use a variety of methods to attract customers. They may display their products and services in their storefront, place an advertisement in the newspaper, distribute a circular to potential customer's homes, or rely on word of mouth, using current customers as salespeople. Organizations use a variety of methods to attract potential applicants for job vacancies. They may display a "help wanted" sign in their storefront, place an advertisement in the local or national newspaper, post the job on their corporate Web page or rely on employee referrals, using current employees as recruiters.

To attract a customer, the organization has to tell a potential customer what the product or service is and persuade him or her that it is better than competing products, services, and price. To attract an applicant, the organization has to tell a potential applicant what the job is and persuade him or her that it is better than jobs at other organizations (e.g., compensation, opportunities for advancement, flexible work hours). For example, Ryan, Horvath, and Kriska (2005) found that applicants' decisions to apply for a firefighter job were related to recruiting source informativeness and organizational familiarity.

Potential applicants find out about job vacancies through a variety of methods. There are formal methods, such as newspaper advertisements, college recruiting, employment agencies, job fairs, company Web pages ("Careers"), and Internet job boards. There are also informal methods, such as employee referral, self-initiated contact (walk-ins), and recommendations from friends and family. A typical job posting contains two key elements: the job description and the job specification. The job description is the statement of the job requirements: tasks, duties, responsibilities, working conditions, reporting relationships, and supervisory responsibilities. The job specification is the statement of the person requirements: knowledge, skills, abilities, experience, and education required to do the job.

To Do

Find four different recruitment advertisements from four different recruitment sources (e.g., Internet job board, local newspaper, national newspaper, company Web page, etc.). Identify and record the job description and the job specification in the form "Am I Qualified? Four Job Descriptions and Specifications." For each job, state whether you would be qualified or not qualified for the job and give the reasons.

(Continued)

(Continued)

Am I Qualified? Four Job Descriptions and Specifications

Job Title:	1. 2. 3. 4.
Job Description:	1. 2. 3. 4.
Job Specification:	1. 2. 3. 4.
Qualified or Not Qualified? Reasons:	1. 2. 3. 4.

Resources

Barclay, L. A., & Bass, A. R. (1994). Get the most from recruitment efforts. *HR Magazine, 39*(6), 70-72.

Brown, D. J., Cober, R. T., Kane, K., Levy, P. E., & Shalhoop, J. (2006). Proactive personality and the successful job search: A field investigation with college graduates. *Journal of Applied Psychology, 91*(3), 717-726.

CareerBank.com. http://www.careerbank.com/

CareerBuilder.com. http://www.careerbuilder.com/

CareerJournal.com. *The Wall Street Journal Executive Career Site*. http://www.careerjournal.com/

Marchal, E., Mellet, K., Rieucau, G. (2007). Job board toolkits: Internet matchmaking and changes in job advertisements. *Human Relations, 60*(7), 1091-1113.

Maurer, S. D., & Liu, Y. (2007). Developing effective e-recruiting websites: Insights for managers from marketers. *Business Horizons, 50*(4), 305-314.

Monster.com. www.monster.com

Ryan, A. M., Horvath, M., & Kriska, S. D. (2005). The role of recruiting source informativeness and organizational perceptions in decisions to apply. *International Journal of Selection and Assessment, 13*(4), 235-249.

Swaroff, P. G., Barlcay, L. A., & Bass, A. R. (1985). Recruiting sources: Another look. *Journal of Applied Psychology, 70*(4), 720-728.

Yahoo! HotJobs.com. http://hotjobs.yahoo.com/

APPLICANT POOLS FOR PART-TIME WORKERS

According to a Society for Human Resource Management survey of HRM professionals, 33% said that their organization has formal, part-time employees, 39% said part-timers are hired on a case-by-case basis, and 67% said that employing part-timers has helped their organization keep employees who might otherwise have been lost (Grensing-Pophal, 2007). The food service industry employs more than 12 million workers; for restauranteurs, their top challenge is not food costs but the recruiting and training of employees (Gerst, 2005). Recruiting for permanent part-time employees can be more challenging than recruiting for full-time employees because these positions are attractive only to potential applicants who are not interested in a full-time job and who are willing to take a job that has fewer or lesser benefits. The job attributes that are attractive to people looking for part-time jobs may be different from the job attributes that are attractive to people looking for full-time jobs (Martin, 1974; Nkomo & Fields, 1994).

Part-time employees comprise nearly 20% of the U.S. workforce (Bureau of Labor Statistics, 2006b; Tilly, 1991). The Bureau of Labor Statistics collects data on the reasons people work part-time; more people work part-time for noneconomic than economic reasons. The noneconomic reasons include child care problems, other family or personal obligations, health or medical limitations, retirement, or Social Security limit on earnings; the most frequently stated reason is being in school or in a training program. For example, people pursuing an acting career might take a part-time job as a server in a restaurant until they get their big break, because they can work evening hours, leaving their days free for auditions and acting classes. For these permanent part-time jobs, organizations might need to seek applicants in ways other than newspaper advertisements, corporate careers Web pages, and Internet job boards.

To Do

For each of the permanent part-time jobs shown in the table on the next page, list at least two nontraditional potential applicant pools to target for recruitment and briefly describe the recruiting plan to get the job posting noticed by people in the target audience.

Resources

Bureau of Labor Statistics. (2006). *Labor force statistics from the Current Population Survey.* http://www.bls.gov/cps/lfcharacteristics.htm#fullpart

Davey, S. R. (1998). Virtual staffing. *Occupational Health & Safety, 67*(8), 28.

Gerst, V. (2005). The ten minute manager's guide to nontraditional hiring. *Restaurants & Institutions, 115*(17), 22-23.

Grensing-Pophal, L. (2007). Committing to part-timers. *HR Magazine, 52*(4), 84-88.

Martin, V. H. (1974). Recruiting women managers through flexible hours. *S.A.M. Advanced Management Journal, 39*(3), 46-53.

McShulskis, E. (1996). The best recruiting sources. *HR Magazine, 41*(3), 16-17.

Nkomo, S. M., & Fields, D. M. (1994). A field study of demographic characteristics and job attribute preferences of new part-time employees. *Journal of Business and Psychology, 8*(3), 365-375.

Rau, B. L., & Adams, G. A. (2005). Attracting retirees to apply: Desired organizational characteristics of bridge employment. *Journal of Organizational Behavior, 26*(6), 649-660.

Rau, B. L., & Hyland, M. M. (2002). Role conflict and flexible work arrangements: The effects on applicant attraction. *Personnel Psychology, 55*(1), 111-136.

Tilly, C. (1991). Reasons for the continuing growth of part-time employment. *Monthly Labor Review, 114*(3), 10-18.

Ulrich, L. B., & Brott, P. E. (2005). Older workers and bridge employment: Redefining retirement. *Journal of Employment Counseling, 42*(4), 159-170.

Applicant Pools and Recruiting Plans for Permanent Part-Time Jobs

Organization and Job	*Target Audience*	*Recruiting Plan*
Fast food restaurant server	Postretirement workers	• Place advertisements on bulletin boards of senior centers • Sponsor a prize at Bingo night
	College students	• Place advertisements in the school paper • Point-of-sale advertisements on tray liners
Retail store clerk		
Coffee shop team member		
Mail-order sales customer service representative		
Credit union teller		
Limousine service driver		
Nursery and lawn center grower		

Experiential Exercises

REALISTIC JOB PREVIEWS

A Realistic Job Preview (RJP) is a recruitment tool in which applicants are given realistic information about both positives and negatives of the job before they are given the job offer. Applicants are given realistic information about the work itself, pay, coworkers, workload, working conditions, and generally what it is like working in the organization. Because organizations try to look attractive to applicants and recruiters' job performance is often evaluated on job offer acceptances, applicants can have unrealistically positive expectations about the job and what it will be like working for the organization. When these unrealistic expectations collide with reality, turnover can result.

The idea underlying the RJP is that when applicants have more realistic expectations as new hires, they are less likely to quit (Breaugh & Starke, 2000). For example, Wanous (1973) found that new telephone company employees who received an RJP had more realistic job expectations, fewer thoughts of quitting, and slightly higher job survival rates than those who didn't get the preview. In their meta-analysis of 21 RJP experiments, Premack and Wanous (1985) found that RJPs tend to lower initial job expectations, while increasing self-selection, organizational commitment, job satisfaction, performance, and job survival. In their meta-analysis of 40 RJP studies, Phillips (1998) concluded that RJPs were related to higher performance, lower attrition from the recruitment process, and lower turnover. RJPs and Realistic Living Conditions Previews have been found to be positively related to general adjustment for employees on expatriate assignments (Templer, Tay, & Chandrasekar, 2006).

Although providing applicants with RJPs appears to reduce turnover, there are other reasons to conduct RJPs. Based on a longitudinal study of more than 700 salespeople in 54 companies, Barksdale, Bellenger, Boles, and Brashear (2003) concluded that providing an RJP directly helps to improve a salesperson's role clarity and results in more positive perceptions of training, which tends to reduce salesperson role stress, which is negatively related

To Do

Write an RJP—including the positive and negative aspects—for one of jobs listed below. Then, write an RJP for your current job or any job you have had in the past.

Amusement and Recreation Attendants

O*Net: 39-3091.00
Perform variety of attending duties at amusement or recreation facility. May schedule use of recreation facilities, maintain and provide equipment to participants of sporting events or recreational pursuits, or operate amusement concessions and rides.

Slaughterers and Meat Packers

O*Net: 51-3023.00
Work in slaughtering, meat packing, or wholesale establishments performing precision functions involving the preparation of meat. Work may include specialized slaughtering tasks, cutting standard or premium cuts of meat for marketing, making sausage, or wrapping meats.

Emergency Medical Technicians and Paramedics

O*Net: 29-2041.00
Assess injuries, administer emergency medical care, and extricate trapped individuals. Transport injured or sick persons to medical facilities.

Riggers

O*Net: 49-9096.00
Set up or repair rigging for construction projects, manufacturing plants, logging yards, ships and shipyards, or for the entertainment industry.

Musical Instrument Repairers and Tuners

O*Net: 49-9063.00
Repair percussion, stringed, reed, or wind instruments. May specialize in one area, such as piano tuning.

Fish and Game Wardens

O*Net: 33-3031.00
Patrol assigned area to prevent fish and game law violations. Investigate reports of damage to crops or property by wildlife. Compile biological data.

Police Detectives

O*Net: 33-3021.01
Conduct investigations to prevent crimes or solve criminal cases.

Forest Fire Fighting and Prevention Supervisors

O*Net: 33-1021.02
Supervise fire fighters who control and suppress fires in forests or vacant public land.

Resources

Adidam, P. T. (2006). Causes and consequences of high turnover by sales professionals. *Journal of American Academy of Business, 10*(1), 137-141.

Barksdale, H. C., Bellenger, D. N., Boles, J. S., & Brashear, T. G. (2003). The impact of realistic job previews and perceptions of training on sales force performance and continuance commitment: A longitudinal test. *Journal of Personal Selling & Sales Management, 23*(2), 125-138.

Breaugh, J. A. (1983). Realistic job previews: A critical appraisal and future research directions. *Academy of Management Review, 8*(4), 612-619.

Breaugh, J. A., & Starke, M. (2000). Research on employee recruitment: So many studies, so many remaining questions. *Journal of Management, 26*(3), 405-434.

(Continued)

(Continued)

Bretz, R. D., Jr., & Judge, T. A. (1998). Realistic job previews: A test of the adverse self-selection hypothesis. *Journal of Applied Psychology, 83*(2), 330-337.

Buckley, M. R., Fedor, D. B., Carraher, S. M., Frink, D. D., & Marvin, D. (1997). The ethical imperative to provide recruits realistic job previews. *Journal of Managerial Issues, 9*(4), 468-484.

Dean, R. A., & Wanous, J. P. (1984). Effects of realistic job previews on hiring bank tellers. *Journal of Applied Psychology, 69*(1), 61-68.

Dugoni, B. L., & Ilgen, D. R. (1981). Realistic job previews and adjustment of new employees. *Academy of Management Journal, 24*(3), 579-591.

Ganzach, Y., Pazy, A., Ohayun, Y., & Brainin, E. (2002). Social exchange and organizational commitment: Decision-making training for job choice as an alternative to the realistic job preview. *Personnel Psychology, 55*(3), 613-637.

Gravelle, M. (2004). The five most common hiring mistakes and how to avoid them. *Canadian Manager, 29*(3), 11-13.

Jackson, S. (1999). Realistic job previews help screen applicants and reduce turnover. *Canadian HR Reporter, 12*(14), 10.

McEvoy, G. M., & Cascio, W. F. (1985). Strategies for reducing employee turnover: A meta-analysis. *Journal of Applied Psychology, 70*(2), 342-353.

Nicholson, N., & Arnold, J. (1991). From expectation to experience: Graduates entering a large corporation. *Journal of Organizational Behavior, 12*(5), 413-429.

O*Net. *Occupational Information Network*. http://online.onetcenter.org/

Phillips, J. M. (1998). Effects of realistic job previews on multiple organizational outcomes: A meta-analysis. *Academy of Management Journal, 41*(6), 673-690.

Reilly, R. R., Brown, B., Blood, M. R., & Malatesta, C. Z. (1981). The effects of realistic previews: A study and discussion of the literature. *Personnel Psychology, 34*(4), 823-834.

Taylor, G. S. (1994). Realistic job previews in the trucking industry. *Journal of Managerial Issues, 6*(4), 457-473.

Templer, K. J., Tay, C., & Chandrasekar, N. A. (2006). Motivational cultural intelligence, realistic job preview, realistic living conditions preview, and cross-cultural adjustment. *Group & Organization Management, 31*(1), 154.

Wanous, J. P. (1973). Effects of a realistic job preview on job acceptance, job attitudes, and job survival. *Journal of Applied Psychology, 58*(3), 327-332.

to performance. Buckley, Fedor, Carraher, Frink, and Marvin (1997) claim that RJPs are an ethically required practice and that the effect of RJPs on turnover, job satisfaction, and other outcomes is just a fortuitous benefit of dealing fairly and honestly with applicants. In short, RJPs may be one of those HRM processes that ought to be done as a matter of fairness to employees and that benefit both applicants and the organization.

WRITING AN EFFECTIVE RADIO ADVERTISEMENT

A recruitment advertisement contains two parts. The job description is a list of the job duties and tasks. This gives potential applicants an idea of what the job entails, what responsibilities they would have, and what day-to-day tasks they would be performing. The job specification is a list of the knowledge, skills, and abilities required to do the job tasks.

This gives potential applicants an idea of whether they are qualified for the position.

The purpose of a recruitment advertisement is to turn potential applicants into actual applicants. There are other organizations trying to attract potential applicants to apply for similar or different jobs, so the organization's recruitment message must compete with other organizations' recruitment messages. The degree of recruitment message specificity is one factor that has been found to affect potential applicants' attitude toward the advertisement and the company and intentions to apply (Feldman, Bearden, & Hardesty, 2006). Corporate image has also been shown to influence the likelihood that a potential applicant will pursue a job (Belt & Paolillo, 1982).

There are four basic steps to be followed to write an effective recruitment advertisement:

Step 1. Attract attention to the advertisement. If potential applicants do not see the advertisement, they cannot become actual applicants. When selling a product or a service, an organization will use a variety of tools to get potential customers' attention, such as music, bright colors, movement, celebrities, or product demonstrations.

Step 2. Develop interest in the job. The recruitment advertisement must tell potential applicants about the job; what they will be doing on the job; and what knowledge, skills, abilities, and experience is required to do the job.

Step 3. Create desire by building on the interest factors. The job might be a career builder by developing certain knowledge, skills, or experience; the job may be especially interesting or challenging; the organization may be in a desirable location; the organization may have a reputation for being a "best" company to work for; or there may be the opportunity to travel extensively.

Step 4. Tell what action should be taken. Potential applicants should be told how to apply online or whom to call or write about their interest in the job.

To Do

Using the four steps outlined above, create a 30-sec. radio recruitment advertisement for one of the jobs listed below.

Mental Health Counselors

O*Net: 21-1014.00
Counsel with emphasis on prevention. Work with individuals and groups to promote optimum mental health. May help individuals deal with addictions and substance abuse; family, parenting, and marital problems; suicide; stress management; problems with self-esteem; and issues associated with aging and mental and emotional health.

(Continued)

(Continued)

Air Traffic Controllers

O*Net: 53-2021.00
Control air traffic on and within vicinity of airport and movement of air traffic between altitude sectors and control centers according to established procedures and policies. Authorize, regulate, and control commercial airline flights according to government or company regulations to expedite and ensure flight safety.

Radio and Television Announcers

O*Net: 27-3011.00
Talk on radio or television. May interview guests, act as master of ceremonies, read news flashes, identify station by giving call letters, or announce song title and artist.

Travel Guides

O*Net: 39-6022.00
Plan, organize, and conduct long distance cruises, tours, and expeditions for individuals and groups.

Gaming Dealers

O*Net: 39-3011.00
Operate table games. Stand or sit behind table and operate games of chance by dispensing the appropriate number of cards or blocks to players, or operating other gaming equipment. Compare the house's hand against players' hands and payoff or collect players' money or chips.

Pilots, Ship

O*Net: 53-5021.03
Command ships to steer them into and out of harbors, estuaries, straits, and sounds, and on rivers, lakes, and bays. Must be licensed by U.S. Coast Guard with limitations indicating class and tonnage of vessels for which license is valid and route and waters that may be piloted.

Nuclear Engineers

O*Net: 17-2161.00
Conduct research on nuclear engineering problems or apply principles and theory of nuclear science to problems concerned with release, control, and utilization of nuclear energy and nuclear waste disposal.

Environmental Engineers

O*Net: 17-2081.00
Design, plan, or perform engineering duties in the prevention, control, and remediation of environmental health hazards utilizing various engineering disciplines. Work may include waste treatment, site remediation, or pollution control technology.

Probation Officers and Correctional Treatment Specialists

O*Net: 21-1092.00
Provide social services to assist in rehabilitation of law offenders in custody or on probation or parole. Make recommendations for actions involving formulation of rehabilitation plan and treatment of offender, including conditional release and education and employment stipulations.

Personal Financial Advisors

O*Net: 13-2052.00
Advise clients on financial plans utilizing knowledge of tax and investment strategies, securities, insurance, pension plans, and real estate. Duties include assessing clients' assets, liabilities, cash flow, insurance coverage, tax status, and financial objectives to establish investment strategies.

Resources

Avery, D. R. (2003). Reactions to diversity in recruitment advertising—the differences black and white? *Journal of Applied Psychology, 88*(4), 672-679.

Belt, J. A., & Paolillo, J. G. P. (1982). The influence of corporate image and specificity of candidate qualifications on response to recruitment advertisement. *Journal of Management, 8*(1), 105-112.

Blackman, A. (2006). Graduating students' responses to recruitment advertisements. *Journal of Business Communication, 43*(4), 367-388.

Feldman, D. C., Bearden, W. O., & Hardesty, D. M. (2006). Varying the content of job advertisements: The effect of message specificity. *Journal of Advertising, 35*(1), 123-141.

Georgia, B. (2000). How to create a killer job ad. *Network World, 17*(9), 53.

O*Net. *Occupational Information Network.* http://online.onetcenter.org/

Perkins, L. A., Thomas, K. M., & Taylor, G. A. (2000). Advertising and recruitment: Marketing to minorities. *Psychology & Marketing, 17*(3), 235-255.

Redman, T., & Mathews, B. P. (1992). Advertising for effective managerial recruitment. *Journal of General Management, 18*(2), 29-44.

Smith, R. E., & Swinyard, W. R. (1982). Information response models: An integrated approach. *Journal of Marketing, 46*(1), 81-93.

Creative Exercises

SOCIALIZATION OF NEWCOMERS

Once an applicant has been hired, the new employee joins the organization. New employees go through a socialization process, both formal and informal, as they adjust to their new surroundings and learn what it is like to work in their new organization and the organization's preferred ways of doing things. Every organization has an informal socialization process, where new employees "learn the ropes" by observing and interacting with their coworkers. Some organizations also have a formal socialization process that gives the organization greater (although still incomplete) control over the messages given to new employees. Formal socialization processes have been found to be negatively related to role ambiguity, role conflict, and intentions to quit, and positively related to P-O Fit perceptions, job satisfaction, organizational commitment, job performance, and custodial role orientation (Jones, 1986; Saks, Uggerslev, & Fassina, 2007). Formal socialization has also been found to be positively associated with newcomer adjustment (Ashforth, Saks, & Lee, 1998), higher levels of affective organizational commitment (Allen & Meyer, 1990; Klein & Weaver, 2000), and positively related to job satisfaction and negatively related to intentions to quit (Ashforth & Saks, 1996). Turnover is often highest among new employees, but socialization processes serve to embed new employees into the organization and are negatively related to turnover (Allen, 2006).

There is a wide variety of socialization methods that organizations might use to help new employees become socialized, including relationship building (Ashford & Black, 1996), task-oriented and social-oriented information seeking (Bauer & Green, 1998), formal and informal mentorship (Chao, Walz, & Gardner, 1992), performance and social feedback (Morrison, 1993), self-observation and self-goal setting (Saks & Ashforth, 1996), and use of intraorganizational and extraorganizational referents (Settoon & Adkins, 1997). By whatever means, socialization is the process of being made a member of a group and being taught how one must communicate and interact to get things done (Pascale, 1985).

To Do

Part 1: Create a socialization plan for incoming freshmen. The plan should include monthly events to help the new students become familiar with the organization's way of doing things and develop a better understanding of the goals, values, history, and people in the organization. The socialization plan is a year-long process to prepare the students for their first year at college by showing them how to behave in their new organization and giving them an opportunity to practice the appropriate behaviors. Any aspect of college or university life may be the focus, including appropriate and inappropriate classroom behavior, appropriate and inappropriate outside-the-classroom behavior, relationships with roommates, work on team projects, sexual harassment, student organizations, credit cards, exams, library research, papers and other assignments, registration, time management, financial aid, use of university health services, cheating, plagiarism, emergency procedures, and so forth.

Part 2: Make a presentation of your socialization plan for your college or university for incoming freshman and demonstrate one socialization experience. Use the other students in the class as test subjects for the "dress rehearsal."

Resources

Allen, D. G. (2006). Do socialization tactics influence newcomer embeddedness and turnover? *Journal of Management, 32*(2), 237-256.

Allen, N. J., & Meyer, J. P. (1990). Organizational socialization tactics: A longitudinal analysis of links to newcomers' commitment and role orientation. *Academy of Management Journal, 33*(4), 847-858.

Ashford, S. J., & Black, J. S. (1996). Proactivity during organizational entry: A role of desire for control. *Journal of Applied Psychology, 81*(2), 199-214.

Ashforth, B. E., & Saks, A. M. (1996). Socialization tactics: Longitudinal effects on newcomer adjustment. *Academy of Management Journal, 39*(1), 149-178.

Ashforth, B. E., Saks, A. M., & Lee, R. T. (1998). Socialization and newcomer adjustment: The role of organizational context. *Human Relations, 51*(7), 897-926.

Bauer, T. N., & Green, S. G. (1998). Testing the combined effects of newcomer information seeking and manager behavior on socialization. *Journal of Applied Psychology, 83*(1), 72-83.

Chao, G. T., Walz, P. M., & Gardner, P. D. (1992). Formal and informal mentorships: A comparison on mentoring functions and contrast with non-mentored counterparts. *Personnel Psychology, 45*(3), 619-636.

Griffin, A. E. C., Colella, A., & Goparaju, S. (2000). Newcomer and organizational socialization tactics: An interactionist perspective. *Human Resource Management Review, 10*(4), 453-474.

Jones, G. R. (1986). Socialization tactics, self-efficacy, and newcomers' adjustments to organizations. *Academy of Management Journal, 29*(2), 262-279.

Klein, H. J., & Weaver, N. A. (2000). The effectiveness of an organizational level orientation training program in the socialization of new hires. *Personnel Psychology, 53*(1), 47-66.

Morrison, E. W. (1993). Newcomer information seeking: Exploring types, modes, sources, and outcomes. *Academy of Management Journal, 36*(3), 557-589.

Pascale, R. T. (1985). The paradox of "corporate culture": Reconciling ourselves to socialization. *California Management Review, 27*(2), 26-41.

Saks, A. M., & Ashforth, B. E. (1996). Proactive socialization and behavioral self-management. *Journal of Vocational Behavior, 48*(3), 301-323.

Saks, A. M., Uggerslev, K. L, & Fassina, N. E. (2007). Socialization tactics and newcomer adjustment: A meta-analytic review and test of a model. *Journal of Vocational Behavior, 70*(3), 413-446.

Settoon, R. P., & Adkins, C. L. (1997). Newcomer socialization: The role of supervisors, coworkers, friends and family members. *Journal of Business and Psychology, 11*(4), 112-124.

Wesson, M. J., & Gogus, C. I. (2005). Shaking hands with a computer: An examination of two methods of organizational newcomer orientation. *Journal of Applied Psychology, 90*(5), 1018-1026.

MEASURING THE EFFECTIVENESS OF RECRUITMENT

Employers may use a number of different recruitment sources to build an applicant pool. They may put a job posting on the company "Careers" Web page, do campus recruiting, post the job to an Internet job board, place an advertisement in the local newspaper, participate in a job fair, use employee referrals, or use an employment agency or an executive search firm. Different recruiting methods will produce different results. How can the effectiveness of recruitment be measured?

The most basic measure of recruitment success is that potential applicants heard about the job opening and applied for it, so the effectiveness of the recruitment method can be measured by the number of applicants who say they found out about the job through each source. Another way to measure recruitment success is to measure the percentage of job offers that are accepted (acceptance to offer ratio); in filling job vacancies, it is not effective to have a recruitment source that generates a large number of applicants but has only few applicants who are willing to accept the job offer.

The purpose of recruitment is to generate a pool of qualified applicants, so the number of applicants and the number of qualified applicants generated by the recruitment source is another measure of its effectiveness. By this measure, the better recruitment source is the one that generates more qualified applicants. Because the organization must compete with other organizations for employees, timeliness of the source in providing applicants is also important. The more quickly qualified applicants can be generated and the fewer days required to fill job openings, the better the recruitment source. Different recruitment sources will also have different costs. Placing an ad in a local newspaper may be considerably more expensive than posting a job on the company's Web page. The cost-effectiveness of different recruitment methods can be evaluated by determining the cost of each method to generate each qualified applicant.

Just filling an open position doesn't get at the heart of the matter; the primary goal of recruitment is to fill each position with a satisfactory performer. A recruiting source that leads to employees with poor job performance is not an effective recruitment source. Another measure of recruiting effectiveness is the job performance of employees recruited from different sources. The most effective recruiting source is the one that results in the highest percentage of satisfactory performers (Wiley, 1992; Williams, Labig, & Stone, 1993). Job performance can be measured in multiple ways, and employees might have both internal and external customers. The most effective recruitment source will result in employees who are more motivated and satisfied in their jobs and stay with the organization for a longer period of time, which reduces recruitment and selection costs and brings a greater return on investment in the employees' training and development.

To Do

Develop a plan to measure the recruitment effectiveness for the job listed below. Applicants for this job were recruited using a variety of recruitment sources with different costs. The plan should evaluate the effectiveness of each recruitment source with multiple measures of recruitment effectiveness, including multiple aspects of worker attitudes and job performance.

Advertising sales agent

Sell or solicit advertising, including graphic art, advertising space in publications, custom-made signs, or TV and radio advertising time. May obtain leases for outdoor advertising sites or persuade a retailer to use sales promotion display items.

Resources

Carlson, K. D., Connerley, M. L., & Mecham, R. L., III. (2002). Recruitment evaluation: The case for assessing the quality of applicants attracted. *Personnel Psychology, 55*(2), 461-490.

Connor, R. A., Hillson, S. D., & Kralewski, J. E. (1995). An analysis of physician recruitment strategies in rural hospitals. *Health Care Management Review, 20*(1), 7-18.

Martin, S. L. (1992). Determining cutoff scores that optimize utility: A recognition of recruiting costs. *Journal of Applied Psychology, 77*(1), 15-23.

Swaroff, P. G., Barlcay, L. A., & Bass, A. R. (1985). Recruiting sources: Another look. *Journal of Applied Psychology, 70*(4), 720-728.

Wiley, C. (1992). Recruitment research revisited: Effective recruiting methods according to employment outcomes. *Journal of Applied Business Research, 8*(2), 74-79.

Williams, C. R., Labig, C. E., Jr., & Stone, T. H. (1993). Recruitment sources and posthire outcomes for job applicants and new hires: A test of two hypotheses. *Journal of Applied Psychology, 78*(2), 163-172.

5 Selection

Strategic Objective

The purpose of selection is to fill available job openings with qualified applicants and avoid discriminating on the basis of race, color, religion, sex, national origin, age, or disability. A pool of qualified applicants is created by using job analysis information to specify the knowledge, skills, and abilities required to do the job, and applicants not meeting the minimum qualifications are screened out. Tests may also be used to determine whether applicants meet reasonable expectations of proficiency in the workforce. For a selection test to be useful, applicants who score higher on the test should show better performance on the job than applicants who score lower on the test (i.e., there should be a statistically significant correlation between test scores and job performance).

The selection process begins with the job analysis, which defines the essential and nonessential job tasks (the job description) and defines the minimum qualifications needed for job success (the job specification). The job analysis information is used to recruit applicants for the job opening so that applicants will know what kinds of tasks the job entails and whether they are qualified to do the job. Applicants not meeting the minimum qualifications are screened out, leaving a pool of qualified applicants. In some cases, tests may be used to determine whether applicants meet the minimum qualifications, such as a knowledge test of different types of fires and how to put them out for the job of firefighter (see Buster, Roth, & Bobko, 2005). Any of the applicants in the qualified applicant pool can be hired, and if there is underrepresentation of a minority group in that job, a minority applicant may be chosen as part of the Affirmative Action Plan to eliminate or reduce the underrepresentation. If there is no underrepresentation, then a top-down selection method is most commonly used; based on the test scores, applicants are hired from the highest test score on down until all of the available positions are filled.

Although the person to be hired could be randomly selected from the qualified applicant pool, many organizations use tests. The idea is to give applicants a test today that will predict their job performance 6 months or a year from today. It is difficult to predict human behavior and so the predictive validities of tests are never perfect. Any improvement in selection above random selection will improve the quality of the workforce, and the organization should determine both the validity of the test and whether the increase in productivity due to testing is greater than the cost of the test. Utility Analysis can be used to determine the dollar gain in productivity from using the test compared to random selection or of using a new-and-improved but more expensive test.

One of the most commonly used selection tests is the employment interview in its various forms (structured, unstructured, panel, situational, behavioral). Some of the early research on the validity of the selection interview found that it was a weak to modest predictor of job behavior. Wiesner and Cronshaw's (1988) meta-analysis of a large number of studies from the United States, Australia, and Europe found an average validity coefficient of .26; and McDaniel, Whetzel, Schmidt, and Maurer's (1994) analysis of data from the U.S. Office of Personnel Management found an average validity coefficient of .22. However, Harris (1989), Jelf (1999), and Huffcutt and Arthur (1994) reviewed research since these two studies and concluded that the selection interview has at least modest levels of validity, close to that of cognitive ability tests.

The selection process is regulated by Title VII of the Civil Rights Act of 1964, which prohibits discrimination on the basis of race, color, religion, sex, and national origin. Some states have expanded the scope of equal employment opportunity laws to include additional protected groups. The administrative rules that are used to interpret Title VII are the Uniform Guidelines on Employee Selection Procedures (EEOC, 1978) and are enforced by the EEOC, the Civil Service Commission, the Department of Labor, and the Department of Justice. Employers with more than 100 employees must also file EEO Reports with the EEOC annually, reporting the number and percentage of employees in each job by race and sex.

Strategic Issues in HRM

EQUAL EMPLOYMENT OPPORTUNITY POSTURES

In addition to evidence of adverse impact and test validity, the agencies that enforce the Civil Rights Act of 1964 (the EEOC, the Civil Service Commission, the Department of Labor, and the Department of Justice) also take into consideration the equal employment opportunity posture of the organization. The Uniform Guidelines on Employee Selection Procedures, Section 1607.4 states this information on impact:

> E. *Consideration of user's equal employment opportunity posture.* In carrying out their obligations, the Federal enforcement agencies will consider the general posture of the user with respect to equal employment opportunity for the job or group of jobs in question. Where a user has adopted an affirmative action program, the Federal enforcement agencies will consider the provisions of that program, including the goals and timetables which the user has adopted and the progress which the user has made in carrying out that program and in meeting the goals and timetables. While such affirmative action programs may in design and execution be race, color, sex, or ethnic conscious, selection procedures under such programs should be based upon the ability or relative ability to do the work.

The equal employment opportunity posture is based on whether the organization has adopted and implemented an Affirmative Action Plan (EEOC, 1979), including goals and timetables for jobs in which minorities are underrepresented and the progress the organization has made in reducing the underrepresentation. The Four-Fifths Rule is used to determine whether there is adverse impact, but if an employer can show that the company is making progress in reducing underrepresentation, the enforcement agency may exercise its discretion and not begin enforcement proceedings, even if there is adverse impact. There are four distinctly different equal employment opportunity postures that an organization might have for selection (Seligman, 1973):

Passive Nondiscrimination. The organization is an equal employment opportunity employer, but does not make any special effort to recruit minority applicants. Minority applicants are not discriminated against in hiring or promotion, but the organization does no active recruiting of minorities.

Pure Affirmative Action. The organization is an equal employment opportunity employer, and actively recruits minority applicants. Minority applicants are not preferentially hired or promoted, but the organization's affirmative action efforts are directed at increasing the number of minority applicants in the pool of qualified applicants.

Affirmative Action With Preferential Hiring. The organization actively recruits minority applicants, and gives minority applicants preference in hiring and promotion. No quotas for minority hires are set, but minority status is an advantage.

Hard Quotas. The organization hires and promotes according to a strict percentage of minorities for each job. Quotas have generally been held to be illegal (see *University of California Regents v. Bakke*, 1978), but may sometimes be part of a conciliation or settlement agreement, or be court-ordered (Local 28 of the Sheet Metal Workers' International Association et al. v. Equal Employment Opportunity Commission, 1986; McCrary, 2007).

In the Supreme Court case of *Grutter v. Bollinger* (2003), the court ruled that the University of Michigan Law School admissions program was legal because it did not set a quota for the number of minority applicants admitted, race was used only as a "plus factor" in the selection process in addition to applicants' personal statements and undergraduate coursework. Based on this ruling, employers will be able to use race as a plus factor in hiring to ensure diversity, as long as the selection process is not a quota (Witlin & Sloane, 2003).

Strategic Questions

1. Which is the best Equal Employment Opportunity posture to have if the organization has discriminated in the past and minorities are underrepresented in several job categories?

2. Which is the best Equal Employment Opportunity posture to have if the organization has no history of discrimination and minorities are not underrepresented in any job categories?

3. What will be the race and sex makeup of the workforces of two similar organizations that hire workers from the same labor market, one with a Passive Nondiscrimination posture and one with a Pure Affirmative Action posture?

4. Describe how the four Equal Employment Opportunity postures would apply to access to a training program.

5. Which Equal Employment Opportunity posture was used by the University of Michigan Law School's admission program?

Resources

Grutter v. Bollinger, 539 U.S. 306 (U.S. Supreme Court, 2003).

Local 28 of the Sheet Metal Workers' International Association et al. v. Equal Employment Opportunity Commission, 478 U.S. 421 (U.S. Supreme Court, 1986).

Ouseley, L. H. (2006). Not a numbers game. *People Management, 12*(23), 7.

Seligman, D. (1973). How equal opportunity turned into employment quotas. *Fortune, 87*(3), 160-168.

U.S. Equal Employment Opportunity Commission. (1978). *Uniform guidelines on employee selection procedures.* http://www.access.gpo.gov/nara/cfr/waisidx_03/29cfr1607_03.html

U.S. Equal Employment Opportunity Commission. (2006). *Section 15: Race & color discrimination.* http://www.eeoc.gov/policy/docs/race-color.html

University of California Regents v. Bakke, 438 U.S. 265 (U.S. Supreme Court, 1978).

Unzueta, M. M., Lowery, B. S., & Knowles, E. D. (2008). How believing in affirmative action quotas protects white men's self-esteem. *Organizational Behavior and Human Decision Processes, 105*(1), 1-13.

Witlin, S. J., & Sloane, J. (2003). The Supreme Court's recent Affirmative Action decisions may provide some guidance for the workplace. *Employment Relations Today, 30*(3), 85-90.

ADVERSE IMPACT IN MORTGAGE LENDING

To test whether a selection procedure discriminates against women or minorities, the Four-Fifths (80%) Rule is used. If the selection ratio of the minority group is less than 80% of the selection ratio of the majority group (e.g., women vs. men), then the test has adverse impact, which is evidence of discrimination. Table 5.1 shows adverse impact on women because the women's selection ratio is less than 80% of the men's selection ratio.

An organization's defense is to show that the test is valid (i.e., that there is a statistically significant correlation between the test scores and job performance). In other words, even though the selection procedure has adverse impact, it is defensible because people who do better on the test do better on the job.

Adverse impact (i.e., evidence of discrimination) can also be found in other situations. The same logic of race discrimination in selection decisions applies to race discrimination in mortgage approval decisions. Adverse impact can be calculated on mortgage applications by comparing the rejection rate for the minority group to the rejection rate for the majority group. Significant differences in rejection rates by race or sex (i.e., mortgage test selection rates) demand some reasonable justification or business necessity to defend the procedure used to decide whether a mortgage application is accepted or rejected (i.e., mortgage approval test validity). In the case of adverse impact in selection decisions, business necessity is established by showing that the test scores have a statistically significant correlation with job performance. In the case of adverse impact

Table 5.1 Adverse Impact Test on Applicant Flow Data Using the Four-Fifths Rule

	Women	*Men*	*Total*
Hired	10	20	30
Not hired	90	80	170
Total	100	100	200
Selection ratios	.10	.20	.10/.20 = .50
Conclusion: Adverse Impact on Women			

in mortgage lending, business necessity is established by showing that the mortgage applications that are rejected are more likely to default than the mortgage applications that are accepted. A mortgage loan policy is fair if the default rate is the same for women versus men or for different races.

For example, if a race minority has a mortgage rejection rate of 28%, compared to the White rejection rate of 20%, is a 140% higher mortgage rejection rate evidence of adverse impact in mortgage lending? If so, the lender must show a legitimate business reason for the difference, such as credit risk (e.g., although there is a difference in mortgage rejection rates by race, there is no difference in mortgage default rates by race).

Black (1999) suggests that if the average default rate on loans to Black borrowers were lower than that for loans to White borrowers, the implication is that Black borrowers are being held to a higher credit standard. Testing this idea, Anderson and VanderHoff (1999) analyzed a national sample of conventional mortgages and found that Black households have higher marginal default rates, controlling for differences in borrower and property characteristics.

Strategic Questions

1. Does a large difference in mortgage rejection rates prove discrimination by lending institutions?
2. If a lending institution is charged with discrimination in mortgage lending, what statistics could it use to defend itself?
3. Should Whites and Blacks be expected to have similar rejection rates for mortgage loan applications? Should men and women be expected to have similar rejection rates?
4. If Hispanic applicants are rejected for mortgages at a higher rate than White applicants, what should the relative default rates be for successful Hispanic and White applicants?
5. If Black and White applicants for mortgage loans have the same rejection rates, but Whites have a higher default rate than Blacks, does this indicate discrimination?

Resources

Anderson, R., & VanderHoff, J. (1999). Mortgage default rates and borrower race. *Journal of Real Estate Research, 18*(2), 279-289.

Black, H. A. (1999). Is there discrimination in mortgage lending? What does the research tell us? *Review of Black Political Economy, 27*(1), 23-30.

Blackburn, M., & Vermilyea, T. (2006). A comparison of unexplained racial disparities in bank-level models of mortgage lending. *Journal of Financial Services Research, 29*(2), 125-147.

Buist, H., Linneman, P. D., & Megbolugbe, I. F. (1999). Residential-mortgage lending discrimination and lender-risk-compensating policies. *Real Estate Economics, 27*(4), 695-717.

Ferguson, M. F., & Peters, S. R. (1995). What constitutes evidence of discrimination in lending? *Journal of Finance, 1*(2), 739-748.

Harrison, G. W. (1998). Mortgage lending in Boston: A reconsideration of the evidence. *Economic Inquiry, 36*(1), 29-38.

Munnell, A. H., Tootell, G. M. B., Browne, L. E., & McEneaney, J. (1996). Mortgage lending in Boston: Interpreting HMDA data. *American Economic Review, 86*(1), 25-53.

U.S. Equal Employment Opportunity Commission. (1978). *Uniform guidelines on employee selection procedures*. http://www.access.gpo.gov/nara/cfr/waisidx_03/29cfr1607_03.html

WHAT IS A FAIR SELECTION TEST?

The Civil Rights Act of 1964 made it illegal to discriminate in employment on the basis of race, color, religion, sex, and national origin. The Age Discrimination in Employment Act and the Americans with Disabilities Act expanded the scope of fair employment practices legislation by making it illegal to discriminate on the basis of age and disability. The key question for the management of human resources is, what is a fair selection test?

Logical relationship of the test to the job. Job analysis is used to determine the essential tasks of a job, and the knowledge, skills, and abilities required to do those tasks. A selection test that measures whether applicants have the knowledge, skills, and abilities required to do the job should be a fair test. If the job is data entry clerk, a test that gives applicants a sample of data to input and measures the applicants' speed and accuracy of inputting, it has a tight logical relationship between the test and the job. If the job is assistant manager, a general cognitive skills test has a less clear link between the test and the job, but general cognitive skills predict job performance on a wide variety of jobs (Hunter & Hunter, 1984; Schmidt & Hunter, 1977, 2003).

Statistical relationship of the test to the job. If minority applicants consistently get significantly lower scores than majority applicants, adverse impact is indicated. However, if people who do better on the test also tend to do better on the job and people who do worse on the test also tend to do worse on the job, then the test is fair because it is job related. When a test has been shown to be valid, test scores are a predictor of job success and the test serves a legitimate business purpose. If a test is valid but has adverse impact, an employer should look for other tests that are as valid (and thereby meet the business purpose of using tests for selection) and have less or no adverse impact (and thereby meet the social purpose of the Civil Rights Act).

Similar test validity for minority and majority groups. If the validity of a test is calculated for the minority and majority groups, the test should be valid for each group. Theoretically, a test could be valid for the majority group but not for the minority group; this is called Single Group Validity (Griffin, 1989). A test with Single Group Validity predicts job performance for the majority group but not for the minority group (i.e., low test scores for minority applicants do not predict poor job performance, but this is highly unlikely; Hunter & Schmidt, 1978). When a test is valid for the majority group, not valid for the minority group, and there is a statistically significant difference between the two validity coefficients, this is called Differential Validity (Katzell & Dyer, 1977). If the minority group tends to get lower mean scores than the majority group, use of a test with Single Group or Differential Validity is likely to have adverse impact.

Strategic Questions

1. Should an organization use a test that is valid but has adverse impact?
2. How might an applicant react to a selection test that is statistically valid (i.e., predicts later job performance) but does not have a clear logical relationship to the job? How might rejected applicants react?
3. Should an organization use a general cognitive skills test that can be used for a number of jobs or different tests for each job that have a clearer, logical relationship to the job?
4. If a test has single-group validity (valid for the majority group and not for the minority group), why is this test unfair to members of the minority group?
5. If the regression line for the minority group has the same slope and intercept as the regression line for the majority group, is the test fair?
6. If the regression line for the minority group has the same slope but a lower intercept than the regression line for the majority group, is the test fair?
7. If the regression line for the minority group has the same slope but a lower intercept than the regression line for the majority group, and the raw scores are transformed into predicted scores based on the common regression line, is the test fair?

Resources

Arvey, R. D., & Faley, R. H. (1988). *Fairness in selecting employees.* Reading, MA: Addison-Wesley.

Bartlett, C. J., Bobko, P., Mosier, S. B., & Hannan, R. (1978). Testing for fairness with a moderated multiple regression strategy: An alternative to differential analysis. *Personnel Psychology, 31*(2), 233-241.

Griffin, M. E. (1989). Personnel research on testing, selection, and performance appraisal. *Public Personnel Management, 18*(2), 127-137.

Hunter, J. E., & Hunter, R. F. (1984). Validity and utility of alternative predictors of job performance. *Psychological Bulletin, 96*(1), 72-98.

Katzell, R. A., & Dyer, F. J. (1977). Differential validity revived. *Journal of Applied Psychology, 62*(2), 137-145.

Kuncel, N. R., Hezlett, S. A., & Ones, D. S. (2004). Academic performance, career potential, and job performance: Can one construct predict them all? *Journal of Personality and Social Psychology, 86*(1), 148-161.

Ployhart, R. E., & Holtz, B. C. (2008). The diversity-validity dilemma: Strategies for reducing racioethnic and sex subgroup differences and adverse impact in selection. *Personnel Psychology, 61*(1), 153-172.

Schmidt, F. L. (1988). The problem of group differences in ability test scores in employment selection. *Journal of Vocational Behavior, 33*(3), 272-292.

Schmidt, F. L., & Hunter, J. E. (1977). Development of a general solution to the problem of validity generalization. *Journal of Applied Psychology, 62*(5), 529-540.

Schmidt, F. L., & Hunter, J. E. (2003). History, development, evolution, and impact of validity generalization and meta-analysis methods, 1975-2001. In K. R. Murphy (Ed.), *Validity generalization: A critical review* (pp. 31-65). Mahwah, NJ: Lawrence Erlbaum.

Schoenfelt, E. L., & Pedigo, L. C. (2005). A review of court decisions on cognitive ability testing, 1992-2004. *Review of Public Personnel Administration, 25*(3), 271-287.

WHEN IS AN APPLICANT REALLY AN APPLICANT?

In the past, defining when someone becomes an applicant was fairly straightforward. When someone comes to a place of business, fills out an application, and submits a resume printed on heavy-bond paper, that individual becomes an applicant. When a person indicates an interest in being considered for hiring, promotion, or other employment opportunities, that person becomes an applicant. But technology advances and changes the application process. Now, jobs are posted on corporate Web sites, university placement Web sites, and independent job search Web sites such as Monster.com. Because it is so much easier to submit a resume over the Web, applicants submit more resumes to more employers, and companies that recruit over the Web receive large numbers of resumes. For example, Air Products has 16,000 employees worldwide, including 9,000 in the United States, and gets 20,000 to 40,000 resumes each year, many unsolicited (Roberts, 2002). Is a resume submitted over the Web an expression of interest? Does someone only become an applicant when the company accepts the resume? Is everyone in the resume database an applicant, even applicants for positions without current openings? Because electronic data-processing technologies make it is so easy to apply for positions, it is difficult to determine when an "Internet applicant" becomes an actual applicant.

The definition of "applicant" is important, because employers with 100 or more employees are required to keep data on the impact of their selection procedures on the employment opportunities of applicants and file annual EEO-1 reports, as outlined in the Uniform Guidelines on Employee Selection Procedures Section 1607.4:

> A. *Records concerning impact.* Each user should maintain and have available for inspection records or other information which will disclose the impact which its tests and other selection procedures have upon employment opportunities of persons by identifiable race, sex, or ethnic group as set forth in paragraph B of this section, in order to determine compliance with these guidelines. Where there are large numbers of applicants and procedures

are administered frequently, such information may be retained on a sample basis, provided that the sample is appropriate in terms of the applicant population and adequate in size.

B. *Applicable race, sex, and ethnic groups for recordkeeping.* The records called for by this section are to be maintained by sex, and the following races and ethnic groups: Blacks (Negroes), American Indians (including Alaskan Natives), Asians (including Pacific Islanders), Hispanic (including persons of Mexican, Puerto Rican, Cuban, Central or South American, or other Spanish origin or culture regardless of race), whites (Caucasians) other than Hispanic, and totals. The race, sex, and ethnic classifications called for by this section are consistent with the Equal Employment Opportunity Standard Form 100, Employer Information Report EEO-1 series of reports.

The Office of Federal Contract Compliance Programs' (U.S. Department of Labor, 2005) definition of an "Internet Applicant," effective February 6, 2006:

(1) Internet Applicant means any individual as to whom the following four criteria are satisfied:
   (i) The individual submits an expression of interest in employment through the Internet or related electronic data technologies;
   (ii) The contractor considers the individual for employment in a particular position;
   (iii) The individual's expression of interest indicates the individual possesses the basic qualifications for the position; and,
   (iv) The individual at no point in the contractor's selection process prior to receiving an offer of employment from the contractor, removes himself or herself from further consideration or otherwise indicates that he or she is no longer interested in the position.

(2) For purposes of paragraph (1)(i) of this definition, "submits an expression of interest in employment through the Internet or related electronic data technologies," includes all expressions of interest, regardless of the means or manner in which the expression of interest is made, if the contractor considers expressions of interest made through the Internet or related electronic data technologies in the recruiting or selection processes for that particular position.

Strategic Questions

1. An employer posts on its Web site an opening for a mechanical engineer position and encourages potential applicants to complete an online profile if they are interested in being considered for that position. The Web site also advises potential applicants that they can send a hard-copy resume to the HR manager with a cover letter identifying the position for which they would like to be considered. Are people who complete this personal profile applicants? Are people who send a paper resume and cover letter applicants?

2. An employer advertises for mechanics in a local newspaper and instructs interested candidates to mail their resumes to the employer's address. Walk-in applications also are permitted. The employer considers only paper resumes and application forms for the mechanic position. If someone e-mails a resume to the employer, is he or she an applicant?

3. If an organization receives 1,000 applications for an open position, should it change the minimum qualifications from 2 to 5 years of experience to get a smaller pool of applicants?

Resources

Frauenheim, E. (2006). Federal Internet data rule: Cloudy, but with a silver lining. *Workforce Management, 85*(6), 44-46.

Leichtling, E. A., & Ploor, P. M. (2004). When applicants apply through the Internet. *Employee Relations Law Journal, 30*(2), 3-12.

Mullich, J. (2004). A new definition could cast Internet hiring processes in a new light. *Workforce Management, 83*(9), 72-76.

Roberts, B. (2002). System addresses 'applicant' dilemma. *HR Magazine, 47*(9), 111-119.

Smith, A. (2007). Guidance on internet applicants updated. *HR Magazine, 52*(1), 28-29.

U.S. Equal Employment Opportunity Commission. (2007). *EEO surveys.* http://www.eeoc.gov/employers/surveys.html

HONESTY TESTING

Employee theft (also known as "inventory shrinkage," "pilferage," "shortage," or "unaccounted loss") has been estimated at $200 billion annually in the United States (Appelbaum, Cottin, Paré, & Shapiro, 2006). Theft can also take the form of top-management fraud, workers compensation fraud (Wang & Kleiner, 2005), cash embezzlement, theft of office supplies and equipment, and excessive personal photocopies and phone calls (Gross-Schaefer, Trigilio, Negus, & Ro, 2000).

One approach for attempting to screen out applicants who might steal from the organization is a polygraph. This machine collects three kinds physiological data (respiratory activity, electrodermal activity, and cardiovascular activity; i.e., changes in a person's breathing rate, galvanic skin response, and pulse and blood pressure). The underlying theory of the polygraph test is that these physiological measures change when a person lies. But like any test, accuracy is never 100%, so there will be false positives (the examiner concluding that the person is lying when he or she is actually telling the truth) and false negatives (the examiner concluding that the person is telling the truth when he or she is actually lying). Also, the Employee Polygraph Protection Act of 1988 (EPPA) generally prevents employers from using lie detector tests, either for pre-employment screening or during the course of employment, with certain exemptions. Employers generally may not require or request any employee or job applicant to take a lie detector test; or discharge, discipline, or discriminate against an employee or job applicant for refusing to take a test or for exercising other rights under the Act. In addition, employers are required to display the EPPA poster in the workplace for their employees.

Federal, state, and local governments are excluded from EPPA, as are lie detector tests administered by the federal government to employees of federal contractors engaged in national security intelligence or counter-intelligence functions. The Act also includes limited exemptions in which polygraph tests (but no other lie detector tests) may be administered in the private sector, subject to certain restrictions:

- To employees who are reasonably suspected of involvement in a workplace incident that results in economic loss to the employer and who had access to the property that is the subject of an investigation; and
- To prospective employees of armored car, security alarm, and security guard firms who protect facilities, materials, or operations affecting health or safety, national security, or currency and other like instruments; and
- To prospective employees of pharmaceutical and other firms authorized to manufacture, distribute, or dispense controlled substances, who will have direct access to such controlled substances, as well as current employees who had access to persons or property that are the subject of an ongoing investigation.

Another approach to reducing shrinkage is to administer a paper-and-pencil test to applicants that attempts to measure an employee's propensity to steal as an aspect of his or her personality. As many as five million honesty tests are administered each year (Heller, 2005). The underlying theory of honesty (or integrity) tests is that honesty is a stable personality trait that can be measured and can be used to predict later workplace behavior (Berry, Sackett, & Weimann, 2007; Markus, Lee, & Ashton, 2007; Wanek, Sackett, Ones, & Deniz, 2003). Although some research shows that honesty tests can predict employee theft and other organizationally disruptive behaviors (Bernardin & Cooke, 1993; Ones, Viswesvaran, & Schmidt, 1993), other research shows that they can be faked, have high false positive rates, and low correlations with employee behavior (Guastello & Rieke, 1991; Hurtz & Alliger, 2002; Moore, 1990). Employers who use personality tests also risk litigation. In *Karraker v. Rent-A-Center* (2005), the appellate court ruled that a furniture rental company violated the Americans with Disabilities Act by requiring applicants for promotions to take the Minnesota Multiphasic Personality Inventory.

Strategic Questions

1. How is an honesty test different from a Polygraph Test?
2. Should an employer use an honesty test to screen applicants?
3. Does an employer have a right to measure aspects of an applicant's personality and use that as the basis for selection decisions?
4. Can applicants learn to "fake good" on an honesty test like they can learn to "interview well"?
5. If passing an integrity test is a condition of employment, will this encourage applicants to lie?

Resources

Appelbaum, S. H., Cottin, J., Paré, R., & Shapiro, B. T. (2006). Employee theft: From behavioural causation and prevention to managerial detection and remedies. *Journal of American Academy of Business, 9*(2), 175-182.

Bernardin, H. J., & Cooke, D. K. (1993). Validity of an honesty test in predicting theft among convenience store employees. *Academy of Management Journal, 36*(5), 1097-1108.

Berry, C. M., Sackett, P. R., & Wiemann, S. (2007). A review of recent developments in integrity test research. *Personnel Psychology, 60*(2), 271-301.

Employee Polygraph Protection Act. (1988). *Public Law 100-347.* http://www.dol.gov/compliance/laws/comp-eppa.htm

Employee Polygraph Protection Act Poster. (1988). http://www.dol.gov/esa/whd/regs/compliance/posters/eppa.htm

Garaventa, E. (1986). The polygraph: A dubious pre-employment screening technique. *Review of Business, 7*(4), 26-27.

Gross-Schaefer, A., Trigilio, J., Negus, J., & Ro, C. (2000). Ethics education in the workplace: An effective tool to combat employee theft. *Journal of Business Ethics, 26*(2), 89-100.

Guastello, S. J., & Rieke, M. L. (1991). A review and critique of honesty test research. *Behavioral Sciences & the Law, 9*(4), 501-523.

Harris, M. M., & Sackett, P. R. (1987). A factor analysis and item response theory analysis of an employee honesty test. *Journal of Business and Psychology, 2*(2), 122-135.

Heller, M. (2005). Court ruling that employer's integrity test violated ADA could open door to litigation. *Workforce Management, 84*(9), 74-77.

Hurtz, G. M., & Alliger, G. M. (2002). Influence of coaching on integrity test performance and unlikely virtues scale scores. *Human Performance, 15*(3), 255-273.

Karraker v. Rent-A-Center, Inc., 411 F.3d 831. (United States Court of Appeals for the Seventh Circuit, 2005).

Marcus, B., Lee, K., & Ashton, M. C. (2007). Personality dimensions explaining relationships between integrity tests and counterproductive behavior: Big five, or one in addition? *Personnel Psychology, 60*(1), 1-34.

Moore, R. W. (1990). Instructional effects on the Phase II Profile honesty test. *Psychological Reports, 67*(1), 291-294.

Mulvihill, M. E. (2006). Karraker v. Rent-A-Center: Testing the limits of the ADA, personality tests, and employer pre-employment screening. *Loyola University Chicago Law Journal, 37*, 865.

Ones, D. S., Viswesvaran, C., & Schmidt, F. L. (1993). Comprehensive meta-analysis of integrity test validities: Findings and implications for personnel selection and theories of job performance. *Journal of Applied Psychology, 78*(4), 679-703.

(Continued)

(Continued)

Sackett, P. R., & Wanek, J. E. (1996). New developments in the use of measures of honesty, integrity, conscientiousness, dependability, trustworthiness, and reliability for personnel selection. *Personnel Psychology, 49*(4), 787-829.

Wanek, J. E., Sackett, P. R., Ones, D. S., & Deniz, S. (2003). Towards an understanding of integrity test similarities and differences: An item-level analysis of seven tests. *Personnel Psychology, 56*(4), 873-894.

Wang, Y., & Kleiner, B. H. (2005). Defining employee dishonesty. *Management Research News, 28*(2/3), 11-22.

PREDICTIVE AND CONCURRENT VALIDATION STUDIES

The Uniform Guidelines on Employee Selection Procedures (EEOC, 1978) apply to tests and other selection procedures that are used to make employment decisions.

Section 1607.2 (B) Employment decisions. These guidelines apply to tests and other selection procedures which are used as a basis for any employment decision. Employment decisions include but are not limited to hiring, promotion, demotion, membership (for example, in a labor organization), referral, retention, and licensing and certification, to the extent that licensing and certification may be covered by Federal equal employment opportunity law. Other selection decisions, such as selection for training or transfer, may also be considered employment decisions if they lead to any of the decisions listed above.

If a test has adverse impact, employers are allowed to use the test only if the test has been validated (i.e., shown to be job related).

Section 1607.3 (A). Procedure having adverse impact constitutes discrimination unless justified. The use of any selection procedure which has adverse impact on the hiring, promotion, or other employment or membership opportunities of members of any race, sex, or ethnic group will be considered to be discriminatory and inconsistent with these guidelines, unless the procedure has been validated in accordance with these guidelines, or the provisions of section 6 below are satisfied.

To validate a test, employers can use one of three test validation study designs, criterion-related, content, or construct.

Section 1607.5 (A). Acceptable types of validity studies. For the purposes of satisfying these guidelines, users may rely upon criterion-related validity studies, content validity studies or construct validity studies, in accordance with the standards set forth in the technical standards of these guidelines, section 14 below. New strategies for showing the validity of selection procedures will be evaluated as they become accepted by the psychological profession.

The purpose of a validation study is to determine whether the test scores predict job performance (i.e., that there is a statistically significant correlation between the test scores and one or more measures of job performance). There are two general approaches, each with advantages and disadvantages. For a Predictive Validity study, the employer administers the test to a group of applicants, makes hiring decisions without regard to these test scores (either selecting all of the applicants or selecting based on the old test), waits for employees to learn the job and their performance to stabilize (anywhere from a few weeks to 6 months, depending on the complexity of the job), and then measures the employees' job performance. For a Concurrent Validity study, the employer measures a group of current employees' job performance and administers the test at the same time.

For the Predictive Validity approach, the employer must wait a period of time between the administration of the test and collection of job performance data. During this time, some of the applicants who took the test may no longer be employees (having since quit or been fired). This is called "subject attrition," and the longer the period of time between test administration and collection of job performance data, the greater the number of data points lost. This is a problem, because the smaller the sample size, the less power the statistical test has. If most of the attrition is concentrated in the lower test scores (or mostly in the higher test scores), the correlation will be reduced due to attenuation. For the Concurrent Validity approach, the test is given to current employees, but when the test is actually used for selection, it will be given to applicants. There may be substantial differences between the applicant pool and employees, and the test validation results may be misleading.

Section 1607.14 (4) Representativeness of the sample. Whether the study is predictive or concurrent, the sample subjects should insofar as feasible be representative of the candidates normally available in the relevant labor market for the job or group of jobs in question, and should insofar as feasible include the races, sexes, and ethnic groups normally available in the relevant job market. In determining the representativeness of the sample in a concurrent validity study, the user should take into account the extent to which the specific knowledges or skills which are the primary focus of the test are those which employees learn on the job.

Strategic Questions

1. Is it better to do a validation study using a Predictive or Concurrent approach?
2. Which kinds of tests will have the smallest differences between Predictive and Concurrent approaches to test validation?
3. If your organization has a high rate of turnover from high-level performers, would it be better to use a Predictive or Concurrent approach for the validation study?

(Continued)

(Continued)

4. If the test currently being used is valid but has adverse impact, which method of test validation should be used to determine if a newly developed test has adverse impact?

Resources

Barrett, G. V., Phillips, J. S., & Alexander, R. A. (1981). Concurrent and predictive validity designs: A critical reanalysis. *Journal of Applied Psychology, 66*, 1-6.

Guion, R. M., & Cranny, C. J. (1982). A note on concurrent and predictive validity designs: A critical reanalysis. *Journal of Applied Psychology, 67*(2), 239-244.

Society for Industrial/Organizational Psychology. (2003). *Principles for the validation and use of personnel selection procedures*. http://www.siop.org/_Principles/principles.pdf

Thompson, D. E., & Thompson, T. A. (1982). Court standards for job analysis in test validation. *Personnel Psychology, 35*(4), 865-874.

U.S. Equal Employment Opportunity Commission. (1978). *Uniform guidelines on employee selection procedures*. http://www.access.gpo.gov/nara/cfr/waisidx_03/29cfr1607_03.html

Applications

USING THE MENTAL MEASUREMENT YEARBOOK TO CHOOSE A SELECTION TEST

If an organization lacks the expertise or financial resources to develop its own selection tests in-house, the expertise can be purchased in the form of commercially available tests. As with the purchase of any product, the better informed the consumer is, the more likely it is that the purchase will meet the requirements. However, simply relying on the test publisher's claims of reliability and validity may be insufficient for making a wise purchase decision.

The consumer's handbook of commercially published tests is the *Mental Measurement Yearbook*. The *Mental Measurement Yearbook* provides reliability, validity, and appropriate use information for most commercially available tests, and is available in printed form and on CD-ROM. Although extensive in the number of tests reviewed, it is not exhaustive; some newer tests may not be included. The tests are indexed according to the test title, publisher, scales, names of reviewers, and test authors; and grouped according to the type of test, such as Achievement, Intelligence and General Aptitude, Personality, and Interest tests. There is a detailed descriptive entry for each test, and for many tests, there are critical reviews of the tests and references to the published research using the test.

To Do

For each of the jobs listed in the Data Collection Form, find two tests that might be used for selection. For each test, record in the Data Collection Form the test title, publisher, the cost per test and for manuals, reliability, and validity. Then make a decision about which one to use and write a supportive argument for it.

Job Test Data Collection Form

Job	*Test Title*	*Publisher*	*Cost*	*Reliability*	*Validity*	*Reason*
Accountant						
Firefighter						
Sales representative						
Marketing analyst						
Computer programmer						

(Continued)

(Continued)

Resources

American Psychological Association. (2006). *FAQ/Finding information about psychological tests.* http://www.apa.org/science/faq-findtests.html

Buros Center for Testing. *Mental Measurement Yearbook.* http://www.unl.edu/buros/

Nitko, A. J. (n.d.). *Using a Mental Measurements Yearbook review to evaluate a test.* http://www.unl.edu/buros/bimm/html/lesson01.html

Nitko, A. J. (n.d.). *Using a Mental Measurements Yearbook review and other materials to evaluate a test.* http://www.unl.edu/buros/bimm/html/lesson02.html

MEASURING THE RELIABILITY OF A SELECTION TEST

There are two fundamental properties that all selection tests must have. To be useful, the test must predict job performance (i.e., validity); otherwise, applicants could be selected at random. And to be able to predict job performance, the test must be a consistent measure. If a test cannot measure something consistently, it cannot measure it accurately. Reliability is a necessary but not sufficient condition for validity; for a test to be valid, it has to be reliable.

One way to measure the reliability of a test is to measure its stability over time. To measure test-retest reliability, a test is given to the same sample of people at two points in time, and the correlation between test scores from Time 1 to Time 2 is a measure of stability. Although this is a straightforward way to measure the reliability of a test, it tends to produce reliability estimates that are inflated by a number of factors. First, the test takers' memory; when they take the test a second time, people may remember the questions and the answers they gave the first time. Second, when dealing with a question in which they are unsure of the answer, people may use the same decision rules ("when in doubt, pick C"; "never pick an answer with the word *never* in it") at Time 1 and Time 2. Both of these factors tend to make people give the same answers at Time 1 and Time 2, but the consistency is more in the person taking the test than in the test itself.

A better way to measure the reliability of a test, which avoids the factors that affect test-retest reliability, is to measure the test's internal consistency by a split-half correlation. The test is given to a sample of people only once, and their scores on one half of the test are correlated with their scores on the other half. The higher the correlation between scores on Half 1 and Half 2, the more internally consistent the test is. The halves may be odd-even items or randomly selected items. But this reliability estimate needs to be corrected, because the correlation is based on half as many items as are in the full test. The Spearman-Brown prophecy formula corrects the split-half correlation (upward) to be what the reliability would be for the full test.

For tests with multiple forms, reliability is an estimate of consistency across the different forms. If the test is reliable, it does not matter which form is taken; the score is consistent across the forms. An Analysis of Variance is used to test whether the multiple forms are equivalent; if the *F* Ratio is statistically significant, the forms are not equivalent.

To Do

Use the data in Table 5.2a to calculate the split-half reliability, using the Spearman-Brown prophecy formula. Use the data in Table 5.2b to determine whether the multiple forms of the test are reliable.

Table 5.2a

Applicant	*Odd Items*	*Even Items*
1	87	60
2	79	66
3	89	64
4	77	56
5	87	69
6	51	46
7	68	57
8	60	46
9	88	70
10	74	58
11	79	67
12	61	53
13	69	57
14	59	49
15	52	51
16	66	59
17	82	63
18	90	69
19	81	68
20	73	55

Table 5.2b

Applicant	*Form A*	*Form B*	*Form C*
1	64	69	51
2	58	59	62
3	55	52	56
4	60	52	54
5	62	66	52
6	51	68	58
7	63	65	49
8	59	62	52
9	56	59	57
10	51	52	65

Resources

Burch, G. S., & Anderson, N. (2004). Measuring person-team fit: Development and validation of the team selection inventory. *Journal of Managerial Psychology, 19*(4), 406-426.

Mount, M., Muchinsky, P. M., & Hanser, L. M. (1977). The predictive validity of a work sample: A laboratory study. *Personnel Psychology, 30*(4), 637-645.

Spicer, D. P., & Sadler-Smith, E. (2005). An examination of the general decision making style questionnaire in two UK samples. *Journal of Managerial Psychology, 20*(1-2), 137-149.

MEASURING THE VALIDITY OF A SELECTION TEST

The purpose of testing applicants is to gather data that predicts job performance 6 months or a year in the future. The degree to which a test predicts future job performance is the criterion-related validity of a test and is measured by the correlation between applicants' test scores and job performance. The measure of job performance is typically performance appraisal ratings but can be any measurement of how well the employee is performing the essential tasks of the job as determined by the job analysis. For a test to be valid, there must be a statistically significant correlation between test scores and job performance.

To determine whether a test is valid, the Pearson Correlation Coefficient between the applicants' test scores and job performance is calculated, then this coefficient is tested for statistical significance using $\alpha = .05$ and $df = N - 2$. For the example given in Table 5.3a, the correlation was calculated using Microsoft Excel's Analysis Tools Regression. In this case, the validity of the test is $R = .37$, $F_{(1, 18)} = 2.90$, $p = .106$, indicating that the test is not a significant predictor of job performance and therefore is not a valid test. The Excel output is shown in Table 5.3b.

Table 5.3a Application: Measuring the Validity of a Selection Test

Applicant	*Test Score*	*Job Performance*
1	56	550
2	65	649
3	59	644
4	53	289
5	54	173
6	62	392
7	53	393
8	63	388
9	63	399
10	57	432
11	57	150
12	65	605
13	63	145
14	51	400
15	60	448
16	63	528
17	55	290
18	64	252
19	52	192
20	57	229

Table 5.3b Summary Output for Data in Table 5.3a

Regression Statistics	
Multiple R	0.372750303
R Square	0.138942789
Adjusted R Square	0.091106277
Standard Error	153.6779884
Observations	20

ANOVA					
	df	*SS*	*MS*	*F*	*Significance F*
Regression	1	68596.16596	68596.16596	2.904534292	0.105531232
Residual	18	425104.634	23616.92411		
Total	19	493700.8			

	Coefficients	*Standard Error*	*t Stat*	*p-value*	*Lower 95%*	*Upper 95%*	*Lower 95.0%*	*Upper 95.0%*
Intercept	–376.1779171	443.5039204	–0.848195246	0.407467511	–1307.945077	555.5892428	–1307.945077	555.5892428
Score	2.85969142	7.545574184	1.704269431	0.105531232	–2.992971666	28.7123545	–2.992971666	28.7123545

NOTE: "Multiple R" is the multiple correlation between the test scores and job performance, "F" is the *F* Ratio, and "Significance F" is the probability associated with the correlation.

To Do

Another set of test scores and job performance is given in Table 5.4. Determine whether this selection test is valid.

Table 5.4 Application: Measuring the Validity of a Selection Test

Applicant	*Test Score*	*Job Performance*
1	56	165
2	65	630
3	59	357
4	53	613
5	54	161
6	62	521
7	53	304
8	63	504
9	63	512
10	57	483
11	57	321
12	65	718
13	63	373
14	51	403
15	60	246
16	63	648
17	55	123
18	64	340
19	52	430
20	57	304

Resources

Arthur, W., Jr., Strong, M. H., & Williamson, J. (1994). Validation of a visual attention test as a predictor of driving accident involvement. *Journal of Occupational and Organizational Psychology, 67*(2), 173-182.

Brown, S. H. (1979). Validity distortions associated with a test in use. *Journal of Applied Psychology, 64*(4), 460-462.

Hoffman, C. C., & McPhail, S. M. (1998). Exploring options for supporting test use in situations precluding local validation. *Personnel Psychology, 51*(4), 987-1003.

Hoffman, C. C., & Thornton, G. C., III (1997). Examining selection utility where competing predictors differ in adverse impact. *Personnel Psychology, 50*(2), 455-470.

Schmitt, N., & Ostroff, C. (1986). Operationalizing the "behavioral consistency" approach: Selection test development based on a content-oriented strategy. *Personnel Psychology, 39*(1), 91-108.

Sussmann, M., & Robertson, D. U. (1986). The validity of validity: An analysis of validation study designs. *Journal of Applied Psychology, 71*(3), 461-468.

Walsh, R. J., & Hess, L. R. (1974). The small company, EEOC, and test validation alternatives—Do you know your options? *Personnel Journal, 53*(11), 840-845.

DETERMINING WHETHER A SELECTION TEST HAS ADVERSE IMPACT

The Civil Rights Act of 1964 makes it illegal to discriminate in employment on the basis of race, color, religion, sex, and national origin. The administrative rules that the EEOC, the Civil Service Commission, the Department of Labor, and the Department of Justice use to enforce the Civil Right Act of 1964 are the Uniform Guidelines on Employee Selection Procedures (EEOC, 1978). When applicant flow data are available, the test for adverse impact is the Four-Fifths Rule.

> Section 1607.4 (D). *Adverse impact and the "four-fifths rule."* A selection rate for any race, sex, or ethnic group which is less than four-fifths (4/5) (or eighty percent) of the rate for the group with the highest rate will generally be regarded by the Federal enforcement agencies as evidence of adverse impact, while a greater than four-fifths rate will generally not be regarded by Federal enforcement agencies as evidence of adverse impact. Smaller differences in selection rate may nevertheless constitute adverse impact, where they are significant in both statistical and practical terms or where a user's actions have discouraged applicants disproportionately on grounds of race, sex, or ethnic group.

The selection ratio of the minority group to be tested (e.g., Black, Hispanic, Asian, Native American, female) is the number of minority applicants hired divided by the total number of minority applicants; the selection ratio of the majority group is the number of majority applicants hired divided by the total number of majority applicants; and the Adverse Impact Ratio is the selection ratio of the minority group divided by the selection ratio of the majority group. If the Adverse Impact Ratio is less than .80 (i.e., 80%), there is adverse impact. With larger sample sizes, a chi-square test (χ^2) may be calculated to test for a statistically significant difference between the selection ratios of the minority group tested and the majority group.

If there is a multistep selection procedure, adverse impact is calculated for each step in the selection process, not just the bottom line of who is actually hired. For example, in *Connecticut v. Teal* (1982), applicants for the position of welfare eligibility supervisor had to pass a written exam and then were

Table 5.5 Application: Determining Whether a Selection Test Has Adverse Impact

Applicant Flow Data			
	Minority	*Majority*	*Total*
Hired	20	30	50
Not Hired	40	50	90
Total	60	80	140
SR	0.33	0.38	

Adverse Impact Calculations			
Adverse Impact Ratio (AIR)	0.89		No Adverse Impact
Chi Square Test (df = 1)	0.26	0.6106	No Adverse Impact

selected based on a combination of past work performance, recommendations from the candidates' supervisors, and seniority. In this case, adverse impact is calculated for each test: the written exam and the final selection.

To Do

Determine whether data in Table 5.6a from the selection test used has adverse impact using the Four-Fifths Rule. Determine whether data in Table 5.6b from the selection test used has adverse impact using the chi-square test.

Table 5.6 Application: Determining Whether a Selection Test Has Adverse Impact

Table 5.6a

	Applicant Flow Data		
	Asian	*White*	*Total*
Hired	8	22	30
Not hired	30	50	80
Total	38	72	110

Table 5.6b

	Applicant Flow Data		
	Hispanic	*White*	*Total*
Hired	40	99	139
Not hired	15	14	29
Total	55	113	168

Resources

Boardman, A. E. (1979). Another analysis of the EEOCC "Four-fifths" rule. *Management Science, 25*(8), 770-776.

Connecticut v. Teal, 457 U.S. 440 (U.S. Supreme Court, 1982).

Gastwirth, J. L. (1975). Statistical methods for analyzing claims of employment discrimination. *Industrial and Labor Relations Review, 38*(1), 75-86.

Greenberg, I. (1979). An analysis of the EEOCC "Four-fifths" rule. *Management Science, 25*(8), 762-769.

Ironson, G. H., Guion, R. M., & Ostrander, M. (1991). Adverse impact from a psychometric perspective. *Journal of Applied Psychology, 67*(4), 419-432.

Jackson v. Nassau County Civil Service Commission, 424 F.Supp.1162 (Eastern District of New York 1976).

Jones, G. F. (1981). Usefulness of different statistical techniques for determining adverse impact in small jurisdictions. *Review of Public Personnel Administration, 2*(1), 85-89.

Schoben, E. W. (1978). Differential pass-fail rates in employment testing: Statistical proof under Title VII. *Harvard Law Review, 91*, 793-813.

U.S. Equal Employment Opportunity Commission. (1978). *Uniform guidelines on employee selection procedures.* http://www.access.gpo.gov/nara/cfr/waisidx_03/29cfr1607_03.html

York, K. M. (2002). Disparate results in adverse impact tests: The 4/5ths rule and the chi square test. *Public Personnel Management, 31*(2), 253-262.

EVALUATING WHETHER TO UPGRADE TO A NEW TEST

Commercial test publishers constantly work to improve the reliability and validity of their tests so that they can sell more copies. However, if a new version of a test is published, which has greater validity than the previous version but also costs more, should the organization upgrade to the new version of the test? Although "new and improved" sounds like there will be a financial advantage to upgrading to the new version, what will be the actual dollar gain (if any)?

The dollar gain in productivity of switching to the new test will depend on a number of factors in addition to the validity and the actual cost of the test. It will also be affected by the variability in job performance, the selection ratio, and the number of people hired. The Utility for Selection formula to use when comparing an old test to a new test is as follows:

$$\text{Utility} = N_s \times (r_1 - r_2) \times SD_y \times \text{Mean}(Z_x) - N_s \times (\text{Cost}_1 - \text{Cost}_2)/SR$$

Where:

Utility = Total productivity gain in dollars of new test compared to old test

N_s = Number of selectees (number hired)

r_1 = Validity of the new selection procedure

r_2 = Validity of the old selection procedure

SD_y = Variability in job performance in dollars per year

Mean (Z_x) = Mean Z-Score of selectees on the selection procedure

Cost_1 = Cost per applicant for the new selection procedure

Cost_2 = Cost per applicant for the old selection procedure

SR = Selection ratio (percentage of applicants hired)

To Do

Compute the Utility of Selection for the new test compared to the current test. Should you buy the new test? What is the dollar gain in productivity in upgrading to the new test? Also compute the utility of the new test compared to the current test under the "What if?" conditions listed in the exercise form. When should you buy the new test? What is the dollar gain in productivity under each of the "What if?" conditions?

(Continued)

(Continued)

Utility of Selection Exercise

Utility component	*Current Test*	*New Test*	*What if…*
N_s	100		200
r_1	.35		.40
r_2		.40	
SD_y	$10,000	$12,000	$20,000
Mean (Z_x)	0.5		1.0
$Cost_1$	$20		
$Cost_2$			$100
SR	.20	.20	.10

Resources

Cascio, W. F., & Ramos, R. A. (1986). Development and application of a new method for assessing job performance in behavioral/economic terms. *Journal of Applied Psychology, 71*(1), 20-28.

Hakstian R. A., Scratchley, L. S., MacLeod, A. A., Tweed, R. G., & Siddarth S. (1997). Selection of telemarketing employees by standardized assessment procedures. *Psychology & Marketing, 14*(7), 703-726.

Harel, G. H., Arditi-Vogel, A., & Janz, T. (2003). Comparing the validity and utility of behavior description interview versus assessment center ratings. *Journal of Managerial Psychology, 18*(1/2), 94-104.

Hoffman, C. C., & Thornton, G. C., III (1997). Examining selection utility where competing predictors differ in adverse impact. *Personnel Psychology, 50*(2), 455-470.

Hunter, J. E., & Hunter, R. F. (1984). Validity and utility of alternative predictors of job performance. *Psychological Bulletin, 96*(1), 72-98.

Raju, N. S., Burke, M. J., & Normand, J. (1990). A new approach for utility analysis. *Journal of Applied Psychology, 75*(1), 3-12.

Schmidt, F. L., Mack, M. J., & Hunter, J. E. (1984). Selection utility in the occupation of U.S. park ranger for three modes of test use. *Journal of Applied Psychology, 69*(3), 490-497.

Schultz, C. B. (1984). Saving millions through judicious selection of employees. *Public Personnel Management, 13*(4), 409-415.

Whyte, G., & Latham, G. (1997). The futility of utility analysis revisited: When even an expert fails. *Personnel Psychology, 50*(3), 601-610.

USING AN AFFIRMATIVE ACTION PLAN

The Civil Rights Act of 1964 makes it illegal to discriminate in employment on the basis of race, color, religion, sex, and national origin. If an organization has underrepresentation of women or minorities in a particular job category, it may create an Affirmative Action Plan to reduce the underrepresentation. Underrepresentation of women and minorities in specific job categories can be identified by a comparison between the employer's workforce and the labor market. All else being equal, the employer's workforce should mirror the race and sex composition of the labor market that the organization is hiring from.

The purpose of Affirmative Action is to redress past or current discrimination, and Affirmative Action Plans will include goals and timetables to give greater access to job opportunities for specific jobs and specific minority groups (Hollander, 1975; Siniscalco, 1981; U.S. Department of Labor, 2004). Affirmative Action Plans may be designed to increase the recruitment and selection of women or minorities or to give women and minorities greater access to training programs.

To Do

According to their adverse impact calculations, Blacks are underrepresented in the data entry clerk I position, as well as in all of the other clerical positions. As a result, *Art & Architecture Magazine* wrote an Affirmative Action Plan to increase the representation of Blacks in all clerical positions.

Art & Architecture Magazine has an opening for a data entry clerk I. An advertisement in the local newspaper brought in eight applicants. Each applicant was given the Data Entry Test, and the results are given in Table 5.7.

Apply the *Art & Architecture Magazine* Affirmative Action Plan, and decide who to hire for the position of Data Entry Clerk I. Record your reasons for making that hiring decision.

Table 5.7 Data Entry Clerk I Test Results

Position: Data Entry Clerk I				
Applicant	*Test Score*	*Pass/Fail (Cutoff = 60)*	*Race*	*Sex*
1	90	Pass	White	Female
2	88	Pass	Black	Male
3	81	Pass	White	Male
4	80	Pass	Black	Female
5	75	Pass	White	Female
6	72	Pass	White	Male
7	58	Fail	Black	Female
8	54	Fail	White	Female

Resources

Combs, G. M., Nadkarni, S., & Combs, M. W. (2005). Implementing affirmative action plans in multinational corporations. *Organizational Dynamics, 34*(4), 346-360.

Estlund, C. L. (2005). Putting Grutter to work: Diversity, integration, and affirmative action in the workplace. *Berkeley Journal of Employment and Labor Law, 26*(1), 1-39.

(Continued)

(Continued)

Hollander, J. (1975, Fall). A step-by-step guide to corporate affirmative-action. *Business and Society Review, 15*, 67-73.

Johnson v. Transportation Agency, Santa Clara County, California, 480 U.S. 616; 107 S. Ct. 1442. (Supreme Court 1986).

Moore, D. P., & Hass, M. (1990). When Affirmative Action cloaks management bias in selection. *Academy of Management Executive, 4*(1), 84-89.

Siniscalco, G. (1981). Affirmative Action Plan for the XYZ Company. *EEO Today, 8*(1), 73-90.

U.S. Department of Labor. (2004). *Sample Affirmative Action Program.* http://www.dol.gov/esa/regs/compliance/ofccp/pdf/sampleaap.pdf

U.S. Equal Employment Opportunity Commission. (1978). *Uniform guidelines on employee selection procedures.* http://www.access.gpo.gov/nara/cfr/waisidx_03/29cfr1607_03.html

U.S. Equal Employment Opportunity Commission. (2006). *Affirmative action appropriate under title vii of the civil rights act of 1964, as amended.* http://www.access.gpo.gov/nara/cfr/waisidx_06/29cfr1608_06.html

EXPANDED PROTECTION FOR WORKERS IN STATE EQUAL EMPLOYMENT OPPORTUNITY LAWS

The Civil Rights Act of 1964 makes it illegal to discriminate in employment on the basis of race, color, religion, sex, and national origin; the Age Discrimination in Employment Act protects workers over 40 years old, and the Americans with Disabilities Act protects workers with disabilities. There are also state equal employment opportunity laws that provide protections beyond these "protected groups." For example, Michigan's Elliott-Larsen Civil Rights Act prohibits discrimination on the basis of religion, race, color, national origin, age, sex, height, weight, familial status, or marital status, in employment, housing and other real estate, and the full and equal utilization of public accommodations, public service, and educational facilities. Sex discrimination includes sexual harassment. Michigan's Persons with Disabilities Civil Rights Act guarantees persons with disabilities the opportunity to obtain employment, housing, and other real estate and full and equal utilization of public accommodations, public services, and educational facilities without discrimination because of a disability.

To Do

Find out whether your state has additional civil rights laws that expand protection for workers beyond the federal laws. In the form provided or on your own paper, list the protections available to workers or applicants in your state or city.

Does Your State Have Expanded Protection for Workers?

State:	
Law	*Discrimination prohibited on the basis of. . . .*

(Continued)

(Continued)

Resources

Human Rights Campaign. http://www.hrc.org/

Michigan's Elliott-Larsen Civil Rights Act of 1977. http://www.michigan.gov/documents/act_453_elliott_larsen_8772_7.pdf

Michigan's Persons with Disabilities Civil Rights Act of 1976. http://www.michigan.gov/documents/act-220-of-1976_8771_7.pdf

Experiential Exercises

TEST VALIDATION

A selection test that has adverse impact must be shown to be job related; otherwise, it is an illegal employment practice to use the test to make selection decisions. It is also important to know the validity of a test, because a test with very low validity may yield only a marginal productivity gain over random selection. In some cases, the productivity gain from using a test with low validity may be less than the cost of administering the test.

There are three methods of test construction, which mirror the three methods of test validation described in the Uniform Guidelines on Employee Selection Procedures (EEOC, 1978). In the Criterion-related method, the goal is to create a test that has a statistically significant correlation with the measure of job performance. The test questions in general should be answered differently by satisfactory performers versus unsatisfactory performers, no matter what the content of the questions is. In the Content-related method, a test is created to be a representative sample of the job. The content of the test mirrors the content of the job. In the Construct-related method, the test is designed to measure some hypothetical construct or trait, which has a statistically significant correlation with the measure of job performance. The construct could be cognitive skills or leadership or any trait correlated to job success.

To Do

Write a test of no more than 25 items to predict the undergraduate GPA of the students in the class. Your test should produce higher scores for students with higher GPAs and lower scores for those with lower GPAs. You may ask anything you want in the items except, "What is your college GPA?" or similar questions. Try to keep the questions from being extremely difficult because in one class period, everyone will be taking everyone else's test. Test items can be free response, completion, true-false, matching, multiple choice... anything you want, so long as you can administer and score the tests in one class period.

You might base your test items on the theory that more intelligent students will have higher GPAs than less intelligent students (construct validity), and write a test in which more intelligent students will tend to get higher scores than less intelligent students. Or you might base your test on a job analysis of the job of student (content validity) and write a test in which students with better study habits will get higher scores on the test. Or you might base your test on questions that higher and lower GPA students will tend to answer differently (criterion-related validity).

Come to class prepared with everything needed to administer the test: copies of the test, answer sheets, and so forth. Your instructor will give you an ID number, which you record on each of the tests that you take. Record your GPA on the instructor's Master Scoresheet, next to your ID number. After everyone has taken all of the tests (except their own), calculate the raw score for each person who took your test and record it on the Test Validation Scoresheet. Make sure you match the subjects' ID number on the tests with the ID number on the Test Validation Scoresheet. You do not need to transform the raw score into GPA; you will only need to report the raw score.

Your instructor will give you a copy of the Master Scoresheet with the GPA data so that you can calculate the validity of your test.

Test Validation Scoresheet

Test Validation Scoresheet		
ID Number	*GPA*	*Raw Score*
1	__ . __ __	
2	__ . __ __	
3	__ . __ __	
4	__ . __ __	
5	__ . __ __	
6	__ . __ __	
7	__ . __ __	
8	__ . __ __	
9	__ . __ __	
10	__ . __ __	
11	__ . __ __	
12	__ . __ __	
13	__ . __ __	
14	__ . __ __	
15	__ . __ __	
...		

Resources

Barrett, R. S. (1992). Content validation form. *Public Personnel Management, 21*(1), 41-51.

DuBois, D. A., & DuBois, C. L. Z. (2000). An alternate method for content-oriented test construction: An empirical evaluation. *Journal of Business and Psychology, 15*(2), 197-214.

Harrick, E. (1993). De-mystifying employment test validation: A process to get high validity coefficients. *Consulting Psychology Journal, 45*(3), 1-6.

(Continued)

(Continued)

Society for Industrial/Organizational Psychology. (2003). *Principles for the validation and use of personnel selection procedures.* http://www.siop.org/_Principles/principles.pdf

Sproule, C. F., & Berkley, S. (2001). The selection of entry-level corrections officers: Pennsylvania research. *Public Personnel Management, 30*(3), 377-417.

Stevens, M. (1999). Staffing work teams: Development and validation of a selection test for teamwork settings. *Journal of Management, 25*(2), 207-228.

U.S. Equal Employment Opportunity Commission. (1978). *Uniform guidelines on employee selection procedures.* http://www.access.gpo.gov/nara/cfr/waisidx_03/29cfr1607_03.html

York, K. M. (2002, April). *Is this test valid? A pair of experiential exercises to teach test validation.* Paper presented at the Midwest Academy of Management Conference, Indianapolis, IN.

CREATING AND USING A STRUCTURED INTERVIEW GUIDE

The interview is a commonly used method for selection (Pulakos, Schmitt, Whitney, & Smith, 1996), even though research shows that interviews are only moderately good predictors of job performance (Harris, 1989; Wiesner & Cronshaw, 1988). Some interviewers are better than others. A study of approximately 1,000 interviews conducted by 64 interviewers showed considerable variation in interviewer validity coefficients in relation to multiple performance criteria (Van Iddekinge, Sager, Burnfield, & Heffner, 2006). Some interview formats are better than others. Interviews can be improved if they are structured so that every applicant is asked the same questions, providing a common basis of comparison (Conway, Jako, & Goodman, 1995; Schmidt & Rader, 1999; Van der Zee, Bakker, & Bakker, 2002; Wiesner & Cronshaw, 1988; Wright, Lichtenfels, & Pursell, 1989). Unstructured interviews also present the greatest risk of the interviewer asking the applicant an illegal pre-employment inquiry, because there is no predetermined list of interview questions. In their review of research on the interview for selection, McDaniel et al. (1994) concluded that the validity of the interview depends on the content of the interview (situational, job related, or psychological), how the interview is conducted (structured or unstructured, panel or individual), and the nature of the criterion of job success (job performance, training performance, or tenure; research or administrative ratings).

To Do

You work for a production company making an indie feature film *The HRM House of Horror*. You have the following positions to fill: Grip, film editor, sound engineer, screenwriter, actor, special effects specialist, makeup artist, and camera operator.

Part 1. Choose one of the jobs and write a list of 10 to 12 questions to ask in a structured interview. Make sure that the questions are job related. The questions should be directed to determining whether the applicant can do the job.

Part 2. In small groups, have one person play the role of the interviewer; the other people will play the role of applicant. The interviewer will interview each of the applicants, asking the same questions in the same order for each applicant.

*Grips and set-up workers, motion picture sets, studios, and stages (O*Net: 53-7062.02)*

Arrange equipment; raise and lower scenery; move dollies, cranes, and booms; and perform other duties for the motion picture, recording, or television industry.

- Arranges equipment preparatory to sessions and performances following work order specifications and handles props during performances.
- Rigs and dismantles stage or set equipment such as frames, scaffolding, platforms, or backdrops, using carpenter's hand tools.
- Adjusts controls to raise and lower scenery and stage curtain during performance, following cues. Adjusts controls to guide, position, and move equipment such as cranes, booms, and cameras.
- Erects canvas covers to protect equipment from weather.
- Reads work orders and follows oral instructions to determine specified material and equipment to be moved and its relocation.
- Connects electrical equipment to power source and tests equipment before performance. Orders equipment and maintains equipment storage areas.
- Sews and repairs items using materials and hand tools such as canvas and sewing machines.
- Produces special lighting and sound effects during performances, using various machines and devices.

*Film and video editors (O*Net: 27-4032.00)*

Edit motion picture soundtracks, film, and video.

- Cut shot sequences to different angles at specific points in scenes, making each individual cut as fluid and seamless as possible.
- Study scripts to become familiar with production concepts and requirements.
- Edit films and videotapes to insert music, dialogue, and sound effects, to arrange films into sequences, and to correct errors, using editing equipment.
- Select and combine the most effective shots of each scene in order to form a logical and smoothly running story.
- Mark frames where a particular shot or piece of sound is to begin or end.
- Determine the specific audio and visual effects and music necessary to complete films.

(Continued)

(Continued)

- Verify key numbers and time codes on materials.
- Organize and string together raw footage into a continuous whole according to scripts and/or the instructions of directors and producers.
- Review assembled films or edited videotapes on screens or monitors in order to determine if corrections are necessary.
- Program computerized graphic effects.

*Sound engineering technician (O*Net: 27-4014.00)*

Operate machines and equipment to record, synchronize, mix, or reproduce music, voices, or sound effects in sporting arenas, theater productions, recording studios, or movie and video productions.

- Confer with producers, performers, and others in order to determine and achieve the desired sound for a production such as a musical recording or a film.
- Set up, test, and adjust recording equipment for recording sessions and live performances; tear down equipment after event completion.
- Regulate volume level and sound quality during recording sessions, using control consoles.
- Prepare for recording sessions by performing activities such as selecting and setting up microphones.
- Report equipment problems, and ensure that required repairs are made.
- Mix and edit voices, music, and taped sound effects for live performances and for prerecorded events, using sound mixing boards.
- Synchronize and equalize prerecorded dialogue, music, and sound effects with visual action of motion pictures or television productions, using control consoles.
- Record speech, music, and other sounds on recording media, using recording equipment.
- Reproduce and duplicate sound recordings from original recording media, using sound editing and duplication equipment.
- Separate instruments, vocals, and other sounds, then combine sounds later during the mixing or post-production stage.

*Creative writer (O*Net: 27-3043.02)*

Create original written works, such as plays or prose, for publication or performance.

- Writes fiction or nonfiction prose work, such as short story, novel, biography, article, descriptive or critical analysis, or essay.
- Writes play or script for moving pictures or television, based on original ideas or adapted from fictional, historical, or narrative sources.
- Organizes material for project, plans arrangement or outline, and writes synopsis.

- Collaborates with other writers on specific projects.
- Confers with client, publisher, or producer to discuss development changes or revisions.
- Conducts research to obtain factual information and authentic detail, utilizing sources such as newspaper accounts, diaries, and interviews.
- Reviews, submits for approval, and revises written material to meet personal standards and satisfy needs of client, publisher, director, or producer.
- Selects subject or theme for writing project based on personal interest and writing specialty, or assignment from publisher, client, producer, or director.
- Develops factors, such as theme, plot, characterization, psychological analysis, historical environment, action, and dialogue, to create material.
- Writes humorous material for publication or performance, such as comedy routines, gags, comedy shows, or scripts for entertainers.

*Actor (O*Net: 27-2011.00)*

Play parts in stage, television, radio, video, or motion picture productions for entertainment, information, or instruction. Interpret serious or comic role by speech, gesture, and body movement to entertain or inform audience. May dance and sing.

- Study and rehearse roles from scripts in order to interpret, learn and memorize lines, stunts, and cues as directed.
- Work closely with directors, other actors, and playwrights to find the interpretation most suited to the role.
- Learn about characters in scripts and their relationships to each other in order to develop role interpretations.
- Collaborate with other actors as part of an ensemble.
- Perform humorous and serious interpretations of emotions, actions, and situations, using body movements, facial expressions, and gestures.
- Attend auditions and casting calls in order to audition for roles.
- Portray and interpret roles, using speech, gestures, and body movements in order to entertain, inform, or instruct radio, film, television, or live audiences.
- Work with other crewmembers responsible for lighting, costumes, makeup, and props.
- Sing and/or dance during dramatic or comedic performances.
- Read from scripts or books to narrate action or to inform or entertain audiences, utilizing few or no stage props.

*Multimedia artist and animator (O*Net: 27-1014.00)*

Create special effects, animation, or other visual images using film, video, computers, or other electronic tools and media for use in products or creations, such as computer games, movies, music videos, and commercials.

(Continued)

(Continued)

- Design complex graphics and animation, using independent judgment, creativity, and computer equipment.
- Create two-dimensional and three-dimensional images depicting objects in motion or illustrating a process, using computer animation or modeling programs.
- Make objects or characters appear lifelike by manipulating light, color, texture, shadow, and transparency, and/or manipulating static images to give the illusion of motion.
- Assemble, typeset, scan and produce digital camera-ready art or film negatives and printer's proofs.
- Apply story development, directing, cinematography, and editing to animation to create storyboards that show the flow of the animation and map out key scenes and characters.
- Script, plan, and create animated narrative sequences under tight deadlines, using computer software and hand drawing techniques.
- Create basic designs, drawings, and illustrations for product labels, cartons, direct mail, or television.
- Create pen-and-paper images to be scanned, edited, colored, textured or animated by computer.
- Develop briefings, brochures, multimedia presentations, web pages, promotional products, technical illustrations, and computer artwork for use in products, technical manuals, literature, newsletters and slide shows.
- Use models to simulate the behavior of animated objects in the finished sequence.

*Makeup artist, theatrical and performance (O*Net: 39-5091.00)*

Apply makeup to performers to reflect period, setting, and situation of their role.

- Alter or maintain makeup during productions as necessary to compensate for lighting changes or to achieve continuity of effect.
- Analyze a script, noting events that affect each character's appearance, so that plans can be made for each scene.
- Apply makeup to enhance, and/or alter the appearance of people appearing in productions such as movies.
- Assess performers' skin-type in order to ensure that make-up will not cause break-outs or skin irritations.
- Attach prostheses to performers and apply makeup in order to create special features or effects such as scars, aging, or illness.
- Cleanse and tone the skin in order to prepare it for makeup application.
- Confer with stage or motion picture officials and performers in order to determine desired effects.
- Design rubber or plastic prostheses that can be used to change performers' appearances.

- Duplicate work precisely in order to replicate characters' appearances on a daily basis.
- Evaluate environmental characteristics such as venue size and lighting plans in order to determine makeup requirements.

*Camera operator, television, video, and motion picture (O*Net: 27-4031.00)*

Operate television, video, or motion picture camera to photograph images or scenes for various purposes, such as TV broadcasts, advertising, video production, or motion pictures.

- Operate television or motion picture cameras to record scenes for television broadcasts, advertising, or motion pictures.
- Compose and frame each shot, applying the technical aspects of light, lenses, film, filters, and camera settings in order to achieve the effects sought by directors.
- Operate zoom lenses, changing images according to specifications and rehearsal instructions.
- Use cameras in any of several different camera mounts such as stationary, track-mounted, or crane-mounted.
- Test, clean, and maintain equipment to ensure proper working condition.
- Adjust positions and controls of cameras, printers, and related equipment in order to change focus, exposure, and lighting.
- Gather and edit raw footage on location to send to television affiliates for broadcast, using electronic news-gathering or film-production equipment.
- Confer with directors, sound and lighting technicians, electricians, and other crew members to discuss assignments and determine filming sequences, desired effects, camera movements, and lighting requirements.
- Observe sets or locations for potential problems and to determine filming and lighting requirements.
- Instruct camera operators regarding camera setups, angles, distances, movement, and variables and cues for starting and stopping filming.

Resources

Conway, J. M., Jako, R. A., & Goodman, D. F. (1995). A meta-analysis of interrater and internal consistency reliability of selection interviews. *Journal of Applied Psychology, 80*(5), 565-579.

Harris, M. M. (1989). Reconsidering the employment interview: A review of recent literature and suggestions for future research. *Personnel Psychology, 42*(4), 691-726.

Maurer, T. J., & Salamon, J. M. (2006). The science and practice of a structured employment interview coaching program. *Personnel Psychology, 59*(2), 433-456.

McDaniel, M. A., Whetzel, D. L., Schmidt, F. L., & Maurer, S. D. (1994). The validity of employment interviews: A comprehensive review and meta-analysis. *Journal of Applied Psychology, 79*(4), 599-616.

Morgeson, F. P., Reider, M. H., & Campion, M. A. (2005). Selecting individuals in team settings: The importance of social skills, personality characteristics, and teamwork knowledge. *Personnel Psychology, 58*(3), 583-611.

O*Net. *Occupational Information Network.* http://online.onetcenter.org/

(Continued)

(Continued)

Pulakos, E. D., Schmitt, N., Whitney, D., & Smith, M. (1996). Individual differences in interviewer ratings: The impact of standardization, consensus discussion, and sampling error on the validity of a structured interview. *Personnel Psychology, 49*(1), 85-102.

Schmidt, F. L., & Rader, M. (1999). Exploring the boundary conditions for interview validity: Meta-analytic validity findings for a new interview type. *Personnel Psychology, 52*(2), 445-464.

Van der Zee, K. I., Bakker, A. B., & Bakker, P. (2002). Why are structured interviews so rarely used in personnel selection? *Journal of Applied Psychology, 87*(1), 176-184.

Van Iddekinge, C. H., Sager, C. E., Burnfield, J. L., & Heffner, T. S. (2006). The variability of criterion-related validity estimates among interviewers and interview panels. *International Journal of Selection and Assessment, 14*(3), 193-205.

Wiesner, W. H., & Cronshaw, S. F. (1988). A meta-analytic investigation of the impact of interview format and degree of structure on the validity of the employment interview. *Journal of Occupational Psychology, 61*(4), 275-290.

Wright, P. M., Lichtenfels, P. A., & Pursell, E. D. (1989). The structured interview: Additional studies and a meta-analysis. *Journal of Occupational Psychology, 62*(3), 191-199.

Creative Exercises

DEVELOPING AN IN-BASKET

One approach to developing an In-Basket is to make it generalized for a range of jobs, typically management positions (Joines, 1991). The In-Basket generally requires that candidates indicate the action they would take for each item (e.g., writing a memo, creating a meeting agenda, making a decision, delegating some task), but a multiple-choice response format can be used (Joines, 1987; York, Strubler, & Smith, 2005). By making a generalized management In-Basket that can be used for a number of jobs, development and administration costs can be reduced.

Another approach to developing an In-Basket is to make it specific for a particular job. This makes the In-Basket more realistic, because candidates deal with the same kinds of documents and issues that they would on the job. Situational exercises can be created to assess how the candidate would deal with typical problems encountered in the job or how they would interact with coworkers or people external to the organization.

To Do

Develop an In-Basket of 10 to 20 items for the O*Net job of first-line supervisor/manager of construction trades and extraction workers. Also write the In-Basket "Instructions for the Candidates," so that the candidates know what the exercise is about, a response sheet for candidates to indicate what action they will take on each item, and "Instructions for the Assessors," so the assessors know how the candidates' performance in the exercise should be assessed.

*First-line supervisor/manager of construction trades and extraction worker (O*Net: 47-1011.00)*

Directly supervise and coordinate activities of construction or extraction workers.

- Examine and inspect work progress, equipment, and construction sites to verify safety and to ensure that specifications are met.
- Read specifications such as blueprints to determine construction requirements and to plan procedures.
- Estimate material and worker requirements to complete jobs.
- Supervise, coordinate, and schedule the activities of construction or extractive workers.
- Confer with managerial and technical personnel, other departments, and contractors in order to resolve problems and to coordinate activities.
- Coordinate work activities with other construction project activities.
- Order or requisition materials and supplies.
- Locate, measure, and mark site locations and placement of structures and equipment, using measuring and marking equipment.
- Record information such as personnel, production, and operational data on specified forms and reports.
- Assign work to employees, based on material and worker requirements of specific jobs.

Resources

Barclay, L. A., & York, K. M. (1999). Electronic communication skills in the classroom: An email in-basket exercise. *Journal of Education for Business, 74*(4), 249-253.

Frederiksen, N., Saunders, D. R., & Wand, B. (1957). The In-Basket test. *Psychological Monographs: General and Applied, 71*(9), 1-28.

Joines, R. C. (1987, October). *The item-by-item scored General Management In-Basket.* Paper presented at the International Personnel Management Association Assessment Council Conference, Philadelphia.

Joines, R. C. (1991). *Innovations in In-Basket technology: The General Management In-Basket.* Toronto, Ontario, Canada: International Congress on the Assessment Center Method.

Management & Personnel Systems, Inc. (n.d.). *General Management In-Basket* (GMIB). http://www.mps-corp.com/04gmib.html

Salem, B., Ellis, D., & Johnson, D. (1981). Development and use of an in-basket promotional exam for police sergeant. *Review of Public Personnel Administration, 1*(2), 23-35.

Schippmann, J. S., Prien, E. P., & Katz, J. A. (1990). Reliability and validity of in-basket performance measures. *Personnel Psychology, 43*(4), 837-859.

CREATING AN ASSESSMENT CENTER

Assessment centers have been used as both predictors of job performance (for selection) and as diagnostic measures of job skills (for development), primarily for management positions (Arthur, Day, McNelly, & Edens, 2003;

Bray, 1985; Campbell & Bray, 1993; Munchus & McArthur, 1991). The basic idea of the Assessment Center is to simulate management jobs with realistic tasks and situations—the more realistic the simulation, the greater the content and predictive validity. The Assessment Center is able to achieve high validities because it uses multiple assessment methods, such as tests of cognitive ability tests, situational tests, and interest inventories; it uses standardized methods for evaluating candidate performance in the tests, and the assessors are trained in how to assess the candidates; and the judgments from multiple assessors are pooled to produce more reliable and valid assessments.

A common type Assessment Center Exercise puts candidates in a realistic management situation, and the candidates are evaluated on how they deal with the situation. In an In-Basket Exercise, candidates are given background information about an organization and a collection of materials that might accumulate in the In-Basket of a manager, such as letters, memos, and phone messages. The In-Basket Exercise is typically used to evaluate the candidates' organizational planning, organizing, prioritizing, and delegating skills. In a Management Presentation Exercise, candidates are given materials and asked to make an oral presentation based on the materials. Candidates are assessed on their oral communication skills and on how well they are able to interpret the materials. In a Performance Appraisal Interview, the candidates interact with a role player, described as an employee whose performance has been satisfactory in the past but whose recent performance has declined sharply. Candidates may be evaluated on their interpersonal skills such as building trust and respect, as well as how they handle the interview, such as focusing on performance, identifying barriers to effective performance, listening to the employee's explanation for the decline in performance, and working with the employee to develop a Performance Improvement Plan. In a Selection Interview, the candidates also interact with a role player acting as an applicant. Candidates may be assessed on their skills of eliciting job-relevant information from the applicant and avoiding any illegal pre-employment inquiries. In a Leaderless Group Discussion, a group of candidates are given a topic to discuss or a problem to solve. Candidates may be assessed on their positive and negative contributions to the discussion and how well they keep the discussion on track, with assessors evaluating their interpersonal and group decision-making skills.

Developing a set of realistic tasks and situations can be costly, but the cost is balanced by the greater predictability of job performance and greater face validity compared to single-component selection procedures (Gaugler, Rosenthal, Thornton, & Bentson, 1987; Woehr, 2003). Moreover, the content of the Assessment Center can be tailored to the specific characteristics of the job, making it a very flexible method to select or develop management talent. The first assessment center developed in the United States was used by the Office of Strategic Services (which later became the Central Intelligence Agency) to select spies (Office of Strategic Services, 1948). Also, assessors are typically trained in interviewing methods and behavioral observation, which improves the standardization and fairness of the Assessment Center. The higher validity of Assessment Centers compared to paper-and-pencil tests is based on the use of multiple assessors whose judgments are pooled (which increases the reliability of the exercises) and the use of multiple exercises each measuring a different knowledge, skill, or ability important for job success (which increases the validity).

If the Assessment Center is used for selection, the measurements are used to identify candidates to hire or promote, and the measurements must be sensitive to differences among candidates. If the Assessment Center is used for development, the measurements are used to identify management skills where the candidate is weak and where additional skill development is needed, and the measurements must be diagnostic of different skill levels (Boehm, 1985; Cochran, Hinkle, & Dusenberry, 1987; Rupp et al., 2006).

To Do

The class will be divided into small groups, and each group will create an assessment center that the people in the other groups will be candidates in. The Assessment Center is to select for the job of advertising and promotions manager. Create five exercises, one for each of Senge's (1990) Five Disciplines (Personal Mastery, Mental Models, Shared Vision, Team Learning, and Systems Thinking), and they must fit into the time allotted by your instructor. You may have as many assessors per exercise as you want, but there should be at least one person serving as the assessment center administrator, to keep the assessment center running smoothly. For each exercise, candidates must be given feedback that includes an overall ranking and identification of one strength and one weakness.

Design the assessment center for the job of advertising and promotions manager for a large advertising agency. The agency handles TV, radio, and print advertisements for *Fortune 100* companies. This job requires high levels of communication skills (oral and written) and interpersonal skills because the job requires working as part of a creative team to develop advertisements.

*Advertising and promotions manager (O*Net: 11-2011.00)*

Plan and direct advertising policies and programs or produce collateral materials, such as posters, contests, coupons, or give-aways, to create extra interest in the purchase of a product or service for a department, an entire organization, or on an account basis.

- Prepare budgets and submit estimates for program costs as part of campaign plan development.

(Continued)

(Continued)

- Plan and prepare advertising and promotional material to increase sales of products or services, working with customers, company officials, sales departments and advertising agencies.
- Assist with annual budget development.
- Inspect layouts and advertising copy and edit scripts, audio and video tapes, and other promotional material for adherence to specifications.
- Coordinate activities of departments, such as sales, graphic arts, media, finance, and research.
- Prepare and negotiate advertising and sales contracts.
- Identify and develop contacts for promotional campaigns and industry programs that meet identified buyer targets such as dealers, distributors, or consumers.
- Gather and organize information to plan advertising campaigns.
- Confer with department heads or staff to discuss topics such as contracts, selection of advertising media, or product to be advertised.
- Confer with clients to provide marketing or technical advice.

Because time is limited, you must design the Assessment Center exercises so that there is time for all of the candidates to go through all of the exercises. One solution is to make the exercises fairly short (e.g., for 15 candidates to individually go through a 5-min. exercise requires 75 minutes). Another solution is to create an exercise that multiple candidates can do at the same time. Fifteen candidates can simultaneously do an In-Basket Exercise in 15 minutes (see the example of an Assessment Center Exercise Schedule).

Assessment Center Exercise Schedule

Assessment Center Exercise Schedule								
	Candidates							
Time	*1*	*2*	*3*	*4*	*5*	*6*	*7*	*8*
7:00	IB	IB	Prep	Prep	Prep			
7:05	IB	IB	PA	SI	Prep	Prep	Prep	Prep
7:10	IB	IB			EP	SI	PA	Prep
7:15			IB	IB				MP
7:20		Prep	IB	IB	Prep	Prep		
7:25	Prep	Prep	IB	IB	SI	PA	Prep	Prep
7:30	SI	Prep					Prep	PA
7:35		MP	Prep	Prep	IB	IB	MP	
7:40	Prep		SI	PA	IB	IB		Prep
7:45	Prep	Prep			IB	IB	Prep	SI
7:50	MP	PA		Prep			SI	
7:55			Prep	Prep	Prep			
8:00	Prep	Prep	Prep	MP	PA	Prep	IB	IB

Assessment Center Exercise Schedule								
	Candidates							
Time	1	2	3	4	5	6	7	8
8:05	PA	SI	MP		Prep	Prep	IB	IB
8:10					MP	MP	IB	IB
8:15								
8:20	GD	GD	GD	GD	GD	GD	GD	GD
8:25	GD	GD	GD	GD	GD	GD	GD	GD
8:30	GD	GD	GD	GD	GD	GD	GD	GD
8:35	GD	GD	GD	GD	GD	GD	GD	GD
8:40								
8:45								
8:50								
8:55	Final Results of Assessment Center and Feedback							
9:00								

NOTE: An empty cell indicates break time; GD = Group Discussion; IB = In-Basket; MP = Management Presentation; PA = Performance Appraisal; Prep = Preparation time; SI = Selection Interview.

You must prepare all of the materials the candidates will need to do the exercises and the assessors will need to evaluate the candidates, as well as a schedule, so that assessors and candidates know where they are supposed to be and what they are supposed to be doing at what times. Copies of the exercise materials and the schedule are to be handed in at the beginning of class.

Senge's Five Disciplines of Learning Organizations

Building a Shared Vision: The capacity of people in the organization to hold a shared picture of the future they want to create. When there is a genuine vision, people excel and learn, not because they are told to, but because they want to. The practice of shared vision involves the skills of unearthing shared "pictures of the future" that foster genuine commitment and enrollment rather than compliance.

Mental Models: Mental models are deeply ingrained assumptions, generalizations, or even pictures or images that influence how we understand the world and how we take action. Very often we are not consciously aware of our mental models or the effects they have on our behavior.

Personal Mastery: Personal mastery is the discipline of continually clarifying and deepening our personal vision, of focusing our energies, of developing patience, and of seeing reality objectively. Personal mastery is the cornerstone of the learning organization.

Team Learning: The discipline of team learning starts with dialogue, the capacity of members of a team to suspend assumptions and enter into a genuine "thinking together." The discipline of dialogue also involves learning how to recognize the patterns of interaction in teams that undermine learning. Team learning is vital, because teams are the fundamental learning units in modern organizations.

(Continued)

(Continued)

Systems Thinking: Businesses and organizations are systems, made up of a number of processes that interact. Some of the effects on processes can take years to play out. Systems thinking is a conceptual framework, a body of knowledge and tools that has been developed over the past 50 years to make the full patterns clearer and to help us see how to change them effectively.

Resources

Arthur, W., Jr., Day, E. A., McNelly, T. L., & Edens, P. S. (2003). A meta-analysis of the criterion-related validity of assessment center dimensions. *Personnel Psychology, 56*(1), 125-154.

Arthur, W., Jr., & Woehr, D. J., & Maldegen, R. (2000). Convergent and discriminant validity of Assessment Center dimensions: A conceptual and empirical re-examination of the Assessment Center construct-related validity paradox. *Journal of Management, 26*(4), 813-835.

Boehm, V. R. (1985). Using assessment centres for management development—Five applications. *Journal of Management Development, 4*(4), 40-53.

Bray, D. W. (1985). Fifty years of assessment centres: A retrospective and prospective view. *Journal of Management Development, 4*(4), 4-12.

Campbell, R. J., & Bray, D. W. (1993). Use of an assessment center as an aid in management selection. *Personnel Psychology, 46*(3), 691-699.

Cochran, D. S., Hinkle, T. W., & Dusenberry, D. (1987). Designing a developmental assessment center in a government agency: A case study. *Public Personnel Management, 16*(2), 145-152.

Dayan, K., Kasten, R., & Fox, S. (2002). Entry-level police candidate assessment center: An efficient tool for a hammer to kill a fly? *Personnel Psychology, 55*(4), 827-849.

Gaugler, B. B., Rosenthal, D. B., Thornton, G. C., III, & Bentson, C. (1987). Meta-analysis of assessment center validity. *Journal of Applied Psychology, 72*(3), 493-511.

Munchus, G., III., & McArthur, B. (1991). Revisiting the historical use of the assessment centre in management selection and development. *Journal of Management Development, 10*(1), 5-13.

Office of Strategic Services. (1948). *Assessment of men: Selection of personnel for the Office of Strategic Services*. New York: Rinehart.

Rupp, D. E., Gibbons, A. M., Baldwin, A. M., & Snyder, L. A., Spain, S. M., Sang, E. W., et al. (2006). An initial validation of developmental assessment centers as accurate assessments and effective training interventions. *Psychological Manager Journal, 9*(2), 171-200.

Senge, P. M. (1990). *The fifth discipline: The art and practice of the learning organization*. New York: Doubleday/Currency.

Woehr, D. J. (2003). The construct-related validity of assessment center ratings: A review and meta-analysis of the role of methodological factors. *Journal of Management, 29*(2), 231-258.

York, K. M. (1995). Experiential and creative management exercises using an assessment center. *Journal of Education for Business, 70*(3), 141-145.

Performance Appraisal 6

Strategic Objective

The most important purpose of performance appraisal is to evaluate the employee's job performance as the basis for employment decisions such as continued employment, merit pay, and bonuses. Job performance information might also be used to identify training and development needs where an employee's performance needs improvement and to evaluate the effectiveness of training and development programs. Another purpose is to give the employee feedback on his or her job performance, to motivate improved performance in the future. When employees get no feedback on their performance, they may become demotivated, because they do not know whether they are doing a good job, or they may interpret the lack of feedback as indicating that their performance is satisfactory, even when it needs improvement.

The micro view of performance appraisal is focused on an individual employee's performance of specific job tasks. Job analysis is used to determine the important job tasks and to set standards of effective job performance. The employee's performance is evaluated compared to these performance objectives and expectations, and the employee is given feedback on where the performance objectives and expectations have been met and where job performance needs to be improved. The intent of linking the performance objectives to incentive pay or bonuses is to reward past performance and motivate future performance, although the intent and the effect may sometimes diverge (Kohn, 1993).

The macro view of performance appraisal is focused on how the individual's job fits into the rest of the organization. Employees may have specific individual responsibilities and also serve on teams; therefore, an evaluation of an employee's job performance should include individual and team performance. Every employee's performance objectives should be linked to the organization's business objectives, because each employee contributes to meeting organizational objectives. Incentive pay should be based on individual performance as well as organizational performance. No matter what an individual's job tasks are, the most fundamental responsibility is to attract and retain customers.

An organization that does performance management well gains a competitive advantage, because no matter what other resources the organization has, the work of the organization is planned and done by people (Buhler, 2007; Longenecker, & Waldeck, 2004). To create an effective performance management system, an organization must determine what aspects of each employee's job performance are to be evaluated, how they are to be evaluated, and who will be doing the evaluation. An organization may evaluate its sales representatives on performance-based measures such as dollar volume of sales, number of new customers, percentage of retained customers, as well as buyer–supplier relations. The performance-based measures may be tracked continuously as departmental indicators, and buyer–supplier relations may be evaluated by the customers.

Strategic Issues in HRM

REWARD, DEVELOP, PROMOTE

Performance appraisal has three basic functions: reward, develop, and promote. The job analysis sets the standards for satisfactory job performance, and performance appraisal evaluates the employee's job performance against these standards. This evaluation can then be used for making administrative decisions about continued employment, transfer, promotion, merit pay, bonuses, profit sharing, incentives, and other organizational rewards. The develop function is to give employees feedback on their job performance, which can be used for career planning and employee development. Where the performance appraisal indicates areas of unsatisfactory performance, this may be used to identify training or development needs. Where the performance appraisal indicates areas of superior performance, this may be used to identify strengths the employee can build on to be more effective in the future. The third function is to identify candidates for promotion by using the performance appraisal data to predict the future job performance of an employee in a higher level position. Organizations need a plan prepared for replacing key personnel when they retire or seek other career opportunities outside the organization or other contingencies. With a succession plan in place, the evaluation is made in advance rather than under time pressure from an unexpected event.

There are four requirements for an effective performance appraisal system (Cascio, 1982): relevance, sensitivity, reliability, and acceptability. Relevance means that there are clear links between the performance standards for jobs and the organization's goals and between the performance standards for jobs and the performance dimensions evaluated in the performance appraisal. Sensitivity means that the performance appraisal system can distinguish effective from ineffective performers. Reliability means that there is consistency in the performance appraisal process. Different raters should agree with each other about the performance of a given employee; if they are evaluating the employee on the same performance dimensions, they should give the same score. Acceptability means that the performance appraisal system has the support of the managers and employees who use it. If the system is not acceptable, it may be undermined or used ineffectively.

Managers succeed through the work of others—namely, their employees. Therefore, it is in managers' self-interest to accurately evaluate the job performance of their employees and develop their knowledge and skills. The more capable the manager's team of employees, the more they can achieve and the more successful the manager will be in meeting organizational objectives. The "big picture" of performance appraisal is that to achieve strategic performance appraisal, a manager's overall performance score can be tied to the appraisal score that his or her team receives (Falcone, 2007).

Although many organizations have a performance appraisal system, it has been estimated that less than 20% of all performance appraisals are effective (Longenecker & Goff, 1990). According to their survey, there is agreement among managers and employees on some of the reasons that performance appraisals fail. The performance standards against which employees are to be evaluated may be unclear, the manager may not have had opportunities to observe the employee's job performance, the manager may lack skill in conducting the appraisal, or the appraisal is not taken seriously by the person doing the rating.

There are negative consequences of ineffective performance appraisals. Failure to reward better performing employees reduces their motivation to exert higher levels of effort. Failure to identify employees who are ready for promotion leads to less effective promotion decisions. Failure to identify areas of employees' job performance that need improvement makes employees less productive than they could be. Pickett (2003) reports the results of an international survey of senior executives, which showed that they regard performance appraisal as one of the most difficult things they are required to do; nearly half of the employees surveyed said that their manager was not clear about what he or she thought of their work performance, and a third said that their manager provided little or no assistance in improving their job performance. Longenecker and Gioia's (1992) interviews of executives across manufacturing and service industries revealed that the higher the employees rise in an organization, the less likely they are to receive quality feedback about job performance. They also found that the executive performance appraisal process was often infrequently and haphazardly done.

Strategic Questions

1. Why do managers think that performance appraisal is difficult to do? What can organizations do to make performance appraisal easier for managers to do?
2. Should part of managers' performance appraisal be how well they do performance appraisal for their employees? What data should be collected?
3. What are some possible consequences of managers being held accountable for the accuracy of their performance appraisal ratings? For the career planning and development of their employees? For the performance of their employees who have been promoted on their recommendation?
4. Some organizations don't train managers how to do performance appraisal—what are some possible reasons?
5. What message do upper level managers send to lower level managers when upper level managers do not conduct effective performance appraisals with the lower level managers who work for them?
6. If an employee works as part of a team, how should his or her job performance be evaluated?

Resources

Abraham, S. E., Karns, L. A., Shaw, K., & Mena, M. A. (2001). Managerial competencies and the managerial performance appraisal process. *Journal of Management Development, 20*(9/10), 842-852.

Cascio, W. F. (1982). Scientific, legal, and operational imperatives of workable performance appraisal systems. *Public Personnel Management, 11*(4), 367-375.

Curtis, A. B., Harvey, R. D., & Ravden, D. (2005). Sources of political distortions in performance appraisals: Appraisal purpose and appraiser accountability. *Group & Organization Management, 30*(1), 42-60.

Falcone, P. (2007). Big-picture performance appraisal. *HR Magazine, 52*(8), 97-100.

Kerr, S. (1975). On the folly of rewarding A, while hoping for B: More on the folly. *Academy of Management Executive, 9*(1), 7-16.

Longenecker, C. O., & Gioia, D. A. (1992). The executive appraisal paradox. *Academy of Management Executive, 6*(2), 18-28.

Longenecker, C. O., & Goff, S. J. (1990). Why performance appraisals still fail. *Journal of Compensation & Benefits, 6*(3), 36-41.

Pickett, L. (2003). Transforming the annual fiasco. *Industrial and Commercial Training, 35*(6/7), 237-240.

GRAPHIC RATING SCALES VERSUS BEHAVIORALLY ANCHORED RATING SCALES

There are five common ways of conducting a performance appraisal. A Checklist is a list of job tasks that the employee is expected to perform, and the manager checks off whether the employee has accomplished those tasks. Rank Ordering requires the manager to rank-order a group of employees from highest performer to lowest. Narrative Appraisals require managers to write an essay about each employee's job performance. Graphic Rating Scales (GRS) require the manager to evaluate the employee's job performance on a scale across a number of performance dimensions. A Behaviorally Anchored Rating Scale (BARS) is a type of GRS in which the points on the scale are behaviors.

A Checklist contains a list of job tasks, and the manager conducting the performance appraisal checks off those tasks that have been completed satisfactorily. The employee's score on the performance appraisal is the number of items on the Checklist that have been checked off. Essentially, each job task is evaluated as satisfactory or unsatisfactory, although relatively more important job tasks can be given more weight in the total score. Checklists are easy for the supervisor to use and for the employee to understand, but they are relatively insensitive to differences between employees and within an employee over time, because it is only a 2-point scale.

Rank Ordering a group of employees on their job performance is easy for the manager to do, as long as the number of employees is not too large. With larger numbers of employees, it may be easy for the manager to determine which employees should get the highest and lowest ranks, but deciding on appropriate rankings for employees in between can be more difficult. Also, a rank ordering is an ordinal scale, which hides differences between groups of employees evaluated by different managers. If one manager had three employees, one a superior performer and two below-average performers on an absolute measure of performance, they would be ranked first, second, and third. If another manager had three employees, two superior performers and one below-average performer, they would also be ranked first, second, and third.

Narrative Appraisals require managers to write an essay about the job performance of the employee. Although this has the advantage of providing a richer description of the employee's performance (e.g., the mitigating and aggravating circumstances, the situational constraints, and unexpected events), the result is words, not numbers. Administrative decisions about continued employment, transfer, promotion, and merit pay must still be made, and these decisions are easier to make when they are based on numbers. Also, the quality of narrative appraisals depends on the writing skills of the manager doing the appraisal.

Table 6.1 Graphic Rating Scale

Ability to learn: Consider the ease with which this employee is able to learn new methods and to follow directions.				
Very Superior	*Learns With Ease*	*Ordinary*	*Slow to Learn*	*Dull*
Knowledge of work: Consider present knowledge of job and of work related to it.				
Complete	*Well Informed*	*Moderate*	*Meager*	*Lacking*

A widely used method of performance appraisal is GRS. Managers evaluate an employee's performance on a number of performance dimensions, using a scale with definitions for each point on the scale. The primary advantage of GRS over other performance appraisal methods is that they are easy to develop, easy for supervisors to learn to use, and easy for employees to understand. Other methods of performance appraisal cannot match these advantages.

Graphic Rating Scales have been used for many years. Paterson (1923) provides an example created for the Scott Company, for rating the efficiency of factory workers (see Table 6.1).

A BARS is a kind of GRS in which the definitions of the points on the scale (the anchors) are behaviors (Smith & Kendall, 1963). To evaluate the employee's job performance, the manager matches the behavior on the scale that is typical of the employee. This improves the response clarity of the scale, because raters do not have to interpret a subjective term such as "outstanding" or "satisfactory." A BARS is typically more than a 5-point scale, which improves its sensitivity to differences in job performance between employees and within an employee over time.

Cocanougher and Ivancevich (1978) created a BARS for a sales position (see Table 6.2). One of the performance dimensions was Cooperative Relations with Other Sales Team Members.

To develop a BARS, a large number of critical incidents (i.e., examples of effective and ineffective job performance) is generated, typically by job incumbents and their supervisors, which are then clustered into a set of performance dimensions. A group of subject matter experts then reallocate (or retranslate) the original critical incidents into the clusters, looking for a good match between the cluster to which they assign each critical incident and the cluster it was supposed to be assigned to. The subject matter experts then scale each of the critical incidents according to how effective or ineffective the performance is on its performance dimension. A subset of critical incidents is used as anchors for the BARS (see, e.g., Cocanougher, & Ivancevich, 1978; Maiorca, 1997; Rarick & Baxter, 1984). A BARS is difficult and time-consuming to develop, requiring the time to collect a large number of critical incidents, clustering and reallocating the critical incidents, and then scaling the critical incidents.

Table 6.2 Behaviorally Anchored Rating Scale

	Cooperative Relations With Other Sales Team Members
10	Could be expected to cooperate whenever help or aid is requested by other team members.
9	Could be expected to go out of his or her way to help the team achieve its goals.
8	
7	Is usually willing to lend a helping hand and can be expected to try hard to help the team.
6	
5	Could be expected to occasionally support the team on problems encountered in the field.
4	
3	Could be expected to half-heartedly contribute to the team effort to accomplish goals.
2	
1	Could be expected to not care much about the team and its members.
0	

Strategic Questions

1. Movie reviewers write essays about movies, telling readers why they might enjoy or hate them and then giving the movies 4 stars (or fewer). What is the advantage of using both methods to evaluate movies?
2. For what jobs would Narrative Appraisals be appropriate or better than GRS? For what jobs would Checklists be more appropriate than GRS?
3. What factors should be considered when deciding which performance appraisal method to use?
4. Where should HRM's effort be focused, on using rating scales that produce more accurate ratings or training raters to be more accurate using the rating scales that are currently being used?
5. Would BARS be easier to develop and use for the job of sales representative or sales manager (i.e., manager of a group of sales representatives)? Why?

(Continued)

(Continued)

Resources

Bernardin, H. J., & Smith, P. C. (1981). A clarification of some issues regarding the development and use of Behaviorally Anchored Rating Scales (BARS). *Journal of Applied Psychology, 66*(4), 458-463.

Cocanougher, A. B., & Ivancevich, J. M. (1978). BARS performance rating for sales force personnel. *Journal of Marketing, 42*(3), 87-95.

Jacobs, R., Kafry, D., & Zedeck, S. (1980). Expectations of Behaviorally Anchored Rating Scales. *Personnel Psychology, 33*, 595-640.

Kingstrom, P. O., & Bass, A. R. (1981). A critical analysis of studies comparing Behaviorally Anchored Rating Scales (BARS) and other rating formats. *Personnel Psychology, 34*, 263-289.

Kunin, T. (1955). The construction of a new type of attitude measure. *Personnel Psychology, 8*, 65-77.

Maiorca, J. (1997). How to construct behaviorally anchored rating scales (BARS) for employee evaluations. *Supervision, 58*(8), 15-18.

Paterson, D. G. (1923). The Scott Company Graphic Rating Scale. *Journal of Personnel Research, 1*(8), 361-376.

Rarick, C., & Baxter, G. (1984). Behaviorally anchored rating scales (BARS): An effective performance appraisal approach. S.A.M. *Advanced Management Journal, 51*, 36-39.

Schwab, D. P., Heneman, H. G., III, & DeCotiis, T. A. (1975). Behaviorally Anchored Rating Scales: A review of the literature. *Personnel Psychology, 28*(4), 549-562.

Smith, P. C., & Kendall, L. M. (1963). Retranslation of expectations: An approach to the construction of unambiguous anchors for rating scales. *Journal of Applied Psychology, 47*(2), 149-155.

Tziner, A., Joanis, C., & Murphy, K. R. (2000). A comparison of three methods of performance appraisal with regard to goal properties, goal perception, and ratee satisfaction. *Group & Organization Management, 25*(2), 175-190.

RATER ERROR TRAINING VERSUS RATER ACCURACY TRAINING

When subjective ratings by managers are used for performance appraisal, the ratings should be accurate (i.e., employees with better job performance should get higher performance appraisal ratings than employees with worse job performance). But performance appraisal ratings can be affected by rating errors such as leniency (the manager makes too many high ratings), severity (the manager makes too many low ratings), or central tendency (the manager makes too many ratings at the middle of the scale). Collectively, these rating errors are called "restriction in range," because the rater is using only part of the entire rating scale. What can be done to prevent these rating errors?

Rater Error Training is designed to reduce rating errors by showing managers what distributions of performance ratings look like when they show leniency, severity, or central tendency. Managers may be given an opportunity to practice making ratings and be given feedback on their ratings, indicating whether their ratings had a normal distribution or exhibited one of these rating errors. The end result of the training is that managers learn how to "grade on a curve," producing a normal distribution of performance ratings. Although Rater Error Training may reduce rating errors, it may also negatively affect the accuracy of the ratings (Hedge & Kavanagh, 1988).

Rater Accuracy Training (also called Frame of Reference Training) is designed to improve the manager's observation skills, so that when a certain level of job performance is observed, every manager will give the same rating (i.e., every manager is evaluating their employees from a common frame of reference). Managers do not always have a common point of reference; for example, Hauenstein and Foti (1989) found in two law enforcement agency samples that supervisors and patrol officers differed on their evaluation of poor-performance incidents. Instead of focusing on errors to avoid in making ratings, Rater Accuracy Training focuses on making accurate ratings (i.e., ratings that reflect the actual level job performance observed, regardless of the shape of the distribution; Bernardin & Buckley, 1981; Chirico et al., 2004; Day & Sulsky, 1995).

Strategic Questions

1. Should managers be expected to know how to do performance appraisal as part of their job's requirements, or should they be trained by the organization in how to do performance appraisal?
2. Why is it important for managers to avoid making rating errors when they do performance appraisal?
3. If managers are given Rater Accuracy Training and their ratings do not have a normal distribution, how will that affect a merit pay system based on the performance appraisal ratings?
4. Will managers be less likely to make rating errors if the organization has a policy of pay secrecy?

Resources

Bernardin, H. J., & Buckley, M. R. (1981). Strategies of rater training. *Academy of Management Review, 6*(2), 205-212.

Chirico, K. E., Buckley, M. R., Wheeler, A. R., Facteau, J. D., Bernardin, H. J., & Beu, D. S. (2004). A note on the need for true scores in Frame-of-Reference (FOR) training research. *Journal of Managerial Issues, 16*(3), 382-395.

(Continued)

(Continued)

Curtis, A. B., Harvey, R. D., & Ravden, D. (2005). Sources of political distortions in performance appraisals: Appraisal purpose and appraiser accountability. *Group & Organization Management, 30*(1), 42-60.

Day, D. V., & Sulsky, L. M. (1995). Effects of Frame-of-Reference training and information configuration on memory organization and rating accuracy. *Journal of Applied Psychology, 80*(1), 158-167.

Hauenstein, M. A., & Foti, R. J. (1989). From laboratory to practice: Neglected issues in implementing Frame-of-Reference rater training. *Personnel Psychology, 42*(2), 359-378.

Hedge, J. W., & Kavanagh, M. J. (1988). Improving the accuracy of performance evaluations: Comparison of three methods of performance appraiser training. *Journal of Applied Psychology, 73*(1), 68-73.

Pulakos, E. D. (1984). A comparison of rater training programs: Error training and accuracy training. *Journal of Applied Psychology, 69*(4), 581-588.

Schleicher, D. J., & Day, D. V. (1998). A cognitive evaluation of Frame-of-Reference rater training: Content and process issues. *Organizational Behavior and Human Decision Processes, 73*(1), 76-101.

Stamoulis, D. T., & Hauenstein, M. A. (1993). Rater training and rating accuracy: Training for dimensional accuracy versus training for ratee differentiation. *Journal of Applied Psychology, 78*(6), 994-1003.

Woehr, D. J., & Huffcutt, A. I. (1994). Rater training for performance appraisal: A quantitative review. *Journal of Occupational and Organizational Psychology, 67*(3), 189-206.

Zalesny, M. D., & Highhouse, S. (1992). Accuracy in performance evaluations. *Organizational Behavior and Human Decision Processes, 51*(1), 22-50.

SEX DISCRIMINATION IN PERFORMANCE APPRAISAL

Although employee performance on some jobs can be evaluated with direct measures of performance such as dollar volume of sales, number of loan applications processed, and percentage retention of current customers, many jobs are evaluated using subjective evaluations of job performance. Whenever a subjective evaluation of job performance is used, there is danger of discrimination.

Sex discrimination in performance appraisal has been a topic of research over multiple decades. Mobley (1982) found a small effect of sex in a field study of a supply distribution company; Pulakos, White, Oppler, and Borman (1989) also found a small amount sex bias in performance appraisals. In looking at wage differences between men and women, Drazin and Auster (1987) did not find sex discrimination in performance appraisals but did find sex discrimination in the salary allocation process. Some field studies have found that gender does not adversely affect the rate of promotion (Powell & Butterfield, 1994; Tsui & Gutek, 1984).

But even if the sex of the ratee has little effect on performance appraisal ratings, gender-related stereotypes may have an effect (Maurer & Taylor, 1994). Women in leadership positions are devalued relative to their male counterparts when they have a stereotypically masculine leadership style, especially when female leaders are in male-dominated roles (Eagly, Makhijani, & Klonsky, 1992). Powell, Butterfield, and Parent (2002) compared two studies 13 years apart and found that although managerial stereotypes now place less emphasis on masculine characteristics, a good manager is still seen as predominantly masculine. Lyness and Heilman (2006), based on their study of archival data, concluded that gender bias against women results from the perceived lack of person–job fit (i.e., negative expectations of women in management roles affects how their work is evaluated in traditionally male jobs). The term "glass ceiling" refers to the smaller percentage of women than men in management positions (Bible & Hill, 2007).

In their amicus curiae brief for the *Price Waterhouse v. Hopkins* (1989) case, the American Psychological Association (1991) identified three conditions that contribute to the reduction of stereotypic thought and discriminatory action: (a) additional information, (b) increased attention to that information, and (c) motivational incentives that support increased attention and indicate consensual disapproval of stereotyping. Information about a particular individual undermines the use of stereotypes, particularly if that information is inconsistent with a category (like the individual's sex). Therefore, stereotypes are less likely to affect evaluative judgments such as performance appraisal ratings when specific information about the employee's job performance is made available and is expected to be used to make the evaluations.

To motivate managers to avoid stereotypical judgments when doing performance appraisal, the American Psychological Association (1991) brief suggests that three types of organizational incentives should be in place. First, interdependence undercuts stereotyping by giving people more accurate, individual-specific (rather than group-stereotyped) impressions. Organizations should make teamwork explicit, make promotions depend on group products, and hold supervisors responsible for the success of their employees. Second, the organization should emphasize accuracy of performance appraisal judgments, to encourage decision makers to make less stereotyped evaluations. Decision makers need to be reminded that their employees' futures depend on their judgments. Third, adding the opinion of a third party to the evaluation process can exert a positive influence on the decision-making process. Therefore, the organization should seek other opinions, especially from a superior or a colleague.

Strategic Questions

1. For which jobs in an organization are sex stereotypes most likely to have an effect on performance appraisal judgments?
2. Performance appraisal data are used to make many administrative decisions other than continued employment. What other measures could be tracked to determine whether there is discrimination against women in the organization?
3. What should the training objectives be for a performance appraisal training program for managers? How can fairness in performance appraisal evaluations be assessed at the completion of the training?

(Continued)

(Continued)

4. Which methods of performance appraisal are less likely to result in discrimination against women?
5. What is the "glass ceiling"? How could you tell whether an organization has a glass ceiling?
6. What are the long-term consequences of systematic organization-wide sex discrimination against women in performance appraisal? What is the likely impact on productivity, job satisfaction, turnover, recruitment, and so forth?

Resources

American Psychological Association. (1991). In the Supreme Court of the United States: Price Waterhouse v. Ann B. Hopkins: Amicus curiae brief for the American Psychological Association. *American Psychologist, 46*(10), 1061-1070.

Bible, D., & Hill, K. L. (2007). Discrimination: Women in business. *Journal of Organizational Culture, Communication and Conflict, 11*(1), 65-76.

Drazin, R., & Auster, E. R. (1987). Wage differences between men and women: Performance appraisal ratings vs. salary allocation as a locus of bias. *Human Resource Management, 26*(2), 157-168.

Eagly, A. H., Makhijani, M. G., & Klonsky, B. G. (1992). Gender and the evaluation of leaders: A meta-analysis. *Psychological Bulletin, 111*(1), 3-22.

Maurer, T. J., & Taylor, M. E. (1994). Is sex by itself enough? An exploration of gender bias issues in performance appraisal. *Organizational Behavior and Human Decision Processes, 60*(2), 231-251.

Mobley, W. H. (1982). Supervisor and employee race and sex effects on performance appraisals: A field study of adverse impact and generalizability. *Academy of Management Journal, 25*(3), 598-606.

Powell, G. N., & Butterfield, D. A. (1994). Investigating the "glass ceiling" phenomenon: An empirical study of actual promotions to top management. *Academy of Management Journal, 37*(1), 68-86.

Powell, G. N., Butterfield, D. A., & Parent, J. D. (2002). Gender and managerial stereotypes: Have times changed? *Journal of Management, 28*(2), 177-193.

Price Waterhouse v. Hopkins, 490 U.S. 228 (1989).

Pulakos, E. D., White, L. A., Oppler, S. H., & Borman, W. C. (1989). Examination of race and sex effects on performance ratings. *Journal of Applied Psychology, 74*(5), 770-780.

Tsui, A. S., & Gutek, B. A. (1984). A role set analysis of gender differences in performance, affective relationships, and career success of industrial middle managers. *Academy of Management Journal, 27*(3), 619-635.

Applications

DEVELOPING PERFORMANCE DIMENSIONS

Whatever performance appraisal method is used, the manager evaluates the employee's performance on the aspects of the job that are most important for job success. For most jobs, the most important job tasks are the tasks that are done most frequently. For a few jobs, what the employee spends the most time doing are not the most critical tasks. According to O*Net, Firefighters (Municipal Fire Fighter [33-2011.01]) "control and extinguish municipal fires, protect life and property and conduct rescue efforts," but may actually spend more of their work time maintaining the firefighting equipment, conducting or participating in firefighting drills, and presenting fire safety programs to elementary schoolchildren.

The performance dimensions are developed from the job analysis. Once the important job tasks have been identified, a list of performance dimensions to be evaluated in the performance appraisal can be developed. For example, Day and Silverman (1989) developed a set of performance dimensions for the job of accountant based on critical incidents and interviews. Included in their list of performance dimensions were:

1. Technical ability—understands technical aspects of the job;
2. Timeliness of work—completes work within time budgets;
3. Client relations—gains the confidence, respect, and cooperation of clients;
4. Cooperation—demonstrates a positive and professional manner in working with personnel at all levels;
5. Work ethic—willing to work long hours and complete assigned tasks.

There are many other applications of performance appraisal beyond evaluating the job performance of employees. In some sports, the winner is easy to determine; fastest to the finish line, lifted the most weight, jumped the highest. But the winner of many sporting events is determined by a subjective evaluation by expert judges. Judging the performance of an athlete in a sporting event is a kind of performance appraisal, similar to evaluating the performance of an employee in a job. The first step is to develop the performance dimensions that are to be measured. In figure skating, for example, a panel of judges evaluates each skater on five performance dimensions.

Skating skills: Overall skating quality; edge control and flow over the ice surface demonstrated by a command of the skating vocabulary (edges, steps, turns, etc.), the clarity of technique, and use of effortless power to accelerate and vary speed.

Transitions and linking footwork and movement: The varied and/or intricate footwork, positions, movements, and holds that link all elements. In singles, pairs, and synchronized, this also includes the entrances and exits of technical elements.

Performance and execution: Performance is the involvement of the skater/couple/teams physically, emotionally, and intellectually, as they translate the intent of the music and choreography. Execution is the quality of movement and precision in delivery.

Choreography and composition: An intentional, developed, and/or original arrangement of all types of movements according to the principles of proportion, unity, space, pattern, structure, and phrasing.

Interpretation: The personal and creative translation of the music to movement on ice.

To Do

Choose one of the jobs listed below, and use the O*Net job description to develop between five and seven performance dimensions for that job. For each performance dimension, describe what would be "excellent" or "poor" job performance on that performance dimension. For example, if the performance dimension is knowledge of technical specifications of products for a computer sales representative, "excellent" job performance would be "always knows the answer to customers' questions about the specifications of a product," and "poor" job performance would be "rarely knows the answer to customer's questions about the specifications of a product."

*Food science technician (O*Net: 19-4011.02)*

Perform standardized qualitative and quantitative tests to determine physical or chemical properties of food or beverage products.

- Conduct standardized tests on food, beverages, additives, and preservatives in order to ensure compliance with standards and regulations regarding factors such as color, texture, and nutrients.
- Provide assistance to food scientists and technologists in research and development, production technology, and quality control.
- Compute moisture or salt content, percentages of ingredients, formulas, or other product factors, using mathematical and chemical procedures.
- Record and compile test results, and prepare graphs, charts, and reports.
- Clean and sterilize laboratory equipment.
- Analyze test results to classify products, or compare results with standard tables.
- Taste or smell foods or beverages in order to ensure that flavors meet specifications, or to select samples with specific characteristics.
- Examine chemical and biological samples in order to identify cell structures, and to locate bacteria, or extraneous material, using microscope.

- Mix, blend, or cultivate ingredients in order to make reagents or to manufacture food or beverage products.
- Measure, test, and weigh bottles, cans, and other containers in order to ensure hardness, strength, and dimensions that meet specifications.

*Sales manager (O*Net: 11-2022.00)*

Direct the actual distribution or movement of a product or service to the customer. Coordinate sales distribution by establishing sales territories, quotas, and goals and establish training programs for sales representatives. Analyze sales statistics gathered by staff to determine sales potential and inventory requirements and monitor the preferences of customers.

- Resolve customer complaints regarding sales and service.
- Monitor customer preferences to determine focus of sales efforts.
- Direct and coordinate activities involving sales of manufactured products, services, commodities, real estate or other subjects of sale.
- Determine price schedules and discount rates.
- Review operational records and reports to project sales and determine profitability.
- Direct, coordinate, and review activities in sales and service accounting and record-keeping, and in receiving and shipping operations.
- Confer or consult with department heads to plan advertising services and to secure information on equipment and customer specifications.
- Advise dealers and distributors on policies and operating procedures to ensure functional effectiveness of business.
- Prepare budgets and approve budget expenditures.
- Represent company at trade association meetings to promote products.

*Registered nurse (O*Net: 29-1111.00)*

Assess patient health problems and needs, develop and implement nursing care plans, and maintain medical records. Administer nursing care to ill, injured, convalescent, or disabled patients. May advise patients on health maintenance and disease prevention or provide case management. Licensing or registration required. Includes advance practice nurses such as: nurse practitioners, clinical nurse specialists, certified nurse midwives, and certified registered nurse anesthetists. Advanced practice nursing is practiced by RNs who have specialized formal, post-basic education and who function in highly autonomous and specialized roles.

- Maintain accurate, detailed reports and records.
- Monitor, record and report symptoms and changes in patients' conditions.

(Continued)

(Continued)

- Record patients' medical information and vital signs.
- Modify patient treatment plans as indicated by patients' responses and conditions.
- Consult and coordinate with health care team members to assess, plan, implement and evaluate patient care plans.
- Order, interpret, and evaluate diagnostic tests to identify and assess patient's condition.
- Monitor all aspects of patient care, including diet and physical activity.
- Direct and supervise less skilled nursing or health care personnel or supervise a particular unit.
- Prepare patients for, and assist with, examinations and treatments.
- Observe nurses and visit patients to ensure proper nursing care.

*Motion picture projectionist (O*Net: 39-3021.00)*

Set up and operate motion picture projection and related sound reproduction equipment.

- Insert film into top magazine reel, or thread film through a series of sprockets and guide rollers, attaching the end to a take-up reel.
- Start projectors and open shutters to project images onto screens.
- Monitor operations to ensure that standards for sound and image projection quality are met.
- Operate equipment in order to show films in a number of theaters simultaneously.
- Splice separate film reels, advertisements, and movie trailers together to form a feature-length presentation on one continuous reel.
- Inspect movie films to ensure that they are complete and in good condition.
- Set up and adjust picture projectors and screens to achieve proper size, illumination, and focus of images, and proper volume and tone of sound.
- Inspect projection equipment prior to operation in order to ensure proper working order.
- Perform regular maintenance tasks such as rotating or replacing xenon bulbs, cleaning lenses, lubricating machinery, and keeping electrical contacts clean and tight.
- Remove film splicing in order to prepare films for shipment after showings, and return films to their sources.

*Waiter and waitress (O*Net: 35-3031.00)*

Take orders and serve food and beverages to patrons at tables in dining establishment.

- Check patrons' identification to ensure that they meet minimum age requirements for consumption of alcoholic beverages.

- Collect payments from customers.
- Write patrons' food orders on order slips, memorize orders, or enter orders into computers for transmittal to kitchen staff.
- Take orders from patrons for food or beverages.
- Check with customers to ensure that they are enjoying their meals and take action to correct any problems.
- Serve food or beverages to patrons, and prepare or serve specialty dishes at tables as required.
- Prepare checks that itemize and total meal costs and sales taxes.
- Remove dishes and glasses from tables or counters, and take them to kitchen for cleaning.
- Present menus to patrons and answer questions about menu items, making recommendations upon request.
- Inform customers of daily specials.

*Biomedical engineers (O*Net: 17-2031.00)*

Apply knowledge of engineering, biology, and biomechanical principles to the design, development, and evaluation of biological and health systems and products, such as artificial organs, prostheses, instrumentation, medical information systems, and health management and care delivery systems.

- Evaluate the safety, efficiency, and effectiveness of biomedical equipment.
- Install, adjust, maintain, and/or repair biomedical equipment.
- Advise hospital administrators on the planning, acquisition, and use of medical equipment.
- Advise and assist in the application of instrumentation in clinical environments.
- Research new materials to be used for products such as implanted artificial organs.
- Develop models or computer simulations of human bio-behavioral systems in order to obtain data for measuring or controlling life processes.
- Design and develop medical diagnostic and clinical instrumentation, equipment, and procedures, utilizing the principles of engineering and bio-behavioral sciences.
- Conduct research, along with life scientists, chemists, and medical scientists, on the engineering aspects of the biological systems of humans and animals.
- Teach biomedical engineering, or disseminate knowledge about field through writing or consulting.
- Design and deliver technology to assist people with disabilities.

(Continued)

(Continued)

Resources

Arvey, R. D., & Murphy, K. R. (1998). Performance evaluation in work settings. *Annual Review of Psychology, 49*, 141-168.

Day, D. V., & Silverman, S. B. (1989). Personality and job performance: Evidence of incremental validity. *Personnel Psychology, 42*, 25-26.

MyBallroomDancing.com. *Ballroom dancing—judging criteria.* http://myballroomdancing.com/Ballroom Dancing - Judging Criteria.php

Ronan, W. W., Talbert, T. L., Mullet, G. M. (1977). Prediction of job performance dimensions—police officers. *Public Personnel Management, 6*(3), 173-180.

Schmitt, N., Noe, R. A., Meritt, R., & Fitzgerald, M. P. (1984). Validity of assessment center ratings for the prediction of performance ratings and school climate of school administrators. *Journal of Applied Psychology, 69*(2), 207-213.

U.S. Figure Skating. http://www.usfigureskating.org/New_Judging.asp?id=280

RATING ERRORS IN PERFORMANCE APPRAISAL

Whenever a subjective evaluation of employee job performance is used, such as a Graphic Rating Scale, the supervisor's ratings may fall into frequency distributions called rating errors. If a supervisor is doing performance appraisals on a number of employees and makes too many high ratings, that supervisor is displaying a Leniency Bias. If a supervisor is making too many low ratings, there is a Severity Bias. Alternatively, if the supervisor is making too many ratings in the middle of the scale, there is a Central Tendency. Collectively, these rating biases are types of restriction in range in the criterion, because the rater is not using the entire scale. The underlying assumption is that when a group of employees is evaluated, there should be a normal distribution, and whenever a rater's ratings cluster toward the top, bottom, or middle of a rating scale, that is an error in the ratings.

Why would managers make these rating errors? Managers may vary in their perceptions of satisfactory or unsatisfactory performance, with some managers having a higher or lower standard than others. A lenient rater sees a greater range of employee job performance as satisfactory; a severe rater sees a smaller range. Some managers may have difficulty distinguishing between different employees' levels of job performance and therefore rate all of the employees about the same.

There are other rating errors that raters might make, such as Contrast Effect, Halo Effect, Recency Error, and Similarity. When a rater evaluates a number of employees at once, the ratings made on one employee can affect the ratings on the next employee that is evaluated. That is, an average employee who is evaluated just after an above-average employee may be evaluated as less than average. An average employee who is evaluated just after a below-average employee is evaluated as better than average. Halo Effect occurs when raters let an overall impression of an employee affect their ratings across a set of performance dimensions (i.e., an employee receives higher ratings; or lower ratings, if there is a negative impression) so that the ratings they make tend to be consistent with the rater's overall impression. Recency Error occurs when the rater focuses only on recent performance, instead of evaluating the employee's job performance over the entire evaluation period. Similarity is the tendency for raters to judge more favorably those perceived to be similar to themselves (i.e., employees are rated more favorably if they are similar in background, attitudes, or other characteristics).

The assumption that a set of ratings should have a normal distribution is why some organizations use a forced distribution, where supervisors are not allowed to deviate from a strict percentage of ratings at each point on the rating scale, so that a normal distribution of ratings is guaranteed. Or a set of ratings may be mathematically transformed to have a normal distribution (e.g., *z* scores). Similarly, some teachers choose to grade on a curve, transforming raw test scores into grades that have a normal distribution, so that a fixed percentage of students are assigned a grade of "A."

Rater Error Training teaches raters to recognize and avoid errors in ratings (Hedge & Kavanaugh, 1988; Stamoulis, & Hauenstein, 1993; Woehr & Huffcutt, 1994). Raters are asked to make a set of ratings. Then the raters are given feedback on the ratings they have made, so that they can see where the ratings show leniency, severity, or central tendency. With practice, raters can learn to make ratings without these rating errors and produce ratings that have a normal distribution.

The term "rating errors" contains the assumption that a nonnormal distribution itself indicates a rating error, because a normal distribution is expected. Alternatively, rating errors can be defined as deviations from the correct ratings or true scores. If the true scores have a nonnormal distribution, a matching nonnormal distribution of ratings does not have rating errors but accurate ratings instead. Therefore, instead of training focused on teaching raters to recognize rating errors and avoid making them, rater training should be focused on getting raters to make accurate ratings. Performance Dimension Training trains raters to recognize and use the appropriate performance dimensions on which their ratings will be made rather than on more global judgments. Behavioral Observation Training trains raters to be better observers of behavior. Rater Accuracy Training teaches raters to use a common frame of reference so that their ratings are more accurate, regardless of the shape of distribution of the true scores.

To Do

There are seven district sales managers, and each has done performance appraisals on 20 sales representatives. The overall performance rating scale is a 5-point scale, with 1 being the lowest and 5 being the highest. For each of the managers in Table 6.3, identify whether they are displaying leniency, severity, central tendency, or no rating error in their overall performance ratings. Make a bar chart showing the frequency of each rating for each of the seven district sales managers.

Table 6.3a Overall Manager Performance Ratings

Overall Performance Ratings							
	Raters						
Employee	*Anctil*	*Brent*	*Cianciolo*	*DelGreco*	*Enfield*	*Frederick*	*Garcia*
1	4	1	2	1	1	3	1
2	5	2	3	2	1	4	1
3	5	2	3	3	3	3	2
4	4	1	3	1	3	4	2
5	5	1	3	2	2	3	2
6	2	1	3	3	2	3	2
7	5	2	2	1	2	3	5
8	4	1	3	2	2	3	5
9	5	4	4	3	2	3	4
10	3	1	3	1	2	3	4
11	4	2	2	2	3	3	4
12	5	1	3	3	3	3	4
13	4	1	4	1	3	3	3
14	5	2	3	2	3	3	3
15	5	1	2	3	3	3	3
16	4	1	3	4	3	3	3
17	5	2	4	2	3	4	3
18	3	1	3	2	3	4	3
19	4	2	2	2	3	4	3
20	5	3	3	2	3	3	3

Table 6.3b Raters

	Actil	*Brent*	*Cianciolo*	*Delgreco*	*Enfield*	*Frederick*	*Garcia*
N	20	20	20	20	20	20	20
Minimum	2	1	2	1	1	3	1
Maximum	5	4	4	4	3	4	5
M	4.3	1.6	2.9	2.1	2.5	3.25	3
SD	0.865	0.821	0.641	0.852	0.688	0.444	1.124
Skewness (G1)	−1.206	1.548	0.08	0.363	−1.076	1.251	0
Kurtosis (G2)	1.137	2.609	−0.25	−0.303	0.083	−0.497	−0.279

Resources

DeNisi, A. S., Robbins, T. L., & Summers, T. P. (1997). Organization, processing, and use of performance information: A cognitive role for appraisal instruments. *Journal of Applied Social Psychology, 27*(21), 1884-1905.

Hedge, J., & Kavanaugh, M. J. (1988). Improving the accuracy of performance evaluations: Comparison of three methods of performance appraiser training. *Journal of Applied Psychology, 73*(1), 68-73.

Heneman, R. L. (1986). The relationship between supervisory ratings and results-oriented measures of performance: A meta-analysis. *Personnel Psychology, 39*, 811-826.

Kasten, R., & Weintraub, Z. (1999). Rating errors and rating accuracy: A field experiment. *Human Performance, 12*(2), 137-153.

Latham, G. P., Wexley, K. N., & Pursell, E. D. (1975). Training managers to minimize rating errors in the observation of behavior. *Journal of Applied Psychology, 60*(5), 550-555.

Murphy, K. R., & Balzer, W. K. (1989). Rater errors and rating accuracy. *Journal of Applied Psychology, 74*(4), 619-624.

Pulakos, E. D. (1984). A comparison of rater training programs: Error training and accuracy training. *Journal of Applied Psychology, 69*(4), 581-588.

Sackett, P. R., Laczo, R. M., & Arvey, R. D. (2002). The effects of range restriction on estimates of criterion interrater reliability: Implications for validation research. *Personnel Psychology, 55*, 807-825.

Stamoulis, D. T., & Hauenstein, M. A. (1993). Rater training and rating accuracy: Training for dimensional accuracy versus training for ratee differentiation. *Journal of Applied Psychology, 78*(6), 994-1003.

Sulsky, L. M., & Balzer, W. K. (1988). Meaning and measurement of performance rating accuracy: Some methodological and theoretical concerns. *Journal of Applied Psychology, 73*(3), 497-506.

Woehr, D. J., & Huffcutt, A. I. (1994). Rater training for performance appraisal: A quantitative review. *Journal of Occupational and Organizational Psychology, 67*, 189-205.

Experiential Exercises

SELECTING PLAYERS FOR THE ALL-STAR GAME

The All-Star Game is a promotional event for Major League Baseball, in which the fans get an opportunity to see many of the best players (or at least, their favorite players) all on one field at the same time. One year there was no All-Star Game (1945), and some years there have been two (1959-1962). Although the game does not affect the standings, since 2003, it has been used to determine home field advantage for the upcoming World Series. Under the current system, players are selected by fan vote for the starting position players and by the managers from the previous year's World Series for pitchers and reserve players. Allowing the fans to select the players for the All-Star game achieves the strategic goal of maintaining and building fan interest in the game. But if the strategic goal was to have the best performing players compete against each other so that "All-Star" was defined by on-the-field performance rather than by popularity with the fans, how should the players be selected?

Baseball players' game performance can be measured by many statistics. It has been said that statistics are the lifeblood of baseball. Statistics to measure offensive performance include runs scored, hits, doubles, triples, home runs, runs batted in, total bases, walks, strikeouts, stolen bases, caught stealing, on-base percentage, slugging percentage, and batting average. These are just the basics; there are more, including isolated power (extra bases per at bats), runs created (on base percentage times total bases), and strikeout ratio (number of strikeouts divided by number of at bats), as well as defensive statistics and statistics just for pitchers. There is even a popular pastime called "Fantasy Baseball," in which people manage imaginary baseball teams based on the statistics of real-life baseball players and compete against other players using their players' statistics.

To Do

Step 1. Choose a position: Pitcher (P), Catcher (C), First Base (1B), Second Base (2B), Shortstop (SS), Third Base (3B), Left Fielder (LF), Center Fielder (CF), Right Fielder (RF).

Step 2. Develop a performance appraisal method for this position. Use any combination of offensive and defensive statistics as direct measures of performance to appraise the performance of the players in that position (see ESPN and Major League Baseball Web sites for various statistics and their definitions). For example, a right fielder might be evaluated on Home Runs (HR) and Runs Batted In (RBI).

Step 3. Collect statistical data for each of the players from the American and National League at that position last season (see ESPN and Major League Baseball Web sites for individual player statistics).

Step 4. Apply your scoring system to American and National League players at that position last season. Determine each player's rank order on each of the statistics and add their rank orders together to get an overall rank for each player at that position, according to your scoring system. If your performance appraisal method for right fielder was Batting Average + HR + RBI, then in the 2007 season Magglio Ordonez's (Detroit) ranks were: 1 + 3 + 1 = 5.

Who did your scoring system select (i.e., who was ranked first) for the position you selected? What ranking did the player whom the fans selected get on your scoring system? Did the fans select the best player for the All-Star Game? Would a Graphic Rating Scale work better to evaluate players' performance?

Resources

Baseball Almanac. http://www.baseball-almanac.com/index.shtml, http://www.baseball-almanac.com/bstatmen.shtml

Bennett, J. M. (2001). The game of statistics. *Quality Progress, 34*(8), 43-47.

ESPN. *MLB—Statistics index.* sports.espn.go.com/mlb/statistics

Harder, J. W. (1991). Equity Theory versus Expectancy Theory: The case of Major League Baseball free agents. *Journal of Applied Psychology, 76*(3), 458-464.

Holden, E. C., & Sommers, P. M. (2005). The influence of free-agent filing on MLB player performance. *Atlantic Economic Journal, 33*(4), 489.

Koop, G. (2002). Comparing the performance of baseball players: A multiple-output approach. *Journal of the American Statistical Association, 97*(459), 710-720.

Koppett, L. (1967). *A thinking man's guide to baseball.* New York: Dutton.

Major League Baseball. http://mlb.mlb.com

USING A GRAPHIC RATING SCALE

In evaluating the job performance of employees, managers must consistently observe the employee's performance over the entire evaluation period. When managers rely only on recent observations, they do not have a representative sample of job performance on which to base their evaluation. To avoid this Recency Error, managers should keep a performance diary on each employee, noting examples of effective and ineffective work performance that can be referred to when doing the performance appraisal. Using a performance diary as an aid to performance appraisal has been shown to give raters more positive reactions to the appraisal process, better ability to recall performance information, and better ability to distinguish between different employees' job performance and differences in an employee's job performance over time (DeNisi & Peters, 1996; DeNisi, Robbins, & Cafferty, 1989).

To Do

Use the Performance Diary to observe the job performance of a salesperson on one of the shopping channels (e.g., QVC, HSN, Jewelry Television), or an infomercial, over at least three 15-min. periods. When you have completed your Performance Diary, evaluate the job performance of the salesperson, using the Graphic Rating Scale (derived from Babakus, Cravens, Grant, Ingram, & LaForge, 1996).

*Retail salesperson (O*Net: 41-2031.00)*

Sell merchandise, such as furniture, motor vehicles, appliances, or apparel in a retail establishment.

- Greet customers and ascertain what each customer wants or needs.
- Open and close cash registers, performing tasks such as counting money, separating charge slips, coupons, and vouchers, balancing cash drawers, and making deposits.
- Maintain knowledge of current sales and promotions, policies regarding payment and exchanges, and security practices.
- Compute sales prices, total purchases and receive and process cash or credit payment.
- Maintain records related to sales.
- Watch for and recognize security risks and thefts, and know how to prevent or handle these situations.
- Recommend, select, and help locate or obtain merchandise based on customer needs and desires.
- Answer questions regarding the store and its merchandise.
- Describe merchandise and explain use, operation, and care of merchandise to customers.
- Ticket, arrange and display merchandise to promote sales.

(Continued)

(Continued)

Performance Diary

Performance Diary			*Performance Level*	
Date	*Time*	*Description of Performance*	*Ineffective*	*Effective*

Performance Appraisal

Performance Appraisal: Retail Salesperson					
	Unsatisfactory	*Improvement Needed*	*Good*	*Very Good*	*Outstanding*
Generating a high level of dollar sales					
Knowing the design and specification of products					
Knowing the applications and functions of products					
Experimenting with different sales approaches					
Being flexible in the selling approaches used					
Varying sales style from situation to situation					
Building strong working relationships with other people in the company					
Listening attentively to identify and understand the real concerns of customers					
Convincing customers that they understand their unique problems and concerns					
Communicating their sales presentation clearly and concisely					

Resources

Babakus, E., Cravens, D. W., Grant, K., Ingram, T. N., & LaForge, R. W. (1996). Investigating the relationships among sales, management control, sales territory design, salesperson performance, and sales organization effectiveness. *International Journal of Research in Marketing, 13*(4), 345-363.

DeNisi, A. S., Robbins, T., & Cafferty, T. P. (1989). Organization of information used for performance appraisals: Role of diary-keeping. *Journal of Applied Psychology, 74*(1), 124-129.

Creative Exercises

DEVELOPING A GRAPHIC RATING SCALE

A GRS is a commonly used method of performance appraisal. Compared to a BARS, it is easier to develop and more sensitive to differences between employees than checklists or ranking. The format is flexible so that a GRS can be developed for most jobs. The steps to develop a GRS are as follows: (1) job analysis to determine the important job tasks and the expected level of performance, (2) definition of the performance dimensions to be measured by the GRS, and (3) definition of the points on the GRS (i.e., the anchors).

The job description for police officer can be found on O*Net. The O*Net job summary and job tasks for Police Patrol Officer are as follows:

Police patrol officer (O*Net: 33-3051.01)

Patrol assigned area to enforce laws and ordinances, regulate traffic, control crowds, prevent crime, and arrest violators.

- Provide for public safety by maintaining order, responding to emergencies, protecting people and property, enforcing motor vehicle and criminal laws, and promoting good community relations.
- Identify, pursue, and arrest suspects and perpetrators of criminal acts.
- Record facts to prepare reports that document incidents and activities.
- Review facts of incidents to determine if criminal act or statute violations were involved.

- Render aid to accident victims and other persons requiring first aid for physical injuries.
- Testify in court to present evidence or act as witness in traffic and criminal cases.
- Evaluate complaint and emergency-request information to determine response requirements.
- Patrol specific area on foot, horseback, or motorized conveyance, responding promptly to calls for assistance.
- Monitor, note, report, and investigate suspicious persons and situations, safety hazards, and unusual or illegal activity in patrol area.
- Investigate traffic accidents and other accidents to determine causes and to determine if a crime has been committed.

Landy, Farr, Saal, and Freytag (1976) identified the following performance dimensions for the performance appraisal of municipal police officers:

1. Job Knowledge: Awareness of procedures, laws, and court rulings, and changes in them.
2. Judgment: Observation and assessment of the situation and taking appropriate action.
3. Initiative: Individual personal performance conducted without either direct supervision or commands, including suggestions for improved departmental procedures.
4. Dependability: Predictable job behavior, including attendance, promptness, and reaction to boredom, stress, and criticism.
5. Demeanor: Professional bearing as determined by overall neatness of uniform, personal grooming, and general physical condition.
6. Attitude: General orientation toward the law enforcement profession and the department.
7. Relations with Others: Dealing with people, including the public, fellow officers, and supervisory personnel.
8. Communication: Making oneself understood, gathering and transmiting information, both in oral and written fashion.

Using the performance dimension Judgment, a GRS item could be developed to measure this performance dimension, such as that shown in Table 6.4 (Rosinger et al., 1982).

Table 6.4 GRS Item Using the Performance Dimension Judgment

Judgment:	1	2	3
Stops vehicles for a variety of violations	Concentrates on one or two kinds of violations and spends too little time on the others.	Concentrates on speed violations, but stops vehicles for other violations also.	Stops vehicles for a variety of traffic and other violations.
Comments:			

To Do

Part 1. Develop a GRS item for each of the eight performance dimensions listed above for police officer.

Part 2. Choose one of the jobs in this exercise, your current job (if it is in O*Net), or any other job in O*Net. Create a set of six to eight performance appraisal items using a Graphic Rating Scale. Each item should have a definition of the performance dimension to be evaluated and definitions of each point on the scale. Each item should have between three and seven units, depending on what is appropriate for the performance dimension being evaluated.

*Human resources managers (O*Net: 11-3040.00)*

Plan, direct, and coordinate human resource management activities of an organization to maximize the strategic use of human resources and maintain functions such as employee compensation, recruitment, personnel policies, and regulatory compliance.

*Refuse and recyclable material collectors (O*Net: 53-7081.00)*

Collect and dump refuse or recyclable materials from containers into truck. May drive truck.

*Architectural drafters (O*Net: 17-3011.01)*

Prepare detailed drawings of architectural designs and plans for buildings and structures according to specifications provided by architect.

*Web administrators (O*Net: 15-1099.05)*

Manage web environment design, deployment, development and maintenance activities. Perform testing and quality assurance of web sites and web applications.

*Budget analysts (O*Net: 13-2031.00)*

Examine budget estimates for completeness, accuracy, and conformance with procedures and regulations. Analyze budgeting and accounting reports for the purpose of maintaining expenditure controls.

(Continued)

(Continued)

*Waiters and waitresses (O*Net: 35-3031.00)*

Take orders and serve food and beverages to patrons at tables in dining establishment.

Resources

Landy, F. J., Farr, J. L., Saal, F. E., & Freytag, W. R. (1976). Behaviorally anchored scales for rating the performance of police officers. *Journal of Applied Psychology, 61*(6), 750-758.

Rosinger, G., Myers, L. B., Levy, G. W., Loar, M., Mohrman, S. A., & Stock, J. R (1982). Development of a behaviorally based performance appraisal system. *Personnel Psychology, 35*, 75-88.

CREATING A FACULTY EVALUATION FORM

Many universities use student evaluations as part of the appraisal process for professors. The student evaluations, along with other information, are then used to make decisions about merit pay, tenure, and promotion. Other aspects of a professor's job performance are research (journal articles, books, conference presentations, and other scholarly work) and service (to the university, to the community, and to their profession). Although students are most familiar with the part of a professor's job that relates to teaching, only some aspects of teaching are readily observable by students. Therefore, student evaluations of professors should focus on those aspects of teaching that students are able to evaluate, because they see that aspect of the job being done in the classroom or see the work product.

To create a Faculty Evaluation Form, the first step is to do a job analysis of the job of university professor, so that all of the job tasks are known. The products of the job analysis are the job description (a list of the job tasks) and the job specification (a list of the knowledge, skill, and ability requirements to do the job tasks). These are what will be evaluated by the Faculty Evaluation Form. The next step is to use the job analysis information to identify the performance dimensions to be measured by the Faculty Evaluation Form. Then, items are written for the Faculty Evaluation Form to measure those performance dimensions. Finally, the items are put into the Faculty Evaluation form, using a GRS.

There are three parts to a GRS. The performance dimensions are the aspects of job performance that are being measured with the scale. The anchors are the definitions of the points on the rating scale. The units are the number of points on the rating scale; if there are five possible ratings, it is a 5-point rating scale. Response clarity is the degree to which it is clear what is being evaluated and refers to the performance dimensions and the anchors.

To Do

Step 1. Do a job analysis of the job of university professor of a Business School. Start with the O*Net job description for business teacher, postsecondary. The job analysis must include interviews with students from other classes in a variety of majors. These students are being used as subject matter experts, because they have some understanding of the job from their experience as students (Boex, 2000; Mueller & Belcher, 2000; Toland, 2005; Umble & Whitten, 1977). Develop a job analysis interview guide to find out what they think are the most important tasks in the job and what tasks are done most frequently. Document these interviews and summarize your conclusions.

Step 2. Based on the job analysis, develop a set of performance dimensions to evaluate teaching performance. The performance dimension that students would be most familiar with and have the most behavioral observations on which to base their ratings would be "Effective Classroom Performance." Few students would be able to evaluate, for example, curriculum development or instructional innovations. The performance dimension of Effective Classroom Performance might include the professor's attitude toward students (e.g., does the professor expect students to succeed or to fail?), relevance of the class (e.g., does the professor show how the material is relevant for running a successful business?), use of class time (e.g., are discussions focused and productive?), organization and preparation (e.g., is the professor fully prepared for each class?), speed and depth of coverage (e.g., does the professor try to cover too much material too fast?), grading (e.g., is grading based on sufficient opportunities for student performance evaluation?).

Step 3. Develop a Faculty Evaluation Form with a GRS, to measure the performance dimensions you identified earlier, to be used by students to evaluate the performance of their instructors. There should be no performance dimensions without items to measure it, and there should be no items unrelated to any of the performance dimensions. To improve the response clarity of the items on the form, use descriptive anchors, rather than vague terms such as "superior performance" or "needs improvement." There should be clear links between the job analysis and the performance dimensions and between the performance dimensions and the Faculty Evaluation Form.

Step 4. Write a short report on your work, including (a) the data you collected for the job analysis, (b) the job description and job specification, (c) the list of performance dimensions and definitions of each of the performance dimensions, and (d) the Faculty Evaluation Form.

Resources

Boex, L. F. J. (2000). Attributes of effective economics instructors: An Analysis of Student Evaluations. *Journal of Economic Education, 31*(3), 211-227.

Kim, E. J., & Buschmann, M. T. (2006). Reliability and validity of the Faces Pain Scale with older adults. *International Journal of Nursing Studies, 43*, 447-456.

Lowenberg, G. (1979). Interindividual consistencies in determining behavior-based dimensions of teaching effectiveness. *Journal of Applied Psychology, 64*(5), 492-501.

Mueller, M., & Belcher, G. (2000). Observed divergence in the attitudes of incumbents and supervisors as subject matter experts in job analysis: A study of the fire captain rank. *Public Personnel Management,* 29(4), 529-556.

(Continued)

(Continued)

O*Net On-Line. *Occupational Information Network*. http://online.onetcenter.org/

Toland, M. (2005). A multilevel factor analysis of students' evaluations of teaching. *Educational and Psychological Measurement, 65*(2), 272-296.

Tziner, A., Joanis, C., & Murphy, K. R. (2000). A comparison of three methods of performance appraisal with regard to goal properties, goal perception, and ratee satisfaction. *Group & Organization Management, 25*(2), 175-190.

Umble, M., & Whitten, B. J. (1977). The significant dimensions of teaching behavior and their relative importance for instructor evaluations. *Educational and Psychological Measurement, 37*(4), 1023-1030.

Wright, R. E. (2006). Student evaluations of faculty: Concerns raised in the literature, and possible solutions. *College Student Journal, 40*(2), 417-422.

Training and Developing Employees 7

Strategic Objective

All organizations must manage four resources: money, equipment, information, and people. Investments in better equipment may speed up production or reduce waste. Information is power; data about products, prices, and customers are essential to every business. Investments in training and development of employees can make them more productive or more effective in their jobs, directly contributing to the bottom line. Burke and Day's (1986) meta-analysis of managerial training effects (across six training content areas, seven training methods, and four types of training outcomes) showed that managerial training is moderately effective. Collins and Holton (2004), in their evaluation of 83 studies from 1982 to 2001, including education, government, medical, and military organizations, came to a similar conclusion. Even a moderately effective training program can have a substantial effect. A training program for 65 bank supervisors was found to cost $50,500, but the utility to the organization was over $34,600 in the first year, $108,600 by the third year, and more than $148,000 by the fifth year (Mathieu & Leonard, 1987).

The purpose of training and management development programs is to improve employee capabilities and organizational capabilities. When the organization invests in improving the knowledge and skills of its employees, the investment is returned in the form of more productive and effective employees. Training and development programs may be focused on individual performance or team performance. The creation and implementation of training and management development programs should be based on training and management development needs identified by a training needs analysis so that the time and money invested in training and management development is linked to the mission or core business of the organization (Watad & Ospina, 1999).

To be effective, training and management development programs need to take into account that employees are adult learners (Forrest & Peterson, 2006). Knowles's (1990) theory of adult learning or "Andragogy" is based on five ideas: (a) adults need to know why they are learning something, (b) adults need to be self-directed, (c) adults bring more work-related experiences into the learning situation, (d) adults enter into a learning experience with a problem-centered approach to learning, and (e) adults are motivated to learn by both extrinsic and intrinsic motivators. Having a problem-centered approach means that workers will learn better when they can see how learning will help them perform tasks or deal with problems that they confront in their work (Aik & Tway, 2006).

At different stages of their careers, employees need different kinds of training and different kinds of development experiences. Although a business degree might prepare students for their first job, they will need to gain knowledge and skills through education and experience as they progress through their career. Peters (2006) suggests that there are four stages of management education with different learning outcomes:

1. Functional competence, an understanding of finance, accounting, marketing, strategy, information technology, economics, operations, and human resources management;
2. Understanding context and strategy and how organizational processes interrelate, to make sense of societal changes, politics, social values, global issues, and technological change;
3. Ability to influence people, based on a broad understanding of people and motivations; and
4. Reflective skills, to set priorities for work efforts and life goals.

Therefore, to maximize the effectiveness of training and development, organizations must constantly assess their employees' current training and development needs and identify training and development needs to prepare employees for their next position. This requires that organizations recognize that different employees will have different needs and that these needs will change over time as these workers continue in their careers.

Strategic Issues in HRM

EMPLOYEE DEVELOPMENT AND TURNOVER

Investing in human resources through training and management development improves individual employee capabilities and organizational capabilities. But investing in people is not the same as investing in equipment or machinery. When an organization invests in new computers, for example, the cost can be depreciated over multiple years; but when an organization invests in management development, it is a cost for that year and cannot be depreciated. So from an accounting point of view, dollar for dollar, it is better to invest in the equipment that employees use than it is to invest in the employees using that equipment.

If an organization invests in new equipment, it is expected that the equipment will pay for itself in faster production, less waste, lower maintenance costs, and so forth. But if an organization invests in improving the knowledge and skills of its employees, there should be some benefit to the organization. How should the organization measure the effect? As measures of training program success, Kirkpatrick (1959) suggested using four criteria:

1. Reaction: what the trainees thought of the particular program;
2. Learning: what principles, facts, and techniques trainees learned;
3. Behavior: an assessment of changes in trainee job performance; and
4. Results: the impact of the training program on organizational objectives, such as turnover, absence, and costs.

Measuring the return on investment for a training program adds a fifth level to the criteria. Phillips's (1996) summary of the American Society for Training and Development's return on investment for training case studies in a variety of industries notes that the returns on investment ranged from 150% to 2000%.

There is a second reason that organizations have a bias toward investments in equipment rather than employee development. Developing your employees makes them more attractive to other employers, potentially making them more likely to turnover. After they have been developed, employees are free to leave the organization to work for another organization, taking the organization's investment in their improved level of knowledge or skills with them to their new employer. According to this counterproductive logic, it is better not to develop your own employees, to prevent competitors from potentially benefitting from the training.

Strategic Questions

1. Why would an organization be reluctant to invest in training its employees, if it makes their employees more capable? Isn't it better to have more capable employees?
2. If an organization offered to send you to a management development program, with the condition that you agree to work for the organization for 2 years to "pay off" the training, would you accept the offer?
3. If an organization has a high level of turnover, should it invest in training programs?
4. How should an organization measure the outcome of a training or management development program?
5. How should an organization determine the "break-even" point for management development programs (i.e., where the organization's investment is paid for by increased productivity)?
6. Should the government fund training programs to improve the knowledge and skills of citizens? If organizations are reluctant to invest in training their own employees because those trained employees might be working for a competitor one day, should the government have or not have a similar reluctance to fund training programs?

Resources

Alliger, G. M. (1989). Kirkpatrick's levels of training criteria: Thirty years later. *Personnel Psychology, 42*(2), 331-342.

Gattiker. U. E. (1995). Firm and taxpayer returns from training of semiskilled employees. *Academy of Management Journal, 38*(3), 1152-1173.

Kirkpatrick, D. L. (1959). Techniques for evaluating training programs. *Journal of the American Society of Training Directors, 33*(6), 3-9, 21-26.

Kline, S., & Harris, K. (2008). ROI is MIA: Why are hoteliers failing to demand the ROI of training? *International Journal of Contemporary Hospitality Management, 20*(1), 45-59.

Phillips, J. J. (1996). ROI: The search for best practices. *Training & Development, 50*(2), 42-47.

WAYS TO MANAGE

Frederick Winslow Taylor's ideas on Scientific Management were intended to improve workplace efficiency through the systematic application of four principles (Robinson, 1992):

- Develop a science for each element of an individual's work, instead of the old rule-of-thumb method;
- Scientifically select and then train, teach, and develop the worker, rather than expect workers to train themselves;
- Cooperate with the workers so as to ensure that all work is done in accordance with the principles that have been developed; and
- Divide work and responsibility between management and workers.

In more modern terminology, Taylor's principles are to find the best practice, then make the best practice the organization's practice by training employees and replicating it throughout the organization. Insights into better quality products and services or more effective or efficient ways to produce the product or deliver the service can come from employees throughout the organization.

Gosling and Mintzberg (2003) describe two ways to manage. "Heroic Management" is based on the self, and "Engaging Management" is based on collaboration.

Heroic Management:

- Managers are important people, separate from those who develop products and deliver services;
- Higher up managers develop strategy for those lower down to implement;
- Implementation is the problem, because although the higher level managers develop it, most others resist it;
- Rewards for increasing performance go to the leaders—what matters is shareholder value; and
- Leadership is thrust on those who thrust their will on others.

Engaging Management:

- Managers are important to the extent that other people do the important work of developing products and services;
- Effective leaders work throughout the organization, and engaged people often grow little problems into big initiatives;
- Implementation is the problem, because it cannot be separated from formulation, and committed insiders are necessary to come up with key changes;
- Rewards for making the organization better go to everyone—what matters is human values; and
- Leadership is a sacred trust earned through the respect of others.

Heroic Management is based on the idea of command and control (i.e., someone with position power makes the decisions, and the people with less power implement them). And because making decisions and monitoring their implementation is difficult, decision makers are entitled to greater organizational rewards. Engaging Management is based on the idea of teamwork (i.e., everyone in the organization is responsible for creating customers, not just the employees who deal directly with customers).

Strategic Questions

1. If you were to start a sidewalk shoveling business, should you train your employees to know the optimal number of pounds of snow per shovelful to maximize productivity and minimize injury, or let them decide for themselves?
2. Who are the creators of value in organizations?
3. According to Scientific Management, managers plan the work and workers do the work; so how does an organization figure out the best way to do a job?
4. Which is more important, planning the work or doing the work?
5. If workers are given responsibility for the work, are they managers?
6. Is leadership in a person or in an organization?

Resources

Aurelius, M. (2002). *The emperor's handbook: A new translation of the Meditations* (C. Scot Hicks & David V. Hicks, Trans.). New York: Scribner.

Delinder, J. V. (2005). Taylorism, managerial control strategies, and the ballets of Balanchine and Stravinsky. *American Behavioral Scientist, 48*(11), 1439-1452.

Foley, J. (Director). (1992). *Glengarry Glen Ross* [Motion picture]. Los Angeles, CA: Lion's Gate.

Gosling, J., & Mintzberg, H. (2003). The five minds of a manager. *Harvard Business Review, 81*(11), 54-63.

Raelin, J. (2004). Don't bother putting leadership into people. *Academy of Management Executive, 18*(3), 131-135.

Robinson, T. L. (1992). Revisiting the original management primer: Defending a great productivity innovator. *Industrial Management, 34*(1), 19-20.

THE ROLE OF THE MANAGER

What does a manager do? A manager manages the work and manages the people doing the work. According to the Fair Labor Standards Act, what makes an employee a manager is that he or she directs the work of others and exercises independent judgment. The Fair Labor Standards Act describes an executive as an employee with the primary duty of managing the enterprise in which the employee is employed or of a customarily recognized department or subdivision thereof; customarily and regularly directing the work of two or more other employees; and having the authority to hire or fire other employees or having particular weight given to suggestions and recommendations as to the hiring, firing, advancement, promotion, or any other change of status of other employees. An employee in an administrative position has as his or her primary duty the performance of office or nonmanual work directly related to the management or general business operations of the employer or the employer's customers. The employee's primary duty includes the exercise of discretion and independent judgment with respect to matters of significance.

The most common management tasks involve managing individual performance, instructing subordinates, planning and allocating resources, coordinating interdependent groups, managing group performance, monitoring the business environment, and representing one's staff. The relative importance of these seven management tasks varies by level in the organization (Kraut, Pedigo, McKenna, & Dunnette, 1989). For first-level managers, managing individual performance is the most important activity, which includes motivating and disciplining subordinates, tracking performance and giving feedback, and improving communications and individual productivity. For middle managers, the most important tasks involve planning and allocating resources, including estimating group resource requirements, making decisions about how resources should be distributed, and translating general directives into specific plans and communicating their benefits. For executives, monitoring the business environment is the most important job task, including an increased awareness of sales, business, economic, and social trends. For a self-managed work team, the team takes on the tasks and roles of the manager (Druskat & Wheeler, 2003).

Four management roles result from the influence a middle manager has over others in the organization and the kind of strategic thinking that is required of a middle manager (Floyd & Wooldridge, 1994). "Championing Strategic Alternatives" is bringing entrepreneurial and innovative proposals to top management's attention. "Synthesizing Information" is supplying information to top management about events within and outside the organization. "Facilitating Adaptability" is facilitating the change process. "Implementing Deliberate Strategy" is implementing the organization's strategy.

Strategic Questions

1. What does a manager do? What makes a manager a manager?
2. How does management differ from leadership?
3. What is a manager's role in developing strategy? What is a manager's role in implementing strategies once they have been developed?
4. If a work team becomes a self-managed work team, what does it now have to do that it didn't do when it was just a work team?

(Continued)

(Continued)

Resources

Druskat, V. U., & Wheeler, J. V. (2003). Managing from the boundary: The effective leadership of self-managing work teams. *Academy of Management Journal, 46*(4), 435-457.

Floyd, S. W., & Wooldridge, B. (1994). Dinosaurs or dynamos? Recognizing middle management's strategic role. *Academy of Management Executive, 8*(4), 47-57.

Heimovics, R. D., & Herman, R. D. (1989). The salient management skills: A conceptual framework for a curriculum for managers in nonprofit organizations. *American Review of Public Administration, 19*(4), 295-312.

Kraut, A. I., Pedigo, P. R., McKenna, D. D., & Dunnette, M. D. (1989). The role of manager: What's really important in different management jobs? *Academy of Management Executive, 3*(4), 286-293.

U.S. Department of Labor. (2004). *Defining and delimiting the exemptions for executive, administrative, professional, outside sales and computer employees; final rule, CFR Title 29, Part 541.* http://www.dol.gov/esa/regs/fedreg/final/Regulation_541.pdf

SYSTEMS THINKING

Organizations are complex systems, made up of many interacting processes and people. A decision in one functional area influences other functional areas. Understanding how all of these processes interact with each other is an essential aspect of the job of manager. Making the transition from a nonmanagement to a management position requires a shift in focus from the job to the "big picture" of the organization. This integrative view of the organization, which Senge (1990) calls "Systems Thinking," is methods, tools, and principles oriented to looking at the interrelatedness of forces and seeing them as part of a common process (a system). A system is a perceived whole whose elements "hang together" because they continually affect each other over time and operate toward a common purpose. For example, Wright (1999) describes the highly complex tuition and counseling system at the Open University (United Kingdom), which allocates 900 tutors at 50 study centers to 12,000 students in 190 courses.

HRM can be seen as a system of interrelated processes. The more effectively the organization does recruiting, the larger the pool of qualified applicants there are to select from when making hiring decisions. The more selective the organization can be in making hiring decisions, the better the selection decisions will be and the more effective and productive the employees will be. The longer that effective employees stay with the organization, the lower the turnover and the greater the return on investment for training and development programs.

Pierce (2002) describes the application of Systems Thinking to a safety program at a mid-sized manufacturing company. The case study company had widely varying numbers of recordable injuries per month, which resulted in variable management emphasis on safety, more emphasis in months following a high number of injuries, and less emphasis in other months. The company undertook a systems thinking approach to safety, to give workers a broader perspective than traditional problem-solving techniques focused on determining causes of problems and then fixing them. Systems Thinking looks at the interrelatedness and interdependence of the parts of a system. Workplace safety can then be seen as a system that includes both machines and the people operating the machines. Workplace injuries may be caused by the machine, by the operator of the machine, or a combination of the two.

Cavana, Boyd, and Taylor (2007) report on their study investigating the causal factors of poor retention and recruitment in the electronic technicians trade in the New Zealand Army. Taking a Systems Thinking approach, they examined the interconnections among apprentices, tradesmen, management, and external stakeholders, to identify the issues and develop an action plan to improve retention. Recognizing that recruitment and retention involved a number of interconnected systems, the action plan had three parts. The action plan included two recruiting initiatives (recruiting current polytechnic students and recent graduates and providing educational opportunities to soldiers from other trade groups to prepare them for trade training), a change in training methods (to better address the learning styles of young adults), and a change in the pay progression model to improve pay equity (by reducing the gap between the pay of apprentices and other Army trainees).

Strategic Questions

1. What would be the effect of downsizing 20% of your workforce? On labor costs, work motivation, job satisfaction, recruitment, etc.?
2. If cheap electricity from fusion power were to become a reality tomorrow, how would it affect your business, if your business was in
   - Aluminum manufacturing
   - Heating and air conditioning equipment
   - Home construction
   - Electric utility
   - Automobile manufacturing
   - Petroleum refining

(Continued)

(Continued)

3. Cities compete to host the Super Bowl; what are the effects on the city's economy?
4. If the birthrate continues to fall over the next 20 years, what will be the effect on the typical company's workforce?
5. What would be the effects on businesses of a "carbon footprint" tax, in which greater use of carbon-based fuels brings a higher tax?
6. What organizations would be most adversely affected by a 50% increase in the price of gasoline? What organizations would benefit from a 50% increase in the price of gasoline?
7. What would be the effect of a substantial increase in the federal minimum wage?

Resources

Cavana, R. Y., Boyd, D. M., & Taylor, R. J. (2007). A systems thinking study of retention and recruitment issues for the New Zealand Army Electronic Technician Trade Group. *Systems Research and Behavioral Science, 24*(2), 201-216.

Deming, W. E. (1986). *Out of the crisis.* Cambridge, MA: MIT Center for Advanced Engineering Study.

Flood, R. L. (1998). "Fifth Discipline": Review and discussion. *Systemic Practice and Action Research, 11*(3), 259-273.

Senge, P. M. (1990). *The fifth discipline: The art and practice of the learning organization.* New York: Doubleday/Currency.

Senge, P. M., & Sterman, J. D. (1992). Systems Thinking and Organizational Learning: Acting locally and thinking globally in the organization of the future. *European Journal of Operational Research, 59*(1), 137-151.

Sevcik, P. (2006). Tragedy of the commons. *Business Communications Review, 36*(3), 8-9.

Wright, T. (1999). Systems Thinking and systems practice: Working in the Fifth Dimension. *Systemic Practice and Action Research, 12*(6), 607-631.

Applications

CALCULATING THE UTILITY OF A TRAINING PROGRAM

The purpose of training employees is to improve their knowledge and skills, which improves their individual capability. Whether the training should be done is a kind of cost–benefit calculation; the improvement in the employees' job performance should be greater than the cost of training the employees. The cost of a training program includes the time and costs to develop the course, instructional materials, equipment, the wages of the trainers, and lost productivity of the employees while they are in the training program. The benefits of a training program include time savings, improved productivity, and improved product or service quality. Parry (1996) gives an example of a government agency that ran a project management training program for 120 employees. The posttraining measures included percentage of projects completed on time and within budget, level of client satisfaction, and estimated time and money saved. The conclusion was that the agency's training cost of $95,000 resulted in a savings of $670,000. Training a group of bank supervisors in supervisory skills was found to result in a cost savings to the organization of $34,600 in the first year, $108,600 by the third year, and more than $148,900 by the fifth year (Mathieu & Leonard, 1987).

To effectively manage the training process, the costs and the benefits of training programs must be measured. Just as the dollar value of a new-and-improved selection test can be compared to the dollar value of the current test by comparing the costs of the tests and the benefits in terms of better selection decisions, the dollar value of a training program can also be calculated, to determine the return on the investment in training (Chmielewski & Phillips, 2002; Phillips & Phillips, 2006). Just because employees completed the training program does not guarantee a positive return; some training programs can have negative utility (Morrow, Jarrett, & Rupinski, 1997).

To evaluate the utility of a training program, a number of variables need to be considered (Cascio, 1999). The greater the difference in job performance between trained and untrained employees, the greater the utility of the training program. Every training program has costs, and as the cost of the training program goes up, the utility goes down. If the training program improves trained employees' job performance, the more employees that are trained, the greater the utility. To determine how effective a training program is in dollars gained, a utility analysis can be conducted, using the utility of training equation. For example, in Farrell and Hakstian's (2001) meta-analysis of training programs for sales representatives, they found improvements in sales productivity of 23% and a dollar gain per employee for the duration of their tenure of $64,633 for sales representatives and $93,684 for senior sales representatives.

To Do

Use the utility of training equation and the data in Table 7.1 to create a spreadsheet to calculate the dollar gain of the training program. Next, calculate the utility of the training program under different conditions. What if the cost of the training program was $1,000 per trainee? What if the cost of the training program was $1,000 and the true difference in job performance in standard deviation units was 80? What if the cost of the training program was $1,000 and the true difference in job performance in standard deviation units was 80 and the number of years duration of the training effect on performance was 3 years?

(Continued)

(Continued)

Table 7.1 Data

ΔU	$\Delta U = T \times N \times d_t \times SD_y - N \times C$	Utility of training equation to calculate the dollar value of the training program
T	Number of years duration of the training effect on performance	2 years
N	Number of employees trained	100 employees
d_t	True difference in job performance between the average trained and untrained employee in standard deviation (*SD*) units, corrected for attenuation, due to unreliability in the ratings d = (trained – untrained)/*SD* $d_t = d/\text{SQRT(IRR)}$	• The performance mean for the trained group = 55 • The performance mean for the untrained group = 50 • The *SD* for both groups = 10 • Estimate of interrater reliability (IRR) = .60
SD_y	Standard deviation of job performance in dollars of the untrained group	Estimate of SD_y = \$10,413
C	Cost of training per trainee	\$500 per trainee
Calculate the dollar value of the training program using the utility equation and the data above.		
ΔU		The dollar value of the training program
Now calculate the dollar value of the training program under the following different scenarios with different values from the data above.		
What if....		What if the cost of the training program was \$1,000 per trainee?
What if....		What if the cost of the training program was \$1,000, and the true difference in job performance in *SD* units was 80?
What if....		What if the cost of the training program was \$1,000 and the true difference in job performance in *SD* units was 80 and the number of years duration of the training effect on performance was 3 years?

Resources

Boudreau. J. W. (1983). Economic considerations in estimating the utility of human resource productivity improvement programs. *Personnel Psychology, 36*(3), 551-576.

Cascio, W. F. (1999). *Costing human resources: The financial impact of behavior in organizations.* Mason, OH: South-Western.

Chmielewski, T. L., & Phillips, J. J. (2002). Measuring Return-On-Investment in government: Issues and procedures. *Public Personnel Management, 31*(2), 225-237.

Ferrell, S., & Hakstian, A. R. (2001). Improving salesforce performance: A meta-analytic investigation of the effectiveness and utility of personnel selection procedures and training interventions. *Psychology & Marketing, 18*(3), 281-316.

Latham, G. P., & Whyte, G. (1994). The futility of utility analysis. *Personnel Psychology, 47*(1), 31-46.

Mathieu, J, E., & Leonard, R. L., Jr. (1987). Applying utility concepts to a training program in supervisory skills: A time-based approach. *Academy of Management Journal, 30*(2), 316-335.

Morrow, C. C., Jarrett, M. Q., & Rupinski, M. T. (1997). An investigation of the effect and economic utility of corporate-wide training. *Personnel Psychology, 50*(1), 91-119.

Parry, S. B. (1996). Measuring training's ROI. *Training & Development, 50*(5), 72-77.

Phillips, J., & Phillips, P. (2006). Return on Investment measures success. *Industrial Management, 48*(2), 18-23.

Raju, N. S. (1990). A new approach for utility analysis. *Journal of Applied Psychology, 75*(1), 3-12.

Schmidt, F. L., Hunter, J. E., & Pearlman, K. (1982). Assessing the economic impact of personnel programs on workforce productivity. *Personnel Psychology, 35*(2), 333-347.

MY DREAM JOB

Organizations develop mission statements to clarify their purpose and to make public the organization's goals and values. Strategic plans are then developed to realize the mission. A company may state that its mission is to provide the most reliable wireless communication network, then develop strategic plans to ensure that their customers have few dropped calls or poor connections.

Individuals have career goals, jobs that they always wanted to have. To get this dream job, they need to develop a career plan to get that job. The first step is a personal assessment to discover their abilities, skills, and interests. Some of this information may already be available in performance appraisal evaluations or other assessments made by the employer. The next step is to determine what knowledge and skills are required for the dream job, so that the employee can make plans to acquire the needed knowledge and skills. A career is a sequence of related work experiences and activities, aimed at personal and organizational goals, through which a person passes during his or her lifetime, that are partly under the control of the individual and partly under the control of others. Both individual career management and organizational career management is correlated with career success (Gould, 1979; Orpen, 1994); career plans with specific goals and timetables are more likely to be successful.

If an employee's dream job is a compensation manager, the first source of information about the job is the *Occupational Outlook Handbook*. Under the section for "Occupations: Management" is general information about the nature of the work and then a section dealing with jobs in compensation, which is described as follows:

> NATURE OF THE WORK
>
> Attracting the most qualified employees and matching them to the jobs for which they are best suited is significant for the success of any organization. However, many enterprises are too large to permit close contact between top management and employees. Human resources, training, and labor relations managers and specialists provide this connection. In the past, these workers have been associated with performing the administrative function of an organization, such as handling employee benefits questions or recruiting, interviewing, and hiring new staff in accordance with policies and requirements that have been established in conjunction with top management. Today's human resources workers manage these tasks and, increasingly, consult top executives regarding strategic planning. They have moved from behind-the-scenes staff work to leading the company in suggesting and changing policies. Senior management is recognizing the significance of the human resources department to their financial success.
>
> Compensation, benefits, and job analysis specialists conduct programs for employers and may specialize in specific areas such as position classifications or pensions. Job analysts, occasionally called position classifiers, collect and examine detailed information about job duties in order to prepare job descriptions. These descriptions explain the duties, training, and skills that each job requires. Whenever a large organization introduces a new job or reviews existing jobs, it calls upon the expert knowledge of the job analyst.

Another useful piece of information is the job market for a compensation manager. Is the demand expected to be better or worse than job growth in general? Ideally, the outlook would be higher than average so that the employee would have more opportunities.

> JOB OUTLOOK
>
> The abundant supply of qualified college graduates and experienced workers should create keen competition for jobs. Overall employment of human resources, training, and labor relations managers and specialists is expected to grow faster than the average for all occupations through 2014. In addition to openings due to growth, many job openings will arise from the need to replace workers who transfer to other occupations or leave the labor force.

It would also be helpful to have some idea of what this job pays, because different areas of the country pay more or less for this job. In the following section is general information about earnings.

EARNINGS

Annual salary rates for human resources workers vary according to occupation, level of experience, training, location, and size of the firm, and whether they are union members.

Median annual earnings of compensation and benefits managers were $66,530 in May 2004. The middle 50 percent earned between $49,970 and $89,340. The lowest 10 percent earned less than $39,250, and the highest 10 percent earned more than $118,880. In May 2004, median annual earnings were $81,080 in the management of companies and enterprises industry.

Another source of occupational information that is helpful in career planning is O*Net, which lists the tasks a compensation manager typically performs, and more important, what Knowledge, Skills, and Abilities are required in the job, as well as information on the Work Activities, Work Context, Job Zone, Occupational Interests, Work Styles, and Work Values. If an employee's highest occupational interests were Enterprising and Conventional, O*Net shows that this matches with the occupational interests for people in the job of compensation manager (see Campbell & Holland, 1972; Day, Rounds, & Swaney, 1998; Holland, 1973). There is also a section on Wages and Employment, which gives an estimate of salaries for the United States and for a specific state. The first section gives a summary of the job of compensation manager, and a later section lists the skills someone would need to have to be qualified for the job.

SUMMARY REPORT FOR:

Compensation and benefits manager (O*Net: 11-3041.00)

Plan, direct, or coordinate compensation and benefits activities and staff of an organization.

Sample of reported job titles: Benefits Manager, Human Resources Director, Compensation Manager, Office Manager, Benefits Coordinator, Compensation and Benefits Manager, Business Manager, Corporate Controller, Director of Compensation, Employee Benefits Coordinator.

Skills

Active Listening—Giving full attention to what other people are saying, taking time to understand the points being made, asking questions as appropriate, and not interrupting at inappropriate times.

Critical Thinking—Using logic and reasoning to identify the strengths and weaknesses of alternative solutions, conclusions or approaches to problems.

Time Management—Managing one's own time and the time of others.

Management of Personnel Resources—Motivating, developing, and directing people as they work, identifying the best people for the job.

Reading Comprehension—Understanding written sentences and paragraphs in work related documents.

Social Perceptiveness—Being aware of others' reactions and understanding why they react as they do.

Speaking—Talking to others to convey information effectively.

Writing—Communicating effectively in writing as appropriate for the needs of the audience.

Management of Financial Resources—Determining how money will be spent to get the work done, and accounting for these expenditures.

Monitoring—Monitoring/Assessing performance of yourself, other individuals, or organizations to make improvements or take corrective action.

To Do

Identify your dream job. Your dream job is the job you want to do someday, not just the job that you think you can get. Describe the nature of the work in general, based on information in the Occupational Outlook Handbook. What is the job outlook for this job? What does the job pay? Identify the knowledge, skills, and abilities required to do the job, based on information in O*Net (if you cannot find an exact match in O*Net, choose a close match).

Create a career plan. Develop an action plan to develop the knowledge, skills, and abilities required for this job. The plan should include milestones to be accomplished by some specific point in time in the future. Use the form provided or your own paper to generate your report.

Dream Job Form

Dream Job:		
Nature of the work:		
Outlook:		
Pay:		
Knowledge, skills, abilities needed:	How to develop the knowledge, skills, abilities:	Milestones and time line for developing the knowledge, skills, abilities:

(Continued)

(Continued)

Resources

Campbell, D. P., & Holland, J. (1972). A merger in vocational interest research: Applying Holland's theory to Strong's data. *Journal of Vocational Behavior, 2*(4), 353-376.

Day, S., Rounds, J., & Swaney, K. (1998). The structure of vocational interests for diverse racial-ethnic groups. *Psychological Science, 9*(1), 40-44.

Dooney, J., & Esen, E. (2007). Incentive pay fuels HR salaries. *HR Magazine, 52*(11), 34-43.

Gould, S. (1979). Characteristics of career planners in upwardly mobile occupations. *Academy of Management Journal, 22*(3), 539-550.

Holland, J. (1973). *Making vocational choices: A theory of careers.* Upper Saddle River, NJ: Prentice Hall.

Laker, D. R., & Laker, R. (2007). The five-year resume: A career planning exercise. *Journal of Management Education, 13*(1), 128-141.

Noe, R. A. (1996). Is career management related to employee development and performance? *Journal of Organizational Behavior, 17*(2), 119-133.

O*Net Occupational Information Network. http://online.onetcenter.org/

Occupational Outlook Handbook. http://www.bls.gov/oco/

Orpen, C. (1994). The effects of organizational and individual career management on career success. *International Journal of Manpower, 15*(1), 27-37.

Experiential Exercises

CONDUCTING A TRAINING NEEDS ASSESSMENT

The first step in creating effective training programs is to determine what training employees need. Training Needs Assessment is the process of gathering data to determine what training needs employees have so that training can be developed to improve the effectiveness of employees and thereby help the organization meet its business objectives. There are four reasons why training needs assessment should be done before training programs are developed: (a) to identify specific problem areas in the organization so that the highest priority organizational problems requiring training solutions are addressed; (b) to obtain management support by making certain that the training directly contributes to the bottom line, that the training improves employee job performance; (c) to develop data for evaluation of the success of the training program, when the training has been completed; and (d) to determine the costs and benefits of training, because there are costs to leaving a training need unmet as well as benefits from improved job performance (Brown, 2002).

One outcome of doing a training-needs assessment is identification of gaps between the skills that employees have and the skills required for effective job performance. Another outcome is identification of performance problems that are not training needs, because job performance is a function of both job knowledge, skills, and work motivation (i.e., not every job performance problem has a training solution). There may be organizational practices or incentives that contribute to a lack of employee motivation, a problem that training cannot solve.

To Do

Conduct a training-needs assessment for an employee's job. Use the Training Needs Assessment Survey to identify where the employee has training needs. In pairs, each person should pick one of the following roles:

Employee: Help the manager identify your training needs in your current job. If you are not currently employed, use your most recent job. If you have never been employed, use student as your job.

Manager: Interview the employee to identify training needs in the current job. Ask the employee questions to identify the employee's current training needs. Use the list of management skills in the Training Needs Assessment Survey to get ideas for questions to ask the employee. Take notes on the knowledge, skills, and abilities that the employee identifies as needed in his or her job, and possible training needs, using the Training Needs Assessment Worksheet.

Training Needs Assessment Survey

Training Needs Assessment Survey—Leader Observation System	
Categories	*Behavioral Descriptors*
Planning and coordinating	• Setting goals and objectives • Defining tasks needed to accomplish goals • Scheduling employees, timetables • Assigning tasks and providing routine instructions • Coordinating activities to keep work running smoothly • Organizing the work
Staffing	• Developing job descriptions of position openings • Reviewing applications • Interviewing applicants • Hiring • Contacting applicants to inform them as to whether or not they have been hired • "Filling in" when needed
Training and developing	• Orienting employees, arranging for training seminars, and the like • Clarifying roles, duties, job descriptions • Coaching, acting as a mentor, "walking" subordinates through tasks • Helping subordinates with personal development plans

(Continued)

(Continued)

Decision making and problem solving	• Defining problems • Choosing between two or more alternatives or strategies • Handling day-to-day operational crises as they arise • Weighing tradeoffs, making cost and benefit analyses • Deciding what to do • Developing new procedures to increase efficiency
Processing paperwork	• Processing mail • Reading reports, emptying the in-box • Writing reports, memos, letters, etc. • Routine financial reporting and bookkeeping • General desk work
Exchanging routine information	• Answering routine procedural questions • Receiving and disseminating requested information • Conveying the results of meetings • Giving or receiving routine information over the phone or e-mail • Attending staff meetings of an informational nature (e.g., status updates, new company policies)
Monitoring and controlling performance	• Inspecting work • Walking around and checking things out • Monitoring performance data (e.g., computer printouts, production, financial reports) • Preventive maintenance
Motivating and reinforcing	• Allocating formal organizational rewards • Asking for input, participation • Conveying appreciation, compliments • Giving credit when due • Listening to suggestions • Giving feedback on positive performance • Increasing job challenges • Delegating responsibility and authority • Letting subordinates determine how to do their own work • Sticking up for the group to superiors and others, backing a subordinate
Disciplining and punishing	• Enforcing rules and policies • Nonverbal glaring, harassment • Demotion, firing, layoff • Any formal organizational reprimand or notice • "Chewing out" a subordinate, criticizing a subordinate • Giving feedback on negative performance
Interacting with others	• Public relations • Contacting customers • Contact with suppliers and vendors • External meetings • Community service activities

Managing conflict	• Managing interpersonal conflicts between subordinates or others • Appealing to higher authority to resolve a dispute • Appealing to third-party negotiators • Trying to get cooperation or consensus between conflicting parties • Attempting to resolve conflicts between a subordinate and oneself
Socializing and politicking	• Nonwork-related chit chat (e.g., family or personal matters) • Informal "joking around" • Discussing rumors, hearsay, grapevine • Complaining, griping, putting others down • Politicking, gamesmanship

SOURCE: Luthans, Rosenkrantz, and Hennessey (1985).

Training Needs Assessment Worksheet

Training Needs Assessment Worksheet	
Knowledge, Skill, Ability	*Training Need*

Resources

Brown, J. (2002). Training Needs Assessment: A must for developing an effective training program. *Public Personnel Management, 31*(4), 569-578.

Gorman, P., McDonald, B., Moore, R., Glassman, A., Takeuchi, L., & Henry, M. J. (2003). Custom needs assessment for strategic HR training: The Los Angeles County experience. *Public Personnel Management,* 32(4), 475-495.

Holton, E. F., III. (2000). Large-scale performance-driven training needs assessment. *Public Personnel Management,* 29(2), 249-267.

(Continued)

(Continued)

Luthans, F. (1988). Successful vs. effective real managers. *Academy of Management Executive*, 2(2), 127-132.

Moore, M. L., & Dutton, P. (1978). Training needs analysis: Review and critique. *Academy of Management Review*, 3(3), 532-545.

Patton, W. D., & Pratt, C. (2002). Assessing the training needs of high-potential managers. *Public Personnel Management*, 31(4), 465-484.

Roberson, L., Kulik, C. T., & Pepper, M. B. (2003). Using needs assessment to resolve controversies in diversity training design. *Group & Organization Management*, 28(1), 148-174.

Wircenski, J. L., Sullivan, R. L., & Moore, P. (1989). Assessing training needs at Texas Instruments. *Training & Development Journal*, 43(4), 61-63.

ASSESSMENT CENTER FOR MANAGEMENT DEVELOPMENT

The first Assessment Center in the United States was developed by the Office of Strategic Services (which later became the Central Intelligence Agency) to select spies (Office of Strategic Services, 1948). It was thought that a paper-and-pencil test would be inadequate for selecting people for such a high-risk job and that better prediction of job success would come from putting spy candidates in various situations to see how they would react. The Assessment Center included cognitive skills tests (e.g., Vocabulary Test, Otis Test of Mental Ability), biographical questionnaires (e.g., Health Questionnaire, Work Conditions Survey), personality tests (e.g., Sentence Completion Test, Projective Questionnaire), a variety of situational tests (e.g., Escaped Prisoner, Resourcefulness Test, Belongings Test), and more than 80 measurements of each candidate.

Some of the situational exercises had obvious content validity for the job of covert agent, and other exercises were designed to measure one or more of the performance dimensions without being typical covert agent situations. For example, the Escaped Prisoner test had content validity. Candidates had to interrogate an allied prisoner recently escaped from a prisoner of war camp to find out how many prisoners were detained in the camp, how many guards, and so on; intelligence gathering is an essential job task for a covert agent. On the other hand, in the Wall Problem, candidates had to work together to get every member of their group from one side of a wall to the other. This was a general test of teamwork and leadership in a leaderless group but not specific to the job of the covert agent. The performance dimensions that the Office of Strategic Services Assessment Center was designed to measure are shown in Table 7.2.

Table 7.2 Performance Dimensions: Office of Strategic Services Assessment Center

Motivation for assignment	War morale, interest in proposed job
Energy and initiative	Activity level, zest, effort, initiative
Effective intelligence	Ability to select strategic goals and the most efficient means of attaining them; quick and practical thought—resourcefulness, originality, good judgment—in dealing with things, people, or ideas
Emotional stability	Ability to govern disturbing emotions, steadiness and endurance under pressure, snafu tolerance, freedom from neurotic tendencies
Social relations	Ability to get along well with other people, good will, team play, tact, freedom from disturbing prejudices, freedom from annoying traits
Leadership	Social initiative, ability to evoke cooperation, organizing and administering ability, acceptance of responsibility
Security	Ability to keep secrets; caution, discretion, ability to bluff and mislead

Although assessment centers are most often used for selection, they can also be used for management development (Jones & Whitmore, 1995). Instead of assessing a number of candidates for management positions for the purpose of making a selection decision, the assessors look for each candidate's strengths and weaknesses. Identified weaknesses are areas for management development experiences, and strengths are characteristics that the candidate can build on throughout his or her career.

To Do

This exercise is done in teams of about six people. Each team will create an assessment center that the people in the other teams will be candidates in. The purpose of this assessment center is management development, so the focus is on identifying the strengths and weaknesses of each candidate (rather than trying to identify which candidates to hire or promote). Create two exercises, one standard assessment center exercise (in-basket, management presentation, a selection interview, a performance appraisal interview, a leaderless group discussion) and one nonstandard exercise. The assessment center must fit into the allotted time. You may have as many assessors per exercise as you want (you must have at least one; two is better).

(Continued)

(Continued)

One person must serve as the assessment center administrator, to keep the assessment center running smoothly and be the contact person for the instructor. For each exercise, candidates must be given oral or written feedback, which includes an overall assessment of their performance in the exercise and identification of one strength and one weakness. Design the assessment center for the job of assistant director of media relations.

Assistant Director of Media Relations

Job description: Assist the media relations director in planning and implementing strategic public and media relations plans for the university. Write and disseminate press releases, serve on the campus emergency response team, develop internal and external communication plans, write talking points, speeches and other communication materials, assist with special university projects and events, respond to media inquiries, and act as a university spokesperson.

Job specification: Bachelor's degree in communications, marketing or public relations, or an equivalent combination of education and/or experience. Minimum 4 years experience in media relations, strategic communications, crisis management, or a combination of these areas. Strategic thinking and the ability to handle multiple projects simultaneously. Ability to work independently and as part of a team. Excellent organizational and analytical skills. Excellent oral and written communication skills. Ability to communicate effectively with others.

A key component of an assessment center is the schedule, so that assessors and candidates know where they are supposed to be and what they are supposed to be doing. For a two-exercise assessment center with exercises of approximately the same time allotment, the schedule is simple. When the exercises use differing amounts of time, the schedule becomes more complicated. A simple two-exercise assessment center with equal time allotments looks like Table 7.3.

Table 7.3 Two-Exercise Assessment Center With Equal Time Allotments

Time	*Exercise*	*Candidates*	*Assessors*
1:00-1:20 p.m.	In-Basket	#1, #3, #5, #7, #9	A, B, C, D
	Puzzle Exercise	#2, #4, #6, #8, #10	E, F, G, H
1:20-1:30 p.m.	Break	ALL	ALL
1:30-1:50 p.m.	Puzzle Exercise	#1, #3, #5, #7, #9	E, F, G, H
	In-Basket	#2, #4, #6, #8, #10	A, B, C, D

You must prepare all of the materials that the candidates will need to do the exercises and that the assessors will need to evaluate the candidates, including a schedule so that assessors and candidates know where they are supposed to be, what they are supposed to be doing, and at what times. If the exercise requires a role player (e.g., an applicant to interview for a Selection Interview exercise), a description of the role needs to be written. A copy of all of the exercise materials (Exercises, Instructions for Candidates, Instructions for Assessors, Instructions for Role Players, and the Schedule) must be handed in to the instructor at the beginning of class.

Resources

Barclay, L. A., & York, K. M. (1999). Electronic communication skills in the classroom: An e-mail in-basket exercise. *Journal of Education for Business, 74*(4), 249-253.

Bray, D. W., & Grant, D. L. (1966). The assessment center in the measurement of potential for business management. *Psychological Monographs, 80*(17, whole no. 625), 27.

Briscoe, D. R. (1997). Assessment centers: Cross-cultural and cross-national issues. *Journal of Social Behavior and Personality, 12*(5), 261-270.

Byham, W. C. (1980). The Assessment Center as an aid in management development. *Training & Development Journal, 34*(6), 24-36.

Engelbrecht, A. S., & Fischer, H. (1995). The managerial performance implications of a developmental assessment center process. *Human Relations, 48*(4), 387-404.

Gaugler, B. B., Rosenthal, D. B., Thoron, G. C., III., & Bentson, B. (1987). Meta-analysis of assessment center validity. *Journal of Applied Psychology, 72*(3), 493-511.

Handler, L. (2001). Assessment of Men: Personality assessment goes to war by the Office of Strategic Services assessment staff. *Journal of Personality Assessment, 76*(3), 558–578.

Huck, J. R., & Bray, D. W. (1976). Management assessment-center evaluations and subsequent job-performance of white and black females. *Personnel Psychology, 29*(1), 13-30.

Jansen, P. G. W., & Vinkenburg, C. J. (2006). Predicting management career success from assessment center data: A longitudinal study. *Journal of Vocational Behavior, 68*(2), 253-266.

Jones, R. G., & Whitmore, M. D. (1995). Evaluating developmental assessment centers as interventions. *Personnel Psychology, 48*(2), 377-388.

Office of Strategic Services. (1948). *Assessment of men: Selection of personnel for the Office of Strategic Services.* New York: Rinehart.

Pearson, M. M., Barnes, J. W., & Onken, M. H. (2006). Development of a computerized in-basket exercise for the classroom: A sales management example. *Journal of Marketing Education, 28*(3), 227-236.

Shore, T. H., Tashchian, A., & Adams, J. S. (1997). The role of gender in a developmental assessment center. *Journal of Social Behavior and Personality, 12*(5), 191-203.

Thornton, G. C., & Byham, W. C. (1982). *Assessment centers and managerial performance.* New York: Academic Press.

Waldman, D. A., & Korbar, T. (2004). Student Assessment Center performance in the prediction of early career success. *Academy of Management Learning & Education, 3*(2), 151-167.

York, K. M. (1995). Experiential and creative management exercises using an assessment center. *Journal of Education for Business, 70*(3), 141-145.

DEALING WITH A PLATEAUED EMPLOYEE

Career plateauing occurs when employees reach a point in their career where the likelihood of additional promotion is very low (Ference, Stoner, & Warren, 1977; Veiga, 1981). Career plateauing may also result when there is a lack of potential for career movement generally, including when the likelihood of receiving further assignments of increased responsibility is low (Feldman & Weitz, 1988). Career plateaus are a normal result in hierarchical organizations; with fewer and fewer positions going up the organizational ladder, almost all employees will reach positions from which further promotions are unlikely. There are other factors that contribute to career plateauing, including population demographics, economic growth, and type of organization (Tan & Salomone, 1994).

For employees who view promotions as the measure of success at work, career plateauing can have a negative impact on their job satisfaction, work motivation, and job performance. In addition to job satisfaction, career plateauing can also have an impact on career satisfaction and turnover intentions (Lee, 2003) and may be more common for minority employees (Greenhaus, Parasuraman, & Wormley, 1990). But the attitudes and behaviors of plateaued managers can be more positive, if their job is richer and offers an opportunity to participate in decision making (Tremblay & Roger, 2004), and if they have professional mentors (de Janasz, Sullivan, & Whiting, 2003).

Managers need to understand what career plateauing is for two reasons. First, because most of their employees will reach a point in their career where the chances for promotion are low, they will need to work with each employee to find ways to maintain the employee's interest in the job and satisfactory levels of job performance. Second, managers need to understand career plateauing, because it is likely to happen to every employee in the organization, including themselves.

To Do

In pairs, each person should pick the employee or the manager role. The manager will conduct a career planning session with a plateaued employee. The Career Plateauing Guide can be used to structure the session with the employee. The manager should try to help the employee understand the nature of career plateauing and develop a plan to deal with the situation.

Employee: You have been in your current position for a number of years. You have been hoping for a promotion when the next retirement creates an opening. Your job performance has always been excellent, so you think your chances of getting promoted are good.

Manager: The employee has been in the current position for a number of years and his or her job performance has always been excellent. You are aware that the employee has been expecting to get a promotion, but there are at least three other employees that are more likely to get the promotion because of their skills and experience.

Career Plateauing Guide

Career Plateauing Guide	
Educate	• Explain to the employee what career plateauing is and why it happens. • Remove the stigma of career plateauing by explaining that it is likely to affect nearly every employee.

Career Plateauing Guide	
Inform	• Give the employee information and assistance about second-career development and career changes. • Explain how careers can be spent in one organization (company career) or in a sequence of organizations (individual career). • Identify organizational rewards and recognition for exceptional job performance other than raises and promotions. • Identify other kinds of work experiences that are available, such as lateral moves and special projects, to maintain interest in the job and build knowledge and skills.
Plan	• Discourage workaholic lifestyles; emphasize high productivity, not long work hours. • Help the employee to find additional career development experiences. • Encourage the employee to take the initiative to bring to you ideas about how his or her knowledge and skills might be used more effectively, in the current job and other jobs. • Work with the employee to reassess his or her career goals, identify alternate career paths, and make a career plan.

Resources

Appelbaum, S. H., & Finestone, D. (1994). Revisiting career plateauing: Same old problems—Avant-garde solutions. *Journal of Managerial Psychology, 9*(5), 12-21.

de Janasz, S. C., Sullivan, S. E., & Whiting, V. (2003). Mentor networks and career success: Lessons for turbulent times. *Academy of Management Executive, 17*(4), 78-91.

Feldman, D. C., & Weitz, B. A. (1988). Career plateaus reconsidered. *Journal of Management, 14*(1), 69-80.

Ference, T. P., Stoner, J. A. F., & Warren, E. K. (1977). Managing the career plateau. *Academy of Management Review, 2*(4), 602-612.

Greenhaus, J. H., Parasuraman, S., & Wormley, W. M. (1990). Effects of race on organizational experiences, job performance evaluations, and career outcomes. *Academy of Management Journal, 33*(11), 64-86.

Hall, D. T. (1985). Project work as an antidote to career plateauing in a declining engineering organization. *Human Resource Management, 24*(3), 271-292.

Lee, P. C. B. (2003). Going beyond career plateau: Using professional plateau to account for work outcomes. *Journal of Management Development, 22*(5/6), 538-551.

Nachbagauer, A. G. M., & Riedl, G. (2002). Effects of concepts of career plateaus on performance, work satisfaction and commitment. *International Journal of Manpower, 23*(8), 716-736.

Tan, C. S., & Salomone, P. R. (1994). Understanding career plateauing: Implications for counseling. *Career Development Quarterly, 42*(4), 291-302.

Tremblay, M., & Roger, A. (2004). Career plateauing reactions: The moderating role of job scope, role ambiguity and participation among Canadian managers. *International Journal of Human Resource Management, 15*(6), 996-1017.

Veiga, J. F. (1981). Plateaued versus nonplateaued managers: Career patterns, attitudes, and path potential. *Academy of Management Journal, 24*(3), 566-578.

Creative Exercises

DEVELOPING MANAGEMENT TALENT

According to survey results (Becker et al., 2001), organizations with high HRM quality have a higher percentage of employees in a formal plan for development, and both new and experienced employees spend more hours in training each year. Investing in employee development means increasing the value of the organization's human resources. By improving individual capabilities, organizational capabilities are also improved. And as organizations become flatter, with fewer levels between the top and the bottom and more management responsibilities throughout the organization, investments in developing the management skills of all employees becomes even more important.

Some organizations use coaching to develop skills in strategic thinking, vision, creativity, innovation, decisiveness, and motivating others, especially to high-potential employees early in the development process (Pomeroy, 2006; Romans, 2006). Rather than putting people in management positions and expecting them to develop knowledge and skills on their own, organizations can systematically develop their employees' talents through a combination of succession planning and management development to create a long-term process for managing the talent roster across the organization (Conger & Fulmer, 2003).

Coaching is a combination of training and feedback given to employees, where the employee can learn by doing. The purpose of coaching is to have a more experienced employee show a less experienced employee how to do better. Woodruff (2006) calls coaching a powerful catalyst for transforming performance, because coaching is not just a remedial intervention for poor performers; it is a way to help any employee to perform better. A survey conducted by the Chartered Institute of Personnel and Development found that 88% of organizations expect their line managers to coach as part of their day-to-day job (Horner, 2006).

To Do

Your team is responsible for developing the talent of the most recent winner of a television reality show game-show singing contest. This performer has raw talent but does not have much experience, and there are many aspects of show business that this performer needs to learn to successfully manage a career. Your task is to develop a management development program to teach this singer to become a pop star. Choose from one of the development experiences described below and create the content of a management development experience. Prepare to pitch your idea in a 5-min. presentation.

Like most performers who dream of becoming stars, this performer's primary focus is on the music, so one can expect a short attention span for anything not directly related to performing. Therefore, the best management development experiences will have these characteristics:

1. Clear statement of purpose (and payoff), so the performer knows what to expect from the developmental experience.
2. An opportunity to immediately apply what has been learned, in a role play or experiential exercise.
3. Use of real-life examples to illustrate how performers went from unrecognized obscurity to fame and fortune, or from fame and fortune to obscurity (or both).

Development Experiences

Managing the money. The money flows in, the money flows out; who knows where the money goes? Living large and retirement planning.

Breaking in a new manager. How to handle the transition, when artistic differences lead to the firing of the old manager and the hiring of a new manager.

Creating a cost-efficient entourage. The entourage should create the desired image, at a reasonable price. How to distinguish between value-added expenses and needless cost overruns.

How to identify bad influences. There is only one thing worse than bad publicity, and that is no publicity. Staying edgy without falling from grace.

Making a good red-carpet impression. Building your image; face and name recognition. Standing out in a crowd of people trying to stand out in a crowd.

Dealing with local law enforcement. Making all of your interactions with local police positive and newsworthy. The art of persuading the police to use their discretion.

Providing photo opportunities for the paparazzi. Balancing the need for publicity with the desire for privacy, building working relationships with people who can positively or negatively affect your career.

Doing "entertainment news" interviews. Answering and not answering lite-news questions. How to get the most out of a promotional tour: plugging albums, tour dates, and yourself.

Negotiating and renegotiating contracts. Maximizing current income against expectations of future income, on the way up and on the way down.

Creating your distinctive style. All about the look; clothing, hair, makeup, fitness, and accessories.

(Continued)

(Continued)

Resources

Atchison, D. (Director). (2006). *Akeelah and the bee.* [Motion picture]. Los Angeles, CA: Lion's Gate.

Aversano, S. (Producer), & Linklater, R. (Director). (2003). *School of rock.* [Motion picture]. Hollywood, CA: Paramount.

Becker, B. E., Huselid, M. A., & Ulrich, D. (2001). *The HR Scorecard: Linking people, strategy and performance.* Boston: Harvard Business School Press.

Conger, J. A., & Fulmer, R. M. (2003). Developing your leadership pipeline. *Harvard Business Review, 81*(12), 76-84.

Di Bergi, M. (Producer), & Reiner, R. (Director). (2000). *This is Spinal Tap.* [Motion picture]. Los Angeles, CA: MGM Home Entertainment.

Grazer, B., & Hanson, C. (Producers). (2002). *8 mile.* (2002). [Motion picture]. Universal City, CA: Universal Studios.

Horner, C. (2006). Coaching for the better. *Training & Development Methods,* 20(4), 535-539.

Johnson, J. (2004). Leveraging leadership. *Training, 41*(1), 20-21.

Peters, J. (Producer), & Pierson, F. (Director). (1983). *A star is born.* [Motion picture]. Burbank, CA: Warner Home Video.

Pomeroy, A. (2006). Earlier coaching pays dividends now and in the future. *HRMagazine, 51*(9), 16.

Romans, J. (2006). Developing high-potential talent at Hughes Supply. *Strategic HR Review,* 5(3), 32-35.

Woodruff, C. (2006). Coaching: A powerful catalyst for transforming performance. *Training & Development Methods,* 20(2), 401-406.

CREATING TEAM-BUILDING EXERCISES

Modern organizations are commonly structured around teams, so that for employees in these organizations, most of their work is done in teams. Teams are the fundamental learning unit in organizations. In teams, employees share knowledge and experience and learn from each other, building individual and organizational capability. For example, teams at Whole Foods are structured around products (Produce, Grocery, Prepared Foods), and at the San Diego Zoo, teams are structured around Bioclimatic Zones (Asian Rain Forest, Gorilla Tropics). Organizational learning requires both individuals' competence and organizational culture to work hand in hand, which may require efforts to attain a high level of commitment, trust, and understanding among employees (Yeo, 2005).

When teams are first formed, the team members may not all know each other. Before beginning work, it is useful for team members to build their relationships. Before becoming a fully functioning team, all teams go through five stages of group development: Forming, Storming, Norming, Performing, and Adjourning (Tuckman & Jensen, 1977). Team-building exercises are designed to help the team move through the early stages of group development and arrive at the performing stage. Team-building exercises can be used when a group first forms or as a re-energizer when the team is immersed in a difficult task or experiencing counterproductive conflict among team members. A team-building exercise gives the team a common experience to help build cohesion.

At Certicom, a high-tech provider of cryptography for secure devices and software, team-building activities are part of a total rewards strategy. The team-building activities help create a positive working environment and team atmosphere (Grant, 2005). Based on field interviews with software testing professionals, Cohen, Birkin, Garfield, and Webb (2004) have suggested that team-building activities in conflict handling can be used to improve the software development process. At their European strategy launch, StorageTek (an international provider of data storage and network solutions) used a team-building exercise in which multiple teams each painted one part of a picture. The teams had to interact to match the correct colors and make sure that their part of the picture aligned with the others around it; these parts eventually became part of the "big picture" (Kirby, 2003).

To Do

In teams of four to six members, create an original team-building exercise for the people in the other teams. Although the content of the exercise may vary, the purpose is to improve the working relationships of the people in the team. The exercise should have the following elements:

- Simple directions—simple to explain, simple to understand;
- Minimal equipment, minimal set-up time;
- Difficult enough to be interesting, easy enough for most teams to be successful; and
- A postexercise debriefing to tell team members why they were doing what they were doing.

Resources

Berg, P. (Director), & Aaron, D. (Writer). (2004). *Friday night lights.* [Motion picture]. Universal City, CA: Universal Studios.

Cohen, C. F., Birkin, S. J., Garfield, M. J., & Webb, H. W. (2004). Managing conflict in software testing. *Communications of the Association for Computing Machinery, 47*(1), 76-81.

Fishman, C. (1996, April). Whole Foods is all teams. *Fast Company.* http://www.fastcompany.com/online/02/team1.html

Glines, D. (1994). Do you work in a zoo? *Executive Excellence, 11*(10), 12-13.

Grant, J. (2005). Creating a team atmosphere helps Certicom foster recognition. *Canadian HR Reporter, 18*(1), 13-14.

(Continued)

(Continued)

Kirby, A. (2003). StorageTek expands its employees' horizons. *Training & Management Development Methods, 17*(4), 961-963.

Martin, A. (2006). The campus information game. *Simulation & Gaming, 37*(1), 124-133.

Milestone, L. (Producer and Director). (1960). *Ocean's eleven.* [Motion picture]. Burbank, CA: Warner Home Video.

Miller, B. C. (2007a). Quick activities to improve your team: How to run a successful team-building activity. *Journal for Quality and Participation, 30*(3), 28-32.

Miller, B. C. (2007b). Quick activities to improve your team: Improve performance in under 15 minutes. *Journal for Quality and Participation, 30*(4), 29-30.

Page, D., & Donelan, J. G. (2003). Team-building tools for students. *Journal of Education for Business, 78*(3), 125-128.

Senge, P. M. (1990). *The fifth discipline: The art and practice of the learning organization.* New York: Doubleday/Currency.

Tuckman, B. W., & Jensen, A. C. (1977). Stages of small-group development revisited. *Group & Organization Studies, 2*(4), 419-427.

Watkins, T., Young, M., Johnsen, T., Howard, T., & Hanbery, G. (1997). Recycling: A structured student exercise. *Journal of Management Education, 21*(2), 244-254.

Woodward, N. H. (2006). Make the most of team building. *HR Magazine, 51*(9), 72-76.

Yeo, R. K. (2005). Revisiting the roots of the learning organization: A synthesis of the learning organization literature. *The Learning Organization, 12*(4), 368-382.

8 Compensation and Benefits

Strategic Objective

One of the most important HRM functions is compensation systems. Compensation has a direct impact on recruitment, selection, and retention. If an organization is paying below what the market is paying for jobs, it will be more difficult to attract applicants to apply for job vacancies, and it will be difficult to retain satisfactory performers if they can get paid more for the same work at another organization. Paying below the market also means that the quality of the applicant pool will be less than if the organization is paying at or above the market; and with fewer applicants, the organization cannot be as selective when making hiring decisions. Creating pay scales is an ongoing process, requiring constant monitoring of what the market is paying and what the organization is paying. To track changes in the market rates for jobs, organizations may use salary survey data or share salary information with other organizations, even competitors.

Jobs that experience a sudden increase in demand relative to supply will see market rates for those jobs increase. Changes in demand for some jobs may cause the wages offered to newly hired employees to be nearly the same as the wages paid to current employees, a situation called "salary compression" (Duncan, Krall, Maxcy, & Prus, 2004). Salary compression may be the source of dissatisfaction with pay among current employees. Large changes in demand may cause the wages offered to newly hired employees to be greater than what current employees are earning, a situation called "salary inversion." Salary compression and salary inversion, especially in academic organizations (where salary information is more commonly available), has sometimes been identified as a major contributor to higher turnover and lower productivity (Jennings & McLaughlin, 1997). When current employees see newly hired employees being paid more than they are for the same job, they may be motivated to become newly hired employees at another organization to get the higher "going rate." The effect of this is to create even more demand, a positive feedback loop. Organizations may react to salary inversion by making market adjustments for current employees. Paying current employees more, to be more in alignment with what the market is paying, may be cheaper than losing a satisfactory performer who can find better pay elsewhere, plus the cost to fill the a vacant position.

For a compensation plan to be effective, it must be fair in a number of ways. It must meet minimum wage levels for jobs where the Fair Labor Standard's Act or state minimum wage laws apply. According to the Equal Pay Act, men and women doing the same job should get paid the same, except for differences due to a seniority system, a merit system, a system that measures earnings by quantity or quality of production, or some other differential based on any other factor other than sex. Organizations must make a decision to pay at, above, or below the market for jobs (external competitiveness) and pay different people differently based on what they do, with employees doing "more difficult" jobs—however that is defined—getting paid more (internal equity).

Paying different jobs differently based on the tasks performed is one approach. Another approach is to focus on the knowledge, skills, abilities, and experience of the employee performing the job—paying the person, not the job (Lawler, 1992, 2000). This approach recognizes that different people doing the same job can be different, because they have different skills. A skill-based compensation system gives employees incentives to acquire new skills. What Worley and Lawler (2006) call "built-to-change organizations" use person-based pay to encourage current performance and change to adapt to changing conditions. In work environments with changing task assignments, paying the person rather than the job is a more effective approach for retaining skilled people. Based on data collected over 37 months, Murray and Gerhart (1998) found that a skill-based pay program at a component assembly plant resulted in greater productivity, lower labor cost per part, and a reduced scrap rate.

Organizational rewards drive organizational behavior, so performance-driven organizations must create reward systems that link employee contributions to organizational results and also align closely with the organization's strategic goals (Heneman & Dixon, 2001; Stiffler, 2006). When organizations reward one thing but expect another, they should not be surprised when they get what they reward (Kerr, 1995).

Strategic Issues in HRM

A FAIR DAY'S WORK FOR A FAIR DAY'S PAY

How much a job should be paid is a difficult question for any organization to answer, but it is a critical question for the effective management of human resources and a good illustration of the basic idea that bad HRM has costs to the organization. On the one hand, if an organization systematically pays more for jobs than what other organizations are paying, it will have higher labor costs than its competitors and perhaps be less profitable. But it will make it easier to recruit and retain employees, because pay is one factor that affects applicants' and employees' decisions to accept or stay in a job. On the other hand, if an organization systematically pays less for jobs than what other organizations are paying, the organization will have lower labor costs, which may be essential to its survival if it is a newer or smaller organization, but it will also make it harder to recruit and retain employees, because employees can get paid more at another organization for the same work.

Some organizations may make a strategic decision to pay more than what the market is paying, to attract "the best and the brightest," especially in a tight labor market. To become or remain the premier transportation manufacturer, an organization might choose to pay significantly above the market for engineering jobs, based on the idea that the organization's continued success depends on attracting and retaining the best engineering talent. Organizations that cannot afford to pay what the market is paying must find other ways to attract applicants (e.g., the career development benefits of being in on the ground floor, the offer of an equity stake in the company, or the challenge of taking on "the big guys"). Paying employees fairly based on what other organizations are paying is the concept of external competitiveness.

Different jobs in the organization require different levels of knowledge and skills and have different requirements in supervising workers, handling money, or dealing with the consequences of error. To systematically pay employees fairly within organizations requires a thorough analysis of the jobs within the organization (task requirements and worker requirements) and a list of the compensable factors that the organization is willing to pay more for. Jobs that have more of the compensable factors should be paid more than jobs that have less of the compensable factors. Systematically paying different employees differently based on what they do in their jobs is the concept of internal equity.

To illustrate the concept of internal equity, consider the jobs of licensed practical nurse and registered nurse. Licensed practical nurses earn on average $36,210 per year, and registered nurses earn on average

$56,880 (Bureau of Labor Statistics, 2005d). The jobs are very different from each other. According to O*Net, a licensed practical nurses must

> care for ill, injured, convalescent, or disabled persons in hospitals, nursing homes, clinics, private homes, group homes, and similar institutions. May work under the supervision of a registered nurse. Licensing required.

A registered nurse must, again according to O*Net

> assess patient health problems and needs, develop and implement nursing care plans, and maintain medical records; administer nursing care to ill, injured, convalescent, or disabled patients; may advise patients on health maintenance and disease prevention or provide case management. Licensing or registration required. Includes advance practice nurses such as: nurse practitioners, clinical nurse specialists, certified nurse midwives, and certified registered nurse anesthetists. Advanced practice nursing is practiced by RNs who have specialized formal, post-basic education and who function in highly autonomous and specialized roles.

A salary survey can show concepts of both external competitiveness and internal equity. In Table 8.1 are the mean salaries for three ranks of university professors at three different types of educational institutions representing three different (although somewhat overlapping) labor markets. External competitiveness can be seen by comparing the schools by category. Category I schools recruit faculty from the same labor market, because they have significant doctoral programs, a minimum of 30 doctoral-level degrees per year in three or more unrelated disciplines. Category IIA and IIB recruit from a different labor market, because they are primarily focused on undergraduate education. The mean salaries for the Category IIA and IIB schools are similar for all three professor ranks and are substantially lower than the mean salaries for the Category I schools for all three ranks. Internal equity can be seen by comparing across the three professor ranks. In every school, assistant professors are paid the least, followed by tenured associate professors and then full professors, who are paid the most.

Another aspect of fairness in pay is the psychological contract between the employee and the organization (King & Bu, 2005; Michael, 2001; Robinson, Kraatz, & Rousseau, 1994). A psychological contract is an individual belief in reciprocal obligations between employees and employers and comes in two types: relational obligations of exchanging job security for loyalty and a minimum length of stay, and transactional obligations of high pay and career advancement in exchange for hard work (Rousseau, 1990). Employees, and applicants before they accept a job offer, have an idea about what is a fair day's work for a fair day's pay. Employees judge how hard they should be expected to work for how much

Table 8.1 Faculty Salaries for Minnesota Colleges and Universities

College/University (Minnesota)	*Category*	*Professor*	*Associate*	*Assistant*
Augsburg College	IIB	$67,700	$54,500	$47,800
Bemidji State University	IIB	$74,700	$60,000	$50,500
Bethel University	IIB	$67,900	$58,500	$51,300
Carleton College	IIB	$105,000	$74,600	$65,700
College of Saint Benedict	IIB	$76,200	$61,400	$52,700
College of St. Scholastica	IIB	$73,200	$63,100	$52,800
Concordia College–Morehead	IIB	$72,000	$57,000	$49,600
Gustavus Adolphus	IIB	$76,100	$60,500	$52,700
Macalester College	IIB	$103,000	$76,300	$61,800
Minneapolis College of Art & Design	IIB	$68,400	$57,500	$49,000
Northwestern College	IIB	$60,800	$53,400	$46,500
Saint John's University	IIB	$76,300	$61,100	$50,200
Southwest Minnesota State University	IIB	$77,100	$63,300	$55,700
St. Olaf College	IIB	$81,900	$65,300	$52,800
University of Minnesota–Crookston	IIB	$76,000	$59,800	$53,900
University of Minnesota–Morris	IIB	$73,600	$59,700	$48,200
Bethel University	IIA	$67,900	$58,500	$51,300
College of St. Catherine	IIA	$71,500	$56,800	$48,000
Hamline University	IIA	$69,900	$54,100	$48,600
Metropolitan State University	IIA	$78,500	$61,300	$55,300
Minnesota State University–Mankato	IIA	$79,300	$63,700	$55,500
Minnesota State University–Moorhead	IIA	$75,600	$59,200	$52,200

(Continued)

Table 8.1 (Continued)

College/University (Minnesota)	*Category*	*Professor*	*Associate*	*Assistant*
Saint Mary's University of Minnesota	IIA	$65,200	$52,500	$43,400
St. Cloud State University	IIA	$76,300	$62,200	$54,800
University of Minnesota–Duluth	IIA	$83,400	$67,400	$53,600
Winona State University	IIA	$76,600	$59,300	$51,800
University of Minnesota–Twin Cities	I	$116,600	$80,600	$69,400
University of St. Thomas	I	$83,600	$69,100	$61,400
Means:	IIB	$76,869	$61,625	$52,575
Means:	IIA	$74,420	$59,500	$51,450
Means:	I	$100,100	$74,850	$65,400

SOURCE: American Association University Professors, 2005.

NOTE: Category IIB (Baccaulaureate) = Institutions characterized by their primary emphasis on general undergraduate baccalaureate-level education and not significantly engaged in postbacculaureate education; Category IIA (Master's) = Institutions characterized by diverse postbaccalaureate programs (including first professional), but not engaged in significant doctoral-level education; Category I (Doctoral) = Institutions characterized by a significant level and breadth of activity in a commitment to doctoral-level education.

they are being paid. If they are paid less than the "fair" amount, they may be demotivated and work less hard to establish an equitable amount of work for their pay. Systematically paying employees as low as the market will bear will result in the lowest possible amount of work effort to maintain employment—a race to the bottom.

The idea of fairness in pay also underlies the minimum wage (i.e., to pay less for a job than the minimum wage is legally defined as unfairly low). Someone working full-time and paid the minimum wage could make enough money to "get by." However, the minimum wage has not always kept pace with inflation during the past few decades. In 1968, the minimum wage (adjusted for inflation in 2004 dollars) was $8.78 per hour; but by 2005, the minimum wage of $5.15 per hour was 41% less than it was in 1968 (Muilenburg & Singh, 2007). The law's expectation is that the minimum wage is paid to workers in jobs with low knowledge and skill requirements and that few people will long remain at the minimum wage as they gain in knowledge and skills from working. Where there are labor shortages, employers offering only the minimum wage for jobs may find no applicants, and starting wage rates for entry-level jobs with no skill or experience requirements may be above the minimum wage.

Another concept about fair pay is that employees should be paid enough to support themselves and a family (i.e., to be fair, pay must be enough to be a "living wage"). Living wage levels are often set to what is needed for a family with one full-time, year-round worker to reach the federal poverty line; therefore, the living wage is based on a self-sufficiency standard. In the United States, about 36 million, or 12% of all individuals, earn less than $9 per hour and live below the federal poverty level (Muilenberg & Singh, 2007). The Economic Policy Institute has suggested that a wage sufficient to allow subsistence plus some room for savings would be $15 to $20 per hour, with regional variations (Boushey, Brocht, Gundersen, & Bernstein, 2001). As of 2002, living wage ordinances have been passed in New York City, Jersey City, Milwaukee, and Santa Clara County, California—nearly 100 living wage ordinances in all (Luce, 2002; Noell, 2006). The average living wage of these ordinances was $8.94 with benefits or $10.44 without (Luce, 2002).

Strategic Questions

1. Under what circumstances would it make sense for an organization to pay above the market for some (or all) jobs in the organization?
2. What are the consequences to the organization of paying employees with no data on what the market is paying for those jobs?
3. What are the consequences to the organization of paying employees differently for different jobs, with no data on how the jobs differ from each other in knowledge, skills, and tasks?
4. What are the contents of a newly hired employee's psychological contract with the employer? What are the contents of a long-time employee's psychological contract with the employer? What are the contents of an employee's psychological contract with the employer after a major downsizing?
5. Are there any cities in your state with Living Wage ordinances? What percentage of the minimum wage is the Living Wage? What percentage of the poverty rate is the Living Wage?
6. What is the economic impact of Living Wage ordinances on organizations? Will some organizations be at a competitive disadvantage because of such ordinances?

(Continued)

(Continued)

Resources

Adams, S., & Neumark, D. (2005). Living Wage effects: New and improved evidence. *Economic Development Quarterly, 19*(1), 80-102.

American Association of University Professors. (2005). The annual report on the economic status of the profession 2005-2006. *Academe, 93*(2), 21-105.

Boushey, H., Brocht, C., Gundersen, B., & Bernstein, J. (2001). *Hardships in America: The real story of working families.* Washington, DC: Economic Policy Institute.

Bureau of Labor Statistics. (2005). *May 2005 national occupational employment and wage estimates: United States.* http://www.bls.gov/oes/current/oes_nat.htm#b31-0000

Buss, J. A., & Romeo, A. (2006). The changing employment situation in some cities with Living Wage ordinances. *Review of Social Economy, 64*(3), 349-367.

De Meuse, K. P., Bergman, T. J., & Lester, S. W. (2001). An investigation of the relational component of the psychological contract across time, generation, and employment status. *Journal of Managerial Issues, 13*(1), 102-118.

De Pelsmacker, P., Driesen, L., & Rayp, G. (2005). Do consumers care about ethics? Willingness to pay for fair-trade coffee. *Journal of Consumer Affairs, 39*(2), 363-385.

Ehrenreich, B. (2001). *Nickel and dimed: On (not) getting by in America.* New York: Metropolitan Books.

King, R. C., & Bu, N. (2005). Perceptions of the mutual obligations between employees and employers: A comparative study of new generation IT professionals in China and the United States. *International Journal of Human Resource Management, 16*(1), 46-64.

Luce, S. (2002). "The full fruits of our labor": The rebirth of the Living Wage movement. *Labor History, 43*(4), 401-409.

Michael, J. H. (2001). Perceived obligations of future forest industry employees: A psychological contracts perspective. *Forest Products Journal, 51*(10), 39-46.

Muilenburg, K., & Singh, G. (2007). The modern Living Wage movement. *Compensation and Benefits Review, 39*(1), 21-28.

Noell, E. S. (2006). Smith and a living wage: Competition, economic compulsion, and the Scholastic legacy. *History of Political Economy, 38*(1), 151-174.

Pollin, R. (2005). Evaluating Living Wage laws in the United States: Good intentions and economic reality in conflict? *Economic Development Quarterly, 19*(1), 3-24.

Reynolds, D., & Vortkamp, J. (2005). The effect of Detroit's Living Wage law on nonprofit organizations. *Economic Development Quarterly, 19*(1), 45-61.

Robinson, S., Kraatz, M. S., & Rousseau, D. M. (1994). Changing obligations and the psychological contract: A longitudinal study. *Academy of Management Journal, 37*(1), 137-152.

Rousseau, D. M. (1990). New hire perceptions of their own and their employer's obligations: A study of psychological contracts. *Journal of Organizational Behavior, 11*(5), 389-409.

Singh, R. (1998). Redefining psychological contracts with the U.S. work force: A critical task for strategic human resource management planners in the 1990's. *Human Resource Management, 37*(1), 61-69.

Sparrow, P. R. (1996). Transitions in the psychological contract: Some evidence from the banking sector. *Human Resource Management Journal, 6*(4), 75-92.

U.S. Department of Labor. *Minimum wage poster.* http://www.dol.gov/esa/whd/regs/compliance/posters/flsa.htm

PAY SECRECY

Some organizations make pay information public or publicly available (e.g., sports teams, state-supported universities, and politicians). According to the Congressional Research Service (2007), the president of the United States is paid $400,000, the vice president $215,700, the speaker of the House of Representatives $212,100, and the chief justice of the Supreme Court $215,700. Politicians often set their own pay, and to give themselves a raise, they must overcome their reluctance to see the pay increases they decide to give themselves publicly reported in the media.

Other organizations impose pay secrecy (not making pay information public) with a policy against employees sharing pay information (see *National Labor Relations Board v. Main Street Terrace Center*, 2000). Burroughs (1982) outlined four different levels of pay openness:

1. Type Red: no information is made available to employees except their own pay;
2. Type Orange: information on factors determining pay or pay ranges and medians for certain jobs is made available;
3. Type Yellow: information about size of raises and who gets them is made available; and
4. Type Green: information on specific pay levels for specific individuals is made available.

For example, an organization might have a merit pay system with annual raise letters sent to all employees, listing the factors considered in making the raise decisions and identifying the different percentage merit raises and how many employees were in each level, without identifying specific individuals and their new salaries. This "Yellow" pay policy would become "Green" if salary information identifying specific individuals were made publicly available.

The intent of pay secrecy policies is to avoid employee dissatisfaction with pay when they know what other employees are being paid. If employees are in the dark about what other employees are paid, the logic goes, then they will have no basis for dissatisfaction with their pay (i.e., if you don't talk about the elephant in the room, it's not really there). The single most interesting thing for people in organizations to talk about is how much people get paid, and expecting that people will not discuss pay if you tell them not to is to ignore human nature (Burroughs, 1982). In the absence of accurate information about what other people get paid, employees guess, and their estimates are systematically inaccurate. Managers tend to overestimate the average pay of managers at their own and lower organizational levels and underestimate the average pay of managers above them (Lawler, 1965; Mahoney & Weitzel, 1978; Milkovich & Anderson, 1972). Instead of removing a cause of dissatisfaction with pay, pay secrecy policies appear to be a cause of dissatisfaction with pay. More open pay policies may have a positive impact on job performance and satisfaction with pay (Futrell & Jenkins, 1978).

Strategic Questions

1. Should an organization have a pay secrecy policy? What are the benefits? What are the costs?
2. Should an organization have an open pay policy? What are the benefits? What are the costs?
3. If the organization has a pay secrecy policy, what should the penalty be for an employee who shares salary information?
4. In rolling out an open pay policy in an organization that has had pay secrecy, which employee group should be first?

Resources

AFL-CIO Executive Paywatch. http://www.aflcio.org/corporatewatch/paywatch/

Bierman, L., & Gely, R. (2004). "Love, sex and politics? Sure. Salary? No way": Workplace social norms and the law. *Berkeley Journal of Employment and Labor Law, 25*(1), 167-191.

Burroughs, J. D. (1982). Pay secrecy and performance: The psychological research. *Compensation Review, 14*(3), 44-54.

Case, J. (2001). When salaries aren't secret. *Harvard Business Review, 79*(5), 37-49.

Colella, A., Paetzold, R. L., Zardkoohi, A., & Wesson, M. J. (2007). Exposing pay secrecy. *Academy of Management Review, 33*(1), 55-71.

Congressional Research Service. (2007, February 15). *Legislative, executive, and judicial officials: Process for adjusting pay and current salaries.* http://www.senate.gov/reference/resources/pdf/RL33245.pdf

Edwards, M. A. (2005). The law and social norms of pay secrecy. *Berkeley Journal of Employment and Labor Law, 25*(41), 1-37.

Futrell, C. M., & Jenkins, O. C. (1978). Pay secrecy versus pay disclosure for salesmen: A longitudinal study. *Journal of Marketing Research, 15*(2), 214-219.

Lawler, E. E., III. (1965). Managers' perceptions of their subordinates' pay and of their superiors' pay. *Personnel Psychology, 18*(4), 413-422.

Mahoney, T. A., & Weitzel, W. (1978). Secrecy and managerial compensation. *Industrial Relations, 17*(2), 245-251.

Milkovich, G. T., & Anderson, P. H. (1972). Management compensation and secrecy policies. *Personnel Psychology, 25*(2), 293-302.

National Labor Relations Board v. Main Street Terrace Center, 218 F.3d 531 (Sixth Circuit Court of Appeals, 2000).

Schuster, J. R., & Colletti, J. A. (1978). Pay secrecy: Who is for and against it? *Academy of Management Journal, 16*(1), 35-40.

SHARING SALARY INFORMATION AND ANTITRUST

To achieve the goal of external competitiveness in salaries, organizations must pay near what the market is paying for jobs. To pay what the market is paying requires obtaining data on what the market is paying. Every organization is different, with different job titles and even some jobs unique to the organization. But there are jobs that are common to most organizations, and these provide the basis of comparison. Receptionist, Accountant I, and Payroll Clerk are positions that are common to many organizations; they are benchmark jobs. If salary information is obtained about what the market is paying for these benchmark jobs, then the organization can find out whether it is paying above or below the market for these jobs. Determining whether the organization is paying above or below the market for the rest of the jobs in the organization, the nonbenchmark jobs, requires a second step, using regression analysis to determine pay rates. Using the point method of job evaluation, every job in the organization is evaluated and assigned a number of points based on how much of each of the compensable factors the job has. Now the organization has a set of benchmark jobs, each with their own job evaluation point total, and a set of nonbenchmark jobs, each with their own job evaluation point total. By interpolation between the benchmark jobs, the appropriate salary for the nonbenchmark jobs can be determined.

Salary survey data will be available for the benchmark jobs, but for some organizations, there can be many more nonbenchmark jobs than benchmark jobs. In addition to purchased salary survey data, HRM professionals may share salary data informally with other organizations. The natural result of organizations obtaining and using salary survey data and using job evaluation to determine salaries is a convergence of salaries across many jobs. The key legal question is, is this price fixing for wages?

Representing nurses, the Service Employees International Union filed four class-action lawsuits against hospitals in Chicago, Albany, Memphis, and San Antonio, alleging that the hospitals exchanged compensation information through telephone conversations, meetings, and written surveys, and that this exchange of information suppressed competition among the hospitals and kept wages low in violation of antitrust laws (Lubel, 2006; Marquez, 2006). The National Collegiate Athletics Association (NCAA) promulgated a rule in 1991, imposing caps on the compensation of certain assistant coaches in Division I sports. The district court ruled against the NCAA and permanently enjoined the NCAA from enforcing the rule. The Sherman Antitrust Act prohibits combinations or "trusts" in restraint of trade, most commonly by monopolizing markets, fixing prices, and excluding competitors. But these cases show that antitrust laws may apply to compensation and human resources practices (Skonberg, Notestine, & Sud, 2006).

According to the U.S. Department of Justice and Federal Trade Commission guidelines, federal antitrust agencies will not scrutinize compensation surveys that have four features: (a) the salary survey is conducted by a third party, such as an independent consultant, and not by the competing employers themselves (to avoid direct contact between competitors, which might lead to conspiracy); (b) the information provided by employers who participate in the survey is based on data more than 3 months old (so that the information cannot be used to signal current or future pricing intention); (c) at least five participants have reported data on which each disseminated statistic is based; and (d) any information disseminated is sufficiently aggregated so that recipients cannot attribute specific data to specific participating employers, so that no individual respondent to the survey can be identified (Dennis, 1995).

Strategic Questions

1. All of the gasoline stations between your home and your work have prices within a few pennies of each other. Is this evidence of collusion in setting prices or effective competition?
2. Although there is some variability, most organizations pay benchmark jobs similarly. Is this evidence of collusion in setting wages or effective competition?
3. Should some organizations be exempt from antitrust laws in regard to setting wages?
4. If an organization has an open pay policy (information on specific pay levels for specific individuals is made publicly available) and competitors also saw this information, would this be an antitrust violation?

Resources

Clarke v. Baptist Memorial Healthcare Corp., No. 06-02377 (W.D. Tenn. filed June 20, 2006); Maderazo v. Vanguard Health Sys., No. 06-00535 (W.D. Tex. filed June 20, 2006); Reed v. Advocate Health Care, No. 06-3337 (N.D. Ill. filed June 20, 2006); Unger v. Albany Med. Ctr., No. 06-00765 (N.D.N.Y. filed June 20, 2006).

Dennis, A. J. (1995). Avoiding the antitrust traps. *HR Focus, 72*(9), 11-11.

Federal Trade Commission. (2006, September 20). *Health care antitrust report—policy statements. Statement 6: Provider participation in exchanges of price and cost information.* http://www.ftc.gov/bc/healthcare/industryguide/policy/index.htm, http://www.ftc.gov/bc/healthcare/industryguide/policy/statement6.htm

Friss, L. (1987). External equity and the free market myth. *Review of Public Personnel Administration, 7*(3), 74-91.

Hamilton, B. W. (2003). Class action in price-fixing litigation when the fixed price is a wage rate: Law et al. v. NCAA. *Antitrust Bulletin, 48*(2), 505-529.

Law et al. v. National Collegiate Athletic Association, 167 F.R.D. 464 (United State District Court for the District of Kansas, 1996).

Lubel, J. (2006). Nurses head to court. *Modern Healthcare, 36*(26), 12.
Marquez, J. (2006). Lawsuits could raise scrutiny of pay survey. *Workforce Management, 85*(14), 12.
Monster.com Salary Calculator. http://salary.monster.com/?WT.mc_n=SRCH/?&s_kwcid=salary|640503013
Salary.com. www.salary.com
Salary Expert. www.salaryexpert.com
Skonberg, J., Notestine, K., & Sud, N. (2006, October 5). United States: Sharing compensation or benefit information between competitors may violate antitrust laws. *Mondaq Business Briefing,* 1-5.

EQUAL PAY AND COMPARABLE WORTH

According to the Equal Pay Act of 1963, employers may not discriminate in pay (i.e., men and women doing the same job—requiring equal skill, effort, and responsibility, and performed under similar working conditions—must be paid the same), except for differences due to a seniority system, a merit system, a system that measures earnings by quantity or quality of production, or some other differential based on any other factor other than sex.

According to Bureau of Labor Statistics (2005b) data, women who were full-time wage and salary workers have median weekly earnings of $585, or 81% of the $722 median for men. This ratio has grown since 1979, the first year comparable earnings data were available; that year, women earned about 63% as much as men did. But between 1979 and 2005, the earnings gap between women and men narrowed for most major age groups. The earnings ratio for women to men among 35- to 44-year-olds, for example, rose from 58% in 1979, to 76% in 2005; and the ratio for 45- to 54-year-olds rose from 57% in 1979, to 75% 26 years later (also see Boraas & Rodgers, 2003; Bowler, 1999). There is some evidence that predominantly female occupations (i.e., occupations in which most of the workers are female) pay less than predominantly male occupations (Blau & Kahn, 2000; Kim, 2003). There is evidence of similar earnings gaps in other industrialized countries (Blau & Kahn, 1992; Mumford & Smith, 2007; Shapiro & Stelcner, 1997).

There are a number of possible causes (or multiple causes operating simultaneously) for the earnings differences between men and women. Moore and Abraham (1992) suggest that supervisors subconsciously or consciously undermine female subordinates by not giving them difficult assignments; networking is less available to women, because there are fewer women to act as mentors; women are more likely to choose occupations that pay less; women have more discontinuous work experiences, dropping out of the labor market more frequently than men; women are more likely to bear the brunt of family duties; women are more likely to turn down critical transfers and job relocations for the sake of family; and women tend to work in industries and occupations that are less heavily unionized.

Because of the persistence of the earnings gap between men and women, equal pay for jobs of comparable worth has become a contentious issue in compensation management. Comparable worth is the idea that jobs of equal worth to the organization should be paid the same. In practice, this means that the relationship between job content (what people do on the job; what knowledge, skills, and abilities are required) and wages is the same for all jobs, whether they are predominantly held by men or women (Pierson, Koziara, & Johannesson, 1983). Therefore, according to the idea of comparable worth, employees are not being paid fairly if the relationship between job content and wages is different for predominantly male (i.e., traditionally male jobs) and predominantly female jobs (i.e., traditionally female jobs).

The idea of comparable worth has been adopted at the federal level and in some states, and in some Canadian Provinces, resulting in some modest pay adjustments (Gardner & Daniel, 1998; Killingsworth, 2002). In the state of Minnesota, for example, the cost of pay adjustments as a percentage of payroll was estimated to be between 3.5% and 3.7%. In the Canadian province of Manitoba, the ratio of female to male earnings went from $.82 to $.87, a cost estimated at 3.3% of payroll (Kovach, 1996). Johnson and Solon (1986) estimated that if comparable worth was implemented economy-wide, 8% to 20% of the female-male earnings gap would be closed.

Strategic Questions

1. Are women paid less than men?
2. What would be the effect of implementing comparable worth economy-wide on the organization's payroll?
3. What would be the effect of implementing comparable worth economy-wide on recruitment for what are currently predominantly female jobs?
4. What would be the effect of implementing comparable worth economy-wide on recruitment for what are currently predominantly male jobs?
5. If an organization is implementing comparable worth, what should it do with the wages of jobs that have been underpaid? What should it do with the wages of jobs that have been overpaid?

Resources

Arvey, R. D., & Holt, K. (1988). The cost of alternative comparable worth strategies. *Compensation and Benefits Review, 20*(5), 37-46.

Barrett, G. V., & Sansonetti, D. M. (1988). Issues concerning the use of regression analysis in salary. *Personnel Psychology, 41*(3), 503-516.

Blau, F. D., & Kahn, L. M. (1992). The gender earnings gap: Learning from international comparisons. *American Economic Review, 82*(2), 533-538.

Blau, F. D., & Kahn, L. M. (2000). Gender differences in pay. *Journal of Economic Perspectives, 14*(4), 75-99.

Boraas, S., & Rodgers, W. M., III. (2003). How does gender play a role in the earnings gap? An update. *Monthly Labor Review, 126*(3), 9-14.

Bowler, M. (1999). Women's earnings: An overview. *Monthly Labor Review, 122*(12), 13-21.

Bureau of Labor Statistics. (2005). *Highlights of women's earnings in 2005* (Report 995). http://www.bls.gov/cps/cpswom2005.pdf

Equal Pay Act. (1963). http://www.eeoc.gov/policy/epa.html

Gardner, S. E., & Daniel, C. (1998). Implementing comparable worth/pay equity: Experiences of cutting edge states. *Public Personnel Management, 27*(4), 475-489.

Johnson, G., & Solon, G. (1986). Estimates of direct effects of comparable worth policy. *American Economic Review, 76*(5), 1117-1125.

Kahya, E. (2006). Revising the metal industry job evaluation system for blue-collar jobs. *Compensation and Benefits Review, 38*(6), 49-63.

Killingsworth, M. R. (2002, May). Comparable worth and pay equity: Recent developments in the United States. *Canadian Public Policy, 28*, 171-186.

Kim, J. (2003). Recent pattern of the U.S. gender occupational segregation and earnings gap. *Journal of American Academy of Business, 3*(1/2), 78-84.

Kovach, K. A. (1996). Comparable worth: The Canadian legislation. *Business Horizons, 26*(1), 41-46.

Moore, M. V., & Abraham, Y. T. (1992). Comparable worth: Is it a moot issue? *Public Personnel Management, 21*(4), 455-472.

Moore, M. V., & Abraham, Y. T. (1994). Comparable worth: Is it a moot issue? Part II: The legal and juridical posture. *Public Personnel Management, 23*(2), 263-286.

Moore, M. V., & Abraham, Y. T. (1995). Comparable worth: Is it a moot issue? Part III: controversy, implications, and measurement. *Public Personnel Management, 24*(3), 291-313.

Mumford, K., & Smith, P. N. (2007). The gender earnings gap in Britain: Including the workplace. *The Manchester School, 75*(6), 653-672.

Pierson, D. A., Koziara, K. S., & Johannesson, R. E. (1983). Equal pay for jobs of comparable worth: A quantified job content approach. *Public Personnel Management, 12*(4), 445-460.

Shapiro, D. M., & Stelcner, M. (1997). Language and earnings in Quebec: Trends over twenty years. *Canadian Public Policy, 23*(2), 115-140.

U.S. Department of Labor. *Minimum wage poster.* http://www.dol.gov/esa/whd/regs/compliance/posters/flsa.htm

Applications

FEDERAL AND STATE MINIMUM WAGE LAWS

One provision of the Fair Labor Standards Act (FLSA) is the minimum wage. The 2007 amendments to the FLSA increased the minimum wage to $5.85 per hour effective July 24, 2007; $6.55 per hour effective July 24, 2008; and $7.25 per hour effective July 24, 2009. There are also a number of state minimum wage laws that set the minimum wage higher than the federal minimum wage.

There are some exceptions to the minimum wage law that apply under specific circumstances to workers with disabilities, full-time students, youth under age 20 in their first 90 consecutive calendar days of employment, tipped employees, and student learners. An employer of a tipped employee is only required to pay $2.13 an hour in direct wages if that amount plus the tips received equals at least the federal minimum wage, the employee retains all tips, and the employee customarily and regularly receives more than $30 a month in tips. If an employee's tips combined with the employer's direct wages of at least $2.13 an hour do not equal the federal minimum hourly wage, the employer must make up the difference.

The Full-time Student Program is for full-time students employed in retail or service stores, agriculture, or colleges and universities. The employer that hires students can obtain a certificate from the Department of Labor, which allows the student to be paid not less than 85% of the minimum wage. The certificate also limits the hours that the student may work to 8 hours a day and no more than 20 hours per week when school is in session and 40 hours when school is out, and requires the employer to follow all child labor laws. Once students graduate or leave school for good, they must be paid the minimum wage.

To Do

Although the FLSA sets the minimum wage, this is a federal law, and individual states may have their own minimum wage law with differing provisions and a different minimum wage. The Department of Labor tracks the various state laws.

Part 1. State Minimum Wage Laws

Make a list of the states with minimum wages higher than the federal minimum wage and their minimum wages. Identify the provisions and the minimum wage of the minimum wage law for your state.

Do any nearby or bordering states have a higher minimum wage than the state you live in? If there are, what is the effect on labor costs and labor supply in the state you live in? What is the effect on labor costs and labor supply in the states with a higher minimum wage?

If the federal minimum wage is increased, who would benefit? Who might be adversely affected?

What kinds of workers work for wages at or near the minimum wage?

Part 2. International Minimum Wage Laws

Find at least three other countries with minimum wage laws. Identify the provisions of the laws and the minimum wages.

If there were an international minimum wage law, who would benefit? Who might be adversely affected?

What would be the impact on a multinational organization of an international minimum wage?

Resources

Bureau of Labor Statistics. (2006). *Characteristics of minimum wage workers: 2006.* http://www.bls.gov/cps/minwage2006.htm

Eurostat, Statistical Office of the European Communities. ec.europa.eu/eurostat/

Miller, K. J. (1999). Welfare and the minimum wage: Are workfare participants "employees" under the Fair Labor Standards Act? *University of Chicago Law Review, 66*(1), 183-212.

Samuel, H. D. (2000). Troubled passage: The labour movement and the Fair Labor Standards Act. *Monthly Labor Review, 123*(12), 32-37.

U.S. Department of Labor. (2004, August 23). *Defining and delimiting the exemptions for executive, administrative, professional, outside sales and computer employees* (Final rule. Title 29, Part 541, Code of Federal Regulations). http://www.dol.gov/esa/regs/fedreg/final/Regulation_541.pdf

U.S. Department of Labor. (2006). *Minimum wage laws in the states—January 1, 2008.* http://www.dol.gov/esa/minwage/america.htm

U.S. Department of Labor. *Minimum wage poster.* http://www.dol.gov/esa/whd/regs/compliance/posters/flsa.htm

U.S. Department of Labor. *Questions and answers about the minimum wage.* http://www.dol.gov/esa/minwage/q-a.htm

EVALUATION OF EXEMPT VERSUS NONEXEMPT JOBS

The FLSA sets the rules for overtime pay. More than 130 million American workers are covered by the FLSA, which is enforced by the Wage and Hour Division of the U.S. Department of Labor. For covered, nonexempt employees, the FLSA requires overtime pay at a rate of not less than one and one-half times an employee's regular rate of pay after 40 hours of work in a workweek. Some exceptions to the 40 hours per week standard apply under special circumstances to police officers and firefighters employed by public agencies and to employees of hospitals and nursing homes. Some states have also enacted overtime laws. Where an employee is subject to both the state and federal overtime laws, the employee is entitled to overtime according to the standard that will provide the higher rate of pay (U.S. Department of Labor, n.d.).

To Do

Apply the Fair Labor Standards Act to each of the jobs in Table 8.2. Get the job descriptions for each job from O*Net. Is it a nonexempt job, or is it exempt from the overtime provisions of the FLSA? If the job should be considered exempt, state the reasons for your decision.

(Continued)

(Continued)

Table 8.2 How Does the Fair Labor Standards Act Apply to *The Maltese Falcon?*

Job	*Name*	*Exempt?*	*Reasons for Decision*
Director	John Huston		
Writer	Dashiell Hammett (novel)		
Screenplay	John Huston		
Executive producer	Hal B. Wallis		
Associate producer	Henry Blanke		
Original music (composer)	Adolph Deutsch		
Cinematographer/director of photography	Arthur Edeson		
Film editor	Thomas Richards		
Art director	Robert M. Haas		
Costume designer	Orry-Kelly		
Makeup artist	Perc Westmore		
Sound	Oliver S. Garretson		
Musical director	Leo F. Forbstein		
Dialogue director	Robert Foulk		
Actor	Humphrey Bogart		

Resources

Carroll, S., & Miller, S. R. (2007). New NLRB policy clarification of supervisor. *Employment Relations Today, 33*(4), 59-60.

Clark, M. M. (2003). NLRB still unsure how to define 'supervisor'. *HR Magazine, 48*(9), 23-24.

Fair Labor Standards Act of 1938. http://www.dol.gov/compliance/laws/comp-flsa.htm

IMDB. *Full cast and crew for The Maltese Falcon (1941).* http://www.imdb.com/title/tt0033870/fullcredits#cast

Oakwood Healthcare, Inc. (348 NLRB No. 37, September 23, 2000).

O*Net On-Line. *Occupational Information Network.* http://online.onetcenter.org/

U.S. Department of Labor. (n.d.). *Employment law guide, chapter: Minimum wage and overtime pay.* http://www.dol.gov/compliance/guide/minwage.htm

U.S. Department of Labor. *Fact Sheet #17A: Exemption for executive, administrative, professional, computer & outside sales employees under the Fair Labor Standards Act (FLSA).* http://www.dol.gov/esa/whd/regs/compliance/fairpay/fs17a_overview.pdf

U.S. Department of Labor. *Fact Sheet #17B: Exemption for executive employees under the Fair Labor Standards Act (FLSA).* http://www.dol.gov/esa/whd/regs/compliance/fairpay/fs17b_executive.pdf

U.S. Department of Labor. *Fact Sheet #17C: Exemption for administrative employees under the Fair Labor Standards Act (FLSA).* http://www.dol.gov/esa/whd/regs/compliance/fairpay/fs17c_administrative.pdf

U.S. Department of Labor. *Fact Sheet #17D: Exemption for professional employees under the Fair Labor Standards Act (FLSA).* http://www.dol.gov/esa/whd/regs/compliance/fairpay/fs17d_professional.pdf

U.S. Department of Labor. *Fact Sheet #17E: Exemption for employees in computer-related occupations under the Fair Labor Standards Act (FLSA).* http://www.dol.gov/esa/whd/regs/compliance/fairpay/fs17e_computer.pdf

U.S. Department of Labor. *Fact Sheet #17F: Exemption for outside sales employees under the Fair Labor Standards Act (FLSA).* http://www.dol.gov/esa/whd/regs/compliance/fairpay/fs17f_outsidesales.pdf

U.S. Department of Labor. *Questions and answers about the FLSA.* http://www.dol.gov/esa/whd/flsa/faq.htm

Not all employees are covered by the overtime provisions of the FLSA. Among the employees exempt from the overtime provisions of the FLSA are as follows:

1. Executive, administrative, and professional employees (including teachers and academic administrative personnel in elementary and secondary schools), outside sales employees, and employees in certain computer-related occupations (as defined in Department of Labor regulations);

2. Employees of certain seasonal amusement or recreational establishments, employees of certain small newspapers, seamen employed on foreign vessels, employees engaged in fishing operations, and employees engaged in newspaper delivery;

3. Farm workers employed by anyone who used no more than 500 "man days" of farm labor in any calendar quarter of the preceding calendar year;
4. Casual babysitters and persons employed as companions to the elderly or infirm.

Experiential Exercises

CHOOSE THE INVESTMENTS FOR YOUR 401(K) PLAN

There are two types of pensions: defined benefit and defined contribution. In a defined benefit pension, the retired employee receives a set amount of money as a monthly retirement benefit. The organization must set aside a sufficient amount of money while the employee is working to cover the future obligation to the retired employee. If the pension fund has insufficient funds to pay the promised benefits, and the pension fund is covered by the Pension Benefit Guaranty Corporation (PBGC), the PBCG will take over the payments. The PBGC is a federal corporation created by the Employee Retirement Income Security Act of 1974. It currently protects the pension of nearly 44 million American workers and retirees in more than 30,000 private pension plans (PBGC, 2007).

The PBGC works in much the same way as the Federal Deposit Insurance Corporation to insure bank deposits. Insurance premiums are paid by sponsors of defined benefit plans, and PBGC's assets include investment income, assets from pension plans trusteed by PBCG, and recoveries from the companies formerly responsible for the pension plans. PBGC guarantees "basic benefits" earned by an employee before a defined benefit pension plan ends, including pension benefits at normal retirement age, most early retirement benefits, annuity benefits for survivors of plan participants, and disability benefits for disabilities. PBGC does not guarantee health and welfare benefits, vacation pay, severance benefits, and lump-sum death benefits for a death or disability that occurs after the pension plan's termination date.

Employers can end a pension plan through a process called "plan termination." In a standard termination, the employer can end the plan only after showing PBGC that the plan has enough money to pay all benefits owed to participants. The plan must either purchase an annuity from an insurance company to provide each employee with lifetime benefits when he or she retires, or if the plan allows, issue one lump-sum payment that covers the entire benefit. In a distress termination, the plan is not fully funded, typically because the employer is in financial distress. The employer must prove to a bankruptcy court or to PBGC that the employer cannot remain in business unless the plan is terminated. If the application is granted, PBGC takes over the plan as trustee and pays plan benefits, up to the legal limits, using plan assets and PBGC guarantee funds. Among *Fortune 1000* companies in 2004, 627 had defined-benefit pension plans, but 11% (71 plans) were frozen or terminated plans (Sammer, 2005). To find out whether a specific pension plan is insured by PBGC, the employer or plan administrator can be asked for a copy of the "Summary Plan Description" or SPD. The SPD will state whether your plan is covered by the PBGC program. Although PBGC insures most defined benefit plans, some are not covered. For example, plans offered by "professional service employers" (such as doctors and lawyers) with fewer than 26 employees; by church groups; or by federal, state, or local governments are usually not insured.

In a defined contribution pension, a set amount of money is contributed to a fund each pay period, sometimes including an employer match of the employee's contribution up to a specified maximum percentage. The employee generally has a choice of a number of funds, as part of the organization's 401(k) plan. One reason why 401(k) plans are popular is that employees can easily change their investment choices as their life situation changes. Early in their careers, when they have 30 or more years to make contributions to the plan and for their investments to grow, employees can afford to take greater risks and look for investments with higher rates of return. Later in their careers, when they are planning to retire in a few years, they may be more concerned with principle preservation and look for investments with less risk.

Another reason why 401(k) plans have become so popular is that they are portable. This means that workers can take them to their new employer when they change jobs (with some exceptions). When workers change jobs, they can keep the 401(k) from their former employer and start a new 401(k) with their new employer, or they can rollover the old 401(k) into the new employer's 401(k) plan, or rollover the old 401(k) into an IRA and start a new 401(k) with the new employer.

Investing in a 401(k) plan gives employees the benefit of tax-deferred saving, letting them increase their take-home pay by decreasing their current taxable income. The employees' pretax contributions are not tax-free; rather, the contributions are tax-deferred, which means that they don't pay income tax on the money contributed until they withdraw it from the plan, typically at a time when they are in a lower tax bracket. Each employer's 401(k) plans offers a different collection of investment options. Mutual funds are managed by investment professionals, and they base their investment decisions on research and analysis. The primary advantage of mutual funds is diversification. If employees invest in only one stock (e.g., the company's stock), they are "putting all of their eggs in one basket." If that one stock goes up, they do well; but if it goes down, they do badly. If the money is spread around in a number of stocks, even if some go down, some will go up. A collection of mutual funds with different investment strategies and different stocks will further increase diversification. Some mutual funds take the idea of diversification one step further in index funds, which invest in a very large number of stocks, such as all companies in the S&P 500.

Over time, the different investments in a 401(k) plan will have different rates of growth. The value of an employee's investments in the different funds will no longer mirror what he or she invests in each of the funds each month. This is the time when employees need to rebalance their portfolio, changing their allocations so that their portfolio conforms to their investment plan. Whenever their life situation changes, employees may want to change their allocations to conform to their new investment plan.

To Do

Part 1. The enrollment form for your employer's 401(k) plan lists the available funds you may choose from. Select an allocation for yourself. Divide 100% among the funds; you may put all of your money in one fund, create an equal distribution to all of the funds, or something in between. Use Google to find fund performance data. Enter the symbol and use the Google Finance, Morningstar, Yahoo Finance, MSN Money, Reuters, or AOL Money reports to help you decide how to make your allocations. What were your reasons for the allocation you made? What factors did you consider in making your allocation?

Part 2. Look ahead to your future, about 10 years before you expect to retire. Select an allocation for yourself. Divide 100% among the funds; you may put all of your money in one fund, create an equal distribution to all of the funds, or something in between. Is this allocation the same or different from the allocation you selected in Part 1?

Table 8.3 401(k) Allocation Plan

Fund Name	*Symbol*	*Percentage*
Wells Fargo Advantage Stable Income A	NVSAX	
Fidelity Intermediate Bond	FTHRX	
Van Kampen Equity and Income A	ACEIX	
Van Kampen Growth and Income A	ACGIX	
Fidelity Spartan 500 Index Advantage	FSMAX	
American Funds Growth Fund of America A	AGTHX	
Oppenheimer Main St Small Cap A	OPMSX	
American Funds EuroPacific Growth A	AEPGX	
Jennison Equity Opportunity A	PJIAX	
Total (must sum to 100%)		100%

Resources

Access Education. (2005). *Eight reasons why 401(k) plans are smart.* http://www.accesseducation.org/article.aspx?article=488

Employee Retirement Income Security Act. (1974). http://www.dol.gov/dol/topic/health-plans/erisa.htm

Federal Deposit Insurance Corporation. http://www.fdic.gov/

Jin, L., Mertona, R. C., & Bodie, Z. (2006). Do a firm's equity returns reflect the risk of its pension plan? *Journal of Financial Economics, 81*(1), 1-26.

Moran, A. E., & Tucker, K. (2006). The new Pension Protection Act: More work for plan administrators. *Employee Relations Law Journal, 32*(3), 96-108.

Morningstar. (2005). *Morningstar Investing Classroom Course 205: The Best Investments for Tax Deferred Accounts.* http://news.morningstar.com/classroom2/course.asp?docId=4444&page=1&CN=COM

Pension Benefit Guaranty Corporation. (2007). http://www.pbgc.gov/

Sammer, J. (2005). An uncertain future for defined-benefit plans. *Business Finance, 11*(12), 43-45.

GENDER BIAS IN WAGE RATES

According to Bureau of Labor Statistics (2005e) data, among full-time wage and salary workers, the median usual weekly earnings for men is $722, and for women is $585; women's earnings as percentage of men's is 81.0%. This earnings gap between men and women has many possible causes. One possible cause is that women are concentrated in traditionally low-paying occupations (Pierson, Kozira, & Johannesson, 1983). Another possible cause is that many employers base starting salaries on the wages new employees earned in their previous positions, so if women earned less than men in their previous jobs, this would carry over to affect their salaries in subsequent jobs (Brody & Brito, 2006).

Another possible cause is gender bias in assigning salaries. Both men and women in predominantly female occupations earn less than men and women in male-dominated occupations (Boraas & Rodgers, 2003). Using Current Population Survey data to estimate the relationship between wages and the concentration of females within occupations, Johnson and Solon (1986) found a negative relationship, even after controlling for worker and job characteristics. England (1999) summarized the studies looking at the effect of the sex composition of jobs on wages. Using separate regression analyses to predict men's and women's earnings showed net wage penalties for working in occupations with a higher percentage of female workers (e.g., England, Herbert, Kilbourne, Reid, & Megdal, 1994). Studies examining individuals who moved from occupations with lower to higher percentage female workers found that the decrease in pay was more than could be explained by changes in their occupation and experience (e.g., Macpherson & Hirsch, 1995). In short, predominantly female jobs pay less on average than predominantly male jobs.

To Do

To test the idea that the differences in earnings between men and women is at least in part due to gender bias, do an applied research project. To test the idea, conduct a survey to find out what people think predominantly male and predominantly female jobs should be paid (without telling them that the jobs are predominantly male or predominantly female). If there is no bias against women, there should be no correlation between the salaries that survey respondents suggest for jobs and the percentage of women in those jobs. If there is gender bias, there should be a correlation between the salaries and the percentage of women in those jobs.

Step 1: Collect Information on the Percentage of Women in Various Jobs

Use Bureau of Labor Statistics data from "Women in the Labor Force: A Databook" (Bureau of Labor Statistics, 2006d) to make a list of at least 20 occupations, with varying levels of percentage women in those jobs. The list should include some predominantly male jobs (i.e., a low percentage of women in those jobs), some predominantly female jobs (i.e., a high percentage of women in those jobs), and some with more of a balance between men and women. For example, construction manager is a predominantly male job, with 6.3% women; human resources, training, and labor relations specialist is a predominantly female job, with 70.9% women; and advertising and promotions manager is a nearly equal mix, with 56.1% female.

Step 2: Collect Information on Job Tasks

Find the job summaries for each of the jobs from O*Net. For the three jobs listed above, the O*Net job summaries are below.

Construction Manager: Plan, direct, coordinate, or budget, usually through subordinate supervisory personnel, activities concerned with the construction and maintenance of structures, facilities, and systems. Participate in the conceptual development of a construction project and oversee its organization, scheduling, and implementation.

Human Resources Manager: Plan, direct, and coordinate human resource management activities of an organization to maximize the strategic use of human resources and maintain functions such as employee compensation, recruitment, personnel policies, and regulatory compliance.

Advertising Manager: Plan and direct advertising policies and programs or produce collateral materials, such as posters, contests, coupons, or give-aways, to create extra interest in the purchase of a product or service for a department, an entire organization, or on an account basis.

Step 3: Create a Survey

Use the information you have collected to create a survey. The survey should present each of the jobs, the job summaries, and have a place for respondents to say what they think would be a fair salary for each of the jobs.

Step 4: Collect Data

Administer the survey to a sample of at least 20 students unfamiliar with this project.

Step 5: Data Analysis

Calculate the correlation between percentage female and "fair salary." The independent variable is the percentage of women in each job, and the dependent variable is what the respondents said was a fair salary for each job. To run the correlation analysis, the spreadsheet will look something like Table 8.4. There will be data on at least 20 different occupations from at least 20 different survey respondents.

Table 8.4 Correlation Analysis Spreadsheet

Occupation	*Survey Respondent ID Number*	*Independent Variable: Percentage Female (from Bureau of Labor Statistics)*	*Dependent Variable: "Fair Salary" (from Survey)*
Construction manager	1		
Human resource manager	1		
Advertising manager	1		
. . . 17 other occupations			
Construction manager	2		
Human resource manager	2		
Advertising manager	2		
. . . 17 other occupations			

Step 6: Results

Is the percentage female correlated to salaries? Are the survey respondent's wages for predominantly female jobs above or below O*Net's Wages & Employment Trends, National Median wages? Are the respondent's wages for predominantly male jobs above or below O*Net's Wages & Employment Trends, National Median wages?

Resources

Boraas, S., & Rodgers, W. M., III. (2003, March). How does gender play a role in the earnings gap? An update. *Monthly Labor Review, 126*(3), 9-15.

Brody, H. M., & Brito, C. (2006). When is "unequal" pay not really unequal? *Employment Relations Today, 33*(3), 87-95.

Bureau of Labor Statistics. (2005). *Median usual weekly earnings of full-time wage and salary workers by detailed occupation and sex, 2005 annual averages.* http://www.bls.gov/cps/wlf-table18-2006.pdf

(Continued)

(Continued)

Bureau of Labor Statistics. (2006). *Women in the labor force: A databook.* http://www.bls.gov/cps/wlf-databook2006.htm, http://www.bls.gov/cps/wlf-databook-2007.pdf, http://www.bls.gov/cps/wlf-databook-2007.pdf

England, P. (1999). The case for comparable worth. *Quarterly Review of Economics and Finance, 39,* 743-755.

England, P., Herbert, M. S., Kilbourne, B. S., Reid, L. L., & Megdal, L. M. (1994). The gendered valuation of occupations and skills: Earnings in 1980 census occupations. *Social Forces, 73*(1), 65-101.

Macpherson, D. A., & Hirsch, B. T. (1995). Wages and gender composition: Why do women's jobs pay less? *Journal of Labor Economics, 13*(3), 426-471.

O*Net On-line. *Occupational Information Network.* http://online.onetcenter.org/

Pierson, D. A., Koziara, K. S., & Johannesson, R. E. (1983). Equal pay for jobs of comparable worth: A quantified job content approach. *Public Personnel Management, 12*(4), 445-460.

Remick, H. (1981). The comparable worth controversy. *Public Personnel Management Journal, 10*(4), 371-383.

Creative Exercises

DEVELOPING A MERIT PAY PLAN FOR TEAMS

A variety of incentive compensation methods have been developed, focused on rewarding superior performance of individual employees or teams. More than half of companies use some type of variable pay (Lyons & Ben-Ora, 2002). The use of incentive plans has been found to be positively related to performance (Bucklin & Dickinson, 2001). Stiffler (2006) reports the results of a survey showing that 72% of respondents said that distribution of rewards based on individual performance was the top goal of their organization's performance management program, based on the idea that pay-for-performance motivates employees to achieve outstanding performance in their jobs. But among those same survey respondents, only 29% said that their organization's performance reviews provided a clear explanation for compensation decisions. If pay is not clearly and consistently linked with performance, it cannot have the desired motivating effect.

Organizations are increasingly using teams to improve productivity, improve product or service quality, and improve customer satisfaction (Dzamba, 2001). As the emphasis shifts from individual performance to team performance, many organizations have designed group-based reward systems, to reward employees for a group's success in contributing to the organization's strategy (Heneman & von Hippel, 1995). Giving incentives for individual performance is likely to be counterproductive in a team-based work environment. Instead, team-based incentives need to be developed, to reward both high work performance and teamwork. Gomez-Mejia and Balkin (1989) found that for research and development workers, team-based bonuses were most effective in terms of pay satisfaction, propensity to leave, project performance, and individual performance.

One type of incentive compensation is merit pay. Merit pay is individual pay increases based on the rated performance of individual employees in a previous time period (Heneman, 1992). Merit pay is different from a bonus, which is a one-time payment in addition to the employee's salary. A merit pay increase is added to the employee's base salary, so the merit pay increases are cumulative over time. Merit pay systems are based on the idea that higher levels of employee performance should be rewarded with increases in wages. The link between pay and performance symbolically demonstrates to employees the organization's commitment to reward top performers (Schulz & Tanguay, 2006). Despite its widespread use, there are problems associated with merit pay (Campbell, Campbell, & Chia, 1998). If job performance is not accurately measured, or if noise hides the link between work performance and merit pay, or if there is limited desirability of the merit reward, merit pay systems will be ineffective. There may also be some unintended consequences, such as the loss of job satisfaction and intrinsic motivation.

Hackett and McDermott (1999) list seven steps to successful performance-based rewards programs:

1. Senior management must know what it expects of employees, and based on these expectations, set clearly defined goals;
2. Show employees that their direct efforts will affect the desired results;
3. Tie performance-based rewards to individual or group goals that have a reasonable chance of being achieved;
4. Provide quantitative measures of results;
5. Persuade employees to believe that the goals and rewards are achievable;
6. Make the reward significant (15% to 20% of base pay); and
7. Shorten the time between employee performance and the reward payout, so that employees can quickly feel the impact of their efforts.

To Do

Develop a proposal for implementing a merit pay plan for a cross-functional work team. The plan should clearly identify the team goals, the rewards to team members for achieving the goals, the amount of the reward, and the promised time between measurement of the goals and disbursement of the reward.

(Continued)

(Continued)

Resources

Bartol, K. M., & Srivastava, A. (2002). Encouraging knowledge sharing: The role of organizational reward systems. *Journal of Leadership & Organizational Studies, 9*(1), 64-76.

Bucklin, B. R., & Dickinson, A. M. (2001). Individual monetary incentives: A review of different types of arrangements between performance and pay. *Journal of Organizational Behavior Management, 21*(3), 45-137.

Campbell, D. J., Campbell, K. M., & Chia, H. (1998). Merit pay, performance appraisal, and individual motivation: An analysis and alternative. *Human Resource Management, 37*(2), 131-146.

Day, J. D., Mang, P. Y., Richter, A., & Roberts, J. (2002, January). *The McKinsey Quarterly, 4*, 46-55.

Dzamba, A. (2001). Compensation strategies to use amid organizational change. *Compensation and Benefits Management, 17*(1), 16-29.

Eskew, D., & Heneman, R. L. (1996). A survey of merit pay plan effectiveness: End of the line for merit pay or hope for improvement? *Human Resource Planning, 19*(2), 12-19.

Ganzel, R. (1998). What's wrong with pay for performance? *Training, 35*(12), 34-40.

Gomez-Mejia, L. R., & Balkin, D. B. (1989). Effectiveness of individual and aggregate compensation strategies. *Industrial Relations, 28*(3), 431-445.

Hackett, T. J., & McDermott, D. G. (1999). Seven steps to successful performance-based rewards. *HR Focus, 76*(9), 11-12.

Harris, M. M., Gilbreath, B., & Sunday, J. A. (1998). A longitudinal examination of a merit pay system: Relationships among performance ratings, merit increases, and total pay increases. *Journal of Applied Psychology, 83*(5), 825-832.

Heneman, R. L. (1992). *Merit pay: Linking pay increases to performance ratings*. Reading, MA: Addison-Wesley.

Heneman, R. L., & von Hippel, C. (1995). Balancing group and individual rewards: Rewarding individual contributions to the team. *Compensation and Benefits Review, 27*(4), 63-68.

Johnson, S. T. (1996). High performance work teams: One firm's approach to team incentive pay. *Compensation and Benefits Review, 28*(5), 47-50.

Lyons, F. H., & Ben-Ora, D. (2002). Total rewards strategy: The best foundation of pay for performance. *Compensation and Benefits Review, 34*(2), 34-49.

Schulz, E. R., & Tanguay, D. M. (2006). Merit pay in a public higher education institution: Questions of impact and attitudes. *Public Personnel Management, 35*(1), 71-88.

Schuster, J. R., & Zingheim, P. K. (1996). The network discusses: Broadbanding, merit pay, and team participation. *Compensation and Benefits Review, 28*(3), 21-22.

Stiffler, M. A. (2006). Incentive compensation management: Making pay-for-performance a reality. *Performance Improvement, 45*(1), 25-30.

Weinberger, T. E. (1998). A method for determining the equitable allocation of team-based pay: Rewarding members of a cross-functional accounting team. *Compensation and Benefits Management, 14*(4), 18-26.

JOB EVALUATION FOR UNIVERSITY PROFESSORS

Job evaluation is the process of systematically examining the task requirements of jobs to determine the appropriate rate of pay (Heneman, 2003). Job evaluation is focused on the requirements of the job, not the performance of a given individual within the job. It is taken for granted that individuals are paid different amounts because of differences in merit or seniority (England, 1999). In short, job evaluation looks at the requirements of a job, and performance appraisal looks at how well an individual performed the requirements of a job.

In the point system of job evaluation, benchmark jobs are evaluated on compensable factors. Compensable factors are anything that the organization is willing to pay more for. Some jobs are more hazardous than others or require supervision of more employees or decision making. Some jobs require higher levels of communication skills, interpersonal skills, or problem-solving skills. Other jobs have a greater degree of responsibility or greater consequences of error. The Equal Pay Act lists four compensable factors for determining whether jobs are similar: skill, effort, responsibility, and working conditions. Jobs that have more of these compensable factors are given more points, which translates into higher rates of pay. Job evaluation is used to maintain internal equity in jobs throughout the organization.

Salary survey data are used to determine what the market is paying for the benchmark jobs (i.e., jobs that are common to many organizations). By doing a regression analysis, using the salary survey data as the dependent variable, and the job evaluation point totals as the independent variable, both internal equity and external competitiveness are addressed. Once the regression analysis has been done, the regression line (i.e., the pay line for midpoint salaries) can be used to interpolate or extrapolate from the benchmark jobs to determine the salaries for nonbenchmark jobs.

To Do

Step 1. Job descriptions and job specifications. Write the job description and job specification for assistant professor, associate professor, full professor, department chair, and dean. Use O*Net, the *Dictionary of Occupational Titles* (U.S. Department of Labor, 1991), and interviews of subject matter experts (i.e., individuals who are experts in a particular area, who have expert knowledge of the topic) to do the job analysis. The job descriptions and job specifications for the three professor jobs should not all be the same; the jobs are different.

Step 2. Compensable factors. Create a list of compensable factors for the jobs of assistant professor, associate professor, full professor, department chair, and dean. Define each of the factors. Every compensable factor will fit into one of the three broad categories of research, teaching, or service. Many universities post their compensable factors to publicly available Web pages.

Step 3. Degrees of the compensable factors. Define the degrees of each compensable factor. For each of the compensable factors, set the number of points for each level (or degree) of each compensable factor. Define each degree of each of the compensable factors. The higher the degree (more supervisory responsibility, more effort, etc.), the greater the number of points. The compensable factors may all have the same number of degrees, or the number of degrees may vary across the compensable factors.

(Continued)

(Continued)

Step 4. Evaluate the jobs. Evaluate each of the five jobs. Based on the degrees of each factor, calculate the total number of points for each job. The job evaluation point total for each job should be different, with the job evaluation point total for assistant professor being the smallest and the job evaluation point total for dean being the largest.

Step 5. Salary survey data. Use the salary survey data from the Academe Salary Survey (American Association of University Professors, 2005) for IIB schools and your job evaluation point totals for the three jobs. Do a regression analysis to find the best-fitting line for the midpoint of the salary range. In the regression analysis, the dependent variable is salary (from the salary survey data) and the independent variable is the job evaluation point total for each job. The number of observations for the regression analysis should be 48 (16 schools × 3 jobs).

Step 6. Regression analysis. Determine the midpoint salary for assistant professor, associate professor, and full professor by using the regression output to generate predicted salaries. The formula to generate these predicted scores is Predicted Salary = JETotal × XCoefficient + Intercept.

Step 7. Determine salaries. Determine the midpoint salary for department chair and dean by using the same formula as was used to generate predicted salaries for the three professor salaries. Create a table showing the midpoint salary for each of the five jobs.

Resources

American Association of University Professors. (2005). The annual report on the economic status of the profession 2005-2006. *Academe, 92*(2), 24-105.

Dictionary of Occupational Titles. http://www.wave.net/upg/immigration/dot_index.html

England, P. (1999). The case for comparable worth. *Quarterly Review of Economics and Finance, 39*, 743-755.

Heneman, R. L. (2003). Job and work evaluation: A literature review. *Public Personnel Management, 32*(1), 47-71.

Heneman, R. L., & LeBlanc, P. V. (2002). Developing a more relevant and competitive approach for valuing knowledge work. *Compensation and Benefits Review, 34*(4), 43-47.

Heneman, R. L., LeBlanc, P. V., & Risher, H. (2003). Work valuation addresses shortcomings of both job evaluation and market pricing. *Compensation and Benefits Review, 35*(1), 7-11.

O*Net On-line. *Occupational Information Network.* http://online.onetcenter.org/

Plachy, R. J. (1987). The Point-Factor Job Evaluation System: A step-by-step guide, part 2. *Compensation and Benefits Review, 19*(5), 9-24.

Weinberger, T. E. (1995). Determining the relative importance of compensable factors: The application of dominance analysis to job evaluation. *Compensation and Benefits Management, 11*(2), 17-23.

Occupational Safety and Health 9

Strategic Objective

Before the passage of workplace safety legislation, employees had few legal protections if they suffered an injury at work. Fatality rates for railroad workers were high, particularly for brakemen from falls from cars and striking overhead obstructions (Aldrich, 1997). Brakeman was a dangerous job requiring the worker to climb to the top of each rail car and turn a brake wheel to press a wood block against the train wheel, while the train was in motion. George Westinghouse invented and patented a compressed-air brake system in 1869 to replace the standard manual braking system, which was often faulty. The 1893 Railroad Safety Appliance Act mandated the use of air brakes and automatic couplers. It was the first federal law intended primarily to improve work safety, and by 1900, when the new equipment was widely distributed, risks to trainmen had fallen dramatically (Usselman, 1984).

The Occupational Safety and Health Administration (OSHA) was created by the Occupational Safety and Health Act of 1970. OSHA's purpose is to ensure employee safety and health in the United States by working with employers and employees to create better working environments. Since its inception in 1971, OSHA has helped to cut workplace fatalities by more than 60% and occupational injury and illness rates by 40%. At the same time, U.S. employment has doubled from 58 million workers at 3.5 million work sites to more than 115 million workers at 7.2 million sites (OSHA, 2004).

Nonfatal workplace injuries and illnesses occurred at a rate of 4.6 cases per 100 equivalent full-time workers among private industry employers in 2005, according to the Survey of Occupational Injuries and Illnesses by the Bureau of Labor Statistics. This was a decline from the rate of 4.8 cases per 100 equivalent full-time workers reported by the Bureau of Labor Statistics for 2004. The rate resulted from a total of 4.2 million nonfatal injuries and illnesses in private industry workplaces during 2005, relatively unchanged compared to 2004, and a 2% increase in the number of hours worked. Incidence rates for injuries and illnesses combined declined significantly in 2005 for most case types, with the exception of cases with days away from work (Bureau of Labor Statistics, 2005f). A total of 5,702 fatal work injuries were recorded in the United States in 2005, down about 1% from the revised total of 5,764 fatal work injuries recorded in 2004. The rate at which fatal work injuries occurred in 2005 was 4.0 per 100,000 workers, down slightly from a rate of 4.1 per 100,000 in 2004 (Bureau of Labor Statistics, 2006c). The benefits to the organization of improving workplace safety can be substantial. Hantula, Rajala, Kellerman, and Bragger (2001), using a time-based utility analysis model, found a rate of return of direct costs in worker's compensation of 10:1 in some cases.

According to the Department of Labor's Strategic Plan for 2006-2011 (Department of Labor, 2006), the Department of Labor protects the rights of workers covered under the Occupational Safety and Health Act of 1970 by responding promptly to imminent danger situations; investigating fatalities, catastrophes, and worker complaints; enforcing whistle-blower rights under 14 statutes; and inspecting federal agencies to protect federal workers. To effectively protect workers, OSHA uses a targeted approach, directing inspections and outreach to work sites and industries with the highest injury and illness rates. In addition to workplace inspections, OSHA uses a variety of compliance assistance and educational and outreach programs to improve employer health and safety management systems. By focusing on emergency preparedness, OSHA is also helping employers be ready to respond to workplace emergencies such as natural disasters or terrorist attacks.

About 10 million workers across the European Union have the right to information and consultation on company decisions through their European Works Councils. Walters (2000) analyzed 386 voluntary agreements on European Works Councils and concluded that many of the agreements provide a forum for discussion of the improvement of health and safety standards at the enterprise level throughout Europe. The Federal Republic of Germany has a dual system of health and safety regulation at the national level, with statutory provisions issued by the federal government and accident prevention regulations generated by the professional associations (Koch & Salter, 1999).

Strategic Issues in HRM

SELECTING SAFE EMPLOYEES

There are three main causes of workplace accidents: chance occurrences, unsafe conditions, and unsafe work behaviors by employees. Unsafe conditions include defective equipment, hazardous procedures, unsafe storage, improper illumination, and improper ventilation. The engineering approach to workplace safety attempts to find ways to make equipment safer for employees to use and less likely to cause accidents. Unsafe work behaviors include not using the proper safety equipment or protective clothing and failing to follow safe work procedures. The personnel approach to workplace safety looks at reducing the human causes of accidents (Feggetter, 1982) and focuses on getting employees to use tools and equipment safely.

According to OSHA (2007), a chain saw is one of the most efficient, productive, and dangerous portable power tools used in any industry. It has a number of safety devices built into it (the engineering approach). The chain catcher prevents a broken or dislodged chain from striking the user, a chain brake to stop the chain if kickback occurs, a throttle that will stop the chain when pressure on the throttle is released, and a throttle interlock that prevents the throttle from activating until the interlock is depressed. Chain saws should only be used with additional personal safety equipment, including a hard hat, eye and face protection, hearing protection, foot protection, hand protection if handling wire rope, leg protection, and a first-aid kit. Employees should also use the chain saw safely (personnel approach), including keeping their hands on the handles and maintaining secure footing while operating the chainsaw; clearing the area of obstacles that might interfere with cutting the tree or using the retreat path; not cutting directly overhead; shutting off or releasing the throttle prior to retreating; and shutting off or engaging the chain brake whenever the saw is carried more than 50 feet or on hazardous terrain.

Following the personnel approach, employees can be trained in safe work methods so that they know what the workplace hazards are and how to avoid accidents and injuries. This has limitations, however; training alone is not sufficient. Employees must be motivated to behave safely (Komaki, Heinzmann, & Lawson, 1980). Incentives for unsafe work behavior may be greater than the employee's perceived risk of an accident. The sociotechnical approach to workplace safety recognizes that many aspects of the work environment affect employees' behavior (Barling, Kelloway, & Iverson, 2003; Brown, Willis, & Prussia, 2000; Hoffman & Stetzer, 1996) and focuses on giving employees incentives for safe work behavior. Another option for the personnel approach is to try to identify applicants who are more likely to have an accident and give them additional training or not select them. Accident proneness (Foreman, Ellis, & Beavan, 1983; Rawson, 1944) is a personality construct that might be used to predict workplace accidents based on a person's past accident record (i.e., accident repeater). If a valid test could be developed to measure accident proneness (see, e.g., Matsuoka, 1997), it could be administered to employees, and high-risk employees could be directed to receive additional safety training.

Strategic Questions

1. If 80% of workplace accidents are caused by 20% of the employees, are these employees accident prone?
2. Is it illegal to decide not to hire someone based on his or her past accident record?
3. Which is more likely to have the greatest improvement in workplace safety, the engineering approach or the personnel approach?
4. Why do workers need to be motivated to behave safely? Isn't it in their own best interest to not have a workplace accident?
5. If a valid test of accident proneness could be developed, should it be used as part of the selection process?

Resources

Barling, J., Kelloway, E. K., & Iverson, R. D. (2003). High-quality work, job satisfaction, and occupational injuries. *Journal of Applied Psychology, 88*(2), 276-283.

Brown, K. A., Willis, P. G., & Prussia, G. E. (2000). Predicting safe employee behavior in the steel industry: Development and test of a sociotechnical model. *Journal of Operations Management, 18*(4), 445-465.

Feggetter, A. J. (1982). A method for investigating human factor aspects of aircraft accidents and incidents. *Ergonomics, 25*(11), 1065-1075.

Foreman, E. I., Ellis, H. D., & Beavan, D. (1983). Mea culpa? A study of the relationships among personality traits, life-events and ascribed accident causation. *British Journal of Clinical Psychology, 22*, 223-224.

Hofmann, D. A., & Stetzer, A. (1996). A cross-level investigation of factors influencing unsafe behaviors and accidents. *Personnel Psychology, 49*(2), 307-339.

Komaki, J., Heinzmann, A. T., & Lawson, L. (1980). Effect of training and feedback: Component analysis of a behavioral safety program. *Journal of Applied Psychology, 65*(3), 261-270.

Matsuoka, H. (1997). Development of a short test for accident proneness. *Perceptual and Motor Skills, 85*(3), 903-906.

Occupational Safety and Health Administration. (2007). *Logging eTool: Chain saw.* http://www.osha.gov/SLTC/substanceabuse/index.html

Jacob, I. G. (2006). Depression's impact on safety. *Occupational Health & Safety, 75*(1), 32-40.

Rawson, A. J. (1944). Accident proneness. *Psychosomatic Medicine, 6*, 88-94.

Reynolds, S. H. (1996). Is ADD driving up your worker's comp costs? *HR Magazine, 41*(9), 92-96.

Törner, M., Karlsson, R., Sęthre, H., & Kadefors, R. (1995). Analysis of serious occupational accidents in Swedish fishery. *Safety Science, 21*, 93-111.

REPETITIVE STRAIN INJURY

Repetitive Strain Injury is a general term describing a workplace injury that is caused by repeated physical movements resulting in damage to tendons, nerves, muscles, and other soft body tissues (Cole, Ibrahim, & Shannon, 2005). A number of occupations are at high risk for such injuries, such as meatpackers, musicians, and computer operators. Another name for this condition is Cumulative Trauma Disorder, which highlights the process underlying the injury. The injury does not appear immediately, as it is the accumulation of small injuries or strains over a period of time. Carpal Tunnel Syndrome is a particular kind of repetitive strain injury affecting the wrist. The industries most commonly affected include meat and poultry processing and packing, textiles and apparel, and those that use vibrating tools such as jackhammers (Atkinson, 2002a). According to the Bureau of Labor Statistics (2005c), the median number of lost workdays due to Carpal Tunnel Syndrome was 27, the highest of any occupational injury or illness. The occupations with the highest incidence rates were laborers; freight movers, stock movers, and material movers; customer service representatives; and first-line supervisors or managers of office and administrative support workers.

Carpal Tunnel Syndrome is an occupational injury and not a disability, according to the Supreme Court (Nash, 2002; Zachary, 2002). The Americans with Disabilities Act (ADA) defines a disability as a physical or mental impairment that substantially limits one or more of the major life activities of an individual. In the case of *Toyota Motor Manufacturing, Kentucky, Inc. v. Williams* (2002), Williams was a worker on an assembly line in an automobile manufacturing plant in Kentucky. She developed pain in her hands, wrists, and arms, and was diagnosed with impairments, including Carpal Tunnel Syndrome. Williams was then reassigned to two quality-control inspection jobs. However, when the company added a third job, her condition worsened, and the company refused her request for an accommodation under the ADA. The Supreme Court ruled that for an individual to be substantially limited in performing manual tasks, the individual must have an impairment that prevents or severely restricts the individual from doing activities that are of central importance to most people's daily lives and the impairment's impact must also be permanent or long-term. Although her physical impairment limited her in performing her job, it was an injury and not a disability under the ADA. The impairments did not prevent or restrict her from performing tasks that were of central importance to most people's daily lives (according to the worker's deposition testimony, even after her condition allegedly worsened, she could still brush her teeth, wash her face, bathe, tend her flower garden, fix breakfast, do laundry, and pick up around the house).

Because of the large number of lost workdays with Carpal Tunnel Syndrome cases, the average cost is more than $13,000 per case (Atkinson, 2002). The cause may be in the design of the jobs, if the job requires workers to perform some activity repeatedly, especially when using a tool that vibrates. And if an employee recovers from Carpal Tunnel Syndrome and returns to the same job, more lost worktime is a predictable result.

There are a number of things that employers can do to deal with ADA issues such as those presented by repetitive strain injury (Alvarez, 2002): (a) understand the legal obligations to provide leave of absence or accommodations and write policies to handle these situations, (b) identify the essential job functions for every job and communicate this information to employees and supervisors, (c) train managers and supervisors to recognize medical conditions that might lead to ADA obligations, and (d) develop options to keep employees working when they are unable to perform their original positions.

Strategic Questions

1. According to the Bureau of Labor Statistics, what are the most typical characteristics of an employee with Carpal Tunnel Syndrome (sex, age, occupation, length of service with employer, race or ethnic origin, industry sector, and number of days away from work)?
2. What is the difference between a disability and physical impairment such as Carpal Tunnel Syndrome? What other occupational injuries would not be considered a disability under ADA? What other occupational injuries would be considered a disability under ADA?
3. Using an engineering approach (make changes in the tools or equipment), what changes to a typical assembly line job would make employees less likely to get a repetitive strain injury?
4. Using a personnel approach (make changes in employee behavior), what changes to the design of a job would make employees less likely to get a repetitive strain injury?

Resources

Alvarez, R. (2002). Tighter reins on who is 'disabled.' *Occupational Health & Safety, 71*(4), 93-94.

Americans with Disabilities Act. (1990). http://www.eeoc.gov/policy/ada.html

Atkinson, W. (2002). The carpal tunnel conundrum. *Wordforce, 81*(9), 17.

Bureau of Labor Statistics. (2005a). *Table 9. Number of nonfatal occupational injuries and illnesses involving days away from work1 by selected worker and case characteristics and nature of injury or illness, All United States, private industry, 2005.* http://stats.bls.gov/iif/oshwc/osh/case/ostb1653.pdf

Bureau of Labor Statistics. (2005b). *Table 10. Number and percent of nonfatal occupational injuries and illnesses involving days away from work resulting from carpal tunnel syndrome, by occupation with one percent or more of total cases, 2005.* http://stats.bls.gov/iif/oshwc/osh/case/ostb1654.pdf

Bureau of Labor Statistics. (2005c). *Table 11. Percent distribution of nonfatal occupational injuries and illnesses involving days away from work by selected injury or illness characteristics and number of days away from work, 2005.* http://stats.bls.gov/news.release/osh2.t11.htm

Cole, D. C., Ibrahim, S., & Shannon, H. S. (2005). Predictors of work-related repetitive strain injuries in a population cohort. *American Journal of Public Health, 95*(7), 1233-1237.

Nash, J. J. (2002). Are ergonomic injuries disabling? *Occupational Hazards, 64*(2), 45-48.

Toyota Motor Manufacturing, Kentucky, Inc. v. Williams, 534 U.S. 184 (Supreme Court of the United States, 2002).

Vargas, C. (2002). Select recent court decisions: Disability law: Substantial limitations under the Americans with Disabilities Act—Toyota Motor Manufacturing, Kentucky, Inc. v. Williams, 122 S. Ct. 681 (2002). *American Journal of Law & Medicine, 28*(1), 125–129.

Zachary, M. (2002). Supreme Court clarifies ADA manual task guidelines. *Supervision, 63*(4), 22-25.

DRUG TESTING

According to OSHA (2007), of the 16.7 million illicit drug users aged 18 or older in 2003, 12.4 million (74.3%) were employed either full-time or part-time. Furthermore, research indicates that between 10% and 20% of the nation's workers who die on the job test positive for alcohol or other drugs. In fact, industries with the highest rates of drug use are the same as those at a high risk for occupational injuries, such as construction, mining, manufacturing, and wholesale. More than half of job site accidents are caused by illegal drug use (Gerber & Yacoubian, 2001). The National Institutes of Health estimated the economic cost of drug abuse in 2002 as $180 billion (National Institute on Drug Abuse, 2004). The costs of drug abuse–related workplace accidents include fatalities, injuries, higher insurance costs, and higher worker's compensation claims (Cholakis, 2005).

One possible organizational response to these undesirable outcomes is to institute a drug testing program. Although not required by OSHA, drug-free workplace programs are natural complements to other initiatives that help ensure safe and healthy workplaces and add value to America's businesses and communities. OSHA works closely with the U.S. Department of Labor's Working Partners for an Alcohol- and Drug-Free Workplace program to help employers ensure that their health and safety plans are enhanced through workplace drug prevention (OSHA, 2007). The Drug-Free Workplace Act of 1988 requires some federal contractors and all federal grantees to agree that they will provide drug-free workplaces as a precondition of receiving a contract or grant from a federal agency.

One of the more common methods of drug testing requires applicants or employees to provide a urine sample for testing. However, there are more than 400 products available to "beat" a drug test, including a lifelike prosthetic device that delivers a clean sample, products to dilute or cleanse a drug user's sample, and chemical adulterants in small, easily concealed vials (Fletcher, 2005). Employees have even substituted a dog sample for their own or sent someone else to donate a sample for them (Sunoo, 1998). The most significant problem in drug test administration is chain of custody. To prevent adulteration of the sample or donation of a sample not belonging to the testee, the test administrator must observe the sample donation process, which is invasive.

An alternative is to collect a hair sample, which is less invasive (but not noninvasive). However, a strand of hair records drug use over time (i.e., the longer the strand of hair, the further back in time the record of drug use). Human hair grows about a half-inch per month, so a 1.5 inch hair sample can provide a history of drug use over a period of 3 months (Overman, 1999). Oral fluid testing is the newest drug testing technology. A sample is taken by an oral swab, and test results can be obtained immediately without a round trip to a testing laboratory.

Regardless of the type of sample collected, there is a problem common to all: No drug test is 100% accurate. Even with a test of a very high degree of accuracy (with correct identifications of illegal drug abusers as illegal drug abusers and nondrug abusers as nondrug abusers), there will be two kinds of errors. False positives are nondrug abusers whom the test incorrectly identifies as drug abusers. This leads to an employee relations problem of falsely accusing someone of abusing illegal drugs. Employees may file lawsuits with claims of erroneous test results, and juries have awarded large verdicts for job loss and wages, as well as for reputation damages (Atkinson, 2002b). Even use of a second test may not solve the problem; running a second test on the same sample may reproduce the same error. And there are a variety of reasons for the test to return a false positive result, including prescription drugs and even common foods (the infamous poppy seed bagel).

The second problem with a less than 100% accurate drug test is false negatives. False negatives are drug abusers whom the test incorrectly identifies as nondrug abusers. This may be the result of the presence of other chemicals that mask the presence of the illegal drug or just an error in testing. When this happens, it means that the employer hires or continues to employ someone who is an illegal drug abuser, incorrectly thinking that, based on the test result, he or she is not a drug abuser.

An entirely different approach to drug testing uses a written integrity test (or honesty test) to predict drug use by employees. It avoids the problems of sample collection and chain of custody and may be seen by applicants and employees as less invasive. Employee perceptions of invasiveness may be related to turnover intentions (Mastrangelo & Popovich, 2000). Mastragelo and Jolton's (2001) initial tests with college students found moderate correlations between integrity test scores and alcohol and drug abuse but suggest that the approach may be limited by the high rate of false negatives.

Strategic Questions

1. Which drug testing method is the least invasive of applicants' or employees' privacy?
2. For which drug testing method is it easiest to maintain the chain of custody?
3. If the accuracy of a drug test is 95%, and the base rate for illegal drug abusers is 10%, how many false positives (incorrectly identifying someone as a drug abuser) will there be if 100 people are tested? If the accuracy of a drug test is 99%, how many false positives will there be?
4. If the accuracy of a drug test is 95%, and the base rate for illegal drug abusers is 10%, how many false negatives (failing to identify a drug abuser) will there be if 100 people are tested? If the accuracy of a drug test is 99%, how many false negatives will there be?
5. How could a hair sample give a false positive from external contamination rather than by illegal drugs in the person's blood?
6. How can applicants or employees "beat" a drug test? What steps can an employer take to reduce the chances that an applicant or employee will beat a drug test?

Resources

Atkinson, W. (2002). The liability of employee drug testing. *Risk Management, 49*(9), 40-44.

Cholakis, P. (2005). How to implement a successful drug testing program. *Risk Management, 52*(11), 24-28.

Fletcher, M. (2005). Drug-test cheats frustrate employer screening efforts. *Business Insurance, 39*(31), 26-28.

Gerber, J. K., & Yacoubian G. S., Jr. (2001). Evaluation of drug testing in the workplace: Study of the construction industry. *Journal of Construction Engineering and Management, 127*(6), 438-444.

Griffin, S. O., Keller, A., & Cohn, A. (2001). Developing a drug testing policy at a public university: Participant perspectives. *Public Personnel Management, 30*(4), 467-481.

Mastrangelo, P. M., & Jolton, J. A. (2001). Predicting on-the-job substance abuse with a written Integrity Test. *Employee Responsibilities and Rights Journal, 13*(2), 95-106.

Mastrangelo, P. M., & Popovich, P. M. (2000). Employees' attitudes toward drug testing, perceptions of organizational climate, and withdrawal from the employer. *Journal of Business and Psychology, 15*(1), 3-18.

National Institute on Drug Abuse. (2004). *The economic costs of drug abuse in the United States.* http://www.whitehousedrugpolicy.gov/publications/economic_costs/economic_costs.pdf

Occupational Safety and Health Administration. (2007). *Safety and health topics: Workplace substance abuse.* http://www.osha.gov/SLTC/substanceabuse/index.html

Overman, S. (1999). Splitting hairs. *HRMagazine, 44*(8), 42-48.

Sunoo, B. P. (1998). Top-10 ways employees disguise drug abuse. *Workforce, 77*(5), 16.

BIORHYTHMS AND ACCIDENTS

One type of safe work program requires employees to regularly attend training sessions as refresher courses on workplace hazards and safe work methods. The programs aim at sending frequent and consistent messages to employees that they are valued assets and that safety is the most important work rule. Continuously reminding employees about workplace safety can take a number of forms, such as postings of the number of safe workdays, or number of lost work days due to injury, as well as generic "Work Safe" posters.

But these messages are general in nature. It would be more effective if a way could be found to predict specific times when employees are more at risk for workplace accidents and then remind the employee at this high-risk time to work safely. For example, overtime work is a potential cause of workplace accidents because overtime work leads to fatigue, which increases the likelihood of accidents (O'Rourke, 2004; Schuster & Rhodes, 1985). Therefore, employers could closely monitor employee scheduling so that employees would be warned before they worked an excessive amount of overtime.

It is known that accidents are more likely to occur during some shifts than others and are especially likely around midnight (Folkard, Lombardi, & Spencer, 2006). This is related to people's circadian rhythms, the daily cycle of changes in body temperature, attention, and sleepiness. But constant monitoring of employees' physical states is impractical and intrusive. The theory of biorhythms was briefly explored as a way to predict when employees were more likely to have accidents, and all that was required was calculation of three repetitive fixed sinusoidal cycles: a 23-day physical cycle, a 28-day emotional cycle, and a 33-day intellectual cycle. The "critical days" were when any of the three rhythms crossed the horizontal axis (shifting from "up" days to "down" days, or vice versa), during which times accidents are supposed to be more probable (Persinger, Cooke, & Janes, 1978).

It seems too good to be true, being able to predict when employees have an increased risk of accident just by knowing their birth dates. Research has consistently shown no relationship between biorhythms and accidents, for mining accidents (Persinger et al., 1978), aircraft accidents (Khalil & Kurucz, 1977), and industrial accidents (Soutar, & Weaver, 1984). In the most thorough test of the relationship between biorhythms and accidents, biorhythm data were calculated for 4,000 pilots over the course of a year, and no correlation was found between biorhythms and accident occurrence (Wolcott, McMeekin, Burgin, & Yanowitch, 1977).

Strategic Questions

1. Find a Web site selling safe work programs (or software) based on biorhythms (i.e., tracking employees' biorhythms to identify their at-risk days for workplace accidents). Does the Web page cite any research supporting the link between biorhythms and accidents?
2. If employees are warned before the start of their work day that it is one of their "critical days," on how many days in a month will the organization be warning them to work safely?

3. If employees were reminded to work safely on random days during the month, would this have any effect on their safe work behavior?
4. Is there a scientific basis for the 23-day physical cycle, 28-day emotional cycle, and 33-day intellectual cycles? How was the length of each of the cycles determined?
5. How can an organization determine whether the safe work programs sold by different vendors will be effective?

Resources

Folkard, S., Lombardi, D. A., & Spencer, M. B. (2006). Estimating the circadian rhythm in the risk of occupational injuries and accidents. *Chronobiology International, 23*(6), 1181-1192.

Khalil, T. M., & Kurucz, C. N. (1977). The influence of 'biorhythm' on accident occurrence and performance. *Ergonomics, 20*(4), 389-398.

Persinger, M. A., Cooke, W. J., & Janes, J. T. (1978). No evidence for relationship between biorhythms and industrial accidents. *Perceptual and Motor Skills, 46*(2), 423-426.

Schuster, M., & Rhodes, S. (1985). The impact of overtime work on industrial accident rates. *Industrial Relations, 24*(2), 234-246.

Soutar, G. N., & Weaver, J. R. (1984). Biorhythm and the incidence of industrial accidents. *Journal of Safety Research, 14*(4), 167-172.

O'Rourke, M. (2004). The costs of overtime. *Risk Management, 51*(3), 44-45.

Wolcott, J. H., McMeekin, R. B., Burgin, R. E., & Yanowitch, R. E. (1977). Correlation of general aviation accidents with biorhythm theory. *Human Factors, 19*(3), 283-293.

Applications

WHAT ARE THE MOST HAZARDOUS OCCUPATIONS?

Occupations can be hazardous for many reasons. Sometimes jobs require handling hazardous materials (e.g., lead, asbestos) or equipment (e.g., chain saws, farm equipment). Other jobs put workers in hazardous situations (e.g., taxi driver, smoke jumper). Some workers are injured by workplace violence. In 2004, there were 5,764 fatal occupational injuries: 2,490 in transportation; 809 assaults and violent acts; 1,009 due to contacts with objects and equipment; 822 from falls; 464 from exposure to harmful substances or environments; and 159 from fires and explosions (Bureau of Labor Statistics, 2004a, 2004b).

Some industries are more hazardous than others. In 2004, of the 5,764 fatal occupational injuries there were: 2,566 in goods producing; 825 in natural resources and mining; 673 in agriculture, forestry, fishing, and hunting; 1,278 in construction; 463 in manufacturing; 206 in wholesale trade; 72 in real estate; 234 in education and health services; 148 in accommodation and food services; and 327 in public administration (Bureau of

Labor Statistics, 2004). The industries with the most fatalities were trade, transportation, and utilities, with 26.5% of all fatalities; and construction with 22.2% of all fatalities (Bureau of Labor Statistics, 2004a). But this is just the total number of fatalities, not a percentage of the number of all workers in that industry. The rate of fatal work injuries across all industries in 2004 was 4.1 per 100,000 workers but was much higher in agriculture, forestry, fishing, and hunting (32.5); mining (25.6); and transportation and warehousing (17.6; Bureau of Labor Statistics, 2005a).

Some occupational illnesses are caused by the work environment. Sick Building Syndrome is caused by poor indoor air quality. The symptoms of Sick Building Syndrome include irritation of the eyes, nose, and throat; dry mucous membranes and skin; erythema; mental fatigue and headache; respiratory infections and cough; hoarseness of voice and wheezing; hypersensitivity reactions; and nausea and dizziness. Generally, these conditions are not easily traced to a specific substance but are perceived as resulting from some unidentified contaminant or combination of contaminants. Symptoms are relieved when the employee leaves the building and may be reduced or eliminated by modifying the ventilation system (OSHA, 1994).

Building-Related Illness describes specific medical conditions of known etiology that can often be documented by physical signs and laboratory findings. Such illnesses include sensory irritation when caused by known agents, respiratory allergies, nosocomial infections, humidifier fever, hypersensitivity pneumonitis, Legionnaires' disease, and the symptoms and signs characteristic of exposure to chemical or biologic substances such as carbon monoxide, formaldehyde, pesticides, endotoxins, or mycotoxins. Some of these conditions are caused by exposure to bioaerosols containing whole or parts of viruses, fungi, bacteria, or protozoans. These illnesses are often potentially severe and, in contrast to Sick Building Syndrome complaints, are often traceable to a specific contaminant source, such as mold infestation and/or microbial growth in cooling towers, air handling systems, and water-damaged furnishings. Symptoms may or may not disappear when the employee leaves the building. Susceptibility is influenced by host factors, such as age and immune system status. Mitigation of Building-Related Illnesses requires identification and removal of the source, especially in cases involving hypersensitivity responses (OSHA, 1994).

To Do

Use the data provided on the Bureau of Labor Statistics Web page, "Safety & Health," to answer these questions.

1. What three occupations have the highest fatality rates per 100,000 workers?
2. What is the most frequent event leading to workplace fatalities?
3. What is the most common event leading to a workplace fatality for first-line supervisors and managers of retail sales workers?

4. What is the profile of workplace fatalities, in terms of the age, sex, and race or ethnic origin? In what age group do the most fatalities occur?
5. What are the employer's obligations relating to indoor air quality in the work environment under the Occupational Safety and Health Act?
6. What are the causes of Sick Building Syndrome? What are the causes of Building Related Illness?
7. What can organizations do to evaluate and control the indoor air quality in the workplace?

Resources

Anonymous. (2006). The 9/11 nightmare goes on for "Ground Zero" emergency workers. *Safety & Health Practitioner, 24*(10), 10.

Bureau of Labor Statistics. (2004). *Industry by event or exposure, 2004. TABLE A-1. Fatal occupational injuries by industry and event or exposure.* http://stats.bls.gov/iif/oshwc/cfoi/cftb0196.pdf

Bureau of Labor Statistics. (2004). *Industry by private sector, government workers, and self-employed workers, 2004 TABLE A-3. Fatal occupational injuries to private sector wage and salary workers, government workers, and self-employed workers by industry, All United States.* http://www.bls.gov/iif/oshwc/cfoi/cftb0198.pdf

Bureau of Labor Statistics. (2005). *Census of fatal occupational injuries charts, 1992-2005. Number and rate of fatal occupational injuries by private industry sector, 2005.* http://www.bls.gov/iif/oshwc/cfoi/cfch0004.pdf

Bureau of Labor Statistics. (n.d.). *Overview of BLS statistics on worker safety and health.* http://www.bls.gov/bls/safety.htm

Discovery Channel. (2007). *Dirty jobs, Season 1* [Television broadcast]. United States: Author.

Law, L. (Producer). (2005). *Deadliest catch: Crab fishing in Alaska.* [Television broadcast]. United States: Discovery Channel.

Lioy, P. J., Pellizzari, E., & Prezant, D. (2006). The World Trade Center aftermath and its effects on health: Understanding and learning through human-exposure science. *Environmental Science & Technology, 40*(22), 6876-6885.

Naso, M. (2007). Airing out concerns. *Journal of Property Management, 72*(1), 58-59.

Occupational Safety and Health Administration. (1994). *Indoor air quality—59:15968-16039.* http://www.osha.gov/pls/oshaweb/owadisp.show_document?p_table=FEDERAL_REGISTER&p_id=13369

Occupational Safety and Health Administration. (1998). *Informational booklet on industrial hygiene.* http://www.osha.gov/Publications/OSHA3143/OSHA3143.htm

Thomas-Mobley, L., Roper, K. O., & Oberle, R. (2005). A proactive assessment of Sick Building Syndrome. *Facilities, 23*(1/2), 6-15.

Thörn, A. (2000). Case study of a sick building. Could an integrated biopsychosocial perspective prevent chronicity? *European Journal of Public Health, 10*(2), 133-137.

CALCULATING INCIDENCE RATES

Although the Bureau of Labor Statistics collects data on the number of occupational injuries and illnesses stratified by a number of factors such as sex and age, to get a better idea of how often occupational injuries and illnesses happen, an index number should be calculated based on a ratio of the number of injuries or illnesses to the number of employees and hours worked. This is the Incidence Rate. The Incidence Rate is the number of injuries and/or illnesses per 100 full-time workers, calculated as follows: $(N/EH) \times 200{,}000$, where N = number of injuries and/or illnesses and EH = total hours worked by all employees during the calendar year; and 200,000 = base for 100 full-time equivalent workers working 40 hours per week, 50 weeks per year.

To Do

Use either the Incidence Rate Calculator on the Bureau of Labor Statistics Web page or create a spreadsheet to calculate the Incidence Rate. If you are using the Incidence Rate Calculator, follow the steps below. If you are using a spreadsheet, use the values given in the steps below to create the necessary formulas to calculate the Incidence Rate.

1. Enter the number of hours actually worked by all employees at the organization in the given year. Assume that you have 432 full-time employees, working 2,000 hours per year (40 hours per week, 50 weeks per year).
2. Enter the number of nonfatal work-related injury and illness cases. Assume that you had 27 nonfatal work-related injuries and illnesses.
3. Select the current year and "All ownerships" for your state.
4. Incidence Rate is the (Number of injuries and illnesses × 200,000) divided by total hours worked. Calculate the results.
5. Find the actual numbers for your current employer, or your university, and calculate the Incidence Rate.

Resources

Bureau of Labor Statistics. *Incidence Rate calculator.* http://data.bls.gov/IIRC/

Cable, J. (2006). Workplace injury and illness rate declines. *Occupational Hazards, 68*(11), 8.

Ussif, A. (2004). An international analysis of workplace injuries. *Monthly Labor Review, 127*(3), 41-51.

Experiential Exercises

OSHA COMPLIANCE

The Occupational Safety and Health Act (1970) was passed to ensure safe and healthful working conditions for working men and women by authorizing enforcement of the standards developed under the Act; by assisting and encouraging the states in their efforts to assure safe and healthful working conditions; and by providing for research, information, education, and training in the field of occupational safety and health.

OSHA requires certain employers to prepare and maintain records of work-related injuries and illnesses. There are three forms for reporting occupational injuries and illnesses.

Form 300, Log of Work-Related Injuries and Illnesses, is used to classify work-related injuries and illnesses and to note the extent and severity of each case. When an incident occurs, the form is used to record specific details about what happened and how it happened. *Form 300A, Summary of Work-Related Injuries and Illnesses*, shows the totals for the year in each category. This form is posted in a visible location so that employees are aware of the injuries and illnesses occurring in their workplace. Employees have the right to review their employer's injury and illness records. Employers must keep a log for each establishment or site. If the organization has more than one establishment, it must keep a separate form for each physical location that is expected to be in operation for 1 year or longer. *Form 301, Injury and Illness Incident Report*, is one of the first forms to be filled out when a recordable work-related injury or illness has occurred. Together with the *Log and Summary*, these forms help the employer and OSHA develop a picture of the extent and severity of work-related incidents (OSHA, n.d.).

Within 8 hours after the death of any employee from a work-related incident or the in-patient hospitalization of three or more employees as a result of a work-related incident, the organization must orally report the fatality and multiple hospitalization by telephone or in person to the Area Office of the OSHA, U.S. Department of Labor, that is nearest to the site of the incident, or use the OSHA toll-free central telephone number. The information that the organization must report to OSHA is the establishment name, the location of the incident, the time of the incident, the number of fatalities or hospitalized employees, the names of any injured employees, the organization's contact person and his or her phone number, and a brief description of the incident.

To Do

Part 1. Download *OSHA Form 301: Injury and Illness Incident Report* from the OSHA Web site. Fill out *OSHA Form 301* for a fictitious employee and incident. Download *OSHA Form 300: Log of Work-Related Injuries and Illnesses* and add this incident to *Form 300.*

Part 2. Employees, former employees, and their representatives have the right to review the OSHA *Form 300* in its entirety. Obtain *Form 300A: Summary of Work-Related Injuries and Illnesses* from your current employer, a past employer, or any organization, to share with the class (or copy the data from the posted form). The *Summary of Work-Related Injuries and Illnesses* should be posted in a visible location (from February 1 to April 30 of the year following the year covered by the form) so that the employees are aware of injuries and illnesses occurring in their workplace.

(Continued)

(Continued)

Resources

Occupational Safety and Health Act. (1970). http://www.osha.gov/pls/oshaweb/owasrch.search_form?p_doc_type=OSHACT&p_toc_level=0&p_keyvalue=

Occupational Safety and Health Administration (2001, January 19). *Reporting fatalities and multiple hospitalization incidents to OSHA—1904.39.* http://www.osha.gov/pls/oshaweb/owadisp.show_document?p_table=STANDARDS&p_id=12783

Occupational Safety and Health Administration, U.S. Department of Labor. http://www.osha.gov/, http://www.osha.gov/pls/publications/pubindex.list, http://www.osha.gov/pls/publications/pubindex.list#300

DRUG TESTING

Industries with the highest rates of drug use are the same as those at a high risk for occupational injuries, such as construction, mining, manufacturing, and wholesale (OSHA, n.d.). One approach to improving workplace safety is to create a drug-free workplace. A comprehensive drug-free workplace approach includes five components: a policy, supervisor training, employee education, employee assistance, and drug testing. Such programs, especially when drug testing is included, must be reasonable and take into consideration employees' rights to privacy.

The drug-free workplace policy is the first step in creating a drug-free workplace program. The policy should meet the needs of the organization, and every organization's needs will be different. The policy should include a statement about why the policy is being implemented, such as a general statement about protecting the safety and health of both employees and customers. There should be a clear statement of behaviors that violate the policy (such as the use, possession, transfer, or sale of illegal drugs by employees) and the organizational consequences of violating the policy (from referral for assistance to termination). And the policy should be disseminated to all employees.

Once a policy has been developed, supervisors need to be trained so that they fully understand the drug-free workplace policy, how to deal with employees who have performance problems (that may or may not be drug related), and how to refer employees to available assistance (to the organization's Employee Assistance Program or other assistance).

Employees also need a drug education program so that they understand the organization's drug-free workplace policy, the nature of drug addiction and its impact on work performance and personal life, and help that is available to them to deal with drug-related problems. This information can be given to employees in multiple methods, such as seminars, training sessions, and home mailings.

Employee Assistance is a general term for anything the organization provides to employees related to the prevention, identification, and resolution of personal and productivity issues, including those that may stem from substance abuse. One form of employee assistance is an Employee Assistance Program, which provides confidential help to employees with personal problems, including those related to drug abuse, and may also provide supervisor training and employee education.

Drug testing might be used to deter and detect drug use, as well as provide documentation for referral to treatment or for taking disciplinary action. An employer must decide who will be tested (all employees, job applicants, or employees in safety-sensitive positions), when employees will be tested (postoffer prehire, reasonable suspicion, postaccident, randomly, or periodically), which drugs will be tested for (illegal drugs only or a range of prescription drugs), and how the drug tests will be conducted. At this point, legal counsel will be needed to ensure that the program is in compliance with federal, state, and local laws.

To Do

Choose an organization (past or current employer, your college or university) and develop a Drug-Free Workplace Policy. The policy should include the following:

1. The policy statement:
   - Why the policy is being implemented;
   - Behaviors that violate the policy;
   - Organizational consequences for violating the policy;
   - How the policy will be disseminated to all employees.
2. Supervisor training:
   - Full understanding of the drug-free workplace policy;
   - How to deal with employees who have performance problems;
   - How to refer employees to available assistance.
3. Employee education:
   - An explanation of the organization's drug-free workplace policy;
   - The nature of drug addiction and its impact on work performance and personal life;
   - Assistance available to them to deal with drug-related problems;
   - How the information will be given to employees.

(Continued)

(Continued)

4. Employee assistance:
   - A description of the assistance that will be made available to employees;
   - Providing assistance through an Employee Assistance Program or other sources.
5. Drug testing:
   - Whether drug testing be done;
   - Who will be tested, when, and for which drugs;
   - How the drug tests will be conducted;
   - Getting advice of legal counsel to comply with federal, state, and local laws.

Resources

Bhagat, R. S., Steverson, P. K., & Segovis, J. C. (2007). International and cultural variations in employee assistance programmes: Implications for managerial health and effectiveness. *Journal of Management Studies, 44*(2), 222-242.

Carpenter, C. S. (2007). Workplace drug testing and worker drug use. *Health Research and Educational Trust, 42*(2), 795-810.

Drug Free Workplace. http://www.drugfreeworkplace.com/

Hazelden Foundation. www.hazelden.org

Hoberman, J. M. (2005). *Testosterone dreams: Rejuvenation, aphrodisia, doping.* Berkeley: University of California Press.

Occupational Safety and Health Administration. (n.d.). *Safety and health topics: Workplace substance abuse.* http://www.osha.gov/SLTC/substanceabuse/index.html

Owens, D. M. (2006). EAP's for a diverse world. *HRMagazine, 51*(10), 91-94.

U.S. Code, Title 41, Chapter 10. *Drug Free Workplace Act of 1988.* http://www.law.cornell.edu/uscode/html/uscode41/usc_sup_01_41_10_10.html

U.S. Department of Labor. *Drug-Free Workplace Advisor.* http://www.dol.gov/elaws/asp/drugfree/drugs/screen92.asp

U.S. Department of Labor, Office of the Assistant Secretary for Policy. *Training & Educational Materials.* http://www.dol.gov/asp/programs/drugs/workingpartners/materials/materials.asp

U.S. Department of Labor. *Working partners for an alcohol and drug-free workplace.* http://www.dol.gov/asp/programs/drugs/workingpartners/materials/stepsbroch.pdf

Creative Exercises

STRESS AND BURNOUT

Job stress can be defined as the harmful physical and emotional responses that occur when the requirements of the job do not match the capabilities, resources, or needs of the worker; this can lead to poor health and even injury (National Institute of Occupational Safety and Health, 1999). Job stress is perhaps the most pervasive occupational health problem in the workplace today. An estimated 78% of employees say that work is their biggest source of stress (Farrell & Geist-Martin, 2005). Loss of jobs, outsourcing, jobless recovery, and world events such as war and terrorism are all making workers more anxious, tense, and depressed. Many employees have been forced to do the work of two or three people due to reductions in force. People take this stress home with them, where it has a negative impact on their family and friends. The American Institute of Stress states that illnesses related to stress cost more than $300 billion per year (Losyk, 2006). Surveys show that 25% to 40% of workers report that their jobs are stressful (National Institute of Occupational Safety and Health, 1999).

There are a number of emotional and behavioral results and manifestations of job stress, including depression and anxiety. Stress plays an important role in several types of chronic health problems—especially cardiovascular disease, musculoskeletal disorders, and psychological disorders (National Institute of Occupational Safety and Health, 1999). According to the Occupational Safety and Health Administration (2001), approximately 11 million workers report health-endangering levels of mental stress at work. A large and growing body of literature on occupational stress has identified certain job and organizational characteristics as having deleterious effects on the psychological and physical health of workers, including their mental health. These stressors include high workload demands coupled with low job control; role ambiguity and conflict; lack of job security; poor relationships with coworkers and supervisors; and repetitive, narrow tasks. These include role stressors and demands in excess of control. Decreased performance, less teamwork, low morale, increased health costs and workers' compensation claims, lawsuits, lateness and absenteeism, theft, and sabotage are all results of out-of-control stress levels in workers (Losyk, 2006).

Burnout is the total depletion of physical and mental resources caused by excessive striving to reach some unrealistic work-related goal (Maslach & Jackson, 1981). The symptoms of burnout include being unable to relax; working more but enjoying it less; increased self-medication; and leading an irritable and a workaholic lifestyle. Some jobs are more likely to cause burnout (e.g., nurses, teachers, social workers, firefighters, police officers, paramedics, search and rescue workers, soldiers, and salespeople; Grant & Campbell, 2007; Lewin & Sager, 2007).

Created in 1982, OSHA's Voluntary Protection Programs recognize and partner with businesses and work sites that show excellence in occupational safety and health. Sites are committed to effective employee protection beyond the requirements of OSHA standards. Voluntary Protection Program participants develop and implement systems to effectively identify, evaluate, prevent, and control occupational hazards to prevent employee injuries and illnesses. As a result, the average Voluntary Protection Program work site has a lost workday Incidence Rate at least 50% below the average of its industry. In return, OSHA removes participants from programmed inspection lists and does not issue citations for standards violations that are promptly corrected (OSHA, 2004). 3M Company's manufacturing site in Brookings, South Dakota, was recognized by OSHA for excellence in employee safety and health; the plant was designated a Voluntary Protection Program "Star" site, the highest level of recognition that OSHA's Voluntary Protection Programs offer, because of their exceptional injury prevention program, supplemented by an exemplary employee wellness system that includes on-site medical professionals, physical therapists, and health fairs (OSHA, 2005).

Health and wellness programs have existed in U.S. organizations since the late 1970s. They can be defined as any programs designed to improve an employee's health or eliminate negative health habits. Stress management is a major component and a driver of health and wellness programs, but there are other activities that aid in improving employee health and overall employee well-being, such as diet and nutrition; healthy relationships; time-management training; family-friendly policies (Losyk, 2006); health and fitness programs (Gura, 2002); and programs aimed at improving employees' social health, including building relationships with peers, coworkers, and family (Farrell & Geist-Martin, 2005). The focus of wellness programs can be the individual worker, the working group, the organization of the work, or the organization as a whole (van der Hek & Plomp, 1997). Investment in employee wellness can pay off for both organizations and employees (Bailey, 2006; Schaaf, 2005).

To Do

Create a proposal for a Wellness Program for an organization. The proposal should include the following sections:

1. A description of the proposed program,
2. Anticipated benefits of the proposed program,
3. Costs of the program,
4. Justification of the program (a comparison of the costs and the expected benefits),
5. A list of the first 12 topics for the Monthly Wellness eNewsletter,
6. The first Monthly Wellness eNewsletter.

Resources

American Institute of Stress. http://www.stress.org/

Bailey, G. (2006). Saving justifies the spend. *Occupational Health, 58*(10), 13-15.

Farrell, A., & Geist-Martin, P. (2005). Communicating social health: Perceptions of wellness at work. *Management Communication Quarterly, 18*(4), 543-592.

Foulke, J., & Sherman, B. (2005). Comprehensive workforce health management—not a cost, but a strategic advantage. *Employment Relations Today, 32*(2), 17-29.

Froiland, P. (1993). What cures job stress? *Training, 30*(12), 32-36.

Grant, A. M., & Campbell, E. M. (2007). Doing good, doing harm, being well and burning out: The interactions of perceived prosocial and antisocial impact in service work. *Journal of Occupational and Organizational Psychology, 80*(4), 665-692.

Gura, S. T. (2002). Yoga for stress reduction and injury prevention at work. *Work, 19*(1), 3-7.

Jones, J. W., Barge, B. N., Steffy, B. D., Fay, L. M., Kunz, L. K., & Wuebker, L. J. (1988). Stress and medical malpractice: Organizational risk assessment and intervention. *Journal of Applied Psychology, 73*(4), 727-735.

Kowalski, K. M. (2006). *The effects of disaster on workers: A study of burnout in investigators of serious accidents and fatalities in the U.S. mining industry.* http://www.cdc.gov/niosh/mining/pubs/pdfs/eodow.pdf

Lewin, J. E., & Sager, J. K. (2007). A process model of burnout among salespeople: Some new thoughts. *Journal of Business Research, 60*(12), 1216-1224.

Losyk, B. (2006). Getting a grip on stress: What HR managers must do to prevent burnout and turnover. *Employment Relations Today, 33*(1), 9-17.

Maslach, C., & Jackson, S. E. (1981). The measurement of experienced burnout. *Journal of Occupational Behavior, 2*(2), 99-113.

Michalsen, A., Grossman, P., Acil, A., Langhorst, J., Lüdtke, R., Esch, T., et al. (2005). Rapid stress reduction and anxiolysis among distressed women as a consequence of a three-month intensive yoga program. *Medical Science Monitor, 11*(12), CR555-CR561.

Montana University System Wellness Newsletter. (2007, January). http://www.montana.edu/wellness/CN2007Jan.pdf

National Institute of Occupational Safety and Health. (1999). *Stress at work* (Publication No. 99-101). http://www.cdc.gov/niosh/pdfs/stress.pdf

Occupational Safety and Health Administration. (2001). *Occupational injury and illness recording and reporting requirements.* http://www.osha.gov/pls/oshaweb/owadisp.show_document?p_table=FEDERAL_REGISTER&p_id=16312

Occupational Safety and Health Administration. (2004, April). *OSHA fact sheet: Voluntary protection programs.* http://www.osha.gov/OshDoc/data_General_Facts/factsheet-vpp.pdf

Occupational Safety and Health Administration. (2005, August 24). *3M Company in Brookings recognized by OSHA for excellence in occupational safety and health.* OSHA Regional News Release, Region 8. http://www.osha.gov/pls/oshaweb/owadisp.show_document?p_table=NEWS_RELEASES&p_id=11549

Schaaf, R. (2005). From "sick" care to "health" care: Controlling costs through employee wellness. *Employee Benefit Plan Review, 60*(2), 10-11.

Tufts University Wellness Newsletter. (2005, Spring). http://ase.tufts.edu/healthservice/wellness.htm, http://ase.tufts.edu/healthservice/documents/wellnessSpring05.pdf

van der Hek, H., & Plomp, H. N. (1997). Occupational stress management programmes: A practical overview of published effect studies. *Occupational Medicine, 47*(3), 133-141.

White, M. (2005). The cost-benefit of well employees. *Harvard Business Review, 83*(12), 22.

REDUCING THE RISKS OF HIGH-RISK EMPLOYEES

The mission of the OSHA is to assure the safety and health of America's workers by setting and enforcing standards; providing training, outreach, and education; establishing partnerships; and encouraging continual improvement in workplace safety and health. One of the ways that OSHA does training, outreach, and education is with eTools, which are stand-alone, interactive, Web-based training tools on occupational safety and health topics. They are highly illustrated and use graphical menus, and some also use expert system modules, which enable the user to answer questions and receive reliable advice on how OSHA regulations apply to their work site. Some of the eTools topics include Ammonia Refrigeration, Battery Manufacturing, Construction, Eye and Face Protection, Logging, Noise and Hearing Conservation, Poultry Processing, Scaffolding, and Youth in Agriculture. There are also Ergonomics eTools covering such topics as Baggage Handling, Computer Workstations, and the Printing Industry.

According to the eTool on Scaffolding (Occupational Safety and Health Administration, 2002), an estimated 2.3 million construction workers, or 65% of the construction industry, work on scaffolds frequently. Protecting these workers from scaffold-related accidents would prevent 4,500 injuries and 50 deaths every year, at a savings for American employers of $90 million in workdays not lost. The Scaffolding eTool provides illustrated safety checklists for suspended and supported scaffolds. Its purpose is to identify hazards as well as the controls that keep those hazards from becoming tragedies.

OSHA has also developed PowerPoint Presentations and streaming videos on various occupational safety and health topics, which are useful for training courses. Among the topics:

- Bloodborne pathogens and needlestick prevention
- Eye and face protection
- Logging
- Powered industrial truck operator training standard
- Pump jack and ladder jack scaffold photo compliance guide
- Workplace violence prevention: Health care and social service workers

To Do

Choose any occupational health and safety topic, and create a PowerPoint presentation or eTool that could be used for training, outreach, and education. The presentation or eTool should include what the hazards are, what safety standards apply, solutions to improve workplace safety in that industry, and where to find additional information.

For example, logging is one of the most dangerous occupations in the United States, so there are many topics that could be used for the presentation. The tools and equipment used in logging, such as chain saws and logging machines pose hazards wherever they are used. As loggers use their tools and equipment, they are dealing with massive weights and irresistible momentum of falling, rolling, and sliding trees and logs. The hazards are even more acute when dangerous environmental conditions are factored in, such as uneven, unstable, or rough terrain; inclement weather including rain, snow, lightning, winds, and extreme cold; and/or remote and isolated work sites where health care facilities are not immediately accessible.

Resources

Occupational Safety and Health Administration (2002a). *eTool: Scaffolding.* http://www.osha.gov/SLTC/etools/scaffolding/index.html

Occupational Safety and Health Administration (2002b). *Multimedia: PowerPoint presentations and streaming video.* http://www.osha.gov/SLTC/multimedia.html

Occupational Safety and Health Administration (2002c). *Safety and health topics.* http://www.osha.gov/SLTC/index.html, http://www.osha.gov/SLTC/text_index.html

Occupational Safety and Health Administration. (n.d.). *Safety and health topics: Logging.* http://www.osha.gov/SLTC/logging/index.html

Employee Relations and Labor-Management Relations 10

Strategic Objective

In 2007, 12.1% of employed wage and salary workers were union members, according to the U.S. Department of Labor's Bureau of Labor Statistics. The actual number of employees in a union has remained at about 12% since 2006 (about 15 million workers). The union membership rate has steadily declined from 20% in 1983, the first year for which comparable union data are available. Workers in the public sector have a union membership rate nearly five times that of private sector employees; and education, training, and library occupations have the highest unionization rate among all occupations, at 37.2% (Bureau of Labor Statistics, 2008c).

Shortly after the passage of the National Labor Relations Act of 1935, unions represented more than one third of the workers in the private sector, but today they represent less than 10%. Union membership in the public sector was less than 10%, but today, over 40% of local government and more than a third of state government employees are unionized (Adler, 2006). McCartin (2006) argues that the unsuccessful strike of unionized federal air traffic controllers (Professional Air Traffic Controllers Organization, or PATCO) in 1981 was the most significant single event in accelerating the decline of organized labor in the United States in the late 20th century, primarily because it legitimized the use of permanent replacement workers during strikes. The strike led to the firing of 11,345 striking air traffic controllers and the decertification of their union, the only decertification of a federal union (Shostak, 2006). According to Traynor and Fichtenbaum (1997), following the strike, from 1982 to 1990, total wage payments to union workers were significantly lower than they would have been under pre-PATCO conditions.

Some organizations have employees who belong to labor unions, others have no unions, and some organizations without unionized workers try to avoid becoming unionized (e.g., Cabot, 1997; Koteff, 2006). A report commissioned by the worker advocacy group American Rights at Work (Mehta & Theodore, 2005) claims that a majority of employers use legal and illegal antiunion tactics during union representation elections: 30% of employers fire prounion workers, 49% of employers threaten to close a work site when workers try to form a union, and 82% of employers hire consultants to fight organizing drives.

Since the 1980s, the emergence of the global economy and more progressive management practices have led to significant changes in the relationship between employers and employees. Organizations began to make use of more team-based organizational structures, employee involvement programs, and other forms of worker participation. For example, the electronics industry developed innovative management styles and employee relations techniques as early as the 1930s to deal with recruiting and retaining a highly skilled workforce. These management practices included building collaborative relations between employers and employees by giving substantial autonomy to their engineering staff; organizing research and product development work around teams; involving their professional employees in the decision-making process; and developing unusual financial incentives such as profit-sharing programs, stock ownership, and stock-option plans (Lécuyer, 2003). Organizations have found that employee participation brings many benefits, including fostering consensus decision making, improved commitment to decisions and organizational goals, and improved quality of worklife for employees (e.g., Belanger, 2000; Coopman, 2001; Hodson, 2002; Mohrman, Lawler, & Ledford, 1996).

Strategic Issues in HRM

INTEREST-BASED BARGAINING

Labor-management relations can range from cooperative to adversarial, depending on the attitudes of the organization and the union, and their history of past negotiations. Some labor-management conflicts attract more media attention than others. In 1998-1999, the National Basketball Association cancelled 428 games during a lockout. In 1994, a mid-season strike by Major League Baseball players caused the cancellation of the remainder of the season and the World Series for the first time since 1903 (Greenwood, 1995). And in 2004, the National Hockey League became the first professional sports league to lose an entire season, with 1,230 games lost due to a work stoppage, in the longest lasting shutdown (310 days) in sports history (Staudohar, 2005).

On the other hand, the General Motor's assembly plant at Freemont, California, had significant problems, with unexcused absenteeism running more than 20% and quality and productivity below the General Motors norm, which itself was falling behind Japanese automaker standards (Adler, Goldoftas, & Levine, 1997). There was an accumulated backlog of more than a thousand grievances and a union-management relationship that George Nano, United Auto Workers Shop Committee chair for the plant, called an "ongoing war" (Brown & Reich, 1989). In 1984, General Motors began a joint venture with Toyota at the Freemont plant, with a focus on teamwork between labor and management and a collective bargaining agreement that described the workers as professional partners committed to the New United Motors Manufacturing Inc. (NUMMI) values: Employees were now expected to work as members of a team, participating in setting and meeting team goals, looking for opportunities to make the company more efficient, and helping to meet production goals and schedules (Rehder & Smith, 1986). By 1986, NUMMI's productivity was almost twice that of the Freemont plant and 40% better than the typical GM assembly plant, and had the highest quality levels of any U.S. auto plant (Adler et al., 1997).

The Chrysler New Castle Machining and Forge Plant had a history of adversarial labor-management relations, but when it was put on the list for plant closings, labor and management cooperated to write a Modern Operating Agreement, focused on trust and teamwork rather than antagonism and animosity (Vasilash, 1995). In the year the Agreement was ratified, the plant did $148 million in business and ran a $5 million deficit; eight years later, the plant did $250 million in business and was profitable; work-related injuries decreased; grievances dropped from 800 per year to fewer than 49; and the absenteeism rate dropped to 2.8%, one of the lowest in the company (Leinert, 1994). Production costs became competitive with TRW and Dana, and quality improved by 35% to 50% per year (Vasilash, 1995).

Interest-Based Bargaining (IBB) is a negotiating process developed by the Federal Mediation and Conciliation Service to facilitate non-adversarial negotiations. Instead of each party taking a position and working toward compromise (or at least settlement), IBB is based on discovery and resolution of mutual interests, seeking to improve labor-management relations and contract negotiations through problem solving and consensus decision making (Bohlander & Naber, 1999). According to the Federal Mediation and Conciliation Service, parties that participate in IBB have learned that agreements tend to address issues in more depth than those reached using traditional techniques, because they are the result of a process aimed at satisfying mutual interests by consensus, not just one side's interests at the expense of the other. IBB is a kind of integrative negotiation, which deals with the real needs and interests of the bargaining parties, whereas traditional distributive negotiation deals with positions and resources and how much each side wants (Leventhal, 2006). A survey of union and management negotiators conducted by the Federal Mediation and Conciliation Service found that among respondents who report having used the interest-based approach, 55.8% of union respondents and 80.1% of managers report a preference for it (Cutcher-Gershenfeld, Kochan, & Wells, 1998).

An example of a labor agreement reached through the use of IBB is the Salt River Project. Labor-management relations were close to an impasse because of the adversarial nature of the relationship, so the International Brotherhood of Electrical Workers and Salt River Project management agreed to try the IBB approach (Estes, 1997). After concluding two successful contracts using IBB, the parties reported distinct changes in their labor negotiations, including an absence of "attitudinal" bargaining, reduced number of bargaining issues, and increased information sharing. However, there were some concerns about using the IBB approach: IBB negotiations take longer to complete and are more costly to conduct, bargaining over wages is not as amenable to the IBB method as noneconomic issues, and negotiators need continuous IBB training (Bohlander & Naber, 1999).

Paquet, Gaétan, and Bergeron (2000) compared the changes to collective bargaining agreements in 19 cases that used IBB and 19 that used more traditional forms of negotiation, and they found that clauses dealing with joint governance and organizational innovation underwent more changes when the parties adopted the IBB approach and the IBB approach led to more union concessions.

Strategic Questions

1. Negotiating a contract often centers primarily on money issues. When negotiating about money, is it actually *only* the money?
2. When entering into a contract negotiation, what are the primary interests of labor?
3. When entering into a contract negotiation, what are the primary interests of management?

4. Is IBB likely to work better for the first contract negotiated between the union and the organization, or for a mature contract?

5. What were the mutual interests of the hockey players and the hockey team owners in 2004-2005 that might have formed the basis of a successful contract negotiation using IBB?

Resources

Adler, P. S., Goldoftas, B., & Levine, D. I. (1997). Ergonomics, employee involvement, and the Toyota Production System: A case study of NUMMI's 1993 model introduction. *Industrial and Labor Relations Review, 50*(3), 416-437.

Bohlander, G. W., & Naber, J. (1999). Nonadversarial negotiations: The FMCS Interest-Based Bargaining program. *Journal of Collective Negotiations, 28*(1), 41-52.

Brainerd, R. (1998). Interest-Based Bargaining: Labor and management working together in Ramsey County, Minnesota. *Public Personnel Management, 27*(1), 51-60.

Brown, C., & Reich, M. (1989). When does union-management cooperation work? A look at NUMMI and GM-Van Nuys. *California Management Review, 31*(4), 21-44.

Carlton, P. W. (1995). Interest-based collective bargaining at Youngstown State University: A fresh organizational approach. *Journal of Collective Negotiations, 24*(4), 337-347.

Cutcher-Gershenfeld, J., & Kochan, T. A. (2004). Taking stock: Collective bargaining at the turn of the century. *Industrial and Labor Relations Review, 58*(1), 3-26.

Cutcher-Gershenfeld, J., & Kochan, T. A., & Wells, J. C. (1998). How do labor and management view collective bargaining? *Monthly Labor Review, 121*(10), 23-31.

Cutcher-Gershenfeld, J., & Kochan, T. A., & Wells, J. C. (2001). In whose interest? A first look at national survey data on Interest-Based Bargaining in labor relations. *Industrial Relations, 40*(1), 1-21.

Cronin-Harris, C. (2004). Negotiation strategy: Planning is critical. *CPA Journal, 74*(12), 44-45.

Estes, M. (1997). Adversaries find common ground. *Workforce, 76*(3), 97-102.

Federal Mediation and Conciliation Service. http://www.fmcs.gov/internet/

Federal Mediation and Conciliation Service. *Interest-Based Bargaining: Are you looking for an alternative to traditional collective bargaining?* http://www.fmcs.gov/internet/itemDetail.asp?categoryID=131&itemID=15804

Federal Mediation and Conciliation Service. *Featured case study: Ford Cleveland Engine Plant #2.* http://www.fmcs.gov/internet/categoryList.asp?categoryID=163

Greenwood, J. S. (1995). What Major League Baseball can learn from its international counterparts: Building a model collective-bargaining agreement for Major League Baseball. *George Washington Journal of International Law and Economics, 29*(2), 581-618.

Leventhal, L. (2006). Implementing interest-based negotiations: Conditions for success with evidence from Kaiser Permanente. *Dispute Resolution Journal, 61*(3), 50-58.

Lienert, A. (1994). Forging a new partnership. *Management Review, 83*(10), 39-43.

Paquet, R., Gaétan, I., & Bergeron, J. (2000). Does Interest-Based Bargaining (IBB) really make a difference in collective bargaining outcomes? *Negotiation Journal, 16*(3), 281-296.

Staudohar, P. D. (2005). The hockey lockout of 2004-05. *Monthly Labor Review, 128*(12), 23-29.

Vasilash, G. S. (1995). Chrysler New Castle: How to go from near extinction to world class. *Production, 107*(1), 56-59.

GRADUATE STUDENT UNIONS

According to the Bureau of Labor Statistics (2008d), education, training, and library occupations had the highest unionization rate among all occupations, at 37.2% compared to only 12.1% of all employed wage and salary workers. The University of Iowa's teaching assistants voted to unionize in 1996 (Saltzman, 2000), and graduate students at New York University formed the first graduate student union at a private university in 2001 (Lafer, 2003). Universities with recognized graduate student unions have grown from 10 to at least 30 over the past decade, including major universities such as Temple, Michigan State, and Columbia (Singh, Zinni, & MacLennan, 2006). Approximately 20% of all graduate employees are now covered by collective bargaining agreements (Lafer, 2003).

Economic pressures on universities have caused university administrators to shift increasing amounts of teaching duties away from regular full-time faculty onto graduate students and various types of part-time or adjunct instructors. Lafer (2003) illustrates the point with data showing the incentives and the result: An average full professor in 1999 earned $71,000 per year, a graduate student teacher earned between $5,000 and $20,000; from 1975-1995, overall enrollment expanded significantly, while the number of tenure track faculty decreased by 10% and graduate student teaching assistants increased by nearly 40%. Graduate students make up about 18% of university teachers, part-time faculty make up approximately 32%, and about half of all university teachers are full-time faculty (Coalition of Graduate Employee Unions, 2000). At Yale University, 70% of the undergraduate teaching is done by nonpermanent teachers (i.e., graduate students and instructors not on the tenure track; Graduate Employees and Students Organization, 1999).

University administrators have argued that it is not the money; it is the principle. Graduate students have a unique status as faculty-in-training—that is, their teaching and research work is really part of their education—so graduate students should not be considered employees and allowing graduate students to unionize would violate cherished principles of academic freedom (Lafer, 2003). Although a graduate student union might inhibit the faculty's ability to instruct and advise their graduate students and disrupt the relationship between graduate students and faculty, a survey of about 300 faculty members at five university campuses found that faculty did not have negative attitudes toward graduate student bargaining and believed that it would not interfere would the faculty's ability to advise, instruct, and mentor their graduate students (Hewitt, 2000).

Strategic Questions

1. Why would graduate students want to join a union?
2. Why would some universities (some of which have unionized faculty) not recognize a graduate student union?
3. Are teaching assistants (i.e., graduate student teachers) employees or students?
4. What is the labor market for graduate students just completing their PhD—is the demand greater than the supply, or the supply greater than the demand?
5. What impact does an increasing percentage of classes taught by graduate students and part-time faculty have on the quality of university teaching?
6. How much instruction do graduate students typically get to develop their teaching skills? Are faculty evaluated on how well they develop the teaching skills of their graduate students?

Resources

American Association of University Professors. http://www.aaup.org/aaup

Brown University v. National Labor Relations Board, 342 NLRB (1976). http://www.nlrb.gov/shared_files/Board%20Decisions/342/34242.pdf

Bureau of Labor Statistics. (2008, January 25). *Union members summary* (USDL 08-0092). http://www.bls.gov/news.release/union2.nr0.htm

Coalition of Graduate Employee Unions. (2000). *Casual nation.* http://www.yaleunions.org/geso/reports/Casual_Nation.pdf

Graduate Employees and Students Organization. (1999). *Casual in blue.* http://www.yaleunions.org/geso/reports/Casual_in_Blue.pdf

Hewitt, G. J. (2000). Graduate student employee collective bargaining and the educational relationship between faculty and graduate students. *Journal of Collective Negotiations, 29*(2), 153-166.

Lafer, G. (2003). Graduate student unions: Organizing in a changed academic economy. *Labor Studies Journal, 28*(2), 25-43.

Palmaffy, T. (1999). Class struggle: Union and man at Yale. *New Republic, 220*(23), 17-20.

Saltzman, G. M. (2000). *Union organizing and the law: Part-time faculty and graduate teaching assistants* (NEA 2000 Almanac of Higher Education, 2000, 43-55). http://www2.nea.org/he/healma2k/images/a00p43.pdf

Singh, P., Zinni, D. M., & MacLennan, A. F. (2006). Graduate student unions in the United States. *Journal of Labor Research, 27*(1), 55-73.

Szabó, K., & Négyesi, Á. (2005). The spread of contingent work in the knowledge-based economy. *Human Resource Development Review, 4*(1), 63-85.

Teaching Assistant's Association, University of Wisconsin, Madison. http://www.taa-madison.org/

UNIONS, WAGES, AND FINANCIAL PERFORMANCE

Unionized workers have historically earned more than nonunionized workers, although recently, wages and salaries of nonunion workers have been rising faster than those of union workers (Anderson, Doyle, & Schwenk, 1990; Edwards & Swaim, 1986). For example, unionized faculty receive a premium of between 7% and 14% compared to nonunionized faculty (Monks, 2000). According to Bureau of Labor Statistics data (2008), the median weekly earning for full-time wage and salary workers was $863 for union workers compared to $663 for nonunion workers. This translates into $44,876 per year for union members and $34,476 for nonunion workers, or $2,243,800 versus $1,723,800 for 50 years in the workforce.

If companies with unions are paying higher wages to their unionized workers than other companies without unions are paying to their nonunionized workers, does this have a negative impact on their financial performance? Or do organizations with unionized workers have a greater incentive to control costs other than wages to remain competitive? Other than wages, do unions have a negative effect on an organization's profits or ability to compete? Freeman and Medoff (1984) found that unions reduce profits substantially in highly concentrated industries (i.e., few major competitors in a given industry) but not in low-concentration industries,

Strategic Questions

1. Are unions good for organizations?
2. Are unions good for employees?
3. Are unions good for shareholders?
4. Should an organization without unions try to remain union free?
5. Should an organization with unions try to persuade workers to decertify their unions?

Resources

Anderson, K. E., Doyle, P. M., & Schwenk, A. E. (1990). Measuring union-nonunion earnings differences. *Monthly Labor Review, 113*(6), 26-38.

Becker, B. E., & Olson, C. A. (1989). Unionization and shareholder interests. *Industrial & Labor Relations Review, 42*(2), 246-261.

Bureau of Labor Statistics. (2008, January 25). *Table 2. Median weekly earnings of full-time wage and salary workers by union affiliation and selected characteristics.* http://www.bls.gov/news.release/union2.t02.htm

Edwards, R. M., & Swaim, P. (1986). Union-nonunion earnings differentials and the decline of private-sector unionism. *American Economic Review, 76*(2), 97-102.

Freeman, R., & Medoff, J. (1984). *What do unions do?* New York: Basic Books.

Gittell, J. H., Von Nordenflycht, A., & Kochan, T. A. (2004). Mutual gains or zero sum? Labor relations and firm performance in the airline industry. *Industrial and Labor Relations Review, 57*(2), 163-180.

Hirsch, B. T. (2004). What do unions do for economic performance? *Journal of Labor Research, 25*(3), 415-455.

Kerkvliet, J., & McMullen, B. S. (1997). The impact of unionization on motor carrier costs. *Economic Inquiry, 35*(2), 271-284.

Koteff, E. (2006). Industry must be proactive, organized in efforts to stave off recruitment campaigns by unions. *Nation's Restaurant News, 40*(25), 16.

Machin, S. J., & Stewart, M. B. (1990). Unions and the financial performance of British private sector establishments. *Journal of Applied Econometrics, 5*(4), 327-350.

Monks, J. (2000). Unionization and faculty salaries: New evidence from the 1990s. *Journal of Labor Research, 21*(2), 305-314.

Reinhardt, R. (2005). Avoid unionization with right business climate. *Hotel and Motel Management, 220*(19), 20.

and they concluded that unionism is harmful to the financial well-being of organized enterprises or sectors (Hirsch, 2004). Unionized trucking firms have been found to have higher average costs than nonunion firms, even after controlling for higher unionized labor costs, suggesting that unionized trucking firms are at a competitive disadvantage (Kerkvliet & McMullen, 1997). But in the airline industry, conflict and workplace culture were found to be more important determinants of performance than unionization and wages (Gittell, Von Nordenflycht, & Kochan, 2004). Union representation was found to be associated with higher aircraft productivity, probably due to higher levels of cooperation and discretionary effort that enable aircraft to be turned around more quickly at the gate, a productivity gain that is apparently enough to offset the wage premium.

UNIONIZED PROFESSIONALS

Although some of the most well-known unions represent blue-collar workers, such as International Brotherhood of Teamsters, United Automobile Workers, and United Steelworkers, the union with the most members is the National Education Association. Workers in the public sector have a union membership rate nearly five times that of private sector employees; 35.9% of public sector employees are unionized, 27.8% of federal, 30.2% of state, and 41.9% of local government employees. Education, training, and library occupations have the highest unionization rate among all occupations, at 37.2% (Bureau of Labor Statistics, 2008d).

Strategic Questions

1. What are the consequences of a faculty union and a college or university failing to reach an agreement before classes begin?
2. What workplace issues are college and university professors most concerned about?
3. What workplace issues are college and university administrators most concerned about?
4. What benefits does membership in a union bring to a college or university professor?
5. What are the disadvantages for a college or university with a unionized faculty?
6. What are the advantages for a college or university with a unionized faculty?

Resources

Ashraf, J. (1997). The effect of unions on professor's salaries: The evidence over twenty years. *Journal of Labor Research, 18*(3), 339-450.
Ashraf, J. (1999). Faculty unionism in the 1990s: A comparison of public and private universities. *Journal of Collective Negotiations, 28*(4), 303-310.
American Association of University Professors. http://www.aaup.org/AAUP/
Bureau of Labor Statistics. (2007, January 25). *Union members summary* (USDL 08-0092). http://www.bls.gov/news.release/union2.nr0.htm; http://www.bls.gov/news.release/union2.t03.htm; http://www.bls.gov/news.release/union2.t04.htm.
Friedman, B. A., Abraham, S. E., & Thomas, R. K. (2006). Factors related to employees' desire to join and leave unions. *Industrial Relations, 45*(1), 102-110.
Klaff, D. B., & Ehrenberg, R. G. (2003). Collective bargaining and staff salaries in American colleges and universities. *Industrial and Labor Relations Review, 57*(1), 92-104.
Rees, D. I. (1993). The effect of unionization on faculty salaries and compensation: Estimates from the 1980's. *Journal of Labor Research, 14*(4), 399-422.
Rees, D. I. (1994). Does unionization increase faculty retention? *Industrial Relations, 33*(3), 297-321.
Villa, J., & Blum, A. A. (1996). Collective bargaining in higher education: Prospects for faculty unions. *Journal of Collective Negotiations, 25*(2), 157-169.
Working Life. *Union membership: Largest unions (2003).* http://www.workinglife.org/wiki/Union+Membership:+Largest+Unions+(2003)

The first unionized faculty in higher education occurred in 1963 when the Milwaukee Area Technical College faculty elected the American Federation of Teachers as their bargaining agent, and by the mid-1970s, more than 300 colleges and universities were organized (Rees, 1993). Median weekly earnings for education, training, and library occupations in 2006 were $929 for unionized workers and $725 for nonunion workers. Faculty at unionized universities tend to have higher wages than those at nonunionized universities (Ashraf, 1997; Rees, 1993), although the difference may be primarily in 2-year colleges (Ashraf, 1999). And when salary, benefits, and other factors are held constant, unions increase a school's faculty retention rate for associate and full professors (Rees, 1994). Unionized staff salaries at colleges and universities are 9% to 11% higher, and where faculty members are also covered by a collective bargaining agreement, unionized staff members have an additional 2% to 3% salary gain, a spillover effect from faculty unions to staff unions (Klaff & Ehrenberg, 2003).

Applications

NATIONAL LABOR RELATIONS BOARD CASES

The National Labor Relations Act (1935) states and defines the rights of employees to organize and to bargain collectively with their employers through representatives of their own choosing or not to do so. To ensure that employees can freely choose their own representatives for the purpose of collective bargaining, or choose not to be represented, the Act establishes a procedure by which they can exercise their choice at a secret-ballot election conducted by the National Labor Relations Board (NLRB). Furthermore, to protect the rights of employees and employers, and to prevent labor disputes that would adversely affect the rights of the public, Congress has defined certain practices of employers and unions as unfair labor practices (NLRB, 1997)

The NLRB is an independent federal agency created by Congress in 1935 to administer the National Labor Relations Act, the primary law governing relations between unions and employers in the private sector. The statute guarantees the right of employees to organize and to bargain collectively with their employers and to engage in other protected concerted activity with or without a union, or to refrain from all such activity (NLRB, n.d.).

Some of the rights of employees protected by the NLRB include as follows: forming or attempting to form a union among the employees of a company; joining a union, whether the union is recognized by the employer or not; assisting a union to organize the employees of an employer; going on strike to secure better working conditions; and refraining from activity on behalf of a union.

Some examples of unfair labor practices by employers include as follows:

- Threatening employees with loss of jobs or benefits if they should join or vote for a union.
- Threatening to close down the plant if a union should be organized in it.
- Spying on union gatherings, or pretending to spy.
- Granting wage increases, deliberately timed to discourage employees from forming or joining a union.

- Discharging employees because they urged other employees to join a union.
- Refusing to reinstate employees when jobs they are qualified for are open because they took part in a union's lawful strike.
- Granting of "superseniority" to those hired to replace employees engaged in a lawful strike.
- Discontinuing an operation at one plant and discharging the employees involved followed by opening the same operation at another plant with new employees because the employees at the first plant joined a union.
- Refusing to hire qualified applicants for jobs because they belong to a union. It would also be a violation if the qualified applicants were refused employment because they did not belong to a union or because they belonged to one union rather than another.

Some examples of unfair labor practices by unions include as follows:

- Acts of force or violence on the picket line or in connection with a strike.
- Threats to employees that they will lose their jobs unless they support the union's activities.

To Do

NLRB cases can be found on the NLRB Web site. From the main menu, select "Research, Decisions, Board Decisions." Then use the "Quick Search" to find a decision. Choose "Bound Volumes," because "Slip Opinions" are subject to revision before publication in bound volumes.

1. Find an NLRB case where an employer engaged in an unfair labor practice. Explain the facts of the case, describe the unfair labor practice, and the NLRB ruling in the case. Include a complete citation for the case.
2. Find an NLRB case where a union engaged in an unfair labor practice. Explain the facts of the case, describe the unfair labor practice, and the NLRB ruling in the case. Include a complete citation for the case.

Resources

National Labor Relations Act. (1935). 29 U.S.C. §§ 151-169 [Title 29, Chapter 7, Subchapter II, United States Code] http://www.nlrb.gov/about_us/overview/national_labor_relations_act.aspx

National Labor Relations Board. http://www.nlrb.gov/

National Labor Relations Board. (1997). *Basic guide to the National Labor Relations Act.* http://www.nlrb.gov/nlrb/shared_files/brochures/basicguide.html

National Labor Relations Board. *Board decisions, bound volumes.* http://www.nlrb.gov/research/decisions/board_decisions/bound_volumes.aspx

- Statement to employees who oppose the union that the employees will lose their jobs if the union wins a majority in the plant.
- Fining or expelling members for filing unfair labor practice charges with the Board or for participating in an investigation conducted by the Board.
- Making a contract that requires an employer to hire only members of the union or employees "satisfactory" to the union.
- Causing an employer to reduce employees' seniority because they engaged in antiunion acts.
- Insisting on the inclusion of illegal provisions in a contract, such as a closed shop or a discriminatory hiring hall.
- Striking against an employer who has bargained, and continues to bargain, on a multiemployer basis to compel it to bargain separately.
- Terminating an existing contract and striking for a new one without notifying the employer, the Federal Mediation and Conciliation Service, and the state mediation service, if any.

FAMILY-FRIENDLY WORKPLACES

Just as companies must compete for customers, they must also compete for employees. Applicants might accept a job offer because of the compensation, benefits, opportunities for advancement, job challenge, opportunities for personal growth, the quality of the organization's products and services, or a number of other reasons. For example, the military must compete with the private sector for labor and use social incentives to attract applicants, such as an allowance system that rewards family status (military personnel are more likely to be married and have children than their civilian counterparts), to attract applicants into the service (Cadigan, 2006).

To attract applicants, an organization might adopt family-friendly or work-life balance policies such as flextime, where workers can choose their own starting and ending hours around the core period; telecommuting, where some or all of an employee's work is done at home or at a satellite office; part-time schedule or other reduced work schedule for permanent employees; or job sharing, where two or more employees divide the workload of a single job. The advantages of work-life balance policies include reduced absence and turnover, increased productivity, and reduced overtime (Lewison, 2006); reduced work-family conflict (Frye & Breaugh, 2004); and higher job satisfaction (Ezra & Deckman, 1996; Saltzstein, Ting, & Saltzstein, 2001). Employers that offer flexible sick leave and child care assistance experience measurable reductions in turnover (Baughman, DiNardi, & Holtz-Eakin, 2003). Shareholders appear to think that family-friendly policies are good for the bottom line; firm announcements of work-family initiatives have been found to positively affect shareholder return (Arthur & Cook, 2004).

Hoyman and Duer's (2004) categorization of worker-friendly workplace policies identifies these aspects:

1. Family and personal—pregnancy leaves, paid vacation, flexible use of sick days, flex plans, cafeteria plans;
2. Removing impediments to work—Employee Assistance Programs, telecommuting, flextime, flexplace;
3. Training and education—Skill acquisition, personal development, higher education;
4. Nontraditional incentives—Company car, employee of the month, recognition awards, stress management.

If applicants or employees can see how the organization makes it easier to balance work and family, the organization may gain a competitive advantage in recruitment and retention. Employees who have access to family-responsive policies have greater organizational commitment and have a significantly lower intention to quit their jobs (Grover & Crooker, 1995).

To Do

For an organization's family-friendly or work-life balance policies to be effective in recruiting applicants, potential applicants have to become aware of the policies. Find family-friendly or work-life balance policies on four different organization's Web pages. The organization can be in the private or public sector, small local organization or a global multinational. Use the Organization Family Policy Form to record the details of the policies.

Organization Family Policy Form

Organization	*Industry*	*Family-Friendly Policy*

(Continued)

Resources

Arthur, M. M., & Cook, A. (2004). Taking stock of work-family initiatives: How announcement of "family-friendly" human resource decisions affect shareholder value. *Industrial and Labor Relations Review, 57*(4), 599-613.

Baughman, R., DiNardi, D., & Holtz-Eakin, D. (2003). Productivity and wage effects of "family friendly" fringe benefits. *International Journal of Manpower, 24*(3), 247-259.

Berg, P., Kalleberg, A. L., & Appelbaum, E. (2003). Balancing work and family: The role of high-commitment environments. *Industrial Relations, 42*(2), 168-188.

Cadigan, J. (2006). The impact of family-friendly compensation: An investigation of military personnel policy. *Review of Public Administration, 26*(1), 3-20.

Ezra, M., & Deckman, M. (1996). Balancing work and family responsibilities: Flextime and child care in the federal government. *Public Administration Review, 56*(2), 174-179.

Families and Work Institute. (2006). *Making work "work": New ideas from the winners of the Alfred P. Sloan Awards for Business Excellence in Workplace Flexibility.* http://familiesandwork.org/site/research/reports/3wbooklet.pdf

Frye, N. K., & Breaugh, J. A. (2004). Family-friendly policies, supervisor support, work-family conflict, family-work conflict, and satisfaction: A test of a conceptual model. *Journal of Business and Psychology, 19*(2), 197-220.

Grover, S. L., & Crooker, K. J. (1995). Who appreciates family-responsive human resource policies: The impact of family-friendly policies on the organizational attachment of parents and non-parents. *Personnel Psychology, 48*(2), 271-288.

Hoyman, M., & Duer, H. (2004). A typology of workplace policies: Worker friendly vs. family friendly? *Review of Public Personnel Administration, 24*(2), 113-132.

Jenner, L. (1994). Family-friendly backlash. *Management Review, 83*(5), 7.

Lewison, J. (2006). The work/life balance sheet so far. *Journal of Accountancy, 202*(2), 45-49.

Saltzstein, A. L., Ting, Y., & Saltzstein, G. H. (2001). Work-family balance and job satisfaction: The impact of family-friendly policies on attitudes of federal government employees. *Public Administration Review, 61*(4), 452-467.

Wiley, J. W., Brooks, S. M., & Lundby, K. M. (2006). Put your employees on the other side of the microscope. *Human Resource Planning, 29*(2), 15-21.

Experiential Exercises

ASSESSMENT OF EMPLOYEE OPINIONS

Surveys are used to systematically collect data on people's attitudes and opinions. They are often used in organizations to assess employee perceptions about various aspects of the work environment or the effectiveness of planned organizational change programs. Nearly three out of four companies with more than 10,000 employees conduct employee surveys (Wiley, Brooks, & Lundby, 2006). Surveys are used as an improvement tool, to help identify opportunities for improvement and evaluate the effectiveness of changes already implemented; and as a communication tool, to facilitate

To Do

Choose a functional area of the college or university, and design a survey to collect data on constituents' attitudes. The functional area that you choose could be Registration, Student Billing, Scheduling, Facilities Management, Library, Food Service, Housing, Admissions, Financial Aid, Computer Services, Police, Disability Support Services, Career Services, Human Resources, or some other important college or university function. Collect data from two constituent groups, students and employees working in that functional area or who regularly interact with people in that functional area. Administer the survey to at least five students and five employees. Write a report on your findings, both overall and separately for students and employees. The report should include tables showing means or frequencies of individual survey items or scales and an explanation of the results and what they mean.

The survey questions could ask employees to assess the organization; give their opinions about new policies, procedures, or work methods; rate their satisfaction with their job, the organization, or their relationships with customers or vendors; rate their satisfaction with the training they have received; identify things that prevent them from better satisfying customers; identify improvements that should be made; indicate changes in existing procedures that should be made; evaluate their unit's or the organization's customer orientation; evaluate their unit's or the organization's emphasis on quality; evaluate the adequacy of rewards or recognition for excellent customer service; or identify workplace safety and health concerns (Johnson, 1996; Snee, 1995; Wiley et al., 2006).

Before administering the survey, state the objectives of the survey and ask each person if he or she is willing to answer the questions. Assure confidentiality by not recording the respondent's name, so that no respondent's answers to the survey can be linked to him or her.

Resources

Alreck, P. L., & Settle, R. B. (1995). *The survey research handbook.* Chicago: Irwin.

Baker, G. R., King, H., McDonald, J. L., & Horbar, J. D. (2003). Using organizational assessment surveys for improvement in neonatal intensive care. *Pediatrics, 111*(4), 419-425.

Church, A. H., Margiloff, A., & Coruzzi, C. (1995). Using surveys for change: An applied example in a pharmaceuticals organization. *Leadership and Organization Development Journal, 16*(4), 3-11.

Johnson, J. W. (1996). Linking employee perceptions of service climate to customer satisfaction. *Personnel Psychology, 46*(4), 831-851.

Judge, M. (Director) (1999). *Office space* [Motion picture]. United States: 20th Century Fox.

Hackworth, C. A., King, S. J., & Detwiler, C. A. (2003). *The Employer Attitude Survey 2000: Perspectives on its process and utility* (DOT/FAA/AM-03/11). Washington, DC: U.S. Department of Transportation, Federal Aviation Administration, Office of Aerospace Medicine. http://amelia.db.erau.edu/reports/faa/am/AM03-11.pdf.

Harris, F. J. (1949). The quantification of an industrial employee survey. I: Method. *Journal of Applied Psychology, 33*(2), 103-111.

Kennedy, J. K. (1994). Strategic employee surveys can support change efforts. *Journal for Quality and Participation, 17*(6), 18-20.

Kiedrowski, P. J. (2006). Quantitative assessment of a Senge Learning Organization intervention. *The Learning Organization, 13*(4), 369-383.

(Continued)

(Continued)

Lilienthal, P. (2002). If you give your employees a voice, do you listen? *Journal for Quality and Participation, 25*(3), 38-40.

Roberts, D. R., & Rollins, T. (1995/1996). Employee research is a powerful tool in leading the time-based organization. *Employment Relations Today, 22*(4), 11-17.

Rogelberg, S. G., Church, A. H., Waclawski, J., & Stanton, J. M. (2002). Organizational survey research. In S. G. Rogelberg (Ed.), *Handbook of research methods in industrial and organizational psychology* (pp. 141-160). Malden, MA: Blackwell.

Rollins, T. (1994). Turning employee survey results into high-impact business improvements. *Employment Relations Today, 21*(1), 35-44.

Snee, R. D. (1995). Listening to the voice of the employee. *Quality Progress, 28*(1), 91-95.

Thomas, S. J. (1999). *Designing surveys that work! A step-by-step guide.* Thousand Oaks, CA: Corwin.

dialog between managers and employees (Lilienthal, 2002; Rollins, 1994; Snee, 1995). For example, Kiedrowski (2006) used three employee surveys over 5 years to assess the effectiveness of a Senge Learning Organization intervention, to determine whether it resulted in improved employee satisfaction; and Church, Margiloff, and Coruzzi (1995) used employee surveys to monitor organizational culture change after a merger.

Employee surveys are often focused on job satisfaction or other aspects of the job or the organization. Another use of employee surveys is to ask employees to measure the effectiveness of their workgroups in serving the needs of their customers, data that can be used to determine what changes to make in the organization to have the greatest positive impact (Wiley et al., 2006). For example, Baker, King, MacDonald, and Horbar (2003) used an organizational survey to identify team and organizational issues that impeded improvement in a neonatal intensive care unit. Surveys assist decision makers in three ways: assessing the current state of the organization, acting as a catalyst for change by communicating messages and data, and identifying means for driving organizational change (Church et al., 1995).

INDIE PHENOM MAKES JUMP TO BIG BUCKS PIC

Rates of unionization vary widely across different industries and professions. In the broad categories of motion pictures and sound recording occupations, 10.3% of workers are unionized; and 6.4% of workers in arts, design, entertainment, sports, and media occupations are union members; compared to 4.3% in computer and mathematical occupations and 37.3% in education, training, and library occupations (Bureau of Labor Statistics, 2008c).

When a movie studio makes a major motion picture, many of the workers will be unionized. For example, the Director's Guild of America (DGA) has more than 13,000 members. According to the DGA president, the DGA's purpose is to "protect directorial teams' legal and artistic rights, contend for their creative freedom, and strengthen their ability to develop meaningful and credible careers." The foundation of the DGA's *Creative Rights Handbook* (DGA, 2006-2008) is "Were you consulted about every creative decision?"

Before production begins,

1. Were all the company's script, casting, approvals, and budget commitments revealed to you before you took the assignment?
2. Did you get to choose your first assistant director?

During production,

1. Did you see dailies at a reasonable time?
2. Did you decide the number and placement of monitors?
3. Did all notes to cast and crew come directly from you?

Following production,

1. Did you see the editor's assembly before anyone else?
2. Were you allowed adequate time for preparing your cut?
3. Did you screen your cut for the producer and person with final cutting authority?
4. Were you notified of the date, time, and place of every postproduction operation?

To Do

You are set to begin work on your first big budget Hollywood motion picture after a successful independent low-budget career. For this film, you will be employing unionized workers for many jobs. Use the credits list from a recent big budget Hollywood motion picture to make a list of the positions you need to fill (e.g., director, cinematographer, writer, actor, etc.; use the Position List form on the next page). Then search the Internet to find the unions you will be interacting with that will represent the workers you need. First on your list is the director. You are already familiar with the relevant union here, because you are currently a member of the DGA.

Resources

Bureau of Labor Statistics. (2008, January 25). *Table 3. Union affiliation of employed wage and salary workers by occupation and industry.* http://www.bls.gov/news.release/union2.t03.htm

Director's Guild of America. http://www.dga.org/index2.php3

Internet Movie Database. http://www.imdb.com/

Mamet, D. (Director). (2000). *State and main* [Motion picture]. United States: Green/Renzi Productions.

Yahoo Movies. http://movies.yahoo.com/

Position List

Position	*Union*	*Web Page*
Director	Director's Guild of America	http://www.dga.org/index2.php3

Creative Exercises

REDESIGNING A JOB

A job is a collection of tasks or functions that the employee must perform. Essential job functions are those tasks that the employee must be able to perform, either with or without accommodation. Other tasks that are normally part of the job are nonessential job functions. According to Frederick Winslow Taylor's (1911) ideas on Scientific Management, the way to maximize productivity is to find the one most efficient way of performing the operations required by the job and then make sure that the workers do the job that way. The key to efficiency is work simplification, making the job both easy to learn and easy to do. However, a job that is easy to learn and easy to do can also be monotonous and tedious to do day in and day out.

Hackman and Oldham (1976) developed a model for individual job design (i.e., a model for how to design or redesign jobs to be more motivating and satisfying). Their Job Enrichment model is among the most well known and complete theories for explaining job design characteristics and their relationships to work motivation (Torraco, 2005). According to their Job Characteristics Model, to obtain the desired individual Work Outcomes of high internal work motivation, high growth satisfaction, high general job satisfaction, and high work effectiveness, the three Critical Psychological States must be elicited by the presence in the job of the five Core Job Characteristics. The Core Job Characteristics are Skill Variety (doing a variety of activities requiring multiple skills), Task Identity (completion of a whole and identifiable piece of work), Task Significance (substantial impact on the lives or work of other people), Autonomy (substantial freedom, independence, and discretion in scheduling and doing the work), and Feedback (direct and clear information about the effectiveness of the employee's job performance). Skill Variety, Task Identity, and Task Significance establish Experienced Meaningfulness of the Work (the job is important, valuable, and worthwhile); Autonomy establishes Experienced Responsibility for Work Outcomes (a feeling of personal responsibility); and Feedback establishes Knowledge of the Actual Results of Work Activities (effectiveness of job performance).

To Do

Use the Hackman and Oldham Job Characteristics Model to redesign your current job (or any previous job) to be more motivating and satisfying. First, write the job description and job specification, then describe how the job can be redesigned on each of the five Core Job Characteristics.

(Continued)

(Continued)

Job Redesign Form

Job Title:		
Job Description:		
Job Specification:		
Core Characteristics	*Current Job*	*Redesigned Job*
Skill Variety (Job contains multiple job tasks, requires a variety of job skills)		
Task Identity (Job requires employee to complete a whole piece of work, from beginning to end)		
Task Significance (Job has an impact on other people, inside or outside the organization)		
Autonomy (Job empowers employees to use their discretion to schedule tasks, choose procedures)		
Feedback (Job provides direct and clear information about the effectiveness of employees' performance)		

Resources

de Trevill, S., & Antonakis, J. (2006). Could lean production job design be intrinsically motivating? Contextual, configurational, and levels-of-analysis issues. *Journal of Operations Management, 24*(2), 99-123.

DeVaro, J., Li, R., & Brookshire, D. (2007). Analysing the job characteristics model: New support from a cross-section of establishments. *International Journal of Human Resource Management, 18*(6), 986-1003.

Elsbach, K. D., & Hargadon, A. B. (2006). Enhancing creativity through "mindless" work: A framework of workday design. *Organization Science, 17*(4), 470-483.

Farias, G., & Varma, A. (2000). Integrating job characteristics, sociotechnical systems and reengineering: Presenting a unified approach to work and organizational design. *Organizational Development Journal, 18*(3), 11-24.

Fried, Y., & Ferris, G. R. (1987). The validity of the job characteristics model: A review and meta-analysis. *Personnel Psychology, 40*(2), 287-322.

Hackman, J. R., & Oldham, G. R. (1975). A new strategy for job enrichment. *California Management Review, 17*(4), 57-71.

Hackman, J. R., & Oldham, G. R. (1976). Motivation through design of work: A test of a theory. *Organizational Behavior and Human Performance, 16*, 250-279.

Hackman, J. R., Oldham, G., Janson, R., & Purdy, K. (1975). A new strategy for job enrichment. *California Management Review, 17*(4), 57-71.

Loher, B. T., Noe, R. A., Moeller, N. L., & Fitzpatrick, M. P. (1985). A meta-analysis of the relation of job characteristics to job satisfaction. *Journal of Applied Psychology, 70*(2), 280-289.

Taylor, F. W. (1911). *The principles of scientific management.* New York: Harper & Bros.

Thakor, M. V., & Joshi, A. W. (2005). Motivating salesperson customer orientation: Insights from the Job Characteristics Model. *Journal of Business Research, 58*(5), 584-592.

Tiegs, R. B., Tetrick, L. E., & Fried, Y. (1992). Growth Need Strength and Context Satisfactions as moderators of the relations of the Job Characteristics Model. *Journal of Management, 18*(3), 575-593.

Torraco. R. J. (2005). Work design theory: A review and critique with implications for human resource development. *Human Resource Development Quarterly, 16*(1), 85-109.

Sales is a job where employee motivation is critical. Customer-oriented selling (or customer orientation) creates greater long-term performance benefits for the salesperson compared to sales-orientated selling (or sales orientation). However, it demands greater salesperson motivation to engage in customer relationship development activities. Thakor and Joshi (2005) tested one aspect of the Job Characteristics Model and found that Experienced Meaningfulness had a positive effect on customer orientation. DeVaro, Li, and Brookshire (2007) found that Task Variety and Autonomy were positively associated with productivity and product quality, and Autonomy was associated with worker satisfaction. Elsbach and Hargadon (2006) have suggested redesigning entire workdays to alternate between cognitively challenging and high-pressure work and mindless work, as a way to enhance the creativity of chronically overworked professionals.

DANCING IS LIFE

Employee relations are important to all organizations, but most especially for organizations with highly skilled employees (Lécuyer, 2003). For these organizations, recruiting, retaining, and developing highly skilled employees is the key to competitive success. Creating a positive organizational culture can provide a significant competitive advantage (Sadri & Lees, 2001). When employees identify with the culture, the work environment is more enjoyable, there are increased levels of teamwork, sharing of information, and openness to new ideas (Goffee & Jones, 1996). An examination of companies listed on *Fortune's* "100 Best Companies to Work For" found that employees in these companies had stable and highly positive workforce attitudes and firm-level performance advantages over the broad market (Fulmer, Gerhart, & Scott, 2003).

To Do

You are the owner of *Jacqueline's Stage Door,* a dance studio with about 200 dancers enrolled. Each year, you have a holiday show and a spring recital. Most of the dancers are "competitive dancers" and compete in regional and national dance competitions, where dancers from your studio compete against other dance studios from the United States and Canada. Your goal for this dance season is to place at least one dance team in the top 10 at nationals.

You have just moved into a new facility, a space renovated to be a dance studio. Each classroom is equipped with wood floor and a multimedia computer with plenty of hard disk space to store music and good-quality speakers (and compact stereo system for backup). The studio and the equipment are essential, but they are not your most valuable asset.

Develop a plan to improve employee relations with your dance instructors, using the Improvement Plan form. Choreographing dances and teaching the dancers is a highly creative process. To get the best results, you will need to create a participative organizational culture. Some of the dance instructors are current students, working to help pay for their dance lessons, and the rest are permanent part-time employees, all of whom have been with your studio for at least 3 years. They are not highly compensated employees, but they stay because they are intrinsically motivated.

Employee Relations Improvement Plan—Jacqueline's Stage Door	
Creating a positive organizational culture	
Feedback and communication programs	
Employee involvement strategies	
Teamwork	
Employee development	
Other	

(Continued)

(Continued)

Resources

Arthur, J. B., & Jelf, G. S. (1999). The effects of gainsharing on grievance rates and absenteeism over time. *Journal of Labor Research, 20*(1), 133-145.

Fortune 100 Best Companies to Work For. http://money.cnn.com/magazines/fortune/bestcompanies/2007/full_list/, http://money.cnn.com/magazines/fortune/bestcompanies/2007/

Fulmer, I. S., Gerhart, B., & Scott, K. C. (2003). Are the 100 Best better? An empirical investigation of the relationship between being in a "great place to work" and firm performance. *Personnel Psychology, 56*(4), 965-993.

Goffee, R., & Jones, G. (1996). What holds the modern company together? *Harvard Business Review, 74*(6), 133-148.

Hallowell, R. (1996). Southwest Airlines: A case study linking employee needs satisfaction and organizational capabilities to competitive advantage. *Human Resource Management, 35*(4). 513-534.

Lécuyer, C. (2003). High-tech corporatism: Management-employee relations in U.S. electronic firms, 1920s-1960's. *Enterprise & Society, 4*(3), 502-520.

Sadri, G., & Lees, B. (2001). Developing corporate culture as a competitive advantage. *Journal of Management Development, 20*(9/10), 853-859.

Organizational Change and Development 11

Strategic Objective

Change is a fact of life for all organizations. The capacity for continuous change and improvement is particularly important in today's turbulent environments where technologies, markets, and competitive situations are changing rapidly and unpredictably (Snyder & Cummings, 1998). Mitroff, Mason, and Pearson (1994) have suggested that the world is in transition from the Industrial Age to the information/knowledge/ Systems Age, and organizations must redesign themselves to meet the challenges of crisis management, global competitiveness, environmentalism, and ethics. An organization's capacity for adaptation, flexibility, and innovation may be necessary for survival (Meyer & Stensaker, 2006; Snyder & Cummings, 1998). Because organizations are constantly required to optimize their processes and continuously search for innovative solutions that can give them a competitive advantage, organizations need to proceed from the assumption that change is an ongoing evolutionary process occurring at all levels of the organization (Zaugg & Thom, 2003).

Organizational Development (OD) is the use of planned, behavioral-science interventions in work settings for the purpose of improving organizational functioning and individual development. Its purpose is improvement in the organization's effectiveness, and its scope is overall organizational or systemwide change. Its conceptual underpinnings come from behavioral science, and its targets are the organization's culture, structure, strategy, and processes (Porras & Robertson, 1992). The aim of OD is to increase organizational effectiveness and considers both quantifiable and qualitative factors across the entire organization to improve performance (Rowland, 2007). The series of experiments conducted at the Harwood Manufacturing Corporation from 1939 until the 1970s laid the foundations of OD, focusing on changing group behavior rather than individual behavior, developing innovative training methods such as role play, and testing the effectiveness of participation by allowing workers as a group to decide on their own work methods and set their own pace of work (Burnes, 2007).

OD uses a number of methods (or interventions) to bring about change in the organization. Sensitivity Training is used to change behavior through the use of unstructured group interaction. The purpose is to give participants a better understanding of their own and others' ideas, beliefs, and attitudes. Survey Feedback is the use of surveys to collect information from organization members about their perceptions and attitudes on a variety of issues such as decision making, communication, and coordination with other people in the organization. The data collected by the survey are then analyzed and given back to the members of the organization, which can then be used to identify problems, clarify issues, and seek solutions through informed discussion. In Process Consultation, an outside consultant is called in to observe and suggest changes in organizational processes. Team Building uses high-interaction activities that are designed to increase openness and build trust among team members. Intergroup Development focuses on dealing with counterproductive conflict between groups. Appreciative Inquiry is used to identify the special strengths of an organization, which it can build on to improve performance.

Sociotechnical Systems is another approach to improving organizational performance, which focuses on the interactions between people and technology. Sociotechnical Systems proposes that work design should jointly optimize the social and the technical systems of an organization, because the work group is central, especially for organizations using self-managed teams (Farias & Varma, 2000). As workplaces become increasingly technology driven, Sociotechnical Systems can be the basis of a useful intervention strategy for incorporating technological advancement into organizations (Appelbaum, 1997).

A more radical approach to OD is Business Process Re-engineering, which discards incremental improvement in favor of demolishing old processes to clear the way for new ones (Jarrar & Aspinwall, 1999; McKeown & Philip, 2003; Moosebruker & Loftin, 1998). In Business Process Re-engineering, information technology is used to radically redesign business processes to achieve dramatic improvements in organizational performance, by breaking the old rules about how the business is run and finding imaginative ways to accomplish work (Hammer, 1990).

"New Paradigm Organizations" are able to increase quality while driving down costs and make small production runs at the same cost per unit as long production runs through the use of flexible, multiple-skilled workforces. Their HRM processes show a strong commitment and involvement by top management, consistent goals and objectives communicated to all levels and functions, and effective use of recognition and rewards (Hodgetts, Luthans, & Lee, 1994). This is achieved with cost-effective structures, participative management and employee involvement, an adaptive learning environment, and a focused and shared vision. Hewlett Packard is a classic corporate example of a new paradigm organization. The company reorganized to strategically realign its structure, processes, products, and creative know-how with its fast-changing competitive and economic picture (Burack, Burack, Miller, & Morgan, 1994).

Strategic Issues in HRM

PROFESSIONAL EMPLOYER ORGANIZATIONS

A Professional Employer Organization (PEO) is a company that provides HRM services for client organizations. The services that may be provided include payroll, benefits administration, recruitment, selection, training, and workers' compensation. Small-sized and medium-sized organizations may lack the internal resources to develop and deliver effective human resource services and programs and may choose to outsource these activities to PEOs (Klaas, 2003). PEOs claim that by allowing their clients to focus on their core competencies, their clients can better manage and grow their businesses. When traditional HRM functions such as payroll or recruitment are outsourced to a PEO, the organization's HRM department can concentrate more on strategy and become a facilitator for change (Conklin, 2005). The PEO industry is large and growing and is now a $51-billion industry serving 100,000 small- to mid-sized businesses and as many as three million workers (Basso & Shorten, 2006).

A recent Conference Board study found high levels of satisfaction among executives whose companies have outsourced some or all human resource activities (Shelgren, 2004). The survey identified four reasons for their satisfaction: cost savings, gaining the unique expertise of the service providers, greater control of HRM processes, and improved customer service. Cost reductions are derived from greater economies of scale, lower technology–investment costs, efficient HR processes, and headcount reductions. Organizations that outsource HR activities gain access to expertise that would be difficult and expensive to replicate and sustain on their own. Outsourcing companies gain greater control over human resource activities through improved data accuracy, greater consistency in service delivery, and better handling of compliance issues. And through better technology, process expertise, and adherence to best practices, companies that outsource human resource activities generally obtain an improvement in the service they provide to employees through more customized and accessible information, more responsive customer care centers, and greater self-service capabilities (Shelgren, 2004).

Klaas, Yang, Gainey, and McClendon's (2005) survey of 740 small businesses found that firms not using a PEO reported significantly lower levels of satisfaction with HR outcomes than firms that used a PEO for a limited set of transactional services and firms using a PEO for both transactional and strategic HR services. Among firms using a PEO, satisfaction with HR outcomes was significantly higher among firms that obtained a broader set of transactional and strategic HR services. Gilley, Greer, and Rasheed (2004) found that in a sample of 94 manufacturing firms in 16 different industries, outsourced training had a positive effect on both innovation and stakeholder performance and payroll outsourcing positively influenced firm innovativeness.

However, there are some risks for organizations that lease employees from a PEO. The use of a PEO transfers responsibility for administrative functions such as benefits, payroll, and workers compensation; however, an employer could be sued outside worker's compensation if a leased employee is injured at its worksite (Wojcik, 1998). A PEO and its client have joint responsibility for discrimination, harassment, and compliance with the Fair Labor Standard Act. This joint responsibility could lead to disputes between the organization and the PEO over compensation other than basic hourly salaries and wages, including vacation, bonuses, stock options, and incentive payments (Album & Berkowitz, 2003; Polson, 2002).

Strategic Questions

1. What are the risks of outsourcing the organization's HRM activities to a PEO?
2. What are the advantages of outsourcing the organization's HRM activities to a PEO?
3. What are the disadvantages of outsourcing the organization's HRM activities to a PEO?
4. How does use of a PEO to outsource HRM activities affect the workers in the organization, either positively or negatively?
5. What is the impact on leadership development in HRM if an organization chooses to outsource many HRM activities to a PEO?
6. How should an organization decide which HRM activities to outsource to a PEO?
7. What effects does outsourcing many HRM functions to a PEO have on how HRM is done in organizations?
8. If an organization outsources the entire HRM function to a PEO, what will the HRM people do?

Resources

Album, M. J., & Berkowitz, P. M. (2003). Industry model for Professional Employer Organizations—new NY law outlines responsibilities for PEOs and their clients. *Employment Relations Today, 30*(2), 65-72.

Basso, L., & Shorten, B. (2006). PEO industry continues to grow. *CPA Journal, 76*(8), 66-67.

Brown, M. P., Fink, R. L., & Gillett, J. (2002, Nov/Dec). Managing human resources from the outside in. *Catalyst*, 60-63.

Conklin, D. W. (2005). Risks and rewards in HR business process outsourcing. *Long Range Planning, 38*(6), 579-598.

Cooke, F. L., Shen, J., & McBride, A. (2005). Outsourcing HR as a competitive strategy? A literature review and an assessment of implications. *Human Resource Management, 44*(4), 413-432.

Employer Services Assurance Corporation. http://www.esacorp.org/

Gilley, K. M., Greer, C. R., & Rasheed, A. A. (2004). Human resource outsourcing and organizational performance in manufacturing firms. *Journal of Business Research, 57*(3), 232-240.

Klaas, B. S. (2001). Outsourcing HR: The impact of organizational characteristics. *Human Resource Management, 40*(2), 125-138.

Klaas, B. S., Yang, H., Gainey, T., & McClendon, J. A. (2005). HR in the small business enterprise: Assessing the impact of PEO utilization. *Human Resource Management, 44*(4), 433-448.

National Association of Professional Employer Organizations. http://www.napeo.org/

Pollitt, D., Gelman, L., & Dell, D. (2004). Outsourcing HR: The contrasting experiences of Amex and DuPont. *Human Resource Management International Digest, 12*(6), 8-10.

Polson, J. M. (2002). The PEO phenomenon: Co-employment at work. *Employee Relations Law Journal, 27*(4), 7-25.

Shelgren, D. (2004). Why HR outsourcing continues to expand. *Employment Relations Today, 31*(2), 47-53.

Stopper, W. G. (2005). Outsourcing's effect on HR leadership development. *Human Resource Planning, 28*(4), 11-13.

Wojcik, J. (1998). PEOs don't eliminate employer's risks. *Business Insurance, 32*(19), 21.

ENTROPY IN ORGANIZATIONS

Organizations are collections of individuals working together toward a common goal. Typically, organizations are seen as directed from the top down, with top management collecting data about changes in the environment and making strategic plans to adapt to those changes and meet the organization's goals. These strategic plans are then rolled out to progressively lower levels of management down to the level of the individual worker. This is a rational view of organizations, which seems to ignore that organizations are made up of people who are not always rational.

The paradigm of bounded rationality states that problems are not always clearly defined and decision makers cannot know all of the possible alternatives and their consequences, so decision makers cannot maximize (Simon, 1979). And in the situation where different individuals have different goals and resources are scarce, political processes come into play. Based on their review of the strategic decision-making literature, Eisenhardt and Zbaracki (1992) conclude that organizations are political systems in which strategic partners have partially conflicting objectives and limited cognitive capability, so that strategic decision making is an interweaving of both bounded rationality and political processes. Cohen, March, and Olsen's (1972) "garbage can" model of organizational decision making suggests that an organization is a collection of choices looking for problems; issues and feelings looking for decision situations in which they might be aired; solutions looking for issues to which they might be the answer; and decision makers looking for work.

Organizations may not be a static structure focused on a collection of superordinate objectives (Bryman, 1984). Thus, a bottom-up view of how an organization collectively behaves and changes over time may be more useful (Hensgen, Desouza, & Evaristo, 2004). Complexity theory suggests that managers in organizations should trust workers to self-organize to solve problems, encourage rather than banish informal communication networks, "go with the flow" rather than script procedures, and induce a healthy level of tension and anxiety in the organization to promote creativity and maximize organizational effectiveness (Grobman, 2005).

Organizations often use promotions as incentives to motivate performance, but promotions can have disadvantages, if the promotion transfers an employee to a job that he or she is unable to do well (Fairburn & Malcomson, 2001). The Peter Principle (Peter & Hull, 1969) predicts that satisfactorily performing employees will get promoted until they end up in a position where their performance becomes unsatisfactory (i.e., in a hierarchy, employees tend to rise to their level of incompetence). This seems like a counterproductive thing for a rational organization to do—eventually all of the organization's employees will be incompetent in their positions. So why don't organizations leave employees in their current positions where they are performing satisfactorily? When promoting a satisfactory performer to a higher position, the organization is trying to maximize the difference between the productivity of the employee and the wage rate of the employee; this gap contributes to the profitability of the firm (Schaefer, Massey & Hermanson, 1979). The higher level position has the possibility of higher levels of productivity (or worth to the organization), at a higher multiple of the individual's salary than the lower level position. Lazear (2004) argues that ability appears lower after a promotion purely as a statistical matter (regression to the mean) and that the Peter Principle is therefore a necessary consequence of any promotion process. Cann and Cangemi (1971) have pointed out that the Peter Principle itself is based on the static, pessimistic assumption that an employee's level of competence cannot be changed by education, training, or technology.

To make a successful transition from a nonmanagement role to a management role requires that the individual change his or her thinking about the job from that of a performing role (doing) to a managerial role (supervising the work of others); spend less time on performance activities and more time on supervisory activities; accept the change from a well-known and understood role to an unknown or partially ambiguous role; and accept a change from working on goals that have been previously established for them to having a greater degree of influence in setting those goals (Flamholtz, 1983). All of these things can be learned; incompetence need not be a permanent condition.

Strategic Questions

1. Is the Peter Principle an inevitable result of using promotions as incentives for high levels of job performance?
2. What can an organization do to minimize the number of newly promoted employees from being unsatisfactory performers in their jobs?
3. What is the difference between a plateaued employee and an employee who has reached his or her level of incompetence?
4. If an organization downsizes, and might downsize again, which employees are more likely to remain with the organization—those that have reached their "level of incompetence," or those who have not?

Resources

Appelbaum, S. H., & Finestone, D. (1994). Revisiting career plateauing: Same old problems—Avant-garde solutions. *Journal of Managerial Psychology, 9*(5), 12-21.

Bryman, A. (1984). Organizational studies and the concept of rationality. *Journal of Management Studies, 21*(4), 391-408.

Cohen, M. D., March, J. G., & Olsen, J. P. (1972). A garbage can model of organizational choice. *Administrative Science Quarterly, 17*(1), 1-25.

Eisenhardt, K. M., & Zbaracki, M. J. (1992). Strategic decision making. *Strategic Management Journal, 13*(Special Issue), 17-37.

Elsass, P. M., & Ralston, D. A. (1989). Individual responses to the stress of career plateauing. *Journal of Management, 15*(1), 35-47.

Fairburn, J. A., & Malcomson, J. M. (2001). Performance, promotion, and the Peter Principle. *Review of Economic Studies, 68*(234), 45-66.

Flamholtz, E. G. (1983). Overcoming the Peter Principle: Successful transitions to a new management role. *Journal of Management Development, 2*(2), 51-65.

Grobman, G. M. (2005). Complexity theory: A new way to look at organizational change. *Public Administration Quarterly, 29*(3), 350-382.

Hensgen, T., Desouza, K. C., & Evaristo, J. R. (2004). Ad hoc crisis management and crisis evasion. *International Journal of Technology, Policy and Management, 4*(3), 257-274.

Lazear, E. P. (2004). The Peter Principle: A theory of decline. *Journal of Political Economy, 112*(1), S141-S163.

Peter, L. J., & Hull, R. (1969). *The Peter Principle.* New York: William Morrow.

(Continued)

(Continued)

Riggs, A. J. (1971). Parkinson's Law, the Peter Principle, and the Riggs Hypothesis—A synthesis. *Journal of Accountancy, 132*(1), 95-96.

Schaefer, M. E., Massey, F. A., & Hermanson, R. H. (1979). The Peter Principle revisited: An economic perspective. *Human Resource Management, 18*(4), 1-5.

Simon, H. A. (1979). Rational decision making in business organizations. *American Economic Review, 69*(4), 493-513.

TECHNOLOGY-DRIVEN CHANGE

One of the drivers of change in organizations is technology. Technology can change the way that an individual job's tasks are done or change the way the entire organization functions. Before caller ID and mapping software, employees delivering pizza would have to get directions from the customer to find the house or business. Now, when a customer calls, the pizza restaurant can know who is calling and quickly generate a map with turn-by-turn directions to the location. This kind of change can improve customer satisfaction by reducing the number of pizzas delayed in delivery.

Customers want faster service and real-time tracking, which is putting pressure on shippers. Gordon (2004) lists RFID as one of the mega-trends in modern logistics. RFID is radio frequency identification, a form of wireless communication that allows better tracking and control of valuable assets, enabling tracking of shipments from manufacturing to loading docks, to trucks, to destination (McGinley, 2003). RFID uses readers at each gate location and tags or transponders with a unique ID on each asset. The readers interface with the carrier's computer network to track tagged assets. RFID is a substantial improvement over UPC codes, because an RFID tag is read by radio contact and does not require a line-of-sight contact, a reader can read hundreds of RFID tags simultaneously, and the information collected and stored goes beyond better inventory control to optimize the supply-chain operation (Taghaboni-Dutta & Velthouse, 2006). Wal-Mart uses RFID to track merchandise from suppliers to stores; as soon as goods are unloaded from a truck, it passes a RFID reader at the loading dock door and the store inventory is immediately updated (Troy, 2004). RFID tags attached to trucks can improve security at terminals by helping terminal operators confirm that the drivers of the trucks that call at their facilities are the drivers designated by the trucking company to deliver or pick up containers (Mongelluzzo, 2006). RFID tags attached to trucks also allow the trucking company to track the location of their trucks and drivers.

Introduction of any new technology that brings changes to the workplace might provoke resistance to the change from employees. Organizational change is a function of resolving organizational tensions that arise from the interaction between innovation and inertia (Wong-MingJi & Millette, 2002).

Strategic Questions

1. RFID tags attached to all of an organization's trucks would allow the organization to track the location of each truck in its fleet. What possible reasons could truckers have to resist attaching the RFID tags to their trucks?
2. What can the organization do to overcome resistance from the truckers to the use of RFID tags?
3. What other employees' jobs will change with the implementation of RFID technology to track shipments? What will some employees be spending less time doing? What will some employees be spending more time doing?
4. In what ways could other organizations make use of RFID technology (e.g., railroads, hospitals, law enforcement, toll roads, drive-through restaurants, taxi service, golf courses, airlines, Department of Homeland Security, etc.)? How would jobs in these organizations change?

Resources

Applebaum, S. H. (1997). Socio-technical systems theory: An intervention strategy for organizational development. *Management Decision, 35*(6), 452-463.

Gordon, B. (2004). Seven mega-trends shaping modern logistics. *World Trade, 17*(11), 42-44.

Kirkpatrick, D. (2005). Managing change: Transfer all learning to behavior. *Leadership Excellence, 22*(11), 15-16.

Lengnick-Hall, C. A., & Lengnick-Hall, M. L. (2006). HR, ERP, and knowledge for competitive advantage. *Human Resource Management, 45*(2), 179-194.

McGinley, J. (2003). Do you know where your assets are? *Fleet Equipment, 29*(11), 12.

Mongelluzzo, B. (2006, January 6). PierPass will track trucks with RFID tags. *Journal of Commerce Online Edition*, p. 1.

Moorman, R. W. (2007). RFID: Ready for industry doubters? *Air Transport World, 44*(6), 75-78.

Taghaboni-Dutta, F., & Velthouse, B. (2006). RFID technology is revolutionary: Who should be involved in this game of tag? *Academy of Management Perspectives, 20*(4), 65-78.

Troy, M. (2004). The writing on the wall reads RFID. *DSN Retailing Today, 43*(2), 36, 60, 66.

Wong-MingJi, D. J., & Millette, W. R. (2002). Dealing with the dynamic duo of innovation and inertia: The "In-" theory of organizational change. *Organizational Development Journal, 20*(1), 36-52.

DOWNSIZING

Downsizing is making permanent personnel reductions in an attempt to improve efficiency and/or effectiveness (Budros, 1999). Downsizing is used reactively to avoid bankruptcy and secure survival or proactively to increase productivity and enhance competitiveness (Gandolfi, 2007). These reductions are generally a response to mergers and acquisitions, revenue loss or loss of market share through technological or industrial change, the execution of new organizational structures, and social pressures attributed to the philosophy that smaller is better. Reductions are accomplished by layoffs, attrition, redeployment, early retirement, outsourcing, or reorganization (Mirabal & DeYoung, 2005). More than 85% of the *Fortune 1000* firms downsized their white-collar workforces between 1987 and 1991, affecting more than five million jobs (Cascio, 1993). According to the Bureau of Labor Statistics (2008a), the annual total number of mass layoffs involving at least 50 people from a single establishment across all industries from 1997 to 2006 ranged from 13,998 to 21,467; and the total number of initial claimants for unemployment ranged from 1,542,548 to 2,514,862. Based on the frequency of layoffs, it appears to be regarded by management as one of the preferred routes to turning around declining organizations (Wilkinson, 2005).

The intention of downsizing is an immediate reduction in costs from lower personnel costs, but downsizing does not always have positive effects on performance. Expected beneficial consequences include lower average salaries for the remaining employees, fewer underutilized human resources, resulting in greater production and economic efficiencies; fewer management layers and flatter structures to speed communication and decision making; and increased market responsiveness (Mone, 1994). Although firms anticipate that downsizing will make their firms more productive and efficient in response to increased global competition, when downsized and nondownsized firms are compared, downsized firms are less profitable or no more productive, profitable, or efficient. Downsizing hampers new product development, negatively affects a firm's competitive position, reduces employee commitment, and increases turnover (McKinley, Mone, & Barker, 1998). Cascio, Young, and Morris's (1997) analysis of the impact of downsizing on the performance of more than 3,000 companies over a period of 15 years found that reduction in employment was not translated into improvement in financial performance (i.e., downsizing companies did not show profitability improvements; Morris, Cascio, & Young, 1999).

Downsizing has an impact on the employees who have been downsized as well as those who remain with the organization. Being downsized is an alienating experience, which makes former employees feel powerless, shocked, betrayed, shamed, and socially isolated (Vickers & Parris, 2007). Employees who survive a downsizing exhibit symptoms of survivor syndrome (e.g., anger; insecurity; depression; and decreased levels of commitment, loyalty, motivation, trust, and security; Gandolfi, 2007; Sahdev, 2004). Downsizing organizations may experience increased tardiness, absence, and turnover; reduced performance capabilities; reduced individual and team efforts; and reduced organizational productivity (Mone, 1994). Downsizing also has been found to have a negative effect on the work environment for creativity (Amabile & Conti, 1999). Reynolds-Fisher and White (2000) suggest that downsizing is incompatible with building an organization's learning capacity (i.e., an organization that has invested in its learning capacity as a strategic resource cannot expect to implement across-the-board personnel reductions without risk to its learning investment). Downsizing separates the organization from its most valuable asset: its people (Piturro, 1999).

Organizations have a range of available alternatives to downsizing, including redeployment, freezing recruitment, disengaging contractors and other flexible workers, reducing overtime, job sharing, wage cuts, retraining, increasing labor productivity, and smart cost reduction (Rayburn & Rayburn, 1999; Wilkinson, 2005). For example, when Lincoln Electric faced several economic downturns, it redeployed employees, moving 54 factory workers to sales, and made $10 million in sales in its first year (Piturro, 1999).

Strategic Questions

1. Why do firms downsize? Are downsizing decisions more often made to make the organization more efficient or to achieve a short-term boost in profits?
2. What are the consequences to the organization of downsizing?
3. What should organizations expect to be the result of reducing the number of employees, if the intellectual capital of its employees is its "greatest resource"?
4. If an organization tries to downsize by offering a buyout, which employees are the most likely to take the buyout? Which employees are the least likely?
5. What are the alternatives to downsizing? In what cases are the alternatives preferable to downsizing?
6. If downsizing makes the firm more competitive by reducing the number of employees, how can an organization maximize the cost savings by downsizing?
7. When making decisions about who to downsize, should the organization focus most of the reductions on more senior, more highly compensated employees?

Resources

Amabile, T. M., & Conti, R. (1999). Changes in the work environment for creativity during downsizing. *Academy of Management Journal, 42*(6), 630-640.

Budros, A. (1999). A conceptual framework for analyzing why organizations downsize. *Organization Science, 10*(1), 69-82.

Bureau of Labor Statistics. *Mass layoff statistics.* http://www.bls.gov/mls/home.htm#overview

Cascio, W. F. (1993). Downsizing: What do we know? What have we learned? *The Executive, 7*(1), 95-104.

Gandolfi, F. (2007). Downsizing, corporate survivors, and employability-related issues: A European case study. *Journal of the American Academy of Business, 12*(1), 50-56.

Kleiman, L. S., & Denton, D. (2000). Downsizing: Nine steps to ADEA compliance. *Employment Relations Today, 27*(3), 37-45.

(Continued)

(Continued)

McKinley, W., Mone, M. A., & Barker, V. L., III. (1998). Some ideological foundations of organizational downsizing. *Journal of Management Inquiry, 7*(3), 198-212.

Mirabel, N., & DeYoung, R. (2005). Downsizing as a strategic intervention. *Journal of the American Academy of Business, 6*(1), 39-45.

Mone, M. A. (1994). Relationships between self-concepts, aspirations, emotional responses, and intent to leave a downsizing organization. *Human Resource Development, 33*(2), 281-298.

Morris, J. R., Cascio, W. F., & Young, C. E. (1999). Downsizing after all these years: Questions and answers about who did it, how many did it, and who benefitted from it. *Organizational Dynamics, 27*(3), 78-87.

Piturro, M. (1999). Alternatives to downsizing. *Management Review, 88*(9), 37-41.

Rayburn, J. M., & Rayburn, L. G. (1999). Smart alternatives to downsizing. *Competitiveness Review, 9*(2), 49-57.

Reynolds-Fisher, S., & White, M. (2000). Downsizing in a learning organization: Are there hidden costs? *Academy of Management Review, 25*(1), 244-251.

Sahdev, K. (2004). Revisiting the survivor syndrome: The role of leadership in implementing downsizing. *European Journal of Work and Organizational Psychology, 13*(2), 165-196.

Vickers, M. H., & Parris, M. A. (2007). "Your job no longer exists!": From experiences of alienation to expectations of resilience—A phenomenological study. *Employee Responsibilities and Rights Journal, 19*(2), 113-125.

Wilkinson, A. (2005). Downsizing, rightsizing or dumbsizing? Quality, human resources and the management of sustainability. *Total Quality Management, 16*(8/9), 1079-1088.

Applications

CROSS-FUNCTIONAL ORGANIZATIONAL DEVELOPMENT

OD is planned, behavioral-science interventions in work settings for the purpose of improving organizational functioning and individual development (Porras & Robertson, 1992). The purpose of OD is to improve an organization's visioning, empowerment, learning, and problem-solving processes through an ongoing, collaborative management of organizational culture (French & Bell, 1999). OD is inherently interdisciplinary, encompassing human resource management, organizational behavior, organizational theory, psychology, sociology, anthropology, economics, accounting, finance, strategy, production and operations, and market research (Hay, 2006). With HRM being more of a strategic partner in many organizations (Ulrich, 1997), the boundaries between

OD and HRM are increasingly blurred (Ellis, 2007; Ruona & Gibson, 2004). If an organization decides to go into a new line of business, OD methods can be used to improve the organization's capabilities, both individual knowledge and skills and the ability of employees to work together effectively.

OD can work with Market Research to accelerate the speed and impact of its contributions to strategic planning; Market Research fills the strategy with content, and OD helps to gain employees' commitment for action (Hay, 2006). Before going into a new area of business, the organization needs to develop in its employees the knowledge and skills they will need, and the first step in that process is a training and development needs analysis (Reed & Vakola, 2006).

Disney is well known for its entertainment-related businesses, theme parks, movie and television production, music, toys, and so on. It saw the growth in popularity of cruise vacations, especially for families, and began considering running its own cruise line (Underwood, 1994). Identifying a potential new business to get into was the first step. To run its own cruise line, Disney would need to develop a new set of individual skills and organizational capabilities and learn how to do it the Disney way. Previous experience in running hotels within theme parks would be useful, but running a cruise line would be different, and a Disney cruise line would be as different from other cruise lines as Disney theme parks are from other theme parks (Anderson, 2000). Most cruise lines see their target market as adults, but Disney's target market would be families. Some cruise lines offer on-board gambling while in international waters, but that would not fit with the Disney culture.

To Do

Part 1. In Table 11.1, make a list of seven products and services Disney sells. For example, Disney produces *Disney Channel Original Movies* (e.g., *High School Musical*), which are shown on its television network, DVDs of these movies, and music from these movies. Then make a list of seven products and services that Disney does not sell but might.

Part 2. In Table 11.1, identify the organizational capabilities that would be required to run a successful business selling the products and services Disney does not sell (that were identified in Part 1). This could include individual knowledge and skills or improvement in ways that employees work together.

(Continued)

(Continued)

Table 11.1 Improving on Disney

Part 1: Identify New Business Opportunities	
Products and Services Disney Sells	*Products and Services Disney Does Not Sell*
Part 2: Identify New Organizational Capabilities	
Products and Services Disney Does Not Sell	*Organizational Capabilities Needed*

Resources

Anderson, J. (2000). Discover uncharted magic with Disney Cruise Line. *Incentive, 174*(10), 14.

Disney. http://home.disney.go.com/

Disney Cruise Line. http://disneycruise.disney.go.com/dcl/en_US/home/home

Ellis, F. (2007). The benefits of partnership for OD and HR. *Strategic HR Review, 6*(4), 32-35.

French, W. L., & Bell, C. H. (1999). *Organizational development.* Upper Saddle River, NJ: Prentice Hall.

Hay, G. W. (2006). New partners for strategic change and organizational transformation: The combined effects of market research and organizational development. *Organizational Development Journal, 26*(4), 55-61.

Porras, J. L., & Robertson, P. J. (1992). Organization Development: Theory, practice and research. In M. D. Dunnette & L. M. Hough (Eds.), *Handbook of industrial and organizational psychology* (Vol. 3, 2nd ed., pp. 719-822). Palo Alto, CA: Consulting Psychologist.

Reed, J., & Vakola, M. (2006). What role can a training needs analysis play in organisational change? *Journal of Organizational Change Management, 19*(3), 393-407.

Ruona, W. E. A., & Gibson, S. K. (2004). The making of twenty-first-century HR: An analysis of the convergence of HRM, HRD, and OD. *Human Resource Management, 43*(1), 49-66.

Ulrich, D. (1997). *Human resource champions: The next agenda for adding value and delivering results.* Boston: Harvard Business School Press.

Underwood, E. (1994). Disney charts course to sail into cruises. *Brandweek, 35*(6), 1, 6.

RE-ENGINEER THIS

One approach to OD is Business Process Re-engineering. According to Hammer (1990), to make an organization more competitive, it is not useful to automate outdated processes; instead, the power of modern information technology should be used to redesign business processes to achieve dramatic improvements in performance. A quantum leap in organizational performance comes from finding new ways to meet customer needs, instead of trying to make the old ways more efficient (Jarrar & Apspinwall, 1999; McKeown & Philip, 2003; Moosebruker & Loftin, 1998). Telephone service in areas of difficult terrain and weather can be dramatically improved by replacing land lines with cell phone towers. Music lovers can enjoy more music by buying songs individually, rather than buying an entire album just to get the couple of good songs on the CD.

The focus of Business Process Re-engineering is not just on improving the efficiency of organizational processes; it is also on improving customer value (i.e., the customers' perceptions of how well their needs are being met; Goodstein & Butz, 1998). Business Process Re-engineering can be done for an organizational process with internal customers (employees) or for an organizational process with external customers. For example, in the successful re-engineering of a large, complex, unionized, urban teaching hospital, the focus of change efforts was on improving patient care by developing streamlined patient-focused care centers (Stein, Kruger, & Siegal, 1996), and the focus of re-engineering an unnamed department in the Central Intelligence Agency was to improve internal customer service to thousands of employees (Johnson & Tolchinsky, 1999). Ferris and Hyde (2004) suggest that the dispute process in the Department of Homeland Security needs to be re-engineered. If an arbitrator could be used for one hearing and one decision, multiple forums to resolve basic disputes could be avoided, speeding resolution of disputes and reducing costs.

A common method for developing and bringing new products to the marketplace is Concurrent Engineering, which involves the overlapping of different but previously sequential activities and the early involvement of all functions that contribute to a successful product. Achieving this organization-wide integration requires companies to re-engineer their organizational structures and organizational processes to the Concurrent Engineering approach. Removing organizational barriers is a key to successful Concurrent Engineering; organizations that invest in OD issues are

To Do

Part 1. Re-engineering a process from the point of view of an external customer. Create a flow chart to describe the process of a patient filling a prescription. The start point is the doctor's decision to prescribe a medication for a patient. The end point is when the patient receives the prescription from the pharmacy.

In a flow chart, start and end symbols are represented as ovals or rounded rectangles, usually labeled "Start" or "End."

Arrows show the direction of flow.

Processing steps are represented as rectangles.

Inputs or outputs are represented as parallelograms.

Conditionals (or decisions) are represented as a diamond, with arrows coming out of it.

Part 2. Re-engineering an HRM process from the point of view of an internal customer. From your own work experience (or experience in a social organization), choose any HRM process and re-engineer it to better meet the needs of the employees. For example, the compensation process could be re-engineered for an organization that pays its employees weekly in cash, which requires the manager to make a run to the bank to get the correct combination of bills and coins to give each employee the exact amount they earned for the week. Or re-engineer a college or university admissions process, to be better from the point of view of internal customers at the college or university.

Information technology can be used to simply automate a manual process or eliminate headcount, but that does not lead to "quantum improvements." Information technology can make it possible to re-engineer a process to do something that was impractical to do before or give customers something they couldn't get before.

Resources

Burr, J. T. (1990). The tools of quality—Part I: Going with the flow(chart). *Quality Progress, 23*(6), 64-67.

Ferris, F., & Hyde, A. C. (2004). Federal labor-management relations for the next century—or the last? The case of the Department of Homeland Security. *Review of Public Personnel Administration.* 24(3), 216-233.

Goodstein, L. D., & Butz, H. W. (1998). Customer value: The linchpin of organizational change. *Organizational Dynamics,* 27(1), 21-34.

Hammer, M. (1990). Reengineering work: Don't automate, obliterate. *Harvard Business Review, 68*(4), 104-112.

Haque, B., Pawar, K. S., & Barson, R. J. (2003). The application of business process modelling to organisational analysis of concurrent engineering environments. *Technovation, 23*(2), 147-162.

Jarrar, Y. F., & Aspinwall, E. M. (1999). Integrating Total Quality Management and Business Process Re-engineering: Is it enough? *Total Quality Management, 10*(4/5), S584.

Johnson, M., & Tolchinsky, P. (1999). A redesign in the Central Intelligence Agency. *Journal for Quality and Participation, 22*(2), 31-35.

McKeown, I., & Philip, G. (2003). Business transformation, information technology and competitive strategies: Learning to fly. *International Journal of Information Management, 23*(1), 3-24.

Moosebruker, J. B., & Loftin, R. D. (1998). Business Process Redesign and Organizational Development: Enhancing success by removing the barriers. *Journal of Applied Behavioral Science, 34*(3), 286-304.

Stein, E. J., Kruger, K. F., & Siegal, P. W. (1996). The role of human resources in supporting reengineering. *Health Care Supervisor, 15*(2), 8-16.

more successful at implementing the approach than those that rely only on tools and technology (Haque, Pawar, & Barson, 2003).

Experiential Exercises

THE NEW MANAGER

In a traditional hierarchical organization, top-level managers set direction by formulating strategy and controlling resources; middle-level managers mediate the vertical information process and resource allocation processes by assuming the role of administrative controllers; and front-line managers find themselves in the role of operational implementers (Bartlett & Ghoshal, 1997). A common career path in organizations is for new employees to begin in an entry-level job and, with satisfactory performance and available openings, be promoted to higher level positions. The employee begins by doing a nonmanagement job and at some point transitions to a management job. Instead of doing the work, they are now directing the work of others. For example, an employee begins as an engineer solving technical problems and becomes a manager of engineers solving technical problems. Technical skills have become less important and interpersonal skills have become more important. Not all employees are able to successfully make this transition from a nonmanagement role to a management role.

Although some organizations invest heavily in developing management talent, others do little to help the employee make the transition from a nonmanagement role to a management role, perhaps assuming that if an employee was successful in a nonmanagement role, he or she should be successful in a management role. Anderson, Mehta, and Strong (1997) examined newly selected sales managers making the transition from personal selling to sales management and found that most sales managers receive little or no formal training for their sales management roles and that the training provided often had glaring weaknesses. A comparison of high-quality and low-quality HRM organizations found that 46% of the employees in a high-quality organization were in a formal HRM plan, including recruitment, development, and succession; and experienced employees received an average of 72 hours of training per year, compared to 4% and 35 hours per year for low HRM quality firms (Becker et al., 2001).

What is the nature of managerial work that makes it different from nonmanagerial work? The early work of Mintzberg (1971, 1990) identified 10 basic roles that managers perform, grouped into three categories. Interpersonal roles describe the manager as a figurehead, an external liaison, and leader. Information processing roles describe the manager as the nerve center of this organization's information system. Decision-making roles deal with resource allocation, improvement, and disturbances. Fisher (1986) describes management roles as consisting of leader, facilitator, enabler, and coach. Floyd and Wooldridge's (1994) typology of middle management roles in strategy include championing strategic alternatives, facilitating adaptability, synthesizing information, and implementing deliberate strategy. Bartlett and Ghoshal (1997) claim that the generic manager is a myth and that there are different kinds of management roles and competencies for operating-level, senior-level, and top-level managers: Operating-level managers drive business performance by focusing on productivity, innovation, and growth within front-line units; senior-level managers provide support and coordination; and top-level managers create and embed a sense of direction, commitment, and challenge to people throughout the organization. Mintzberg's (1994) integrated view of the manager's job has three interacting layers of activities. The frame of the job consists of the manager's purpose as to what he or she is supposed to manage; the manager's perspective about the nature of the business; and positions about ways of doing the work, the products produced, the markets served, the structures and systems designed, and the facilities provided. The agenda of the work includes scheduling the work and the current set of issues the manager must deal with in day-to-day work. The manager's role consists of managing by information, managing through people, and managing by "their own direct involvement" in action.

To Do

Interview a manager to learn how management jobs differ from nonmanagement jobs. Use the list of questions in Table 11.2, and develop two additional questions. Report your results.

Table 11.2 Interview With a Manager

Interview Questions	*Manager's Responses*
1. What new things did you have to learn to do in your management job that you had not done in your previous nonmanagement jobs?	
2. What was the most difficult thing for you to learn when you became a manager?	
3. What did the organization do to prepare you for your management role?	
4. What did you do by yourself to prepare for your management role?	
5. Divide up 100 points to indicate how you spend your day, what tasks, what activities, etc.	
6. Divide up 100 points to indicate whom you interact with during your day.	
7. What are you doing now to prepare yourself for your next position?	
8. What are you doing now to prepare your replacement to do your job?	
9. What is the best thing about your job?	
10. What is the worst thing about your job?	
11.	
12.	

(Continued)

(Continued)

Resources

Alreck, P. L., & Settle, R. B. (1995). *The survey research handbook.* Chicago: Irwin.

Anderson, R., Mehta, R., & Strong, J. (1997). An empirical investigation of sales management training programs for sales managers. *Journal of Personal Selling & Sales Management, 17*(3), 53-66.

Bartlett, C. A., & Ghoshal, S. (1997). The myth of the generic manager: New personal competencies for new management roles. *California Management Review, 40*(1), 92-116.

Becker, B. E., Huselid, M. A., & Ulrich, D. (2001). *The HR Scorecard: Linking people, strategy and performance.* Boston: Harvard Business School Press.

Dubinsky, A. J., Anderson, R. E., & Mehta, R. (1999). Selection, training, and performance evaluation of sales managers: An empirical investigation. *Journal of Business-to-Business Marketing, 6*(3), 37-69.

Fisher, K. K. (1986). Management roles in the implementation of participative management systems. *Human Resource Management, 25*(3), 459-480.

Floyd, S. W., & Wooldridge, B. (1994). Dinosaurs or dynamos? Recognizing middle management's strategic role. *Academy of Management Executive, 8*(4), 47-57.

Mintzberg, H. (1971). Managerial work: Analysis from observation. *Management Science, 18*(2), B-97-B110.

Mintzberg, H. (1990). The manager's job: Folklore and fact. *Harvard Business Review, 68*(2), 163-176.

Rogelberg, S. G., Church, A. H., Waclawski, J., & Stanton, J. M. (2002). Organizational survey research. In S. G. Rogelberg (Ed.), *Handbook of research methods in industrial and organizational psychology* (pp. 141-160). Malden, MA: Blackwell.

Thomas, S. J. (1999). *Designing surveys that work! A step-by-step guide.* Thousand Oaks, CA: Corwin.

THE VALUE OF A COLLEGE EDUCATION

The OD method of Appreciative Inquiry is designed to focus on the strengths of an organization rather than its weaknesses, on what can be achieved rather than on problems, and on what works well and how success can be extended throughout the organization. The goal is to increase the collaborative capacity of the organization by giving organization members an opportunity to reflect on existing strengths, discover what is important, and build a collective vision of the preferred future (Carter et al., 2007). Appreciative Inquiry has been used with employees of the U.S. Environmental Protection Agency's Office of Research and Development (Bright, Cooperrider, & Galloway, 2006), a nonprofit metropolitan health care facility (Newman & Fitzgerald, 2001), a coffee roasting company (Babcock, 2005), and the City of Hampton, Virginia (Johnson & Leavitt, 2001). Appreciative Inquiry has also been used to build relationships and develop understanding and trust in a U.S.–India biotechnology alliance (Miller, Fitzgerald, Murrell, Preston, & Ambekar, 2005).

Appreciative Inquiry is designed to induce innovation and collaboration through participatory methods, by providing an opportunity for people to participate in a series of guided conversations that explore a topic of organizational importance (Bright et al., 2006; Carter et al., 2007). The four steps of Appreciative Inquiry are as follows:

1. *Discover.* Intentional conversations among organization members on what is the best that now exists in the organization, how people in the organization should treat each other, and what the organization should represent or strive for. The primary focus is on creating an awareness of images, stories, and capacities that are most likely to inspire future actions. Organizational members may become aware of previously unknown strengths in each other, discover common values, or develop a greater willingness to rethink basic assumptions.
2. *Dream.* The focus of discussion shifts to how the strengths discovered in the Discover step can be leveraged, so that organization members can think about the organization's potential. By creating a sense of continuity across the past, present, and future of the organization, it encourages organizational members to think expansively about the potential future.
3. *Design.* In this step, the major task is to identify concrete, actionable ideas that will move the organization closer to its newly envisioned potential, a shift from reflection to action. Action groups are formed to focus on the implementation of prioritized ideas, and team development activities are planned to build strong, focused teams with a clear sense of purpose and identity.
4. *Destiny.* Organization members now shift from planning to deployment as teams implement their plans to create change. As implementation work continues, teams create small wins to celebrate and motivate organization members to continue the work of implementation (Bright et al., 2006).

To Do

Use Appreciative Inquiry to reflect on the existing strengths, discover what is important, and build a collective vision of the preferred future for your college or university. What have you learned, and how have you changed since you came to the college or university? What have been the best things about your college or university? Begin by discussing the strengths of the organization (Discover), then discuss how these strengths can be built on in the future (Dream). Next, develop specific, concrete ideas that can build on the organization's strengths (Design) and how these ideas could be implemented (Destiny).

(Continued)

(Continued)

Resources

Babcock, P. (2005). A calling for change. *HR Magazine, 50*(9), 46-51.

Barron, J. (2006). Top ten secrets of effective e-learning. *Industrial and Commercial Training, 38*(7), 360-364.

Bright, D. S., Cooperrider, D. L., & Galloway, W. B. (2006). Appreciative Inquiry in the Office of Research and Development: Improving the collaborative capacity of organization. *Public Performance & Management Review, 29*(3), 285-306.

Bushe, G. R. (1998). Appreciative Inquiry with teams. *Organizational Development Journal, 16*(3), 41-50.

Bushe, G. R., & Coetzer, G. (1995). Appreciative Inquiry as a team-development intervention: A controlled experiment. *Journal of Applied Behavioral Science, 31*(1), 13-30.

Bushe, G. R., & Kassam, A. F. (2005). When is Appreciative Inquiry transformational: A meta-case analysis. *Journal of Applied Behavioral Science, 41*(2), 161-181.

Carter, C. A., Ruhe, M. C., Weyer, S., Litaker, D., Frye, R. E., & Stange, K. C. (2007). An Appreciative Inquiry approach to practice improvement and transformative change in health care settings. *Quality Management in Health Care, 16*(3), 194-204.

Fry, R. (2002). *Appreciative inquiry and organizational transformation: Reports from the field.* Westport, CT: Quorum Books.

Johnson, G., & Leavitt, W. (2001). Building on success: Transforming organizations through an Appreciative Inquiry. *Public Personnel Management, 30*(1), 129-136.

Miller, M. G., Fitzgerald, S. P., Murrell, K. L., Preston, J., & Ambekar, R. (2005). Appreciative Inquiry in building a transcultural strategic alliance: The case of a biotech alliance between a U.S. multinational and an Indian family business. *Journal of Applied Behavioral Science, 41*(1), 91-110.

Newman, H. L., & Fitzgerald, S. P. (2001). Appreciative Inquiry with an executive team: Moving along the Action Research continuum. *Organizational Development Journal, 19*(3), 37-44.

Creative Exercises

MANAGING CHANGE

The primary purpose of organizational change is to make fundamental changes in how the organization is run to enable the organization to adapt to changing market conditions (Kotter, 2007). According to Lewin's (1951) model of organizational change, first the organization has to unfreeze its current way of doing things (i.e., the status quo), then organizational changes are put into effect, and then the organization has to refreeze the changes to ensure that the new-and-improved way of doing things becomes the status quo. Driving forces push the organization toward making the changes, and restraining forces hinder the organization from making the changes.

Organizational members' readiness for change (i.e., the opposite of resistance to change) is affected by a number of factors. Holt, Armenakis,

Feild, and Harris (2007) found that readiness for change is influenced by the employees' beliefs that they are capable of implementing the proposed change, that the proposed change is appropriate for the organization, that the leaders are committed to the proposed change, and that the proposed change is beneficial to organizational members.

Kotter (1996) describes an eight-step plan for implementing change:

1. Establish a sense of urgency by creating a compelling reason for why change is needed.
2. Form a coalition with enough power to lead the change.
3. Create a new vision to direct the change and strategies for achieving the vision.
4. Communicate the vision throughout the organization.
5. Empower others to act on the vision by removing barriers to change and encouraging risk taking and creative problem solving.
6. Plan for, create, and reward short-term wins that move the organization toward the new vision.
7. Consolidate improvements, reassess changes, and make necessary adjustments in the new programs.
8. Reinforce the changes by demonstrating the relationship between new behaviors and organizational success.

To Do

You are the owner of *The Pasta Garden*, a small Italian restaurant located in a medium-sized suburban town. The restaurant has been at the same location for more than 20 years, and you have built up a substantial number of regular customers. But as the town has grown over the years, more restaurants have opened up (including two other Italian restaurants), and your daily sales have been steadily declining for the past 3 years. The restaurant business has also changed, because different kinds of "food services" have opened in town over the past few years. One sells gourmet chef-prepared meals that customers pick up and reheat at home, another offers pizza to go in 5 minutes or it's free, and there is a delivery service that will deliver take-out food from most of the restaurants in town. You want to make some changes to your restaurant to get more new customers, but you don't want to do anything that might make you lose any of your long-time regular customers.

Using the form provided, apply Kotter's (1996) eight-step plan for implementing change to create an action plan for making organizational changes at *The Pasta Garden*.

(Continued)

(Continued)

Organizational Changes Using Kotter's Eight-Step Plan

Planned Change: Pasta Garden	*Plan*
Establish a sense of urgency by creating a compelling reason for why change is needed.	
Form a coalition with enough power to lead the change.	
Create a new vision to direct the change and strategies for achieving the vision.	
Communicate the vision throughout the organization.	
Empower others to act on the vision by removing barriers to change and encouraging risk taking and creative problem solving.	
Plan for, create, and reward short-term wins that move the organization toward the new vision.	
Consolidate improvements, reassess changes, and make necessary adjustments in the new programs.	
Reinforce the changes by demonstrating the relationship between new behaviors and organizational success.	

Resources

Burnes, B. (2007). Kurt Lewin and the Harwood Studies: The foundations of OD. *Journal of Applied Behavioral Science, 43*(2), 213-231.

Holt, D. T., Armenakis, A. A., Feild, H. S., & Harris, S. G. (2007). Readiness for organizational change: The systematic development of a scale. *Journal of Applied Behavioral Science, 43*(2), 232-255.

Kotter, J. P. (1996). *Leading change.* Boston: Harvard Business School Press.

Kotter, J. P. (2007). Leading change: Why transformation efforts fail. *Harvard Business Review, 85*(1), 96-103.

Kotter, J. P., & Cohen, D. S. (2002). Creative ways to empower action to change the organization: Cases in point. *Journal of Organizational Excellence, 22*(1), 73-82.

Lewin, K. (1951). *Field theory in social science.* New York: Harper & Row.

Mikaelsson, J. (2002). Managing change in product development organization: Learning from Volvo Car Corporation. *Leadership & Organizational Development Journal, 23*(5/6), 301-313.

Ulrich, D. (1997). *Human resource champions: The next agenda for adding value and delivering results.* Boston: Harvard Business School Press.

DEVELOPING A VALUING DIVERSITY PROGRAM

According to projections based on Bureau of Labor Statistics data, diversity will continue to increase in the 2010 labor force, with a greater proportion of women and Hispanics than in the 2000 labor force and an older workforce (Fullerton & Toossi, 2001). White males comprised nearly 52% of the workforce in 1978, but that percentage had fallen to less than 40% by 1998. Women and minorities are expected to make up over 70% of new entrants into the workforce in 2008. Therefore, diversity is a reality; the key issue is how to deal with it (O'Leary & Weathington, 2006). The business case for valuing diversity is tied to the increasing competition for markets, demand for labor, and the economic imperative to develop new ways of organizing work processes for rapid response to changing conditions (Miller, 1995). Exposure to diverse colleagues helps managers make better decisions and cultivate new ideas by drawing on a larger pool of information and valuable experiences, and helps the organization increase its market share by having a better understanding of how to market to an increasingly diverse customer base (Allen & Montgomery, 2001). Effective management of diversity can lead to improvements in competitiveness and customer satisfaction, such as enhancing corporate image and reputation, and becoming an employer of choice to attract and retain skilled workers (Worman, 2005).

Diversity training has become a popular tool for managing diversity and trying to gain the benefits of diversity, with multinational corporations in the United States beginning to implement diversity programs on a global scale (Holladay & Quiñones, 2005). More than 60% of U.S. employers used diversity training in 2005 (Paluck, 2006) and half of U.S.

companies with more than 100 employees have implemented diversity training at an estimated annual cost of $10 billion (Roberson, Kulik, & Pepper, 2003). Cox and Blake (1991) suggest six areas where effectively managing cultural diversity can create a competitive advantage for the organization: cost, resource acquisition, marketing, creativity, problem solving, and organizational flexibility.

There are a number of different approaches to diversity training. For example, educational interventions to increase trainees' perceptions of perceived similarities and decreasing the perceived dissimilarities (Triandis, 2003); training focused on relationship with self, relationship with the supervisee, and relationship with the organization (Armour, Rubio, & Bain, 2004); informational or educational approaches aim to raise participants' awareness and take the perspective of members of other groups (Pendry, Driscoll, & Field, 2007); and experiential methods that take a personalized and participatory approach to building skills that promote harmonious and productive interactions (Paluck, 2006).

Diversity training also has its risks. Bringing differences among organization members out into the open may build friendships and improve teamwork, or it can lead to group fragmentation and breakdown of friendships (Tomlinson & Egan, 2002). Diversity training is unlikely to be successful without a needs assessment and an evaluation of the success of the training (Hite & McDonald, 2006). Diversity management can lead to devaluation of employees who are perceived as culturally different, reverse discrimination against members of the majority group, and reinforcement of stereotypes (Von Bergen, Soper, & Foster, 2002). Diversity training that includes lesbian, gay, and bisexual issues might conflict with some workers' religious beliefs (Kaplan, 2006).

To Do

Develop a proposal for a Valuing Diversity training program for a specific organization. The proposal could deal with any aspect of diversity in the organization (e.g., race, culture, age, sex, gender, religion, education, work group, etc.). The proposal should include the following sections:

Needs assessment. Needs assessment is an important first step for any training program, so that the training can be developed to meet specific organizational needs rather than creating a one-size-fits-all program. Organizational diversity training programs have frequently been criticized for their lack of attention to the needs assessment process (Roberson et al., 2001). The program could address any aspect of diversity, race, culture, age, gender, religion, education, and so forth. The proposal should include a description of the organization and the results of the needs analysis.

Goals of the training program. What are the objectives of the training program or the mission statement? The objectives may be based on the training needs assessment. Usry and

White's (2000) list of objectives include creating an awareness and sensitivity in participants of the ethnocentrism that is brought to the workplace, developing team-building skills in the participants, creating an awareness in the participants of the value of other cultures in the workplace, enabling individuals to better assess their effect on groups and how groups affect them, enabling participants to assess their behavior with respect to its effect on the customer, and improving communication skills among participants.

Training methods. In what kind of training experiences will organization members participate? Will the focus be on awareness, education, training, skill development, or some combination? Will the training groups be homogeneous or heterogeneous (Roberson, Kulik, & Pepper, 2001)? The training methods could range from interactive dialog, to experiential exercises, to case-based discussions to self-reflection and storytelling (Guillory, 2004; Loo, 1999; Schor, Sims, & Dennehy, 1996; Tang, Hernandez, & Adams, 2004). If the training will involve hiring a consultant, identify the consultant and describe the products and services that will be purchased, and estimate the cost.

Evaluation of the program's effectiveness. Whatever type of diversity training is done, an essential last step is measuring the effectiveness of the program; yet diversity training interventions do not always collect evidence of program impact (Hite & McDonald, 2006; Paluck, 2006). Determine what data will be used to evaluate the effectiveness of the valuing diversity program.

Resources

Allen, R. S., & Montgomery, K. A. (2001). Applying an organizational development approach to creating diversity. *Organizational Dynamics, 30*(2), 149-161.

Armour, M. P., Rubio, R., & Bain, B. (2004). An evaluation study of diversity training for field instructors: A collaborative approach to enhancing cultural competence. *Journal of Social Work Education, 40*(1), 27-38.

Bureau of Labor Statistics. *Current population survey.* http://www.bls.gov/cps/home.htm#charemp

Cox, T. H., & Blake, S. (1991). Managing cultural diversity: Implications for organizational competitiveness. *Academy of Management Executive, 5*(3), 45-56.

Franke, R. H., Hofstede, G., & Bond, M. H. (1991). Cultural roots of economic performance: A research note. *Strategic Management Journal, 12*(Special), 165-173.

Fullerton, H. N., & Toossi, M. (2001). Labor force projections to 2010: Steady growth and changing composition. *Monthly Labor Review, 124*(11), 21-38.

Gilbert, J. A., & Ivancevich, J. M. (2000). Valuing diversity: A tale of two organizations. *Academy of Management Executive, 14*(1), 93-105.

Guillory, W. A. (2004). The roadmap to diversity, inclusion, and high performance. *Healthcare Executive, 19*(4), 24-30.

Hite, L. M., & McDonald, K. S. (2006). Diversity training pitfalls and possibilities: An exploration of small and mid-size U.S. organizations. *Human Resource Development International, 9*(3), 365-377.

Holladay, C. L., & Quiñones, M. A. (2005). Reactions to diversity training: An international comparison. *Human Resource Development Quarterly, 16*(4), 529-545.

Kaplan, D. M. (2006). Can diversity training discriminate? Backlash to lesbian, gay, and bisexual diversity initiatives. *Employee Responsibilities and Rights Journal, 18*(1), 61-72.

Loo, R. (1999). A structured exercise for stimulating cross-cultural sensitivity. *Career Development International, 4*(6), 321-324

(Continued)

(Continued)

Miller, J. (1995). The business case for diversity. *Journal of Education for Business, 71*(1), 7-10.

O'Leary, B. J., & Weathington, B. L. (2006). Beyond the business case for diversity in organizations. *Employee Responsibilities and Rights Journal, 18*(4), 283-292.

Paluck, E. L. (2006). Diversity training and intergroup contact: A call to Action Research. *Journal of Social Issues, 62*(3), 577-595.

Pendry, L. F., Driscoll, D. M., & Field, C. T. (2007). Diversity training: Putting theory into practice. *Journal of Occupational and Organizational Psychology, 80*(1), 27-50.

Roberson, L., Kulik, C. T., & Pepper, M. B. (2001). Designing effective diversity training: Influence of group composition and trainee experience. *Journal of Organizational Behavior, 22*(8), 871-885.

Roberson, L., Kulik, C. T., & Pepper, M. B. (2003). Using needs assessment to resolve controversies in diversity training design. *Group & Organization Management, 28*(1), 148-174.

Schor, S. M., Sims, R. R., & Dennehy, R. F. (1996). Power and diversity: Sensitizing yourself and others through self-reflection and storytelling. *Journal of Management Education, 20*(2), 242-256.

Tang, T. S., Hernandez, E. J., & Adams, B. S. (2004). "Learning by teaching": A peer-teaching model for diversity training in medical school. *Teaching and Learning in Medicine, 16*(1), 60-63.

Tomlinson, F., & Egan, S. (2002). Organizational sensemaking in a culturally diverse setting: Limits to the 'valuing diversity' discourse. *Management Learning, 33*(1), 79-97.

Triandis, H. C. (2003). The future of workforce diversity in international organisations: A commentary. *Applied Psychology: An International Review, 52*(3), 486-495.

Usry, M. L., & White, M. (2000). Multicultural awareness in small businesses. *Business Forum, 25*(1-2), 10-13.

Von Bergen, C. W., Soper, B., & Foster, T. (2002). Unintended negative effects of diversity management. *Public Personnel Management, 31*(2), 239-251.

Washington, C. L. (1993). Diversity without performance is a ticket to mediocrity: A rejoinder. *Human Resource Development Quarterly, 4*(3), 291-293.

Worman, D. (2005, May 17). Is there a business case for diversity? *Personnel Today*, pp. 27-28.

International HRM 12

Strategic Objective

Organizations that do business beyond their own domestic market are international organizations. There are different types of international organizations, categorized by their degree of global integration. Organizations that have fully autonomous units operating in multiple countries are multinational organizations. Global organizations have integrated worldwide operations through a centralized headquarters. Transnational organizations use flexible organizational structures to provide autonomy to independent country operations and various coordination mechanisms to provide global integration and are the least common type (Bartlett & Ghoshal, 1989; Leong & Tan, 1993). Subsidiaries in multinational organizations can play different roles in different organizations. If there is a highly competent national subsidiary in a strategically important market, the subsidiary may be a strategic leader, working with headquarters in developing and implementing strategy to provide global integration. If it is in a less strategically important market, it may be a contributor with its own distinctive capability (Bartlett & Ghoshal, 1986).

In a global organization, home country nationals are citizens of the country in which the organization has its world headquarters. Host country nationals are locals, who are citizens of any country in which the global organization has a subsidiary. Third-country nationals are citizens of a country other than the home country or the host country. Expatriates are noncitizens of the countries in which they are working. Repatriates are expatriates who have returned to the country of which they are a citizen.

International HRM involves the procurement, allocation, and use of the human resources of an organization. Variations in currencies, languages, customs, and culture interact to make International HRM different from traditional HRM (Morgan, 1986). Multinational organizations may take a variety of organizational approaches to HRM. In the ethnocentric approach, key decisions come from headquarters and the subsidiaries follow home country practices; in the polycentric approach, each subsidiary manages on a local basis; and in a geocentric approach, there is a global integrated business strategy and the organization tries to develop a group of international managers from multiple countries (Treven, 2006). A regiocentric approach is used when cultural, consumer, or marketing differences make doing business different in different regions. A strategy suitable for Hong Kong or Taiwan may not automatically translate into success in China (Cui, 1998). Which strategic approach an organization takes seems to be related to corporate success. Caligiuri and Stroh (1995) found that companies that had ethnocentric strategies were less successful than companies using regiocentric, polycentric, or geocentric strategies.

Employees in multinational organizations are sometimes sent on long-term international assignments (i.e., expatriates). Edström and Galbraith (1977) identified three reasons that organizations send their employees to work in other countries: (a) to fill positions, when qualified host country nationals are not available; or (b) for management development, to give employees international experience; or (c) for organizational development, to improve the international capabilities of the organization. Multinational organizations are also seeking alternatives to traditional long-term expatriate assignments, including varying the nature and duration of international assignments (Fenwick, 2004; Forster, 2000). Collings, Scullion, and Morley (2007) suggest that organizations should take a more strategic approach to international staffing and consider other alternatives such as short-term international assignments, frequent flyer assignments, commuter and rotational assignments, and global virtual team assignments.

Brewster, Sparrow, and Harris (2005) identified five organizational drivers of international HRM: efficiency organization, global service provision, information exchange, core business processes, and localization of decision making. In multinational organizations, two HRM activities that are particularly important are compensation and management development. Based on the idea that effort follows reward, compensation systems motivate employees to achieve organizational goals. Therefore, compensation strategy plays an important role in supporting the organization's corporate strategy (Festing, Eidems, & Royer, 2007). Knowledge of global business trends, cultural sensitivity, business knowledge, and understanding of local employment practices are critical for all managers in a multinational organization (Friedman, 2007). This requires more extensive development of management talent, because managers in an international organization will play different management roles than in a domestic organization. Bartlett and Ghoshal (1992) suggest that there is no such thing as a universal global manager and that transnational organizations need to develop three different groups of specialists: (a) the Business Manager must be a strategist, an architect, and a coordinator; (b) the Country Manager must be a sensor, a builder, and a contributor; and (c) the Functional Manager must be a scanner, a cross-pollinator, and a champion.

Strategic Issues in HRM

GLOBAL RECRUITING ON THE INTERNET

Computer technology has affected all areas of business, including the management of human resources. In the past, organizations would place "help wanted" signs in their shop windows or at plant entrances, place an advertisement in the classified section of the local newspaper, or visit a college campus. People searching for jobs might respond to a "help wanted" advertisement or be told about a job opportunity at an organization by someone already working there. Internet technology has changed the way that organizations seek and attract applicants to apply for open positions and the way that applicants search for and pursue job opportunities. Now organizations can post job openings on their own Web pages or post job openings on Internet job boards and search globally for applicants meeting the selection criteria.

It has been estimated that 90% of large U.S. companies recruit via the Internet and that at Monster.com, one of the largest job boards with more than 18 million employee profiles and resumes, about four million people search for work on the busiest days (Cappelli, 2001; Martinez, 2000). A Pew Internet Project survey found that 52 million Americans have looked online for information about jobs and more than 4 million do so on a typical day (Smith, 2005). More than 75% of HRM professionals now use Internet job boards in addition to traditional recruiting methods, and expenditures on newspaper advertisements and headhunter retainer fees have dropped as Internet advertising revenues have increased (Feldman & Klaas, 2002). Nearly half of all HR professionals believe that online job boards are the best resources to find job candidates, compared to traditional sources (Smith, 2005).

CareerBuilder.com runs Internet job boards in Sweden and the Netherlands and has strategic partnerships with Lycos Canada and Naukri.com, India's largest career site with more than 180 million page views per month (Ruiz, 2007). Among the *Fortune Global 500* companies in 2001, 88% had a company Internet recruitment site, up from only 29% in 1998 (Lievens & Harris, 2003). General Electric receives 90% of its resumes electronically, receiving about 10,000 resumes each month through its corporate Web site alone, not including those from positions posted on Internet job board sites (Martinez, 2000). Cisco Systems has received up to 500,000 hits on its job site in a 1-month period and has hired as many as 1,200 people in a 3-month period (Cober, Brown, Blumental, Doverspike, & Levy, 2000).

Internet technology makes it easier for job searchers to look for job opportunities. It is possible to search through thousands of job openings and then apply for jobs simply by sending a resume by e-mail, which allows applicants to apply for many more jobs in a shorter period of time than was possible before (Lievens & Harris, 2003). Because employers use their Web sites to post information about the organization and there are other sources of information about employers that can be found by searching elsewhere on the Internet, potential applicants can know more about the organization they are applying to than they did in the past. Managers and professionals are more likely to use the Internet for job hunting when the geographical scope of the job hunt is wide, when a major salary increase is desired, and when both small and large organizations are being considered as potential employers (Feldman & Klaas, 2002).

There are significant advantages to making use of Internet technology to do recruiting. Job listings can be created in a shorter period of time for an online posting than for a newspaper advertisement, and it provides immediate access to millions of potential job applicants (Greengard, 1995; Stimpson, 2004; Wyld, 1997). Recruiting via the Web allows organizations to better target their specific audience. Although an employment listing in the local newspaper may reach a large number of people, only a small number of them are looking for that type of job (Stimpson, 2004). A study by Recruitsoft/iLogos Research of fifty *Fortune 500* companies found that the average company cut about 6 days off its hiring cycle of 43 days by posting jobs online instead of in newspapers, another 4 days by taking online applications instead of paper ones, and more than a week by screening and processing applications electronically (Cappelli, 2001). Cober et al. (2000) estimate that Internet recruitment is 10% of the cost of traditional methods and that the amount of time between recruitment and selection may be reduced by as much as 25%.

Internet recruitment is essential in a global marketplace. To attract more qualified candidates, recruitment cannot be limited to one country; organizations must search globally (Laabs, 1998). Global recruiting means searching worldwide for qualified applicants regardless of their current location. Using the Internet to recruit makes geography unimportant because contacts between organizations and applicants are made by electronic communication; it doesn't matter where the organization or the applicant is (Wyld, 1997). For example, when Continental Airlines determined that they needed to turn to international markets to survive, they abandoned their labor-intensive domestic recruiting process and implemented a global, Web-enabled, paperless recruitment process that allows them to staff any location worldwide (Hansen, 2006). Because it is so easy for people to post their resume and search for job opportunities online, and for organizations to post job openings and search for potential applicants online, the labor market has become a true market, uncontrolled by individual companies and unconstrained by geography (Cappelli, 2001).

Strategic Questions

1. When should an organization recruit globally instead of just locally?
2. When an organization uses Internet recruiting methods to recruit globally, will the applicant pool be more or less diverse? Is Internet recruitment more or less likely to find potential applicants who are women, minority group members, people with disabilities, or workers over 40 years of age?
3. For what reasons might a potential applicant not use the Internet for job hunting?
4. Should an organization's own employees have the same access to job postings as external job seekers, or more?
5. As an organization makes greater use of Internet recruiting methods, should it continue to use headhunters for high-level positions?
6. Does the ease with which an organization's employees can search for jobs with other organizations decrease their loyalty to their current employer?
7. Does use of Internet recruiting methods make Equal Employment Opportunity compliance and record keeping easier or more difficult?
8. If an organization is recruiting globally, should it post job openings only in the home country language or in multiple languages simultaneously?

Resources

Bartram, D. (2000). Internet recruitment and selection: Kissing frogs to find princes. *International Journal of Selection and Assessment, 8*(4), 261-274.
Brandel, M. (2006). Fishing in the global talent pool. *Computerworld, 40*(47), 33-35.
Cappelli, P. (2001). Making the most of on-line recruiting. *Harvard Business Review, 79*(3), 139-146.
CareerBank.com. http://www.careerbank.com/
CareerBuilder.com. http://www.careerbuilder.com/
CareerJournal.com: The Wall Street Journal Executive Career Site. http://www.careerjournal.com/
Cober, R. T., Brown, D. J., Blumental, A. J., Doverspike, D., & Levy, P. (2000). The quest for the qualified job surfer: It's time the public sector catches the wave. *Public Personnel Management, 29*(4), 479-494.
Feldman, D. C., & Klaas, B. S. (2002). Internet job hunting: A field study of applicant experiences with on-line recruiting. *Human Resources Management, 41*(2), 175-192.
Greengard, S. (1995). Catch the wave as HR goes online. *Personnel Journal, 74*(7), 54-68.
Hansen, F. (2006). Paperless route for recruiting. *Workforce Management, 85*(4), 1, 34-37.
Laabs, J. L. (1998). Like finding a needle in a haystack: Recruiting in the global village. *Workforce, 77*(4), 30-33.

(Continued)

(Continued)

Lievens, F., & Harris, M. M. (2003). Research on Internet recruiting and testing: Current status and future directions. In C. L. Cooper & I. T. Robertson (Eds.), *International Review of Industrial and Organizational Psychology* (Vol. 16, pp. 131-165). Chichester, UK: Wiley & Sons.

Marquardt, M. J., & Sofo, F. (1999). Preparing human resources for the global economy. *Advances in Developing Human Resources, 1*(4), 3-21.

Martinez, M. N. (2000). Get job seekers to come to you. *HR Magazine, 45*(8), 44-52.

Monster.com. http://www.monster.com/

Ruiz, G. (2007). Careerbuilder buys northern European sites. *Workforce Management, 86*(7), 12.

Smith, C. (2005). Finding the "right people" just got easier. *Franchising World, 37*(11), 46-48.

Stimpson, J. (2004). Recruiting via the web. *Practical Accountant, 37*(1), 26-30.

Wyld, D. C. (1997). Recruit@internet.com: The Internet and the future of corporate recruiting. *Equal Opportunities International, 16*(2), 15-24.

Yahoo! HotJobs.com. http://hotjobs.yahoo.com/

GLOBAL COMPENSATION

The effective management of human resources can be a source of competitive advantage, but to achieve that advantage, the organization's reward systems must be aligned with the organization's mission, vision, values, and goals (Chen & Hsieh, 2006). Determining how much employees in specific jobs should be paid and differentiating and rewarding performance are important HRM functions for any organization and can become highly complex for multinational organizations. Global compensation costs between three and five times the total of an employee's home salary, allowances, and taxes (Solomon, 1995).

Global organizations are faced with a two-pronged HRM challenge: to appropriately compensate employees in local markets and facilitate the mobility of skills and expertise to the places worldwide where they are most needed (Dwyer, 1999). It is a significant HRM challenge to find ways to effectively use pay to motivate employees in multiple countries and multiple cultures who are all networked together and can talk in real time about pay issues with each other (Gross & Wingerup, 1999). Also, a compensation strategy that works in one country may not work as well in another. For example, stock options are a common part of compensation plans in the United States and have become common in the United Kingdom, but not in Eastern Europe (Cahill, 2002). There are also legal issues; some practices common in the United States may not be permitted in other countries. For example, some countries prohibit their citizens from holding stock in foreign companies, limiting the use of stock options as a component of incentive pay (Gross & Wingerup, 1999).

Increasing numbers of multinational organizations have implemented transnational corporate strategies that are characterized by global standardization and local responsiveness (Festing, Eidems, & Royer, 2007). Global leveling of compensation may be used to establish internal equity across borders, but with some job rewards that vary from country to country (Powers, 2002). Schuler and Ragovsky (1998) have examined the relationship between compensation practices and national cultures and found that the tendency to use seniority-based and skill-based compensation systems was positively related to Hofstede and Bond's (1988) cultural dimension of "Uncertainty Avoidance." Similarly, in high-power distance cultures, wages and salaries are based on the subjective evaluations of managers who reserve the right to assign differential salaries to employees recruited for the same job. Although pay-for-performance and a focus on individual performance are common in individualistic cultures, there is a greater emphasis on group-based rewards in collectivist cultures (Aycan, 2005).

Strategic Questions

1. Should the organization have a common compensation strategy that is applied across all countries, or should there be local variations?
2. What type of performance incentive plans should be available to all employees? To only selected employees? In which countries?
3. If stock purchase plans are made available to employees in one country, should they be made available to employees in all countries?
4. Should differences in compensation among different international executives be minimized for fairness or allowed for expatriate packages of benefits (e.g., tax equalization, cost of living, housing allowances, repatriation allowances)?
5. In which cultures would an "Employee of the Month" bonus program motivate workers? In which cultures would it not work?

Resources

Aycan, Z. (2005). The interplay between cultural and institutional/structural contingencies in human resource management practices. *International Journal of Human Resource Management, 16*(7), 1083-1119.

Cahill, S. (2002). Global equity plans: Are they costing you too much? *Compensation & Benefits Management, 18*(1), 10-15.

Chen, H., & Hsieh, Y. (2006). Key trends of the total reward system in the 21st century. *Compensation & Benefits Review, 38*(6), 64-70.

de Mesa, A. A., & Mesa-Lago, C. (2006). The structural pension reform in Chile: Effects, comparisons with other Latin American reforms, and lessons. *Oxford Review of Economic Policy, 22*(1), 149-167.

Dwyer, T. D. (1999). Trends in global compensation. *Compensation and Benefits Review, 31*(4), 48-53.

Engle, A. D., Sr., & Mendelhall, M. E. (2004). Transnational roles, transnational rewards: Global integration in compensation. *Employee Relations, 26*(6), 613-625.

(Continued)

(Continued)

Festing, M., Eidems, J., & Royer, S. (2007). Strategic issues and local constraints in transnational compensation strategies: An analysis of cultural, institutional and political influences. *European Management Journal, 25*(2), 118-131.

Gross, S. E., & Wingerup. P. L. (1999). Global pay? Maybe not yet! *Compensation and Benefits Review, 31*(4), 25-34.

Harvey, M. (1993). Empirical evidence of recurring international compensation problems. *Journal of International Business Studies, 24*(4), 785-799.

Hofstede, G., & Bond, M. H. (1988). The Confucius connection: From cultural roots to economic growth. *Organizational Dynamics, 15*(1), 4-21.

Javidan, M., & House, R. J. (2001). Cultural acumen for the global manager: Lessons from Project GLOBE. *Organization Dynamics, 29*(4), 289-305.

Parker, G. (2001). Establishing remuneration practices across culturally diverse environments. *Compensation & Benefits Management, 17*(2), 23-27.

Powers, R. (2002). Ensuring global consistency: The case for job leveling. *Benefits & Compensation International, 31*(8), 14-16, 18-19.

Schuler, R. S., & Rogovsky, N. (1998). Understanding compensation practice variations across firms: The impact of national culture. *Journal of International Business Studies, 29*(1), 159-177.

Solomon, C. M. (1995). Global compensation: Learn the ABCs. *Personnel Journal, 74*(7), 70-76.

GLOBAL VIRTUAL TEAMS

Pucik (1988) argued that the transformation of HRM systems to support the process of organizational learning is the key strategic task facing the HR function in organizations engaged in international co-operative ventures. The process of organizational learning is embedded in people; therefore, many of the necessary capabilities of employees are the focus of HRM strategies and practice, such as HR planning, staffing, training and development, performance appraisal, and reward systems.

Collings et al. (2007) argue that a standardized approach to international assignments is ineffective and that it is essential to develop HR policies and procedures that take into account alternatives to traditional international assignments. The traditional long-term expatriate assignment may not always be the best alternative compared to short-term assignments, frequent flier assignments, commuter or rotational assignments, or global virtual teams (Welch, Welch, & Worm, 2007).

The use of global virtual teams allows the organization to undertake projects without the constraints of geography, time, and physical location, which also allows the organization to conduct business in new ways and new places (McLean, 2007; Nedelko, 2007). A wide variety of computer hardware and software is available to facilitate the work of virtual teams, such as e-mail, discussion boards, and calendars (Gatlin-Watts, Carson, Horton, Maxwell, & Maltby, 2007). However, the cultural diversity of global virtual teams can sometimes lead to task and relationship conflict (Kankanhalli, Tan, & Wei, 2007).

Strategic Questions

1. What are the advantages and disadvantages of traditional expatriate assignments, where employees are sent to another country to work and live for multiyear assignments?
2. What are the advantages and disadvantages of developing host country managers instead of sending expatriates from the home country?
3. What are the advantages and disadvantages of frequent-flier or commuter assignments instead of long-term expatriate assignments?
4. What are the advantages and disadvantages of information technology–supported global virtual teams instead of traditional expatriate assignments?
5. How can global virtual team members build relationships among team members?

Resources

Baruch, Y., & Altman, Y. (2002). Expatriates and repatriation in MNCs: A taxonomy. *Human Resource Management, 41*(2), 239-259.

Frase, M. J. (2007). International commuters. *HR Magazine,* 52(3), 91-95.

Gatlin-Watts, R., Carson, M., Horton, J., Maxwell, L., & Maltby, N. (2007). A guide to global virtual teaming. *Team Performance Management, 13*(1-2), 47-52.

Harris, H., & Holden, L. (2001). Between autonomy and control: Expatriate managers and strategic IHRM in SMEs. *Thunderbird International Business Review, 43*(1), 77-100.

Kankanhalli, A., Tan, B. C. Y., & Wei, K. (2007). Conflict and performance in global virtual teams. *Journal of Management Information Systems,* 23(3), 237-274.

McLean, J. (2007, Summer). Managing global virtual teams. *British Journal of Administrative Management,* 16.

Nedelko, Z. (2007). Videoconferencing in virtual teams. *Business Review, Cambridge,* 7(1), 164-170.

Pucik, V. (1988). Strategic alliances, organizational learning, and competitive advantage: The HRM agenda. *Human Resource Management,* 27(1), 77-93.

Welch, D. E., Welch, L. S., & Worm, V. (2007). The international business traveler: A neglected but strategic human resource. *International Journal of Human Resource Management, 18*(2), 173-184.

ADAPTING TO LIFE IN THE UNITED STATES

As correctly observed by Tung (1981) more than two decades ago, commerce among nations is widespread and likely to increase in the future, which means that there will be an ever-increasing demand for individuals who can function effectively and efficiently in a foreign environment. The number of expatriates crossing international borders has accelerated; about 100,000 U.S. employees are sent on expatriate assignments each year (Baruch & Altman, 2002) and about 80% of mid- and large-sized companies send employees on international assignments (Andreason, 2003; Black & Gregersen, 1999). Stahl, Miller, and Tung (2002) claim that expatriate assignments play an increasingly critical role in the execution of international business strategies and the development of global managers. Although most of the research on expatriates has been conducted on employees from the United States on international assignments to other countries, there are many multinational organizations from Latin America, Europe, and other places outside the United States that also use expatriate assignments, and some of these expatriates are sent to work in the United States.

Despite American culture being widely exported in the form of products and movies, expatriates coming to the United States may face disorienting experiences as they try to adapt to the new culture (Linowes, 1993; Yamazaki & Kayes, 2007). In a study of 53 Taiwanese banking expatriates in the United States, Lee and Liu (2006) found that expatriates who were satisfied with their jobs in the host county were also better cross-culturally adjusted and that organizational socialization in the host country also predicted cross-cultural adjustment. Using a sample of 170 Japanese expatriates working in the United States, Takeuchi, Yun, and Russell (2002) found that language proficiency was positively related to work adjustment, previous knowledge of the host country was related to general and work adjustment, and willingness to communicate was related to interactional adjustment. Past international experience has also been found to affect the relationship between current assignment tenure and general and work adjustment for Japanese expatriates (Takeuchi, Tesluk, Yun, & Lepak, 2005).

Strategic Questions

1. What issues about doing business in the United States should expatriates sent to the United States be aware of? In what ways does doing business in the United States differ from doing business in other countries or cultures?
2. What American cultural issues should expatriates sent to the United States be aware of? What aspects of American culture are distinctively American?
3. In what ways does day-to-day life differ in the United States from other countries, in schools, banking, food, work hours, child care, and so forth?
4. What are the cultural keys to doing business successfully in the United States?

Resources

Andreason, A. W. (2003). Direct and indirect forms of in-country support for expatriates and their families as a means of reducing premature returns and improving job performance. *International Journal of Management, 20*(4), 548-555.

Baruch, Y., & Altman, Y. (2002). Expatriation and repatriation in MNC's: A taxonomy. *Human Resource Management, 41*(2), 239-259.

Black, J. S., & Gregersen, H. B. (1999). The right way to manage expats. *Harvard Business Review, 77*(2), 52-62.

Miller, E. L., & Catteneo, R. J. (1982). Some leadership attitudes of West German expatriate managerial personnel. *Journal of International Business Studies, 13*(1), 39-50.

Lee, H., & Liu, C. (2006). Determinants of the adjustment of expatriate managers in foreign countries: An empirical study. *International Journal of Management, 23*(2), 302-311.

Linowes, R. G. (1993). The Japanese manager's traumatic entry into the United States: Understanding the American-Japanese cultural divide. *Academy of Management Executive, 7*(4), 21-38.

Scullion, H., & Brewster, C. (2001). The management of expatriates: Messages from Europe? *Journal of World Business, 36*(4), 346-365.

Simeon, R., & Fujiu, K. (2000). Cross-cultural adjustment strategies of Japanese spouses in Silicon Valley. *Employee Relations, 22*(6), 594-611.

Stahl, G. K., & Cerdin, J. (2004). Global careers in French and German multinational corporations. *Journal of Management Development, 23*(9), 885-902.

Stahl, G. K., Miller, E. L., & Tung, R. L. (2002). Toward the boundaryless career: A closer look at the expatriate career concept and the perceived implications of an international assignment. *Journal of World Business, 37*(3), 216-227.

Takeuchi, R., Tesluk, P. E., Yun, S., & Lepak, D. P. (2005). An integrative view of international experience. *Academy of Management Journal, 48*(1), 85-100.

Takeuchi, R., Yun, S., & Russell, J. E. A. (2002). Antecedents and consequences of the perceived adjustment of Japanese expatriates in the USA. *International Journal of Human Resource Management, 13*(8), 1224-1244.

Tung, R. L. (1981). Selection and training of personnel for overseas assignments. *Columbia Journal of World Business, 16*(1), 21-25.

Tung, R. L. (1982). Selection and training procedures of U.S., European, and Japanese multinationals. *California Management Review, 25*(1), 57-71.

Yamazaki, Y., & Kayes, D. C. (2007). Expatriate learning: Exploring how Japanese managers adapt in the United States. *International Journal of Human Resource Management, 18*(8), 1373-1395.

Applications

INTERNATIONAL BUSINESS LITERACY

In today's global economy, HRM professionals must continuously show that their function is creating value for the organization, which has led to an emphasis on making human resources a strategic partner and spending less time on traditional HRM activities. However, survey results have shown that HRM professionals are still spending a significant amount of time in transactional HRM activities (Ramlall, 2006). For HRM professionals to become strategic partners in organizations requires a higher level of HRM technical competence and an understanding of the details of the business (Brockbank, Ulrich, & Beatty, 1999; Gangani, McLean, & Braden, 2006). Based on a survey of more than 12,000 employees in 109 firms, Ulrich, Brockbank, Yeung, and Lake (1995) found that when HRM professionals demonstrate competencies in delivery of HRM, management of change, and business knowledge, they are perceived by their associates as more effective.

According to the Human Resource Competency Study (Grossman, 2007), based on responses from more than 10,000 HRM professionals and line managers, there are six major competency domains: "Credible Activist" means that the HRM professional is both credible and active; "Culture and Change Steward" means that the HRM professional appreciates, articulates, and helps shape an organization's culture; "Talent Manager/Organizational Designer" means that the HRM professional masters theory, research, and practice in both talent management and organizational design; "Strategy Architect" means that the HRM professional has a vision for how the organization can win in the future and plays an active role in establishing policy; "Operational Executor" means that the HRM professional executes the operational aspects of managing people and organizations; and "Business Ally" means that the HRM professional contributes to the success of the business by knowing the social and business context in which the organization operates. Quinn and Brockbank (2006) use the case of BAE Systems to illustrate how general competencies for HRM professionals can be applied to the specific needs and circumstances of a particular organization.

The four key HRM competencies are Personal Credibility (being a role model, leading and influencing others), Delivering Results (achieving results by building strong relationships), HRM Knowledge (understanding leading-edge HRM thinking and deciding which HRM process could improve business performance), and Business Knowledge (awareness of the external environment to enhance business performance).

Being a "Business Ally" or having "Business Knowledge" means that HRM professionals understand all the parts of the business, what they must accomplish, and how they need to work together to make the organization successful at what it does. HRM professionals should also know how the business makes money, who their customers are, and why their customers buy the organization's products.

To Do

Choose one U.S. and one non-U.S. global company from the current *Fortune Global 500* list, and answer the business literacy questions listed in the HR Competency form for each company. The answers to the questions may be found in annual reports, corporate Web pages, business publications, or other sources. For each answer, fully document where the information was found.

HRM Competency: Business Literacy

HRM Competency: Business Literacy		
Business Literacy Question	*U.S. Global Company*	*Non-U.S. Global Company*
1. What are the annual revenues of the business?		
2. How does the business "make money"? Of every $100 that the organization takes in, how much comes out the other end as profit, and what happens in between?		
3. What is the company's market value? Price/earnings ratio?		
4. What is the company's type of funding? If equity, what type of stock is it and who are some of the major investors? If debt, who are the major lenders and what is their credit rating for the company?		
5. Who are the company's major customers? Why do they buy from the company (what are their buying criteria)?		
6. What Is the company's market share in its dominant product and service? What is the customer share of the top customers?		
7. What is the company's brand or desired reputation among target customers? How well is the company delivering on this brand promise?		
8. Who are the primary competitors? What are their strengths?		
9. What were the agenda items of a recent meeting of the company's board of directors?		
10. What are the objectives and goals of the top managers of the company?		

SOURCE: Dave Ulrich (cited in Grossman, 2007).

(Continued)

(Continued)

Resources

Brockbank, W., Ulrich, D., & Beatty, R. W. (1999). HR Professional development: Creating the future creators at the University of Michigan Business School. *Human Resource Management, 38*(2), 111-117.

EDGAR. *Securities & Exchange Commission.* http://www.sec.gov/edgar/searchedgar/webusers.htm

Fortune Global 500. http://money.cnn.com/magazines/fortune/global500/2007/

Gangani, N., McLean, G. N., & Braden, R. A. (2006). A competency-based human resource development strategy. *Performance Improvement Quarterly, 19*(1), 127-139.

Graham, M. E., & Tarbell, L. M. (2006). The importance of the employee perspective in the competency development of human resource professionals. *Human Resource Management, 45*(3), 337-355.

Grossman, R. J. (2007). New competencies for HR. *HR Magazine, 52*(6), 58-62.

Hoovers.com. http://www.hoovers.com/free/

Human Resource Competency Study. (2007). *Executive summary.* http://sitemaker.umich.edu/hrcs/executive_summary

Mergent Online. http://www.mergentonline.com/

Quinn, R. W., & Brockbank, W. (2006). The development of strategic human resource professionals at BAE systems. *Human Resource Management, 45*(3), 477-494.

Ramlall, S. J. (2006). HR competencies and their relationship to organizational practices. *Performance Improvement, 45*(5), 32-43.

Ulrich, D., Brockbank, W., Yeung, A. K., & Lake, D. G. (1995). Human resource competencies: An empirical assessment. *Human Resource Management, 34*(4), 473-495.

HOST COUNTRY EMPLOYMENT LAWS

In the United States, there are a number of laws protecting workers. The Civil Rights Act of 1964 prohibits discrimination on the basis of race, color, religion, sex, national origin in hiring and firing; compensation, assignment, or classification of employees; transfer, promotion, layoff, or recall; job advertisements; recruitment; testing; use of the organization's facilities; training and apprenticeship programs; fringe benefits; pay, retirement plans, and disability leave; or other terms and conditions of employment. Discriminatory practices under these laws includes harassment on the basis of race, color, religion, sex, national origin, disability, or age; retaliation against an individual for filing a charge of discrimination, participating in an investigation, or opposing discriminatory practices; employment decisions based on stereotypes or assumptions about the abilities, traits, or performance of individuals of a certain sex, race, age, religion, or ethnic group, or individuals with disabilities; and denying employment opportunities to a person because of marriage to, or association with, an individual of a particular race, religion, national origin, or an individual with a disability. Title VII also prohibits discrimination because of participation in schools or places of worship associated with a particular racial, ethnic, or religious group.

There are other laws to protect workers or to give them specific rights. The Americans with Disabilities Act of 1990 prohibits discrimination on the basis of disability, and the Age Discrimination in Employment Act of 1967 prohibits discrimination on the basis of age. The Equal Pay Act of 1963 prohibits discrimination on the basis of sex in the payment of wages or benefits, in which men and women perform work of similar skill, effort, and responsibility for the same employer under similar working conditions. The Occupational Safety and Health Act of 1970 seeks to assure safe and healthful working conditions. The National Labor Relations Act of 1935 seeks to protect the rights of employees and employers, to encourage collective bargaining, and to curtail certain private sector labor and management practices.

Members of the European Union and some other European countries have a legal right to at least 20 days of paid leave per year, but the legal right to paid leave varies widely across countries. In Japan, there are 10 days of paid annual leave, compared to Austria, where there are 22 days of paid annual leave plus 13 days of paid holidays, compared to the United States where there is no statutory paid leave except for government contractors and subcontractors covered under the Davis-Bacon Act (Ray & Schmitt, 2007).

To Do

Choose any country (other than the United States) and find out what its employment laws are relating to any three of the following areas: employment discrimination, sexual harassment, unionization, wages, hours of work, child labor, benefits, paid leave, family and medical leave, pensions, profit sharing, occupational health and safety, or any other aspect of work. Identify the most significant HRM compliance challenges for a multinational organization operating a subsidiary in that country. Document your findings in a report, including the sources where you obtained the information.

Resources

Age Discrimination in Employment Act. (1967). http://www.eeoc.gov/policy/adea.html

Altonji, J. G., & Oldham, J. (2003). Vacation laws and annual work hours. *Economic Perspectives, 27*(3), 19-29.

Americans with Disabilities Act. (1990). http://www.eeoc.gov/policy/ada.html

Baker & McKenzie: The Global Employer. http://www.bakernet.com/BakerNet/Resources/Publications/Publications+Archive/The+Global+Employer+-+September+2005.htm

Bronstein, A. (2005). The new labour law of the Russian Federation. *International Labour Review, 144*(3), 291-319.

Civil Rights Act of 1964, Title VII (CRA). http://www.eeoc.gov/policy/vii.html

Civil Rights Act of 1991, Title VII (CRA91). http://www.eeoc.gov/policy/cra91.html

Consolidated Omnibus Budget Reconciliation Act (COBRA), Health Benefits. http://www.dol.gov/dol/topic/health-plans/cobra.htm

Copeland Anti-Kickback Act. http://www.dol.gov/compliance/laws/comp-copeland.htm

(Continued)

(Continued)

Davis-Bacon and Related Acts. http://www.dol.gov/esa/programs/dbra/index.htm
Employee Polygraph Protection Act. http://www.dol.gov/compliance/laws/comp-eppa.htm
Employee Retirement Income Security Act. http://www.dol.gov/dol/topic/health-plans/erisa.htm
Equal Pay Act. (1963). http://www.eeoc.gov/policy/epa.html
Fair Labor Standard Act. http://www.dol.gov/compliance/laws/comp-flsa.htm
Family and Medical Leave Act. http://www.dol.gov/dol/topic/benefits-leave/fmla.htm
Federal Unemployment Tax Act. http://www.irs.gov/privacy/article/0,,id=162583,00.html
Health Insurance Portability and Accountability Act of 1996. http://aspe.hhs.gov/admnsimp/pl104191.htm, http://www.dol.gov/dol/topic/health-plans/portability.htm
Husbands, R. (1992). Sexual harassment law in employment: An international perspective. *International Labour Review, 131*(6), 535-559.
Malila, J. (2007). The great look forward: China's HR evolution. *China Business Review, 34*(4), 16-19.
McNamara-O'Hara Service Contract Act. http://www.dol.gov/compliance/laws/comp-sca.htm
National Labor Relations Act. (1935). http://www.nlrb.gov/nlrb/legal/manuals/rules/act.pdf
Occupational Safety and Health Act. (1970). http://www.dol.gov/compliance/laws/comp-osha.htm,http://www.osha.gov/pls/oshaweb/owadisp.show_document?p_table=OSHACT&p_id=2743
Ray, R., & Schmitt, J. (2007). *No-vacation nation.* Washington, DC: Center for Economic and Policy Research.
Social Security Act. http://www.socialsecurity.gov/OP_Home/ssact/ssact.htm
Walsh-Healey Public Contracts Act. http://www.dol.gov/compliance/laws/comp-pca.htm
Worker Adjustment and Retraining Notification Act. http://www.dol.gov/compliance/laws/comp-warn.htm

Experiential Exercises

EXPATRIATE SELECTION

Making successful selection decisions is critical for multinational organizations, for the same reasons that making successful selection decisions is critical for all organizations, and especially so because of the substantial expense of sending employees on expatriate assignments. The cost for a fully loaded expatriate package including benefits and cost-of-living adjustments has been estimated to be $300,000 to $1 million per year (Baruch & Altman, 2002; Black & Gregersen, 1999) and an average one-time cost to relocate an expatriate of $60,000 (McCaughey & Bruning, 2005).

How to create effective selection procedures for expatriate assignments has a long research history in HRM. Hays (1974) interviewed employees on expatriate assignments to identify the factors that they thought lead to job success. The three key factors were job ability (i.e., technical skill, organizational ability, belief in mission), relational ability (i.e., ability to deal with locals, cultural empathy), and family situation (i.e., adaptive and supportive family). Tung (1981) suggested technical competence on the job, personality traits or relational abilities, environmental variables, and family situation. Although these variables were expected to predict success in the job, organizations were slow to implement tests to measure the predictors. Tung's (1982) survey of 144 multinationals showed that tests were administered to determine candidates' technical competence in only 3%, 5%, and 14% of the U.S., European, and Japanese companies, respectively; and tests for relational abilities were used in 5%, 21%, and 0% of companies. In addition, there was no indication that the tests had been validated. More than a decade later, Jordan and Cartwright (1998) concluded that selecting expatriate managers for international assignments had been hindered by the lack of validation studies testing suggested predictors of job success and by the lack of clearly defined traits and competencies that could be tested for their ability to predict job success in expatriate assignments.

A number of researchers have suggested predictors for selection of expatriates, and there is some commonality among the diversity of criteria. Ashamalla (1998) listed cultural empathy, awareness of environmental constraints, interpersonal skills, and managerial and decision-making abilities. Black and Gregersen (1999) listed the will to communicate, broad-based sociability, cultural flexibility, cosmopolitan orientation, and a collaborative negotiation style. Porter and Tansky (1999) suggested learning orientation; Graf (2004) suggested intercultural communication skills, intercultural sensitivity, interpersonal competence; and self-monitoring. Intercultural competence and interpersonal competence has been found to predict success of Master of Business Administration students in an interculturally related organizational scenario (Graf & Harland, 2005). Caligiuri (2000) tested the Big Five personality characteristics (Extroversion, Agreeableness, Conscientiousness, Emotional Stability, and Openness) and found that Extroversion, Agreeableness, and Emotional Stability predicted expatriates' desire to terminate the assignment, but only Conscientiousness predicted job performance.

Collings, Scullion, and Morley (2007) argue that a standardized approach to international assignments is ineffective and that it is essential to develop HRM policies and procedures that take into account alternatives to traditional international assignments. Avril and Magnini (2007), echoing Tung (1981, 2001), suggest a holistic approach for the selection, training, and organizational support of expatriates. Selection should be combined with organizational support for the duration of their assignment and training both before expatriates leave and upon their arrival at their international assignments.

To Do

Design a validation study for an assessment center to select candidates for expatriate assignments. The assessment center should include both pen-and-paper and situational tests. Identify and define the performance dimensions that each test in the assessment center is intended to measure. The criteria of success for the expatriate assignment should include multiple measures of whether the expatriate completes the full-term of his or her assignment, job performance, job satisfaction, and his or her adjustment to the new culture.

Resources

Ashamalla, M. H. (1998). International human resource management practices: The challenge of expatriation. *Competitiveness Review, 8*(2), 54-65.

Avril, A. B., & Magnini, V. P. (2007). A holistic approach to expatriate success. *International Journal of Contemporary Hospitality Management, 19*(11), 53-64.

Baruch, Y., & Altman, Y. (2002). Expatriation and repatriation in MNC's: A taxonomy. *Human Resource Management, 41*(2), 239-259.

Black, J. S., & Gregersen, H. B. (1999). The right way to manage expats. *Harvard Business Review, 77*(2), 52-62.

Caligiuri, P. M. (2000). The Big Five personality characteristics as predictors of expatriate's desire to terminate the assignment and supervisor-rated performance. *Personnel Psychology, 53*(1), 67-88.

Collings, D. G., Scullion, H., & Morley, M. J. (2007). Changing patterns of global staffing in the multinational enterprise: Challenges to the conventional expatriate assignment and emerging alternatives. *Journal of World Business, 42*(2), 198-213.

Graf, A. (2004). Expatriate selection: An empirical study identifying significant skill profiles. *Thunderbird International Business Review, 46*(6), 667-685.

Graf, A., & Harland, L. K. (2005). Expatriate selection: Evaluating the discriminant, convergent, and predictive validity of five measures of interpersonal and intercultural competence. *Journal of Leadership and Organizational Studies, 11*(2), 46-62.

Hays, R. D. (1974). Expatriate selection: Insuring success and avoiding failure. *Journal of International Business Studies, 5*(1), 25-37.

Jordan, J., & Cartwright, S. (1998). Selecting expatriate managers: Key traits and competencies. *Leadership & Organization Development Journal, 19*(2), 89-96.

McCaughey, D., & Bruning, N. S. (2005). Enhancing opportunities for expatriate job satisfaction: HR strategies for foreign assignment success. *HR. Human Resource Planning, 28*(4), 21-29.

Naumann, E. (1993). Antecedents and consequences of satisfaction and commitment among expatriate managers. *Group & Organization Studies, 18*(2), 153-187.

Porter, G., & Tansky, J. W. (1999). Expatriate success may depend on a "learning orientation": Considerations for selection and training. *Human Resource Management, 38*(1), 47-60.

Society for Industrial/Organizational Psychology. (2003). *Principles for the validation and use of personnel selection procedures*. http://www.siop.org/_Principles/principles.pdf

Tung, R. L. (1981). Selection and training of personnel for overseas assignments. *Columbia Journal of World Business, 16*(1), 21-25.

Tung, R. L. (1983). Selection and training procedures of U.S., European, and Japanese multinationals. *California Management Review, 25*(1), 57-71.

Tung, R. L. (2001). A contingency framework of selection and training of expatriates revisited. *Human Resources Management Review, 8*(1), 23-37.

U.S. Equal Employment Opportunity Commission. (1978). *Uniform guidelines on Employee Selection Procedures*. http://www.access.gpo.gov/nara/cfr/waisidx_06/29cfr1607_06.html

Vance, C. M., Paik, Y., & White, J. A. (2006). Tracking bias against the selection of female expatriates:

EXPATRIATE SOCIALIZATION

Socialization in the culture that an expatriate is being sent to work and live in is an important part of the predeparture training for an international assignment but is sometimes overlooked (Lueke & Svyantek, 2000). The inability of expatriates to adjust to the host country's social and business environment is costly in terms of management performance, client relations, and operations efficiency (Katz & Seifer, 1996). Based on their review of 25 years of cross-cultural training, Littrell, Salas, Hess, Paley, and Riedel (2006) concluded that cross-cultural training is effective in facilitating success in expatriate assignments.

In addition to cross-cultural training, expatriates may also benefit from multiple mentors to assist in their adjustment and development during the predeparture, expatriation, and repatriation stages of international assignments (Menzias & Scandura, 2006). For example, Lee and Liu (2006) found in a sample of 53 Taiwanese banking expatriates that organizational socialization in the host country was an important predictor of cross-cultural adjustment.

Although predeparture training is useful, real-time training may be the key driver of expatriate success (Mendenhall & Stahl, 2000). It is impractical to develop and provide predeparture training that covers every possible business and social situation that an expatriate might encounter. Real-time training consists of giving the expatriates resources they can turn to for information and advice as new situations arise (Avril & Magnini, 2007).

To Do

Assume that your instructor is an internationally known scholar from another country on a one-semester sabbatical to your school and is unfamiliar with the culture of American colleges and universities. Develop a 30-min real-time cross-cultural training program to socialize this "new-to-the-U.S." professor, and run the program. The program may include topics such as grading scales, student class participation, teacher-student interactions, feedback to students on work they have turned in, availability to students, testing, and so forth.

Resources

Avril, A. B. (2007). A holistic approach to expatriate success. *International Journal of Contemporary Hospitality Management, 19*(11), 53-64.

Bennett, R., Aston, A., & Colquhoun, T. (2000). Cross-cultural training: A critical step in ensuring the success of international assignments. *Human Resource Management, 39*(2/3), 239-250.

Katz, J. P., & Seifer, D. M. (1996). It's a different world out there: Planning for expatriate success through selection, pre-departure training and on-site socialization. *Human Resource Planning, 19*(2), 32-47.

Lee, H., & Liu, C. (2006). Determinants of the adjustment of expatriate managers in foreign countries: An empirical study. *International Journal of Management, 23*(2), 302-311.

(Continued)

(Continued)

Lee, Y., & Larwood, L. (1983). The socialization of expatriate managers in multinational firms. *Academy of Management Journal, 26*(4), 657-665.

Littrell, L. N., Salas, E., Hess, K. P., Paley, M., & Riedel, S. (2006). Expatriate preparation: A critical analysis of 25 years of cross-cultural training research. *Human Resource Development Review,* 5(3), 355-388.

Lueke, S. B., & Svyantek, D. J. (2000). Organizational socialization in the host country: The missing link in reducing expatriate turnover. *International Journal of Organizational Analysis,* 8(4), 380-400.

Mendenhall, M. E., & Stahl, G. K. (2000). Expatriate training and development: Where do we go from here? *Human Resource Management, 39*(2/3), 251-265.

Menzias, J. M., & Scandura, T. A. (2006). A needs-driven approach to expatriate adjustment and career development: A multiple mentoring perspective. *Journal of International Business Studies, 36*(5), 519-538.

Creative Exercises

TRAINING EMPLOYEES FOR AN INTERNATIONAL ASSIGNMENT

To do business on a global scale, multinational organizations often send their employees on international assignments, either relocating an employee and the family to another country, bringing an employee and the family from another country to the corporate headquarters for management development, or sending employees on short-term assignments. Successful expatriate assignments are critical to the success of multinational organizations.

Black and Gregersen (1999) identify five characteristics that multinational organizations tend to look for in potential expatriates: (a) drive to communicate with local people in their new country; (b) broad-based sociability and willingness to establish social ties with local residents; (c) cultural flexibility and a willingness to experiment with different customs; (d) cosmopolitan orientation and a respect of diverse viewpoints; and (e) collaborative negotiation style. These characteristics might be used when selecting for expatriate assignments or be identified as desired outcomes of training programs. Once established, training programs need to be evaluated for effectiveness. Luthans and Farner (2002) suggest a 360-degree feedback approach to evaluate training effectiveness at the behavioral and performance levels.

Expatriates tend to view their international assignment as an opportunity for personal and professional development and career advancement, despite thinking that their organization's corporate career management systems are inadequate and being skeptical that their international assignment will help them advance in the organization (Stahl & Cerdin, 2004; Stahl, Miller, & Tung, 2002). Management development programs to prepare expatriates for their international assignment often include environmental briefings about the geography, climate, housing, and schools; cultural orientation about the cultural institutions and value systems; language training; sensitivity training to develop attitudinal flexibility; and field experience, where the employee can get some experience living and working in a new culture (Bennett, Aston, & Colquhoun, 2000; Tung, 1982). To maximize the benefits of expatriate assignments, international experience should be rewarded, and the expatriate experience should be a part of the manager's long-term career planning (Downes & Thomas, 1999).

Based on their survey of 459 job changers from 26 countries, Feldman and Tompson (1993) identified six sets of factors related to adjustment of expatriates to their new job assignments. They found that the career development variables most consistently and strongly related to adjustment were having mentors and job assignments that generated opportunities for developing new skills, having realistic job previews, and being given job assignments that fit in with their overall career plans. The types of coping strategies used also had a significant impact on adjustment, such as looking at the positive side of the job rather than psychological withdrawal.

A key component of preparing employees for expatriate assignments is cross-cultural training, to prepare them (and their families) for the cultural adjustments they will need to make. Based on their review of 25 years of cross-cultural training, Littrell et al. (2006) concluded that cross-cultural training is effective in facilitating success in expatriate assignments. Typical components of cross-cultural training are attribution training (learning to explain host national behavior from the host culture point of view), cultural awareness training (teach employees about their own culture so that they will better appreciate cultural differences between host and home countries), interaction training (where incoming expatriates learn from expatriates already occupying the position they will be occupying), language training (if not fluency, as least an ability to exchange common courtesies in the host language), didactic training (information about working conditions, living conditions, and cultural differences), and experiential training (to develop the skills necessary for working and interacting with host nationals). In a study of 251 expatriates from a well-established expatriation program in the United Kingdom, Brewster and Pickard (1994) found that expatriates were positive toward formal training for expatriation and believed that it helped them to make the adjustment to living and working in the host country.

The international assignment cycle (Harzing & Christensen, 2004) begins with recruitment and selection of candidates with the necessary skills and interests, selection of an employee for an international assignment, preparation for the international assignment, expatriation, and repatriation back to the home country. However, a percentage of employees sent on expatriate assignments return home earlier than planned because of job dissatisfaction or difficulties adjusting to a culture in another country. Black and Gregersen (1999) put the estimate for the number of U.S. expatriates who return early at between 10% and 20%, although some published estimates have exaggerated the failure rate (Harzing, 1995, 2002; Tung, 1981, 1982, 1987).

In Tung's (1987) early research on expatriate assignments, seven main reasons for expatriate failure were identified: (a) inability of the manager's spouse to adjust to a different physical or cultural environment, (b) inability of the manager to adapt to a different physical or cultural environment, (c) other family-related problems, (d) the manager's personality or emotional immaturity, (e) the managers' inability to cope with the responsibilities posed by overseas work, (f) the manager's lack of technical competence, and (g) the managers' lack of motivation to work overseas. Other researchers have also found that the adjustment of expatriates' families to the new culture is a key factor in the successful adjustment of expatriates to their international assignment (Andreason, 2003; Simeon & Fujiu, 2000). For example, Lee's (2007) interviews of a small sample of expatriates found that the inability of the expatriate's family to adjust to the foreign environment was the main determinant of expatriate failure.

To Do

Develop a management development program to prepare managers for expatriate assignments. The program should include technical, business, language, cross-cultural training, and ongoing expatriate support. The plan should describe the types of training methods to be used, the content of the training, and how the success of the management development program will be measured.

Resources

Andreason, A. W. (2003). Direct and indirect forms of in-country support for expatriates and their families as a means of reducing premature returns and improving job performance. *International Journal of Management, 20*(4), 548-555.

Arthur, M. B., Khapova, S. N., & Wilderom, C. P. M. (2005). Career success in a boundaryless career world. *Journal of Organizational Behavior, 26*(2), 177-202.

Avril, A. B. (2007). A holistic approach to expatriate success. *International Journal of Contemporary Hospitality Management, 19*(11), 53-64.

Baruch, Y., & Altman, Y. (2002). Expatriation and repatriation in MNC's: A taxonomy. *Human Resource Management, 41*(2), 239-259.

Bennett, R., Aston, A., & Colquhoun, T. (2000). Cross-cultural training: A critical step in ensuring the success of international assignments. *Human Resource Management, 39*(2/3), 239-250.

Black, J. S., & Gregersen, H. B. (1999). The right way to manage expats. *Harvard Business Review, 77*(2), 52-62.

Brewster, C., & Pickard, J. (1994). Evaluating expatriate training. *International Studies of Management & Organization, 24*(3), 18-35.

Downes, M., & Thomas, A. S. (1999). Managing overseas assignments to build organizational knowledge. *Human Resource Planning, 22*(4), 33-48.

Feldman, D. C., & Tompson, H. B. (1993). Expatriation, repatriation, and domestic geographical relocation: An empirical investigation of adjustment to new job assignment. *Journal of International Business Studies, 24*(3), 507-523.

Harzing, A. (1995). The persistent myth of high expatriate failure rates. *International Journal of Human Resource Management, 6*(2), 457-474.

Harzing, A. (2002). Are referencing errors undermining our scholarship and credibility? The case of expatriate failure rates. *Journal of Organizational Behavior, 23*(1), 127-148.

Harzing, A., & Christensen, C. (2004). Expatriate failure: Time to abandon the concept? *Career Development International, 9*(6/7), 616-626.

Jack, D. W., & Stage, V. C. (2005). Success strategies for expats. *T + D, 59*(9), 48-52.

Lee, H. (2007). Factors that influence expatriate failure: An interview study. *International Journal of Management, 24*(3), 403-619.

Lee, L., & Croker, R. (2006). A contingency model to promote the effectiveness of expatriate training. *Industrial Management & Data, 106*(3), 1187-1205.

Littrell, L. N., Salas, E., Hess, K. P., Paley, M., & Riedel, S. (2006). Expatriate preparation: A critical analysis of 25 years of cross-cultural training research. *Human Resource Development Review, 5*(3), 355-388.

Luthans, K. W., & Farner, S. (2002). Expatriate development: The use of 360-degree feedback. *Journal of Management Development, 21*(9/10), 780-793.

McCaughey, D., & Bruning, N. S. (2005). Enhancing opportunities for expatriate job satisfaction: HR strategies for foreign assignment success. *Human Resource Planning, 28*(4), 21-29.

Mendenhall, M. E., & Stahl, G. K. (2000). Expatriate training and development: Where do we go from here? *Human Resource Management, 39*(2/3), 251-265.

Simeon, R., & Fujiu, K. (2000). Cross-cultural adjustment strategies of Japanese spouses in Silicon Valley. *Employee Relations, 22*(6), 594-611.

Stahl, G. K., & Cerdin, J. (2004). Global careers in French and German multinational corporations. *Journal of Management Development, 23*(9), 885-902.

Stahl, G. K., Miller, E. L., & Tung, R. L. (2002). Toward the boundaryless career: A closer look at the expatriate career concept and the perceived implications of an international assignment. *Journal of World Business, 37*(3), 216-227.

Tung, R. L. (1981). Selection and training of personnel for overseas assignments. *Columbia Journal of World Business, 16*(1), 21-25.

Tung, R. L. (1982). Selection and training procedures of U.S., European, and Japanese multinationals. *California Management Review, 25*(1), 57-71.

Tung, R. L. (1987). Expatriate assignments: Enhancing success and minimizing failure. *Academy of Management Executive, 1*(2), 117-126.

Tung, R. L. (1998). A contingency framework of selection and training of expatriates revisited. *Human Resource Management Review, 8*(1), 23-37.

Tyler, K. (2006). Retaining repatriates. *HR Magazine, 51*(3), 97-102.

Wederspahn, G. M. (1992). Costing failures in expatriate human resources management. *Human Resource Planning, 15*(3), 27-35.

RETURNING TO HEADQUARTERS

Many multinational organizations use expatriate assignments, sending their employees to work in another country for months or years at a time. The strategic HRM reasons for sending employees on expatriate assignments include personal and professional development of the employee, which contributes to establishing competitive expertise on an organizational level; and organizational learning about doing business internationally, by knowledge transfer from the expatriate employee (Lazarova & Cerdin, 2007; Lazarova & Tarique, 2005). Daily, Certo, and Dalton (2000) found a positive relationship between CEO international experience and corporate financial performance in *Fortune 500* companies; and Carpenter, Sanders, and Gregersen (2001) found that U.S. multinationals performed better with CEOs who had international assignment experience.

For the organization to gain the full benefits of expatriate assignments, returning expatriates need to stay with the organization after they return home; otherwise, the knowledge and skills may be transferred to another organization. According to a study by PricewaterhouseCoopers and the Cranfield University School of Management, about 25% of repatriates resign within a year or two of their return (Lazarova & Caligiuri, 2001; Tyler, 2006). In one study of a financial services company, 50% of the people left the company within a few years of repatriation (Baruch, 2002). At the end of their assignments, these repatriates may experience similar challenges at re-entry as they did when they began their expatriate assignment. Repatriate support is the mirror image of expatriate support; in both situations, the worker must make an adjustment from living and working in one culture, to living and working in another. The culture shock of returning home may be even more difficult than the culture shock of going overseas (Adler, 1981; Lee & Liu, 2006). A poorly managed repatriation process may lead to high postrepatriation turnover and may make other employees reluctant to accept expatriate assignments (Feldman & Tompson, 1993).

In their study of 133 expatriates from 14 multinational corporations, Lazarova and Cerdin (2007) found that the more repatriation support companies provide, the more likely they will be to retain their internationally experienced workers and that repatriate intentions to turnover was related to perceived employment opportunities and career activism. Repatriation support may include continuous communications with the home office, career planning sessions, financial counseling sessions, reorientation programs about changes in the organization, and visible signs that the organization values international experience. Black, Gregersen, and Mendenhall (1992), developed a framework for repatriation adjustment. According to this framework, there are anticipatory adjustments that expatriates must make before returning to their home country and in-country adjustments that must take place after returning home. The repatriate must adjust to work, interactions with home country nationals, and the environment and culture.

To Do

Write a proposal to create an expatriate re-entry (i.e., repatriate) program. The goals of the program are to reduce re-entry cultural and organizational readjustment problems, reduce the turnover (increase the retention) of expatriates returning to the organization, and improve the knowledge transfer from returning expatriates to the rest of the organization by ensuring that repatriates are placed in jobs in which their newly acquired international knowledge and skills are recognized and used.

Resources

Adler, N. J. (1981). Re-entry: Managing cross-cultural transitions. *Group and Organization Studies, 6*(3), 341-356.

Baruch, Y. (2002). Management of expatriation and reparitation for the novice global player. *International Journal of Manpower, 23*(7), 659-674.

Baruch, Y., & Altman, Y. (2002). Expatriation and repatriation in MNC's: A taxonomy. *Human Resource Management, 41*(2), 239-259.

Black, J. S., Gregersen, H. B., & Mendenhall, M. E. (1992). Toward a theoretical framework of repatriation adjustment. *Journal of International Business Studies, 23*(4), 737-760.

Carpenter, M. A., Sanders, W. G., & Gregersen, H. B. (2001). Bundling human capital with organizational context: The impact of international assignment experience on multinational firm performance and CEO pay. *Academy of Management Journal, 44*(3), 493-511.

Daily, C. M., Certo, S. T., & Dalton, D. R. (2000). International experience in the executive suite: The path to prosperity? *Strategic Management Journal, 21*(4), 515-523.

Feldman, D. C., & Tompson, H. B. (1993). Expatriation, repatriation, and domestic geographical relocation: An empirical investigation of adjustment to new job assignment. *Journal of International Business Studies, 24*(3), 507-523.

Forster, N. (2000). The myth of the international manager. *International Journal of Human Resource Management, 11*(1), 126-142.

Jassawalla, A., Connelly, T., & Slojkowski, L. (2004). Issues of effective repatriation: A model and managerial implications. *S.A.M Advanced Management Journal, 69*(2), 38-46.

Lazarova, M. B., & Caligiuri, P. (2001). Retaining repatriates: The role of organizational support practices. *Journal of World Business, 36*(4), 389-401.

Lazarova, M. B., & Cerdin, J. (2007). Revisiting repatriation concerns: Organizational support versus career and contextual influences. *Journal of International Business Studies, 38*(3), 404-429.

Lazarova, M. B., & Tarique, I. (2005). Knowledge transfer upon repatriation. *Journal of World Business, 40*(4), 361-373.

Lee, H., & Liu, C. (2006). The determinants of repatriate turnover intentions: An empirical analysis. *International Journal of Management, 23*(4), 751-763.

Napier, N. K., & Peterson, R. B. (1991). Expatriate re-entry: What do repatriates have to say? *Human Resource Planning, 14*(1), 19-28.

O'Sullivan, S. L. (2002). The protean approach to managing repatriation transitions. *International Journal of Manpower, 23*(7), 635-648.

Stahl, G. K., Miller, E., & Tung, R. (2002). Toward the boundaryless career: A closer look at the expatriate career concept and the perceived implications of an international assignment. *Journal of World Business, 37*(3), 216-217.

Tyler, K. (2006). Retaining repatriates. *HR Magazine, 51*(3), 97-102.

References

Abelson, M. A. (1987). Examination of avoidable and unavoidable turnover. *Journal of Applied Psychology, 72*(3), 382-386.

Acemoglu, D., & Angrist, J. D. (2001). Consequences of employment protection? The case of the Americans with Disabilities Act. *Journal of Political Economy, 109*(5), 915-957.

Adler, J. (2006). The past as prologue? A brief history of the labor movement in the United States. *Public Personnel Management, 35*(4), 311-329.

Adler, N. J. (1981). Re-entry: Managing cross-cultural transitions. *Group and Organization Studies, 6*(3), 341-356.

Adler, P. S., Goldoftas, B., & Levine, D. I. (1997). Ergonomics, employee involvement, and the Toyota Production System: A case study of NUMMI's 1993 model introduction. *Industrial and Labor Relations Review, 50*(3), 416-437.

Age Discrimination in Employment Act. (1967). http://www.eeoc.gov/policy/adea.html

Aik, C. T., & Tway, D. C. (2006). Elements and principles of training as a performance improvement solution. *Performance Improvement, 45*(3), 28-32.

Aiman-Smith, L., Bauer, T. N., & Cable, D. M. (2001). Are you attracted? Do you intend to pursue? A recruiting policy-capturing study. *Journal of Business and Psychology, 16*(2), 219-237.

Albemarle Paper Co. v. Moody, 422 U.S. 405 (Supreme Court of the United States, 1975).

Albinger, H. S., & Freeman, S. J. (2000). Corporate social performance and attractiveness as an employer to different seeking populations. *Journal of Business Ethics, 28*(3), 243-253.

Album, M. J., & Berkowitz, P. M. (2003). Industry model for Professional Employer Organizations—new NY law outlines responsibilities for PEOs and their clients. *Employment Relations Today, 30*(2), 65-72.

Aldrich, M. (1997). *Safety first: Technology, labor, and business in the building of American work safety, 1870-1939*. Baltimore: Johns Hopkins University Press.

Allen, D. G. (2006). Do socialization tactics influence newcomer embeddedness and turnover? *Journal of Management, 32*(2), 237-256.

Allen, N. J., & Meyer, J. P. (1990). Organizational socialization tactics: A longitudinal analysis of links to newcomers' commitment and role orientation. *Academy of Management Journal, 33*(4), 847-858.

Allen, R. S., & Montgomery, K. A. (2001). Applying an organizational development approach to creating diversity. *Organizational Dynamics, 30*(2), 149-161.

Altman, B. M. (2005). The labor market experience of persons with disabilities: The conundrum. *Work and Occupations, 32*(3), 360-364.

Alvarez, R. (2002). Tighter reins on who is 'disabled.' *Occupational Health & Safety, 71*(4), 93-94.

Amabile, T. M., & Conti, R. (1999). Changes in the work environment for creativity during downsizing. *Academy of Management Journal, 42*(6), 630-640.

American Association of Retired Persons. (2004). *Baby Boomers envision retirement II: Survey of Baby Boomers' expectations for retirement.* Washington, DC: Author.

American Association of University Professors. (2005). The annual report on the economic status of the profession 2005-2006. *Academe, 92*(2), 24-105.

American Physical Therapy Association. (1997). *What you need to know about Carpal Tunnel Syndrome: A physical therapist's perspective.* http://www.apta.org/AM/Images/APTAIMAGES/ContentImages/ptandbody/carpaltunnel/Carpal.pdf

American Psychological Association. (1991). In the Supreme Court of the United States: Price Waterhouse v. Ann B. Hopkins: Amicus curiae brief for the American Psychological Association. *American Psychologist, 46*(10), 1061-1070.

American Society for Training and Development. (2008). [Home page]. http://www.astd.org/

Americans with Disabilities Act. (1990). http://www.eeoc.gov/policy/ada.html

Anderson, J. (2000). Discover uncharted magic with Disney Cruise Line. *Incentive, 174*(10), 14.

Anderson, K. E., Doyle, P. M., & Schwenk, A. E. (1990). Measuring union-nonunion earnings differences. *Monthly Labor Review, 113*(6), 26-38.

Anderson, R., Mehta, R., & Strong, J. (1997). An empirical investigation of sales management training programs for sales managers. *Journal of Personal Selling & Sales Management, 17*(3), 53-66.

Anderson, R., & VanderHoff, J. (1999). Mortgage default rates and borrower race. *Journal of Real Estate Research, 18*(2), 279-289.

Andreason, A. W. (2003). Direct and indirect forms of in-country support for expatriates and their families as a means of reducing premature returns and improving job performance. *International Journal of Management, 20*(4), 548-555.

Appelbaum, S. H. (1997). Socio-technical systems theory: An intervention strategy for organizational development. *Management Decision, 35*(6), 452-463.

Appelbaum, S. H., Cottin, J., Paré, R., & Shapiro, B. T. (2006). Employee theft: From behavioural causation and prevention to managerial detection and remedies. *Journal of American Academy of Business, 9*(2), 175-182.

Armour, M. P., Rubio, R., & Bain, B. (2004). An evaluation study of diversity training for field instructors: A collaborative approach to enhancing cultural competence. *Journal of Social Work Education, 40*(1), 27-38.

Arnold, E. W., & Scott, C. J. (2002). Does broad banding improve pay system effectiveness? *Southern Business Review, 27*(2), 1-8.

Arthur, M. M., & Cook, A. (2004). Taking stock of work-family initiatives: How announcement of "family-friendly" human resource decisions affect shareholder value. *Industrial and Labor Relations Review, 57*(4), 599-613.

Arthur, W., Jr., Day, E. A., McNelly, T. L., & Edens, P. S. (2003). A meta-analysis of the criterion-related validity of assessment center dimensions. *Personnel Psychology, 56*(1), 125-154.

Arvey, R. D., & Begalla, M. E. (1975). Analyzing the homemaker job using the Position Analysis Questionnaire (PAQ). *Journal of Applied Psychology, 60*(4), 513-517.

Ashamalla, M. H. (1998). International human resource management practices: The challenge of expatriation. *Competitiveness Review, 8*(2), 54-65.

Ashenfelter, O., & Card, D. (2002). Did the elimination of mandatory retirement affect faculty retirement? *American Economic Review, 92*(4), 957-980.

Ashford, S. J., & Black, J. S. (1996). Proactivity during organizational entry: A role of desire for control. *Journal of Applied Psychology, 81*(2), 199-214.

Ashforth, B. E., & Saks, A. M. (1996). Socialization tactics: Longitudinal effects on newcomer adjustment. *Academy of Management Journal, 39*(1), 149-178.

Ashforth, B. E., Saks, A. M., & Lee, R. T. (1998). Socialization and newcomer adjustment: The role of organizational context. *Human Relations, 51*(7), 897-926.

Ashraf, J. (1997). The effect of unions on professor's salaries: The evidence over twenty years. *Journal of Labor Research, 18*(3), 339-450.

Ashraf, J. (1999). Faculty unionism in the 1990s: A comparison of public and private universities. *Journal of Collective Negotiations, 28*(4), 303-310.

Association for the Advancement of Collegiate Schools of Business International. (2002). *Management education at risk.* www.aacsb.edu/publications/metf/METFReportFinal-August02.pdf

Atkinson, W. (2002a). The carpal tunnel conundrum. *Wordforce, 81*(9), 17.

Atkinson, W. (2002b). The liability of employee drug testing. *Risk Management, 49*(9), 40-44.

Avery, D. R. (2003). Reactions to diversity in recruitment advertising—are differences black and white? *Journal of Applied Psychology, 88*(4), 672-679.

Avril, A. B., & Magnini, V. P. (2007). A holistic approach to expatriate success. *International Journal of Contemporary Hospitality Management, 19*(11), 53-64.

Aycan, Z. (2005). The interplay between cultural and institutional/structural contingencies in human resource management practices. *International Journal of Human Resource Management, 16*(7), 1083-1119.

Babakus, E., Cravens, D. W., Grant, K., Ingram, T. N., & LaForge, R. W. (1996). Investigating the relationships among sales, management control, sales territory design, salesperson performance, and sales organization effectiveness. *International Journal of Research in Marketing, 13*(4), 345-363.

Babcock, P. (2005). A calling for change. *HR Magazine, 50*(9), 46-51.

Babcock, P. (2006). U.S. union-busting thrives, says report. *HR Magazine, 51*(2), 38-40.

Backhaus, K. B., Stone, B. A., & Heiner, K. (2002). Exploring the relationship between corporate social performance and employer attractiveness. *Business and Society, 41*(3), 292-318.

Bailey, G. (2006). Saving justifies the spend. *Occupational Health, 58*(10), 13-15.

Baker, G. R., King, H., MacDonald, J. L., & Horbar, J. D. (2003). Using organizational assessment surveys for improvement in neonatal intensive care. *Pediatrics, 111*(4), 419-425.

Barber, A. E. (1998). *Recruiting employees: Individual and organizational perspectives.* Thousand Oaks, CA: Sage.

Barclay, L. A., & Bass, A. R. (1994). Get the most from recruitment efforts. *HR Magazine, 39*(6), 70-72.

Barksdale, H. C., Bellenger, D. N., Boles, J. S., & Brashear, T. G. (2003). The impact of realistic job previews and perceptions of training on sales force performance and continuance commitment: A longitudinal test. *Journal of Personal Selling & Sales Management, 23*(2), 125-138.

Barling, J., Kelloway, E. K., & Iverson, R. D. (2003). High-quality work, job satisfaction, and occupational injuries. *Journal of Applied Psychology, 88*(2), 276-283.

Barlow, L. (2006). Talent development: the new imperative? *Development and Learning in Organizations, 20*(3), 6-9.

Barrick, M. R., & Mount, M. K. (1991). The Big Five personality dimensions and job performance: A meta-analysis. *Personnel Psychology, 44*(1), 1-26.

Barrick, M. R., Stewart, G. L., Neubert, M. J., & Mount, M. K. (1998). Relating team member ability and personality to work-team processes and team effectiveness. *Journal of Applied Psychology, 83*(3), 377-391.

Bartlett, C. A., & Ghoshal, S. (1986). Tap your subsidiaries for global reach. *Harvard Business Review, 64*(6), 87-94.

Bartlett, C. A., & Ghoshal, S. (1989). *Managing across borders: The transnational solution.* Boston: Harvard Business School Press.

Bartlett, C. A., & Ghoshal, S. (1992). What is a global manager? *Harvard Business Review, 70*(5), 124-132.

Bartlett, C. A., & Ghoshal, S. (1997). The myth of the generic manager: New personal competencies for new management roles. *California Management Review, 40*(1), 92-116.

Baruch, Y. (2002). Management of expatriation and repatriation for the novice global player. *International Journal of Manpower, 23*(7), 659-674.

Baruch, Y., & Altman, Y. (2002). Expatriates and repatriation in MNCs: A taxonomy. *Human Resource Management, 41*(2), 239-259.

Basso, L., & Shorten, B. (2006). PEO industry continues to grow. *CPA Journal, 76*(8), 66-67.

Bauer, T. N., & Aiman-Smith, L. (1996). Green career choices: The influence of ecological stance on recruiting. *Journal of Business and Psychology, 10*(4), 445-458.

Bauer, T. N., & Green, S. G. (1998). Testing the combined effects of newcomer information seeking and manager behavior on socialization. *Journal of Applied Psychology, 83*(1), 72-83.

Baughman, R., DiNardi, D., & Holtz-Eakin, D. (2003). Productivity and wage effects of "family friendly" fringe benefits. *International Journal of Manpower, 24*(3), 247-259.

Becker, B. E., & Huselid, M. A. (1998). High Performance Work Systems and firm performance: A synthesis of research and managerial implications. *Research in Personnel and Human Resources Management, 16*, 53-101.

Becker, B. E., Huselid, M. A., Pickus, P. S., & Spratt, M. F. (1997). HR as a source of shareholder value: Research and recommendations. *Human Resource Management, 36*(1), 39-47.

Becker, B. E., Huselid, M. A., & Ulrich, D. (2001). *The HR Scorecard: Linking people, strategy and performance.* Boston: Harvard Business School Press.

Beechler, S., Bird, A., & Raghuram, S. (1993). Linking business strategy and human resource management practices in multinational corporations: A theoretical framework. *Advances in International Comparative Management, 8*, 199-215.

Befus, E. F. (2006). New sexual harassment prevention measures. *National Real Estate Investor, 48*(1), 50.

Belanger, J. (2000). *The influence of employee involvement on productivity: A review of the research* (Applied Research Branch Paper, R-00-4E). http://www.hrsdc.gc.ca/en/cs/sp/hrsd/prc/publications/research/2000-002584/r-00-4e.pdf

Belt, J. A., & Paolillo, J. G. P. (1982). The influence of corporate image and specificity of candidate qualifications on response to recruitment advertisement. *Journal of Management, 8*(1), 105-112.

Bender, C., DeVogel, S., & Blomberg, R. (1999). The socialization of newly hired medical staff into a large health system. *Health Care Management Review, 24*(1), 95-108.

Bennett, R., Aston, A., & Colquhoun, T. (2000). Cross-cultural training: A critical step in ensuring the success of international assignments. *Human Resource Management, 39*(2/3), 239-250.

Bernardin, H. J., & Buckley, M. R. (1981). Strategies of rater training. *Academy of Management Review, 6*(2), 205-212.

Bernardin, H. J., & Cooke, D. K. (1993). Validity of an honesty test in predicting theft among convenience store employees. *Academy of Management Journal, 36*(5), 1097-1108.

Berry, C. M., Sackett, P. R., & Wiemann, S. (2007). A review of recent developments in integrity test research. *Personnel Psychology, 60*(2), 271-301.

Berryman-Fink, C. (2001). Women's responses to sexual harassment at work: Organizational policy versus employee practice. *Employment Relations Today, 27*(4), 57-64.

Best, R. B. (1977). Don't forget those reference checks! *Public Personnel Management, 6*(6), 422-426.

Bible, D., & Hill, K. L. (2007). Discrimination: Women in business. *Journal of Organizational Culture, Communication and Conflict, 11*(1), 65-76.

Bingham, B., Ilg, S., & Davidson, N. (2002). Great candidates fast: On-line job application and electronic processing. *Public Personnel Management, 31*(1), 53-64.

blackbaseball.com. (2006). *History of the Negro Baseball Leagues.* http://blackbaseball.com/history/index.htm

Black, H. A. (1999). Is there discrimination in mortgage lending? What does the research tell us? *Review of Black Political Economy, 27*(1), 23-30.

Black, J. S., & Gregersen, H. B. (1999). The right way to manage expats. *Harvard Business Review, 77*(2), 52-62.

Black, J. S., Gregersen, H. B., & Mendenhall, M. E. (1992). Toward a theoretical framework of repatriation adjustment. *Journal of International Business Studies, 23*(4), 737-760.

Blair, H., Taylor, S. G., & Randle, K. (1998). A pernicious panacea: A critical evaluation of business reengineering. *New Technology, Work and Employment, 13*(2), 116-128.

Blanck, P. D. (1996). *Communicating the Americans with Disabilities Act, transcending compliance: 1996 follow-up report on Sears, Roebuck and Co.* Iowa City, IA: Annenberg Program.

Bland, T. S., & Stalcup, S. S. (1999). Build a legal employment application. *HR Magazine, 44*(3), 129-133.

Blankenship v. Martin Marrietta Energy Systems, Inc., 83 F.3d 153 (U.S. Court of Appeals for the Sixth Circuit, 1996).

Blau, F. D., & Kahn, L. M. (1992). The gender earnings gap: Learning from international comparisons. *American Economic Review, 82*(2), 533-538.

Blau, F. D., & Kahn, L. M. (2000). Gender differences in pay. *Journal of Economic Perspectives, 14*(4), 75-99.

Boehm, V. R. (1985). Using assessment centres for management development—Five applications. *Journal of Management Development, 4*(4), 40-53.

Boex, L. F. J. (2000). Attributes of effective economics instructors: An Analysis of Student Evaluations. *Journal of Economic Education, 31*(3), 211-227.

Bohlander, G. W., & Naber, J. (1999). Nonadversarial negotiations: The FMCS Interest-Based Bargaining program. *Journal of Collective Negotiations, 28*(1), 41-52.

Bond, J. T., Galinsky, E., & Swanberg, J. E. (1998). *Executive summary: 1997 national study of the changing workforce.* http://familiesandwork.org/summary/nscw.pdf

Boraas, S., & Rodgers, W. M., III. (2003). How does gender play a role in the earnings gap? An update. *Monthly Labor Review, 126*(3), 9-14.

Borman, W. C., Rosse, R. L., & Abrahams, N. M. (1980). An empirical construct validity approach to studying predictor-job performance links. *Journal of Applied Psychology, 65*(6), 662-671.

Boushey, H., Brocht, C., Gundersen, B., & Bernstein, J. (2001). *Hardships in America: The real story of working families.* Washington, DC: Economic Policy Institute.

Bowen, D. E., Ledford, G. E., Jr., & Nathan, B. R. (1991). Hiring for the organization, not the job. *Academy of Management Executive, 5*(4), 35-51.

Bowler, M. (1999). Women's earnings: An overview. *Monthly Labor Review, 122*(12), 13-21.

Bray, D. W. (1985). Fifty years of assessment centres: A retrospective and prospective view. *Journal of Management Development, 4*(4), 4-12.

Breaugh, J. A., & Starke, M. (2000). Research on employee recruitment: So many studies, so many remaining questions. *Journal of Management, 26*(3), 405-434.

Brewster, C., & Pickard, J. (1994). Evaluating expatriate training. *International Studies of Management & Organization, 24*(3), 18-35.

Brewster, C., Sparrow, P., & Harris, H. (2005). Towards a new model of globalizing HRM. *International Journal of Human Resource Management, 16*(6), 949-970.

Bridges, W. (1994). The end of the job. *Fortune, 130*(6), 62-70.

Bright, D. S., Cooperrider, D. L., & Galloway, W. B. (2006). Appreciative Inquiry in the Office of Research and Development: Improving the collaborative capacity of organization. *Public Performance & Management Review, 29*(3), 285-306.

Brockbank, W. (1999). If HR were really strategically proactive: Present and future directions in HR's contribution to competitive advantage. *Human Resource Management, 38*(4), 337-352.

Brockbank, W., Ulrich, D., & Beatty, R. W. (1999). HR Professional development: Creating the future creators at the University of Michigan Business School. *Human Resource Management, 38*(2), 111-117.

Brodie, J. M. (2006). Getting managers on board. *HR Magazine, 51*(11), 105-108.

Brody, H. M., & Brito, C. (2006). When is "unequal" pay not really unequal? *Employment Relations Today, 33*(3), 87-95.

Brown, C., & Reich, M. (1989). When does union-management cooperation work? A look at NUMMI and GM-Van Nuys. *California Management Review, 31*(4), 21-44.

Brown, J. (2002). Training Needs Assessment: A must for developing an effective training program. *Public Personnel Management, 31*(4), 569-578.

Brown, K. A., Willis, P. G., & Prussia, G. E. (2000). Predicting safe employee behavior in the steel industry: Development and test of a sociotechnical model. *Journal of Operations Management, 18*(4), 445-465.

Bryman, A. (1984). Organizational studies and the concept of rationality. *Journal of Management Studies, 21*(4), 391-408.

Buckley, M. R., Fedor, D. B., Carraher, S. M., Frink, D. D., & Marvin, D. (1997). The ethical imperative to provide recruits realistic job previews. *Journal of Managerial Issues, 9*(4), 468-484.

Bucklin, B. R., & Dickinson, A. M. (2001). Individual monetary incentives: A review of different types of arrangements between performance and pay. *Journal of Organizational Behavior Management, 21*(3), 45-137.

Budros, A. (1999). A conceptual framework for analyzing why organizations downsize. *Organization Science, 10*(1), 69-82.

Buhler, P. M. (2007). Managing in the new millennium. *SuperVision, 68*(5), 18-20.

Burak, E. H., Burack, M. D., Miller, D. M., & Morgan, K. (1994). New paradigm approaches in strategic human resource management. *Group & Organization Management, 16*(2), 141-159.

Bureau of Labor Statistics. (2004a). Industry by event or exposure, 2004. TABLE A-1. Fatal occupational injuries by industry and event or exposure. http://stats.bls.gov/iif/oshwc/cfoi/cftb0196.pdf

Bureau of Labor Statistics. (2004b). Industry by private sector, government workers, and self-employed workers, 2004. TABLE A-3. Fatal occupational injuries to private sector wage and salary workers, government workers, and self-employed workers by industry, All United States. http://www.bls.gov/iif/oshwc/cfoi/cftb0198.pdf

Bureau of Labor Statistics. (2004c, August 25). *Number of jobs held, labor market activity, and earnings growth among younger baby boomers: Recent results from a longitudinal study.* http://www.bls.gov/news.release/History/nlsoy_08252004.txt

Bureau of Labor Statistics. (2005a). Census of fatal occupational injuries charts, 1992-2005. Number and rate of fatal occupational injuries by private industry sector, 2005. http://www.bls.gov/iif/oshwc/cfoi/cfch0004.pdf

Bureau of Labor Statistics. (2005b). *Highlights of women's earnings in 2005* (Report 995). http://www.bls.gov/cps/cpswom2005.pdf

Bureau of Labor Statistics. (2005c). *Lost-worktime injuries and illnesses: Characteristics and resulting time away from work, 2004.* http://www.bls.gov/iif/oshwc/osh/case/osnr0024.pdf

Bureau of Labor Statistics. (2005d). *May 2005 national occupational employment and wage estimates: United States.* http://www.bls.gov/oes/current/oes_nat.htm#b31-0000

Bureau of Labor Statistics. (2005e). Median usual weekly earnings of full-time wage and salary workers by detailed occupation and sex, 2005 annual averages. http://www.bls.gov/cps/wlf-table18-2006.pdf

Bureau of Labor Statistics. (2005f). *Workplace injury and illness summary.* http://www .bls.gov/news.release/osh.nr0.htm

Bureau of Labor Statistics. (2006a, September 8). *Employee tenure summary.* http://www .bls.gov/news.release/tenure.nr0.htm

Bureau of Labor Statistics. (2006b). *Labor force statistics from the Current Population Survey.* http://www.bls.gov/cps/lfcharacteristics.htm#fullpart

Bureau of Labor Statistics. (2006c). *National census of fatal occupational injuries in 2005.* http://www.bls.gov/news.release/archives/cfoi_08102006.pdf

Bureau of Labor Statistics. (2006d). *Women in the labor force: A databook.* http://www.bls.gov/cps/wlf-databook2006.htm, http://www.bls.gov/cps/wlf-databook-2007.pdf, http://www.bls.gov/cps/wlf-databook-2007.pdf

Bureau of Labor Statistics. (2007). *Job openings and labor turnover: July 2007.* http://www.bls.gov/news.release/pdf/jolts.pdf

Bureau of Labor Statistics. (2008a, January 25). *Mass layoffs in 2007.* http://www.bls.gov/opub/ted/2008/jan/wk3/art04.htm

Bureau of Labor Statistics. (2008b, January 25). *Table 2. Median weekly earnings of full-time wage and salary workers by union affiliation and selected characteristics.* http://www.bls.gov/news.release/union2.t02.htm

Bureau of Labor Statistics. (2008c, January 25). *Table 3. Union affiliation of employed wage and salary workers by occupation and industry.* http://www.bls.gov/news.release/union2.t03.htm

Bureau of Labor Statistics. (2008d, January 25). *Union members summary* (USDL 08-0092). http://www.bls.gov/news.release/union2.nr0.htm

Bureau of Labor Statistics. (n.d.). *Collective bargaining agreements file: File location and access.* http://www.dol.gov/esa/olms/regs/compliance/cba/index.htm

Burke, J. (1978). *Connections.* Boston: Little, Brown.

Burke, M. J., & Day, R. R. (1986). A cumulative study of the effectiveness of managerial training. *Journal of Applied Psychology, 71*(2), 232-245.

Burnes, B. (2007). Kurt Lewin and the Harwood Studies: The foundations of OD. *Journal of Applied Behavioral Science, 43*(2), 213-231.

Burrington, D. D. (1982). A review of state government employment application forms for suspect inquiries. *Public Personnel Management Journal, 11*(1), 55-60.

Burroughs, J. D. (1982). Pay secrecy and performance: The psychological research. *Compensation Review, 14*(3), 44-54.

Buster, M. A., Roth, P. L., & Bobko, P. (2005). A process for content validation of education and experienced-based minimum qualifications: An approach resulting in federal court approval. *Personnel Psychology, 58*(3), 771-799.

Buyens, D., & De Vos, A. (2001). Perceptions of the value of the HR function. *Human Resource Management Journal, 11*(3), 70-89.

Cable, D. M., & Turban, D. B. (2003). The value of organizational reputation in the recruitment context: A brand equity perspective. *Journal of Applied Social Psychology, 33*(11), 2244-2266.

Cabot, S. J. (1997). How to avoid (or decertify) a union. *Nursing Homes, 46*(3), 23-24.

Cadigan, J. (2006). The impact of family-friendly compensation: An investigation of military personnel policy. *Review of Public Administration, 26*(1), 3-20.

Cadrain, D. (2004). HR professionals stymied by vanishing job references. *HR Magazine, 49*(11), 31, 40.

Cahill, K. E., Giandrea, M. D., & Quinn, J. F. (2006). Are traditional retirements a thing of the past? New evidence on retirement patterns and bridge jobs. *Business Perspectives, 18*(2), 26-37.

Cahill, S. (2002). Global equity plans: Are they costing you too much? *Compensation & Benefits Management, 18*(1), 10-15.

Caligiuri, P. M. (2000). The Big Five personality characteristics as predictors of expatriate's desire to terminate the assignment and supervisor-rated performance. *Personnel Psychology, 53*(1), 67-88.

Caligiuri, P. M., & Stroh, L. K. (1995). Multinational corporation management strategies and international human resources practices: Bringing IHRM to the bottom line. *International Journal of Human Resource Management, 6*(3), 494-507.

Campbell, D. J., Campbell, K. M., & Chia, H. (1998). Merit pay, performance appraisal, and individual motivation: An analysis and alternative. *Human Resource Management, 37*(2), 131-146.

Campbell, R. J., & Bray, D. W. (1993). Use of an assessment center as an aid in management selection. *Personnel Psychology, 46*(3), 691-699.

Campbell, D. P., & Holland, J. (1972). A merger in vocational interest research: Applying Holland's theory to Strong's data. *Journal of Vocational Behavior, 2*(4), 353-376.

Cann, K. T., & Cangemi, J. P. (1971). Peter's principal principle. *Personnel Journal, 50*(11), 872-877.

Cappelli, P. (2001). Making the most of on-line recruiting. *Harvard Business Review, 79*(3), 139-146.

Carpenter, M. A., Sanders, W. G., & Gregersen, H. B. (2001). Bundling human capital with organizational context: The impact of international assignment experience on multinational firm performance and CEO pay. *Academy of Management Journal, 44*(3), 493-511.

Carter, C. A., Ruhe, M. C., Weyer, S., Litaker, D., Frye, R. E., & Stange, K. C. (2007). An Appreciative Inquiry approach to practice improvement and transformative change in health care settings. *Quality Management in Health Care, 16*(3), 194-204.

Cascio, W. F. (1982). Scientific, legal, and operational imperatives of workable performance appraisal systems. *Public Personnel Management, 11*(4), 367-375.

Cascio, W. F. (1993). Downsizing: What do we know? What have we learned? *The Executive, 7*(1), 95-104.

Cascio, W. F. (1999). Costing human resources: The financial impact of behavior in organizations. Mason, OH: South-Western.

Cascio, W. F., Young, C. E., & Morris, J. R. (1997). Financial consequences of employment-change decisions in major U.S. corporations. *Academy of Management Journal, 40*(5), 1175-1189.

Cashman, K., & Smye, M. (2007). Onboarding: Get on board with it. *Leadership Excellence, 24*(4), 5.

Cassels, L., & Randall, R. L. (1958). Analysis of worker turnover pays off: Three ideas feature new approach to old problem, point to more effective methods. *Nation's Business, 46*(1), 34-38.

Caudron, S. (1994). The de-jobbing of America. *Industry Week, 243*(16), 30-36.

Cavana, R. Y., Boyd, D. M., & Taylor, R. J. (2007). A systems thinking study of retention and recruitment issues for the New Zealand Army Electronic Technician Trade Group. *Systems Research and Behavioral Science, 24*(2), 201-216.

Cederblom, D., & Pemerl, D. E. (2002). From performance appraisal to performance management: One agency's experience. *Public Personnel Management, 31*(2), 131-140.

Chao, G. T., Walz, P. M., & Gardner, P. D. (1992). Formal and informal mentorships: A comparison on mentoring functions and contrast with nonmentored counterparts. *Personnel Psychology, 45*(3), 619-636.

Chapman, D. S., Uggerslev, K. L., Carroll, S. A., Piasentin, K. A., & Jones, D. A. (2005). Applicant attraction to organizations and job choice: A meta-analytic review of the correlates of recruiting outcomes. *Journal of Applied Psychology, 90*(5), 928-944.

Chen, H., & Hsieh, Y. (2006). Key trends of the total reward system in the 21st century. *Compensation & Benefits Review, 38*(6), 64-70.

Chen, M. T. (2003). Project meeting cost analysis. *AACE International Transactions*, PM.07.1.

Chirico, K. E., Buckley, M. R., Wheeler, A. R., Facteau, J. D., Bernardin, H. J., & Beu, D. S. (2004). A note on the need for true scores in Frame-of-Reference (FOR) training research. *Journal of Managerial Issues, 16*(3), 382-395.

Chmielewski, T. L., & Phillips, J. J. (2002). Measuring Return-On-Investment in government: Issues and procedures. *Public Personnel Management, 31*(2), 225-237.

Cholakis, P. (2005). How to implement a successful drug testing program. *Risk Management, 52*(11), 24-28.

Church, A. H., Margiloff, A., & Coruzzi, C. (1995). Using surveys for change: An applied example in a pharmaceuticals organization. *Leadership and Organization Development Journal, 16*(4), 3-11.

Civil Rights Act of 1964, Title VII (CRA). http://www.eeoc.gov/policy/vii.html

Civil Rights Act of 1991. http://www.eeoc.gov/policy/cra91.html

Coalition of Graduate Employee Unions. (2000). *Casual nation.* http://www.yaleunions.org/geso/reports/Casual_Nation.pdf

Cober, R. T., Brown, D. J., Blumental, A. J., Doverspike, D., & Levy, P. (2000). The quest for the qualified job surfer: It's time the public sector catches the wave. *Public Personnel Management, 29*(4), 479-494.

Cober, R. T., Brown, D. J., & Levy, P. E. (2004). Form, content, and function: An evaluative methodology for corporate employment web sites. *Human Resource Management, 43*(2/3), 201-218.

Cochran, D. S., Hinkle, T. W., & Dusenberry, D. (1987). Designing a developmental assessment center in a government agency: A case study. *Public Personnel Management, 16*(2), 145-152.

Cocanougher, A. B., & Ivancevich, J. M. (1978). BARS performance rating for sales force personnel. *Journal of Marketing, 42*(3), 87-95.

Code of Federal Regulations. (1980). *Guidelines on sexual harassment.* 29 C.F.R. Part 1604.11. http://edocket.access.gpo.gov/cfr_2008/julqtr/29cfr1604.11.htm

Cohen, C. F., Birkin, S. J., Garfield, M. J., & Webb, H. W. (2004). Managing conflict in software testing. *Communications of the Association for Computing Machinery, 47*(1), 76-81.

Cohen, M. D., March, J. G., & Olsen, J. P. (1972). A garbage can model of organizational choice. *Administrative Science Quarterly, 17*(1), 1-25.

Cole, D. C., Ibrahim, S., & Shannon, H. S. (2005). Predictors of work-related repetitive strain injuries in a population cohort. *American Journal of Public Health, 95*(7), 1233-1237.

Collings, D. G., Scullion, H., & Morley, M. J. (2007). Changing patterns of global staffing in the multinational enterprise: Challenges to the conventional expatriate assignment and emerging alternatives. *Journal of World Business, 42*(2), 198-213.

Collins, C. J. (2007). The interactive effects of recruitment practices and product awareness on job seekers' employer knowledge and application behaviors. *Journal of Applied Psychology, 92*(1), 180-190.

Collins, C. J., & Han, J. (2004). Exploring applicant pool quantity and quality: The effects of early recruitment practice strategies, corporate advertising, and firm reputation. *Personnel Psychology, 57*(3), 685-717.

Collins, D. B., & Holton, E. F., III. (2004). The effectiveness of managerial leadership development programs: A meta-analysis of studies from 1982 to 2001. *Human Resource Development Quarterly, 15*(2), 217-248.

Collins, C. J., & Stevens, C. K. (2002). The relationship between early recruitment-related activities and the application decisions of new labor-market entrants: A brand equity approach to recruitment. *Journal of Applied Psychology, 87*(6), 1121-1133.

Colquitt, B., & Kleiner, B. H. (1996). How the best companies are preventing sexual harassment in the workplace. *Equal Opportunities International, 15*(3), 12-20.

Conger, J. A., & Fulmer, R. M. (2003). Developing your leadership pipeline. *Harvard Business Review, 81*(12), 76-84.

Congressional Research Service. (2007, February 15). *Legislative, executive, and judicial officials: Process for adjusting pay and current salaries.* http://www.senate.gov/reference/resources/pdf/RL33245.pdf

Conklin, D. W. (2005). Risks and rewards in HR business process outsourcing. *Long Range Planning, 38*(6), 579-598.

Conlon, E. J., & Short, L. O. (1984). Survey Feedback as a large-scale change device: An empirical examination. *Group & Organization Studies, 9*(3), 399-416.

Connecticut v. Teal, 457 U.S. 440 (U.S. Supreme Court, 1982).

Converse, P. D., Oswald, F. L., Gillespie, M. A., Field, K. A., & Bizot, E. B. (2004). Matching individuals to occupations using abilities and the O*Net: Issues and an application in career guidance. *Personnel Psychology, 57*(2), 451-487.

Conway, J. M., Jako, R. A., & Goodman, D. F. (1995). A meta-analysis of interrater and internal consistency reliability of selection interviews. *Journal of Applied Psychology, 80*(5), 565-579.

Coopman, S. J. (2001). Democracy, performance, and outcomes in interdisciplinary health care teams. *Journal of Business Communication, 38*(3), 261-284.

Cornell University's Kheel Center. (2005). *The Triangle Factory Fire.* http://www.ilr.cornell.edu/Trianglefire/

Cox, T. H., & Blake, S. (1991). Managing cultural diversity: Implications for organizational competitiveness. *Academy of Management Executive, 5*(3), 45-56.

Crockett, J. (1999). Minimizing the risk of workplace violence. *Business Insurance, 33*(27), 35-40.

Crosby, P. B. (1979). *Quality is free: The art of making quality certain.* New York: McGraw-Hill.

Cui, G. (1998). The emergence of the Chinese Economic Area (CEA): A regiocentric approach to the markets. *Multinational Business Review, 6*(1), 63-72.

Cutcher-Gershenfeld, J., & Kochan, T. A., & Wells, J. C. (1998). How do labor and management view collective bargaining? *Monthly Labor Review, 121*(10), 23-31.

Daily, C. M., Certo, S. T., & Dalton, D. R. (2000). International experience in the executive suite: The path to prosperity? *Strategic Management Journal, 21*(4), 515-523.

Dalen, L. H., Stanton, N. A., & Roberts, A. D. (2001). Faking personality questionnaires in personnel selection. *Journal of Management Development, 20*(7/8), 729-741.

Dalton, D. R., Krackhardt, D. M., & Porter, L. W. (1981). Functional turnover: An empirical assessment. *Journal of Applied Psychology, 66*(6), 716-721.

Dalton, D. R., & Todor, W. D. (1979). Turnover turned over: An expanded and positive perspective: An expanded and positive perspective. *Academy of Management Review, 4*(2), 225-235.

Day, D. V., & Silverman, S. B. (1989). Personality and job performance: Evidence of incremental validity. *Personnel Psychology, 42*, 25-26.

Day, D. V., & Sulsky, L. M. (1995). Effects of Frame-of-Reference training and information configuration on memory organization and rating accuracy. *Journal of Applied Psychology, 80*(1), 158-167.

Day, S., Rounds, J., & Swaney, K. (1998). The structure of vocational interests for diverse racial-ethnic groups. *Psychological Science, 9*(1), 40-44.

de Janasz, S. C., Sullivan, S. E., & Whiting, V. (2003). Mentor networks and career success: Lessons for turbulent times. *Academy of Management Executive, 17*(4), 78-91.

Delaney, J. T., & Huselid, M. A. (1996). The impact of human resource management practices on perceptions of organizational performance. *Academy of Management Journal, 39*(4), 949-969.

DelVecchio, D., Jarvis, C. B., & Klink, R. R. (2001, February). *Brand equity in resource market exchanges: Extending the value of brands beyond the consumer*. Paper presented at the American Marketing Association Conference, Scottsdale, AZ.

DelVecchio, D., Jarvis, C. B., Klink, R. R., & Dineen, B. R (2007). Leveraging brand equity to attract human capital. *Marketing Letters, 18*(3), 149-164.

Deming, W. E. (1986). *Out of the crisis*. Cambridge, MA: MIT Press.

DeNisi, A. S., & Peters, L. H. (1996). Organization of information in memory and the performance appraisal process: Evidence from the field. *Journal of Applied Psychology, 81*(6), 717-737.

DeNisi, A. S., Robbins, T., & Cafferty, T. P. (1989). Organization of information used for performance appraisals: Role of diary-keeping. *Journal of Applied Psychology, 74*(1), 124-129.

Dennis, A. J. (1995). Avoiding the antitrust traps. *HR Focus, 72*(9), 11-11.

Deshpande, S. P., & Viswesvaran, C. (1992). Is cross-cultural training of expatriate managers effective: A meta-analysis. *International Journal of Intercultural Relations, 16*(3), 295-310.

DeVaro, J., Li, R., & Brookshire, D. (2007). Analysing the job characteristics model: New support from a cross-section of establishments. *International Journal of Human Resource Management, 18*(6), 986-1003.

DeVito, D. (Director), & Mamet, D. (Writer). (1993). *Hoffa* [Motion picture]. Beverly Hills, CA: Fox Video.

Dierdorff, E. C., & Wilson, M. A. (2003). A meta-analysis of job analysis reliability. *Journal of Applied Psychology, 88*(4), 635-646.

Director's Guild of America. (2006-2008). *Creative rights handbook.* Retrieved November 7, 2008, from http://www.dga.org/index2.php3

Doan, H., & Kleiner, B. H. (1999). How to conduct sexual harassment training effectively. *Equal Opportunities International, 18*(5/6), 27-31.

Downes, M., & Thomas, A. S. (1999). Managing overseas assignments to build organizational knowledge. *HR. Human Resource Planning, 22*(4), 33-48.

Drach, R. L. (1992). Making reasonable accommodations under the ADA. *Employment Relations Today, 19*(2), 167-169.

Drazin, R., & Auster, E. R. (1987). Wage differences between men and women: Performance appraisal ratings vs. salary allocation as a locus of bias. *Human Resource Management, 26*(2), 157-168.

Druskat, V. U., & Wheeler, J. V. (2003). Managing from the boundary: The effective leadership of self-managing work teams. *Academy of Management Journal, 46*(4), 435-457.

DuBois, D. A., & DuBois, C. L. Z (2000). An alternate method for content-oriented test construction: An empirical evaluation. *Journal of Business and Psychology, 15*(2), 197-213.

Duncan, K. C., Krall, L., Maxcy, J. G., & Prus, M. J. (2004). Faculty productivity, seniority, and salary compression. *Eastern Economic Journal, 30*(2), 293-310.

Durning v. Duffens Optical, 1996 U.S. Dist. LEXIS 1685 (U.S. District Court for the Eastern District of Louisiana, 1996).

Dutton, G. (2000). The ADA at 10. *Workforce, 79*(12), 40-46.

Dwyer, T. D. (1999). Trends in global compensation. *Compensation and Benefits Review, 31*(4), 48-53.

Dzamba, A. (2001). Compensation strategies to use amid organizational change. *Compensation and Benefits Management, 17*(1), 16-29.

Eagly, A. H., Makhijani, M. G., & Klonsky, B. G. (1992). Gender and the evaluation of leaders: A meta-analysis. *Psychological Bulletin, 111*(1), 3-22.

Edström, A., & Galbraith, J. R. (1977). Transfer of managers as coordination and control strategy in multinational organizations. *Administrative Science Quarterly, 22*(2), 248-263.

Edwards, R. M., & Kleiner, B. H. (2002). Conducting effective and legally safe background and reference checks. *Managerial Law, 44*(1-2), 136-150.

Edwards, R. M., & Swaim, P. (1986). Union-nonunion earnings differentials and the decline of private-sector unionism. *American Economic Review, 76*(2), 97-102.

Eisenhardt, K. M., & Zbaracki, M. J. (1992). Strategic decision making. *Strategic Management Journal, 13*(Special Issue), 17-37.

Ellis, F. (2007). The benefits of partnership for OD and HR. *Strategic HR Review, 6*(4), 32-35.

Elsbach, K. D., & Hargadon, A. B. (2006). Enhancing creativity through "mindless" work: A framework of workday design. *Organization Science, 17*(4), 470-483.

England, P. (1999). The case for comparable worth. *Quarterly Review of Economics and Finance, 39*, 743-755.

England, P., Herbert, M. S., Kilbourne, B. S., Reid, L. L., & Megdal, L. M. (1994). The gendered valuation of occupations and skills: Earnings in 1980 census occupations. *Social Forces, 73*(1), 65-101.

Equal Pay Act. (1963). http://www.eeoc.gov/policy/epa.html

Estes, M. (1997). Adversaries find common ground. *Workforce, 76*(3), 97-102.

Ezra, M., & Deckman, M. (1996). Balancing work and family responsibilities: Flextime and child care in the federal government. *Public Administration Review, 56*(2), 174-179.

Fairburn, J. A., & Malcomson, J. M. (2001). Performance, promotion, and the Peter Principle. *Review of Economic Studies, 68*(234), 45-66.

Faith, M. S., Wong, F. Y., & Carpenter, K. M. (1995). Group sensitivity training: Update, meta-analysis, and recommendations. *Journal of Counseling Psychology, 42*(3), 390-399.

Falcone, P. (2007). Big-picture performance appraisal. *HR Magazine, 52*(8), 97-100.

Farias, G., & Varma, A. (2000). Integrating job characteristics, sociotechnical systems and reengineering: Presenting a unified approach to work and organization. *Organization Development Journal, 18*(3), 11-24.

Farrell, A., & Geist-Martin, P. (2005). Communicating social health: Perceptions of wellness at work. *Management Communication Quarterly, 18*(4), 543-592.

Farrell, S., & Hakstian, A. R. (2001). Improving salesforce performance: A meta-analytic investigation of the effectiveness and utility of personnel selection procedures and training interventions. *Psychology & Marketing, 18*(3), 281-316.

Faure, M. (2006). Problem solving was never this easy: Transformational change through Appreciative Inquiry. *Performance Improvement, 45*(9), 22-32.

Feggetter, A. J. (1982). A method for investigating human factor aspects of aircraft accidents and incidents. *Ergonomics, 25*(11), 1065-1075.

Feild, H. S., Bayley, G. A., & Bayley, S. M. (1977). Employment test validation for minority and nonminority production workers. *Personnel Psychology, 30*(1), 37-46.

Feldman, D. C., Bearden, W. O., & Hardesty, D. M. (2006). Varying the content of job advertisements: The effect of message specificity. *Journal of Advertising, 35*(1), 123-141.

Feldman, D. C., & Kim, S. (2000). Bridge employment during retirement: A field study of individual and organizational experiences with post-retirement employment. *Human Resource Planning, 23*(1), 14-25.

Feldman, D. C., & Klaas, B. S. (2002). Internet job hunting: A field study of applicant experiences with on-line recruiting. *Human Resources Management, 41*(2), 175-192.

Feldman, D. C., & Tompson, H. B. (1993). Expatriation, repatriation, and domestic geographical relocation: An empirical investigation of adjustment to new job assignment. *Journal of International Business Studies, 24*(3), 507-523.

Feldman, D. C., & Weitz, B. A. (1988). Career plateaus reconsidered. *Journal of Management, 14*(1), 69-80.

Fenton, J. W., Jr., & Lawrimore, K. W. (1992). Employment reference checking, firm size, and defamation liability. *Journal of Small Business Management, 30*(4), 88-95.

Fenwick, M. (2004). On international assignment: Is expatriation the only way to go? *Asia Pacific Journal of Human Resources, 42*(3), 356-377.

Ference, T. P., Stoner, J. A. F., & Warren, E. K. (1977). Managing the career plateau. *Academy of Management Review, 2*(4), 602-612.

Ferris, F., & Hyde, A. C. (2004). Federal labor-management relations for the next century—or the last? The case of the Department of Homeland Security. *Review of Public Personnel Administration. 24*(3), 216-233.

Festing, M., Eidems, J., & Royer, S. (2007). Strategic issues and local constraints in transnational compensation strategies: An analysis of cultural, institutional and political influences. *European Management Journal, 25*(2), 118-131.

Fine, C. R., & Schupp, R. W. (2002). Liability exposure trends in recruitment: An assessment and analysis of retail employment applications. *Employee Responsibilities and Rights Journal, 14*(4), 135-143.

Finlay, W., & Coverdill, J. E. (1999). The search game: Organizational conflicts and the use of headhunters. *Sociological Quarterly, 40*(1), 11-30.

Fisher, K. K. (1986). Management roles in the implementation of participative management systems. *Human Resource Management, 25*(3), 459-480.

Fitzgerald, W. K. (1993). Training to become a business partner. *Human Resources Professional, 5*(4), 29-32.

Flamholtz, E. G. (1983). Overcoming the Peter Principle: Successful transitions to a new management role. *Journal of Management Development, 2*(2), 51-65.

Fletcher, M. (2005). Drug-test cheats frustrate employer screening efforts. *Business Insurance, 39*(31), 26-28.

Floyd, S. W., & Wooldridge, B. (1994). Dinosaurs or dynamos? Recognizing middle management's strategic role. *Academy of Management Executive, 8*(4), 47-57.

Folkard, S., Lombardi, D. A., & Spencer, M. B. (2006). Estimating the circadian rhythm in the risk of occupational injuries and accidents. *Chronobiology International, 23*(6), 1181-1192.

Foreman, E. I., Ellis, H. D., & Beavan, D. (1983). Mea culpa? A study of the relationships among personality traits, life-events and ascribed accident causation. *British Journal of Clinical Psychology, 22*, 223-224.

Forrest, S. P., III, & Peterson, T. O. (2006). It's called andragogy. *Academy of Management Learning & Education, 5*(1), 113-122.

Forster, N. (2000). The myth of the "international manager." *International Journal of Human Resource Management, 11*(1), 126-142.

Francis, H., & Keegan, A. (2006). The changing face of HRM: In search of balance. *Human Resource Management Journal, 16*(3), 231-249.

Frankforter, S. A., & Christensen, S. L. (2005). Finding competitive advantage in self-managed work teams. *Business Forum, 27*(1), 20-24.

Freeman, R., & Medoff, J. (1984). *What do unions do?* New York: Basic Books.

French, W. L., & Bell, C. H. (1999). *Organizational development.* Upper Saddle River, NJ: Prentice Hall.

Friedman, B. A. (2007). Globalization implications for human resource management roles. *Employee Responsibilities and Rights Journal, 19*(3), 157-171.

Frierson, J. G. (1989). Reduce the costs of sexual harassment. *Personnel Journal, 68*(11), 79-85.

Frierson, J. G., & Jolly, J. P. (1988). Problems in employment application forms. *Employment Relations Today, 15*(3), 205-217.

Frye, N. K., & Breaugh, J. A. (2004). Family-friendly policies, supervisor support, work-family conflict, family-work conflict, and satisfaction: A test of a conceptual model. *Journal of Business and Psychology, 19*(2), 197-220.

Fullerton, H. N., & Toossi, M. (2001). Labor force projections to 2010: Steady growth and changing composition. *Monthly Labor Review, 124*(11), 21-38.

Fulmer, I. S., Gerhart, B., & Scott, K. C. (2003). Are the 100 Best better? An empirical investigation of the relationship between being in a "great place to work" and firm performance. *Personnel Psychology, 56*(4), 965-993.

Furnham, A. (1990). The fakeability of the 16-PF, Myers-Briggs and FIRO-B personality measures. *Personality and Individual Differences, 11*(7), 711-716.

Futrell, C. M., & Jenkins, O. C. (1978). Pay secrecy versus pay disclosure for salesmen: A longitudinal study. *Journal of Marketing Research, 15*(2), 214-219.

Gandolfi, F. (2007). Downsizing, corporate survivors, and employability-related issues: A European case study. *Journal of the American Academy of Business, 12*(1), 50-56.

Gangani, N., McLean, G. N., & Braden, R. A. (2006). A competency-based human resource development strategy. *Performance Improvement Quarterly, 19*(1), 127-139.

Gardner, S. E., & Daniel, C. (1998). Implementing comparable worth/pay equity: Experiences of cutting edge states. *Public Personnel Management, 27*(4), 475-489.

Gatewood, R. D., Gowan, M. A., & Lautenschlager, G. J. (1993). Corporate image, recruitment image, and initial job choice decisions. *Academy of Management Journal, 36*(2), 414-427.

Gatlin-Watts, R., Carson, M., Horton, J., Maxwell, L., & Maltby, N. (2007). A guide to global virtual teaming. *Team Performance Management, 13*(1-2), 47-52.

Gaugler, B. B., Rosenthal, D. B., Thornton, G. C., III, & Bentson, C. (1987). Meta-analysis of Assessment Center validity. *Journal of Applied Psychology, 72*(3), 493-511.

Gendell, M. (2001). Retirement age declines again in 1990s. *Monthly Labor Review, 124*(10), 12-21.

Gerber, J. K., & Yacoubian G. S., Jr. (2001). Evaluation of drug testing in the workplace: Study of the construction industry. *Journal of Construction Engineering and Management, 127*(6), 438-444.

Gerst, V. (2005). The ten minute manager's guide to nontraditional hiring. *Restaurants & Institutions, 115*(17), 22-23.

Gierden, C. (2007). Get on right track with executive onboarding. *Canadian HR Reporter, 20*(13), 14.

Gilley, K. M., Greer, C. R., & Rasheed, A. A. (2004). Human resource outsourcing and organizational performance in manufacturing firms. *Journal of Business Research, 57*(3), 232-240.

Gittell, J. H., Von Nordenflycht, A., & Kochan, T. A. (2004). Mutual gains or zero sum? Labor relations and firm performance in the airline industry. *Industrial and Labor Relations Review, 57*(2), 163-180.

Goffee, R., & Jones, G. (1996). What holds the modern company together? *Harvard Business Review, 74*(6), 133-148.

Gomez-Mejia, L. R., & Balkin, D. B. (1989). Effectiveness of individual and aggregate compensation strategies. *Industrial Relations, 28*(3), 431-445.

Goodstein, L. D., & Butz, H. W. (1998). Customer value: The linchpin of organizational change. *Organizational Dynamics, 27*(1), 21-34.

Gordon, B. (2004). Seven mega-trends shaping modern logistics. *World Trade, 17*(11), 42-44.

Gosling, J., & Mintzberg, H. (2003). The five minds of a manager. *Harvard Business Review, 81*(11), 54-63.

Gottwals, D. (2006). Implementing sexual harassment training in the workplace. *Employee Benefit Plan Review, 6*(2), 6-9.

Gould, S. (1979). Characteristics of career planners in upwardly mobile occupations. *Academy of Management Journal, 22*(3), 539-550.

Graduate Employees and Students Organization. (1999). *Casual in blue.* http://www.yaleunions.org/geso/reports/Casual_in_Blue.pdf

Graf, A. (2004). Expatriate selection: An empirical study identifying significant skill profiles. *Thunderbird International Business Review, 46*(6), 667-685.

Graf, A., & Harland, L. K. (2005). Expatriate selection: Evaluating the discriminant, convergent, and predictive validity of five measures of interpersonal and intercultural competence. *Journal of Leadership and Organizational Studies, 11*(2), 46-62.

Grant, A. M., & Campbell, E. M. (2007). Doing good, doing harm, being well and burning out: The interactions of perceived prosocial and antisocial impact in service work. *Journal of Occupational and Organizational Psychology, 80*(4), 665-692.

Grant, J. (2005). Creating a team atmosphere helps Certicom foster recognition. *Canadian HR Reporter, 18*(1), 13-14.

Grant, P. C. (1997). Essential or marginal? Job functions and the Americans with Disabilities Act. *Business Horizons, 40*(2), 71-74.

Greengard, S. (1995). Catch the wave as HR goes online. *Personnel Journal, 74*(7), 54-68.

Greenhaus, J. H., Parasuraman, S., & Wormley, W. M. (1990). Effects of race on organizational experiences, job performance evaluations, and career outcomes. *Academy of Management Journal, 33*(11), 64-86.

Greening, D. W., & Turban, D. B. (2000). Corporate social performance as a competitive advantage in attracting a quality workforce. *Business and Society, 39*(3), 254-280.

Greenwood, J. S. (1995). What Major League Baseball can learn from its international counterparts: Building a model collective-bargaining agreement for Major League Baseball. *George Washington Journal of International Law and Economics, 29*(2), 581-618.

Grensing-Pophal, L. (2007). Committing to part-timers. *HR Magazine, 52*(4), 84-88.

Griffin, M. E. (1989). Personnel research on testing, selection, and performance appraisal. *Public Personnel Management, 18*(2), 127-137.

Griggs v. Duke Power Co., 401 U.S. 424 (Supreme Court of the United States, 1971).

Grobman, G. M. (2005). Complexity theory: A new way to look at organizational change. *Public Administration Quarterly, 29*(3), 350-382.

Gross, S. E., & Wingerup, P. L. (1999). Global pay? Maybe not yet! *Compensation and Benefits Review, 31*(4), 25-34.

Gross-Schaefer, A., Trigilio, J., Negus, J., & Ro, C. (2000). Ethics education in the workplace: An effective tool to combat employee theft. *Journal of Business Ethics, 26*(2), 89-100.

Grossman, R. J. (2007). New competencies for HR. *HR Magazine, 52*(6), 58-62.

Grover, S. L., & Crooker, K. J. (1995). Who appreciates family-responsive human resource policies: The impact of family-friendly policies on the organizational attachment of parents and non-parents. *Personnel Psychology, 48*(2), 271-288.

Grutter v. Bollinger, 539 U.S. 306 (U.S. Supreme Court, 2003).

Guastello, S. J., & Rieke, M. L. (1991). A review and critique of honesty test research. *Behavioral Sciences & the Law, 9*(4), 501-523.

Guillory, W. A. (2004). The roadmap to diversity, inclusion, and high performance. *Healthcare Executive, 19*(4), 24-30.

Gura, S. T. (2002). Yoga for stress reduction and injury prevention at work. *Work, 19*(1), 3-7.

Gurchiek, K. (2006). 10 steps for HR to earn its seat at the table. *HR Magazine, 51*(6), 44.

Gwartney, J., & Haworth, C. (1974). Employer costs and discrimination: The case of baseball. *Journal of Political Economy, 82*(4), 873-881.

Hackett, T. J., & McDermott, D. G. (1999). Seven steps to successful performance-based rewards. *HR Focus, 76*(9), 11-12.

Hackman, J. R., & Oldham, G. R. (1976). Motivation through design of work: A test of a theory. *Organizational Behavior and Human Performance, 16*, 250-279.

Hammer, M. (1990). Reengineering work: Don't automate, obliterate. *Harvard Business Review, 68*(4), 104-112.

Hamner, W. C. (1975). How to ruin motivation with pay. *Compensation Review, 7*(3), 17-27.

Hanks, D. (2004). ADA compliance: It's more than "removing barriers." *Nursing Homes, 53*(6), 70-71.

Hansen, F. (2005). The turnover myth. *Workforce Management, 84*(6), 34-40.

Hansen, F. (2006). Paperless route for recruiting. *Workforce Management, 85*(4), 1, 34-37.

Hanssen, A. (1998). The cost of discrimination: A study of Major League baseball. *Southern Economic Journal, 64*(3), 603-627.

Hantula, D. A., Rajala, A. K., Kellerman, E. G. B., & Bragger, J. L. D. (2001). The value of workplace safety: A time-based utility analysis model. *Journal of Organizational Behavior Management, 21*(2), 79-98.

Haque, B., Pawar, K. S., & Barson, R. J. (2003). The application of business process modelling to organisational analysis of concurrent engineering environments. *Technovation, 23*(2), 147-162.

Harris, M. M. (1989). Reconsidering the employment interview: A review of recent literature and suggestions for future research. *Personnel Psychology, 42*(4), 691-726.

Harris, M. M., & Fink, L. S. (1987). A field study of applicant reactions to employment opportunities: Does the recruiter make a difference? *Personnel Psychology, 40*(4), 765-784.

Harvey, R. J., Friedman, L., Hakel, M. D., & Cornelius, E. T. (1988). Dimensionality of the Job Element Inventory, a simplified worker-oriented job analysis questionnaire. *Journal of Applied Psychology, 73*(4), 639-646.

Harzing, A. (1995). The persistent myth of high expatriate failure rates. *International Journal of Human Resource Management, 6*(2), 457-474.

Harzing, A. (2002). Are referencing errors undermining our scholarship and credibility? The case of expatriate failure rates. *Journal of Organizational Behavior, 23*(1), 127-148.

Harzing, A., & Christensen, C. (2004). Expatriate failure: Time to abandon the concept? *Career Development International, 9*(6/7), 616-626.

Hauenstein, M. A., & Foti, R. J. (1989). From laboratory to practice: Neglected issues in implementing Frame-of-Reference rater training. *Personnel Psychology, 42*(2), 359-378.

Hausdorf, P. A., & Duncan, D. (2004). Firm size and Internet recruiting in Canada: A preliminary investigation. *Journal of Small Business Management, 42*(3), 325-334.

Hay, G. W. (2006). New partners for strategic change and organizational transformation: The combined effects of market research and organizational development. *Organizational Development Journal, 26*(4), 55-61.

Hays, R. D. (1974). Expatriate selection: Insuring success and avoiding failure. *Journal of International Business Studies, 5*(1), 25-37.

Hazelwood School District v. U.S., 433 U.S. 299 (United States Supreme Court, 1977).

Hedge, J. W., & Kavanagh, M. J. (1988). Improving the accuracy of performance evaluations: Comparison of three methods of performance appraiser training. *Journal of Applied Psychology, 73*(1), 68-73.

Heller, M. (2005). Court ruling that employer's integrity test violated ADA could open door to litigation. *Workforce Management, 84*(9), 74-77.

Heneman, R. L. (1992). Merit pay: Linking pay increases to performance ratings. Reading, MA: Addison-Wesley.

Heneman, R. L. (2003). Job and work evaluation: A literature review. *Public Personnel Management, 32*(1), 47-71.

Heneman, R. L., & Dixon, K. E. (2001). Reward and organizational systems alignment: An expert system. *Compensation & Benefits Review, 33*(6), 18-29.

Heneman, R. L., & von Hippel, C. (1995). Balancing group and individual rewards: Rewarding individual contributions to the team. *Compensation and Benefits Review, 27*(4), 63-68.

Hensgen, T., Desouza, K. C., & Evaristo, J. R. (2004). Ad hoc crisis management and crisis evasion. *International Journal of Technology, Policy and Management, 4*(3), 257-274.

Henneman, T. (2006). After high court ruling, firms may want to take long look at anti-harassment strategies. *Workforce Management, 85*(14), 33-35.

Herriot, P., & Rothwell, C. (1981). Organizational choice and decision theory: Effects of employers' literature and selection interview. *Journal of Occupational Psychology, 54*(1), 17-31.

Herz, D. E. (1995). Work after early retirement: An increasing trend among men. *Monthly Labor Review, 118*(4), 13-20.

Hewitt, G. J. (2000). Graduate student employee collective bargaining and the educational relationship between faculty and graduate students. *Journal of Collective Negotiations, 29*(2), 153-166.

Hill, J. R., & Spellman, W. (1984). Pay discrimination in baseball: Data from the seventies. *Industrial Relations, 23*(1), 103-112.

Hirsch, B. T. (2004). What do unions do for economic performance? *Journal of Labor Research, 25*(3), 415-455.

Hite, L. M., & McDonald, K. S. (2006). Diversity training pitfalls and possibilities: An exploration of small and mid-size U.S. organizations. *Human Resource Development International, 9*(3), 365-377.

Hodgetts, R. M., Luthans, F., & Lee, S. (1994). New paradigm organizations: From Total Quality to Learning to World-Class. *Organizational Dynamics, 22*(3), 5-19.

Hodson, R. (2002). Worker participation and teams: New evidence from analyzing organizational ethnographies. *Economic and Industrial Democracy, 23*(4), 491-528.

Hofmann, D. A., & Stetzer, A. (1996). A cross-level investigation of factors influencing unsafe behaviors and accidents. *Personnel Psychology, 49*(2), 307-339.

Hoffman, S. J., & Kaplan, D. I. (1997). *Human exploration of Mars: The reference mission of the NASA Mars Exploration Study Team* (NASA Special Publication 6107). ftp://nssdcftp.gsfc.nasa.gov/miscellaneous/planetary/mars_future/mars_ref_mission_sp6107.pdf, http://exploration.jsc.nasa.gov/marsref/contents.html

Hofstede, G., & Bond, M. H. (1988). The Confucius connection: From cultural roots to economic growth. *Organizational Dynamics, 15*(1), 4-21.

Holladay, C. L., & Quiñones, M. A. (2005). Reactions to diversity training: An international comparison. *Human Resource Development Quarterly, 16*(4), 529-545.

Holland, J. (1973). *Making vocational choices: A theory of careers.* Upper Saddle River, NJ: Prentice Hall.

Hollander, J. (1975, Fall). A step-by-step guide to corporate affirmative-action. *Business and Society Review, 15*, 67-73.

Holt, D. T., Armenakis, A. A., Feild, H. S., & Harris, S. G. (2007). Readiness for organizational change: The systematic development of a scale. *Journal of Applied Behavioral Science, 43*(2), 232-255.

Horner, C. (2006). Coaching for the better. *Training & Development Methods, 20*(4), 535-539.

Horrigan, M. W. (2004). Employment projections to 2012: Concepts and context. *Monthly Labor Review, 127*(2), 3-22.

Hoyman, M., & Duer, H. (2004). A typology of workplace policies: Worker friendly vs. family friendly? *Review of Public Personnel Administration, 24*(2), 113-132.

Huffcutt, A. I., & Arthur, W., Jr. (1994). Hunter and Hunter (1984) revisited: Interview validity for entry level jobs. *Journal of Applied Psychology, 79*(2), 184-190.

Human Resource Certification Institute. (2008). *PHR/SPHR/GPHR Handbook, Appendix A, PHR/SPHR Test Specifications.* Retrieved September 3, 2008, from http://www.hrci.org/certification/2008hb/apx-a/

Human Rights Campaign Foundation. (2004). *Transgender issues in the workplace: A tool for managers.* Washington, DC: Author.

Hunter, J. E., & Hunter, R. F. (1984). Validity and utility of alternative predictors of job performance. *Psychological Bulletin, 96*(1), 72-98.

Hunter, J. E., & Schmidt, F. L. (1978). Differential and single-group validity of employment tests by race: A critical analysis of three recent studies. *Journal of Applied Psychology, 63*(1), 1-11.

Hurtz, G. M., & Alliger, G. M. (2002). Influence of coaching on integrity test performance and unlikely virtues scale scores. *Human Performance, 15*(3), 255-273.

Hyland, A. M., & Muchinsky, P. M. (1991). Assessment of the structural validity of Holland's model with job analysis (PAQ) information. *Journal of Applied Psychology, 76*(1), 75-80.

INFOCOMM. (1998). *Meetings in America: A study of trends, costs and attitudes toward business travel, teleconferencing, and their impact on productivity* (MCI Conferencing White Paper). http://e-meetings.verizonbusiness.com/global/en/meetingsinamerica/uswhitepaper.php

Janis, I. L. (1982). *Groupthink: Psychological studies of policy decisions and fiascoes.* Boston: Houghton Mifflin.

Jarrar, Y. F., & Aspinwall, E. M. (1999). Integrating Total Quality Management and Business Process Re-engineering: Is it enough? *Total Quality Management, 10*(4/5), S584-S593.

Jeanneret, P. R., & Strong, M. H. (2003). Linking O*Net job analysis information to job requirement predictors: An O*Net application. *Personnel Psychology, 56*(2), 465-492.

Jelf, G. S. (1999). A narrative review of post-1989 employment interview research. *Journal of Business and Psychology, 14*(1), 25-58.

Jennings, K. M., Jr., & McLaughlin, F. S. (1997). Measuring and correcting inversion in faculty salaries at public universities. *Public Personnel Management, 26*(3), 345-357.

Johnson v. Transportation Agency, Santa Clara County, California, 480 U.S. 616 (Supreme Court of the United States, 1987).

Johnson, G., & Leavitt, W. (2001). Building on success: Transforming organizations through an Appreciative Inquiry. *Public Personnel Management, 30*(1), 129-136.

Johnson, G., & Solon, G. (1986). Estimates of direct effects of comparable worth policy. *American Economic Review, 76*(5), 1117-1125.

Johnson, J. W. (1996). Linking employee perceptions of service climate to customer satisfaction. *Personnel Psychology, 46*(4), 831-851.

Johnson, M., & Tolchinsky, P. (1999). A redesign in the Central Intelligence Agency. *Journal for Quality and Participation, 22*(2), 31-35.

Joines, R. C. (1987, October). *The item-by-item scored General Management In-Basket.* Paper presented at the International Personnel Management Association Assessment Council Conference, Philadelphia.

Joines, R. C. (1991). *Innovations in In-Basket technology: The General Management In-Basket.* Toronto, Ontario, Canada: International Congress on the Assessment Center Method.

Joinson, C. (2000). Capturing turnover costs. *HR Magazine, 45*(7), 107-119.

Jones, G. R. (1986). Socialization tactics, self-efficacy, and newcomers' adjustments to organizations. *Academy of Management Journal, 29*(2), 262-279.

Jones, R. G., & Whitmore, M. D. (1995). Evaluating developmental assessment centers as interventions. *Personnel Psychology, 48*(2), 377-388.

Jordan, J., & Cartwright, S. (1998). Selecting expatriate managers: Key traits and competencies. *Leadership & Organization Development Journal, 19*(2), 89-96.

Kacmar, K. M., Andrews, M. C., Van Rooy, D. L., Steilberg, R. C., & Cerrone, S. (2006). Sure everyone can be replaced . . . but at what cost? Turnover as a predictor of unit-level performance. *Academy of Management Journal, 49*(1), 133-144.

Kahn, L. M. (1992). The effects of race on professional football players' compensation. *Industrial & Labor Relations Review, 45*(2), 295-310.

Kahn, L. M., & Shah, M. (2005). Race, compensation and contract length in the NBA: 2001-2002. *Industrial Relations, 44*(3), 444-462.

Kankanhalli, A., Tan, B. C. Y., & Wei, K. (2007). Conflict and performance in global virtual teams. *Journal of Management Information Systems, 23*(3), 237-274.

Kaplan, D. M. (2006). Can diversity training discriminate? Backlash to lesbian, gay, and bisexual diversity initiatives. *Employee Responsibilities and Rights Journal, 18*(1), 61-72.

Kaplan, R. S., & Norton, D. P. (1992). The Balanced Scorecard—measures that drive performance. *Harvard Business Review, 70*(1), 71-79.

Kaplan, R. S., & Norton, D. P. (1993). Putting the Balanced Scorecard to work. *Harvard Business Review, 71*(5), 134-147.

Karraker v. Rent-A-Center, Inc., 411 F.3d 831. (United States Court of Appeals for the Seventh Circuit, 2005).

Kastl, M. A., & Kleiner, B. H. (2001). New developments concerning discrimination and harassment in universities. *International Journal of Sociology and Social Policy, 21*(8-10), 156-164.

Katz, J. P., & Seifer, D. M. (1996). It's a different world out there: Planning for expatriate success through selection, pre-departure training and on-site socialization. *Human Resource Planning, 19*(2), 32-47.

Katzell, R. A., & Dyer, F. J. (1977). Differential validity revived. *Journal of Applied Psychology, 62*(2), 137-145.

Kegan, R. (1994). *In over our heads: The mental demands of modern life.* Cambridge, MA: Harvard University Press.

Kerkvliet, J., & McMullen, B. S. (1997). The impact of unionization on motor carrier costs. *Economic Inquiry, 35*(2), 271-284.

Kerr, S. (1995). On the folly of rewarding A, while hoping for B. *Academy of Management Executive, 9*(1), 7-14.

Kerr, S., & Ulrich, D. (1995). Creating the boundaryless organization: The radical reconstruction of organizational capabilities. *Planning Review, 23*(5), 41-45.

Kesselman, G. A., & Lopez, F. E. (1979). The impact of job analysis on employment test validation for minority and nonminority accounting personnel. *Personnel Psychology, 32*(1), 91-108.

Kethley, R. B., & Terpstra, D. E. (2005). An analysis of litigation associated with the use of the application form in the selection process. *Public Personnel Management, 34*(4), 357-375.

Keyserling, W. M., Ulin, S. S., Lincoln, A. E., & Baker, S. P. (2003). Using multiple information sources to identify opportunities for ergonomic interventions in automotive parts distribution: A case study. *AIHA Journal, 64*(5), 690-698.

Khalil, T. M., & Kurucz, C. N. (1977). The influence of 'biorhythm' on accident occurrence and performance. *Ergonomics, 20*(4), 389-398.

Kiedrowski, P. J. (2006). Quantitative assessment of a Senge Learning Organization intervention. *The Learning Organization, 13*(4), 369-383.

Killingsworth, M. R. (2002, May). Comparable worth and pay equity: Recent developments in the United States. *Canadian Public Policy, 28*, 171-186.

Kim, J. (2003). Recent pattern of the U.S. gender occupational segregation and earnings gap. *Journal of American Academy of Business, 3*(1/2), 78-84.

Kim, S., & Feldman, D. C. (2000). Working in retirement: The antecedents of bridge employment and its consequences for quality of life in retirement. *Academy of Management Journal, 43*(6), 1195-1210.

King, R. C., & Bu, N. (2005). Perceptions of the mutual obligations between employees and employers: A comparative study of new generation IT professionals in China and the United States. *International Journal of Human Resource Management, 16*(1), 46-64.

Kirby, A. (2003). StorageTek expands its employees' horizons. *Training & Management Development Methods, 17*(4), 961-963.

Kirkpatrick, D. L. (1959). Techniques for evaluating training programs. *Journal of the American Society of Training Directors, 33*(6), 3-9, 21-26.

Klaas, B. S. (2003). Professional Employer Organizations and their role in small and medium enterprises: The impact of HR outsourcing. *Entrepreneurship Theory and Practice, 28*(1), 43-62.

Klaas, B. S., Yang, H., Gainey, T., & McClendon, J. A. (2005). HR in the small business enterprise: Assessing the impact of PEO utilization. *Human Resource Management, 44*(4), 433-448.

Klaff, D. B., & Ehrenberg, R. G. (2003). Collective bargaining and staff salaries in American colleges and universities. *Industrial and Labor Relations Review, 57*(1), 92-104.

Klein, H. J., & Weaver, N. A. (2000). The effectiveness of an organizational level orientation training program in the socialization of new hires. *Personnel Psychology, 53*(1), 47-66.

Knowles, M. S. (1990). *The adult learner: A neglected species 4e.* Houston, TX: Gulf Publishing.

Koch, K., & Salter, N. (1999). The health and safety system in the Federal Republic of Germany. *Industrial Relations Journal, 30*(1), 61-71.

Komaki, J., Heinzmann, A. T., & Lawson, L. (1980). Effect of training and feedback: Component analysis of a behavioral safety program. *Journal of Applied Psychology, 65*(3), 261-270.

Koteff, E. (2006). Industry must be proactive, organized in efforts to stave off recruitment campaigns by unions. *Nation's Restaurant News, 40*(25), 16.

Kotter, J. P. (1996). *Leading change.* Boston: Harvard Business School Press.

Kotter, J. P. (2007). Leading change: Why transformation efforts fail. *Harvard Business Review, 85*(1), 96-103.

Kovach, K. A. (1996). Comparable worth: The Canadian legislation. *Business Horizons, 26*(1), 41-46.

Koch, K., & Salter, N. (1999). The health and safety system in the Federal Republic of Germany. *Industrial Relations Journal, 30*(1), 61-71.

Koen, C. M., Jr. (1995). Guide to pre-employment inquiries. *HR Focus, 72*(6), 4-5.

Kohn, A. (1993). Why incentive plans cannot work. *Harvard Business Review, 74*(5), 54-61.

Kraut, A. I., Pedigo, P. R., McKenna, D. D., & Dunnette, M. D. (1989). The role of manager: What's really important in different management jobs? *Academy of Management Executive, 3*(4), 286-293.

Kruse, D., & Schur, L. (2003). Employment of people with disabilities following the ADA. *Industrial Relations, 42*(1), 31-66.
Laabs, J. L. (1998). Life finding a needle in a haystack: Recruiting in the global village. *Workforce, 77*(4), 30-33.
Laczo, R. M., & Hanisch, K. A. (1999). An examination of behavioral families or organizational withdrawal in volunteer workers and paid employees. *Human Resource Management Review, 9*(4), 453-477.
Lafer, G. (2003). Graduate student unions: Organizing in a changed academic economy. *Labor Studies Journal, 28*(2), 25-43.
Lamont, J. (2007). Employing ECM in human resources. *KM World, 16*(9), 8-9.
Landis, J. (Director). (1988). *Coming to America* [Motion Picture]. Hollywood, CA: Parmount.
Landy, F. J., Farr, J. L., Saal, F. E., & Freytag, W. R. (1976). Behaviorally anchored scales for rating the performance of police officers. *Journal of Applied Psychology, 61*(6), 750-758.
Laurin v. Providence Hospital and Massachusetts Nurses Association, 150 F 3d 52 (Court of Appeals for the First Circuit, 1995).
Lawler, E. E., III. (1965). Managers' perceptions of their subordinates' pay and of their superiors' pay. *Personnel Psychology, 18*(4), 413-422.
Lawler, E. E., III. (1992). Pay the person, not the job. *Industry Week, 241*(23), 18-22.
Lawler, E. E., III. (2000). Pay strategy: New thinking for the new millennium. *Compensation & Benefits Review, 32*(1), 7-12.
Lawler, E. E., III, & Mohrman, S. A. (2003). HR as a strategic partner: What does it take to make it happen? *Human Resource Planning, 26*(3), 15-29.
Lazarova, M. B., & Caligiuri, P. (2001). Retaining repatriates: The role of organizational support practices. *Journal of World Business, 36*(4), 389-401.
Lazarova, M. B., & Cerdin, J. (2007). Revisiting repatriation concerns: Organizational support versus career and contextual influences. *Journal of International Business Studies, 38*(3), 404-429.
Lazarova, M. B., & Tarique, I. (2005). Knowledge transfer upon repatriation. *Journal of World Business, 40*(4), 361-373.
Lazear, E. P. (2004). The Peter Principle: A theory of decline. *Journal of Political Economy, 112*(1), S141-S163.
Le, H., Oh, I., Shaffer, J., & Schmidt, F. (2007). Implications of methodological advances for the practice of personnel selection: How practitioners benefit from meta-analysis. *Academy of Management Perspectives, 21*(3), 6-15.
Lécuyer, C. (2003). High-tech corporatism: Management-employee relations in U.S. electronic firms, 1920s-1960s. *Enterprise & Society, 4*(3), 502-520.
Lee, C. (1998). The adult learner: Neglected no more. *Training, 35*(3), 47-52.
Lee, H. (2007). Factors that influence expatriate failure: An interview study. *International Journal of Management, 24*(3), 403-619.
Lee, H., & Liu, C. (2006). The determinants of repatriate turnover intentions: An empirical analysis. *International Journal of Management, 23*(4), 751-763.
Lee, H., & Liu, C. (2006). Determinants of the adjustment of expatriate managers in foreign countries: An empirical study. *International Journal of Management, 23*(2), 302-311.
Lee, P. C. B. (2003). Going beyond career plateau: Using professional plateau to account for work outcomes. *Journal of Management Development, 22*(5/6), 538-551.

Lemmink, J., Schuijf, A., & Streukens, S. (2003). The role of corporate image and company employment image in explaining application intentions. *Journal of Economic Psychology, 24*(1), 1-15.

Leong, S. M., & Tan, C. T. (1993). Managing across borders: An empirical test of the Bartlett and Ghoshal [1989] typology. *Journal of International Business Studies, 24*(3), 449-464.

Letizia, J. M. (2004). How to avoid a wrongful discharge suit. *Home Health Care Management & Practice, 16*(2), 138-140.

Leventhal, L. (2006). Implementing interest-based negotiations: Conditions for success with evidence from Kaiser Permanente. *Dispute Resolution Journal, 61*(3), 50-58.

Levine, S. R. (2007). Make meetings less dreaded. *HR Magazine, 52*(1), 107-109.

Lewin, J. E., & Sager, J. K. (2007). A process model of burnout among salespeople: Some new thoughts. *Journal of Business Research, 60*(12), 1216-1224.

Lewin, K. (1951). *Field theory in social science.* New York: Harper & Row.

Lewison, J. (2006). The work/life balance sheet so far. *Journal of Accountancy, 202*(2), 45-49.

Lienert, A. (1994). Forging a new partnership. *Management Review, 83*(10), 39-43.

Lievens, F., & Harris, M. M. (2003). Research on Internet recruiting and testing: Current status and future directions. In C. L. Cooper & I. T. Robertson (Eds.), *International Review of Industrial and Organizational Psychology* (Vol. 16, pp. 131-165). Chichester, UK: Wiley & Sons.

Lilienthal, P. (2002). If you give your employees a voice, do you listen? *Journal for Quality and Participation, 25*(3), 38-40.

Lim, G., & Chan, C. (2001). Ethical values of executive search consultants. *Journal of Business Ethics, 29*(3), 213-226.

Linowes, R. G. (1993). The Japanese manager's traumatic entry into the United States: Understanding the American-Japanese cultural divide. *Academy of Management Executive, 7*(4), 21-38.

Little, B. L., & Sipes, D. (2000). Betwixt and between: The dilemma of employee references. *Employee Responsibilities and Rights Journal, 12*(1), 1-8.

Littrell, L. N., Salas, E., Hess, K. P., Paley, M., & Riedel, S. (2006). Expatriate preparation: A critical analysis of 25 years of cross-cultural training research. *Human Resource Development Review, 5*(3), 355-388.

Local 28 of the Sheet Metal Workers' International Association et al. v. Equal Employment Opportunity Commission, 478 U.S. 421 (U.S. Supreme Court, 1986).

Logan, J. (2002). Consultants, lawyers, and the 'union free' movement in the USA since the 1970s. *Industrial Relations Journal, 33*(3), 197-214.

Longenecker, C. O., & Gioia, D. A. (1992). The executive appraisal paradox. *Academy of Management Executive, 6*(2), 18-28.

Longenecker, C. O., & Goff, S. J. (1990). Why performance appraisals still fail. *Journal of Compensation & Benefits, 6*(3), 36-41.

Longenecker, C. O., & Waldeck, N. E. (2004). Benchmarks of effective managerial performance appraisals. *Journal of Compensation and Benefits, 20*(2), 15-23.

Loo, R. (1999). A structured exercise for stimulating cross-cultural sensitivity. *Career Development International, 4*(6), 321-324

Losyk, B. (2006). Getting a grip on stress: What HR managers must do to prevent burnout and turnover. *Employment Relations Today, 33*(1), 9-17.

Lubel, J. (2006). Nurses head to court. *Modern Healthcare, 36*(26), 12-12.

Luce, S. (2002). "The full fruits of our labor": The rebirth of the Living Wage movement. *Labor History, 43*(4), 401-409.

Luebbe, R. L., & Snavely, B. K. (1997). Making effective team decisions with consensus building tools. *Industrial Management, 39*(5), 1-7.

Lueke, S. B., & Svyantek, D. J. (2000). Organizational socialization in the host country: The missing link in reducing expatriate turnover. *International Journal of Organizational Analysis, 8*(4), 380-400.

Luthans, K. W., & Farner, S. (2002). Expatriate development: The use of 360-degree feedback. *Journal of Management Development, 21*(9/10), 780-793.

Luthans, F., Rosenkrantz, S. A., & Hennessey, H. W. (1985). What do successful managers really do? An observation study of managerial activities. *Journal of Applied Behavioral Science, 21*(3), 255-270.

Lyness, K. S., & Heilman, M. E. (2006). When fit is fundamental: Performance evaluations and promotions of upper-level female and male managers. *Journal of Applied Psychology, 91*(4), 777-785.

Lyons, F. H., & Ben-Ora, D. (2002). Total rewards strategy: The best foundation of pay for performance. *Compensation and Benefits Review, 34*(2), 34-49.

MacLaury, J. (1981). The job safety law of 1970: Its passage was perilous. *Monthly Labor Review, 104*(3), 18-24.

Macpherson, D. A., & Hirsch, B. T. (1995). Wages and gender composition: Why do women's jobs pay less? *Journal of Labor Economics, 13*(3), 426-471.

Mahoney, T. A., & Weitzel, W. (1978). Secrecy and managerial compensation. *Industrial Relations, 17*(2), 245-251.

Maiorca, J. (1997). How to construct behaviorally anchored rating scales (BARS) for employee evaluations. *Supervision, 58*(8), 15-18.

Manolatos, T., & Schultz, M. (2003, October 24). Duchane also lied on application to teach; OU says he claimed degree when he taught two-credit course on ethics for $1000. *Detroit News.*

Marcus, B., Lee, K., & Ashton, M. C. (2007). Personality dimensions explaining relationships between integrity tests and counterproductive behavior: Big five, or one in addition? *Personnel Psychology, 60*(1), 1-34.

Marquez, J. (2006). Lawsuits could raise scrutiny of pay survey. *Workforce Management, 85*(14), 12.

Martin, V. H. (1974). Recruiting women managers through flexible hours. *S.A.M. Advanced Management Journal, 39*(3), 46-53.

Martinez, M. N. (2000). Get job seekers to come to you. *HR Magazine, 45*(8), 44-52.

Maslach, C., & Jackson, S. E. (1981). The measurement of experienced burnout. *Journal of Occupational Behavior, 2*(2), 99-113.

Mastrangelo, P. M., & Jolton, J. A. (2001). Predicting on-the-job substance abuse with a written Integrity Test. *Employee Responsibilities and Rights Journal, 13*(2), 95-106.

Mastrangelo, P. M., & Popovich, P. M. (2000). Employees' attitudes toward drug testing, perceptions of organizational climate, and withdrawal from the employer. *Journal of Business and Psychology, 15*(1), 3-18.

Mathieu, J. E., & Leonard, R. L., Jr. (1987). Applying utility concepts to a training program in supervisory skills: A time-based approach. *Academy of Management Journal, 30*(2), 316-335.

Matsuoka, H. (1997). Development of a short test for accident proneness. *Perceptual and Motor Skills, 85*(3), 903-906.

Maurer, T. J., & Taylor, M. E. (1994). Is sex by itself enough? An exploration of gender bias issues in performance appraisal. *Organizational Behavior and Human Decision Processes, 60*(2), 231-251.

Maxwell, G., Rankine, L., Bell, S., & MacVicar, A. (2007). The incidence and impact of flexible working arrangements in smaller businesses. *Employee Relations, 29*(2), 138-161.

May, A. S. (1997). How the gamekeeper can make the most of his poacher. *Career Development International, 2*(5), 254-255.

McCartin, J. A. (2006). A historian's perspective on the PATCO strike, its legacy, and lessons. *Employee Responsibilities and Rights Journal, 18*(3), 215-222.

McCaughey, D., & Bruning, N. S. (2005). Enhancing opportunities for expatriate job satisfaction: HR strategies for foreign assignment success. *HR. Human Resource Planning, 28*(4), 21-29.

McConnell, C. R. (2000). Employment references: Walking scared between the minefield of defamation and the specter of negligent hiring. *The Health Care Manager, 19*(2), 78-90.

McCormick, E. J. (1979). *Job analysis: Methods and applications.* New York: Amacom.

McCormick, E. J., Jeanneret, P. R., & Mecham, R. C. (1969). *The development and background of the Position Analysis Questionnaire.* Lafayette, IN: Purdue University, Occupational Research Center.

McCormick, E. J., Jeanneret, P. R., & Mecham, R. C. (1972). A study of job characteristics and job dimensions as based on the Position Analysis Questionnaire. *Journal of Applied Psychology, 56*(4), 347-368.

McCrary, J. (2007). The effect of court-ordered hiring quotas on the composition and quality of police. *American Economic Review, 97*(1), 318-353.

McDaniel, M. A., Whetzel, D. L., Schmidt, F. L., & Maurer, S. (1994). The validity of employment interviews: A review and meta-analysis. *Journal of Applied Psychology, 79*(4), 599-616.

McElroy, J. C., Morrow, P. C., & Rude, S. N. (2001). Turnover and organizational performance: A comparative analysis of the effects of voluntary, involuntary, and reduction-in-force turnover. *Journal of Applied Psychology, 86*(6), 1294-1299.

McGinley, J. (2003). Do you know where your assets are? *Fleet Equipment, 29*(11), 12.

McKeown, I., & Philip, G. (2003). Business transformation, information technology and competitive strategies: Learning to fly. *International Journal of Information Management, 23*(1), 3-24.

McKinley, W., Mone, M. A., & Barker, V. L., III. (1998). Some ideological foundations of organizational downsizing. *Journal of Management Inquiry, 7*(3), 198-212.

McLean, J. (2007, Summer). Managing global virtual teams. *British Journal of Administrative Management*, 16.

McPherson, R. (2001). ADA integration. *Buildings, 95*(9), 26.

Mehta, C., & Theodore, N. (2005). *Undermining the right to organize: Employer behavior during union representation campaigns.* Retrieved October 3, 2008, from http://www.americanrightsatwork.org/dmdocuments/ARAWReports/UROCUEDcompressedfullreport.pdf

Mendenhall, M. E., & Stahl, G. K. (2000). Expatriate training and development: Where do we go from here? *Human Resource Management, 39*(2/3), 251-265.

Meng, G. J. (1992). Using job descriptions, performance and pay innovations to support quality: A paper company's experience. *National Productivity Review, 11*(2), 247-255.

Menzias, J. M., & Scandura, T. A. (2006). A needs-driven approach to expatriate adjustment and career development: A multiple mentoring perspective. *Journal of International Business Studies, 36*(5), 519-538.

Messmer, M. (2000). Reference checking: A crucial step in the hiring process. *National Public Accountant, 45*(3), 28-29.

Meyer, C. B., & Stensaker, I. G. (2006). Developing capacity for change. *Journal of Change Management, 6*(2), 217-231.

Michael, J. H. (2001). Perceived obligations of future forest industry employees: A psychological contracts perspective. *Forest Products Journal, 51*(10), 39-46.

Milkovich, G. T., & Anderson, P. H. (1972). Management compensation and secrecy policies. *Personnel Psychology, 25*(2), 293-302.

Miller, J. (1995). The business case for diversity. *Journal of Education for Business, 71*(1), 7-10.

Miller, M. G., Fitzgerald, S. P., Murrell, K. L., Preston, J., & Ambekar, R. (2005). Appreciative Inquiry in building a transcultural strategic alliance: The case of a biotech alliance between a U.S. multinational and an Indian family business. *Journal of Applied Behavioral Science, 41*(1), 91-110.

Mintzberg, H. (1971). Managerial work: Analysis from observation. *Management Science, 18*(2), B-97-B110.

Mintzberg, H. (1990). The manager's job: Folklore and fact. *Harvard Business Review, 68*(2), 163-176.

Mintzberg, H. (1994). Rounding out the manager's job. *Sloan Management Review, 36*(1), 11-26.

Mirabel, N., & DeYoung, R. (2005). Downsizing as a strategic intervention. *Journal of the American Academy of Business, 6*(1), 39-45.

Mitroff, I. I., Mason, R. O., & Pearson, C. M. (1994). Radical surgery: What will tomorrow's organizations look like? *Academy of Management Executive, 8*(2), 11-21.

Mobley, W. H. (1982). Supervisor and employee race and sex effects on performance appraisals: A field study of adverse impact and generalizability. *Academy of Management Journal, 25*(3), 598-606.

Mohrman, S. A., & Lawler, E. E., III. (1997). Transforming the human resource function. *Human Resource Management, 36*(1), 157-162.

Mohrman, S. A., Lawler, E. E., III, & Ledford, G. E., Jr. (1996). Do employee involvement and TQM programs work? *Journal for Quality and Participation, 19*(1), 6-10.

Mone, M. A. (1994). Relationships between self-concepts, aspirations, emotional responses, and intent to leave a downsizing organization. *Human Resource Development, 33*(2), 281-298.

Mongelluzzo, B. (2006, January 6). PierPass will track trucks with RFID tags. *Journal of Commerce Online Edition*, p. 1.

Monks, J. (2000). Unionization and faculty salaries: New evidence from the 1990s. *Journal of Labor Research, 21*(2), 305-314.

Monks, J., & Pizer, S. D. (1998). Trends in voluntary and involuntary job turnover. *Industrial Relations, 37*(4), 440-459.

Mook, J. R. (2007). Accommodation paradigm shifts. *HR Magazine, 52*(1), 115-120.

Moore, R. W. (1990). Instructional effects on the Phase II Profile honesty test. *Psychological Reports, 67*(1), 291-294.

Moore, D. P., & Hass, M. (1990). When affirmative action cloaks management bias in selection and promotion decisions. *Academy of Management Executive, 4*(1), 84-90.

Moore, H. L., Gatlin-Watts, R. W., & Cangelosi, J. (1998). Eight steps to a sexual-harassment-free workplace. *Training & Development, 52*(4), 12-13.

Moore, M. V., & Abraham, Y. T. (1992). Comparable worth: Is it a moot issue? *Public Personnel Management, 21*(4), 455-472.

Moosebruker, J. B., & Loftin, R. D. (1998). Business Process Redesign and Organizational Development: Enhancing success by removing the barriers. *Journal of Applied Behavioral Science, 34*(3), 286-304.

Morgan, P. V. (1986). International HRM: Fact or fiction? *Personnel Administrator, 31*(9), 42-47.

Morris, J. R., Cascio, W. F., & Young, C. E. (1999). Downsizing after all these years: Questions and answers about who did it, how many did it, and who benefitted from it. *Organizational Dynamics, 27*(3), 78-87.

Morrison, E. W. (1993). Newcomer information seeking: Exploring types, modes, sources, and outcomes. *Academy of Management Journal, 36*(3), 557-589.

Morrow, C. C., Jarrett, M. Q., & Rupinski, M. T. (1997). An investigation of the effect and economic utility of corporate-wide training. *Personnel Psychology, 50*(1), 91-119.

Mueller, M., & Belcher, G. (2000). Observed divergence in the attitudes of incumbents and supervisors as subject matter experts in job analysis: A study of the fire captain rank. *Public Personnel Management, 29*(4), 529-556.

Muilenburg, K., & Singh, G. (2007). The modern Living Wage movement. *Compensation and Benefits Review, 39*(1), 21-28.

Mumford, K., & Smith, P. N. (2007). The gender earnings gap in Britain: Including the workplace. *The Manchester School, 75*(6), 653-672.

Munchus, G., III. (1985). The status of pre-employment enquiry restrictions on the employment and hiring function. *Employee Relations, 7*(3), 20-26.

Munchus, G., III, & McArthur, B. (1991). Revisiting the historical use of the assessment centre in management selection and development. *Journal of Management Development, 10*(1), 5-13.

Munson, L. J., Hulin, C., & Drasgow, F. (2000). Longitudinal analysis of dispositional influences and sexual harassment: Effects on job and psychological outcomes. *Personnel Psychology, 53*(1), 21-46.

Murray, B., & Gerhart, B. (1998). An empirical analysis of a skill-based pay program and plant performance outcomes. *Academy of Management Journal, 41*(1), 68-78.

Musashi, M. (2005). *The book of five rings*. New York: Overlook.

Muthusamy, S. K., Wheeler, J. V., & Simmons, B. L. (2005). Self-managing work teams: Enhancing organizational effectiveness. *Organization Development Journal, 23*(3), 53-66.

NASA. (1988). NSTS 1988 news reference manual (Vol. 2–Operations). http://science.ksc.nasa.gov/shuttle/technology/sts-newsref/stsref-toc.html

Nash, J. J. (2002). Are ergonomic injuries disabling? *Occupational Hazards, 64*(2), 45-48.

Nathan, B. R., & Alexander, R. A. (1988). A comparison of criteria for test validation: A meta-analytic investigation. *Personnel Psychology, 41*(3), 517-535.

National Institute of Occupational Safety and Health. (1999). *Stress at work* (Publication No. 99-101). http://www.cdc.gov/niosh/pdfs/stress.pdf

National Institute of Standards and Technology. (2008). *Baldrige National Quality Program.* http://www.quality.nist.gov/

National Institute on Drug Abuse. (2004). *The economic costs of drug abuse in the United States.* http://www.whitehousedrugpolicy.gov/publications/economic_costs/economic_costs.pdf

National Labor Relations Act. (1935). 29 U.S.C. §§ 151-169 [Title 29, Chapter 7, Subchapter II, United States Code] http://www.nlrb.gov/about_us/overview/national_labor_relations_act.aspx

National Labor Relations Board. (1997). *Basic guide to the National Labor Relations Act.* http://www.nlrb.gov/nlrb/shared_files/brochures/basicguide.html

National Labor Relations Board v. Main Street Terrace Center, 218 F.3d 531 (Sixth Circuit Court of Appeals, 2000).

Nedelko, Z. (2007). Videoconferencing in virtual teams. *Business Review, Cambridge, 7*(1), 164-170.

Neuman, G. A., Wagner, S. H., & Christiansen, N. D. (1999). The relationship between work-team personality composition and the job performance of teams. *Group & Organization Management, 24*(1), 28-45.

Neuman, G. A., & Wright, J. (1999). Team effectiveness: Beyond skills and cognitive ability. *Journal of Applied Psychology, 84*(3), 376-389.

Neumark, D., & Stock, W. A. (2006). The labor market effects of sex and race discrimination laws. *Economic Inquiry, 44*(3), 385-419.

Newman, H. L., & Fitzgerald, S. P. (2001). Appreciative Inquiry with an executive team: Moving along the Action Research continuum. *Organizational Development Journal, 19*(3), 37-44.

Nkomo, S. M., & Fields, D. M. (1994). A field study of demographic characteristics and job attribute preferences of new part-time employees. *Journal of Business and Psychology, 8*(3), 365-375.

Noell, E. S. (2006). Smith and a living wage: Competition, economic compulsion, and the Scholastic legacy. *History of Political Economy, 38*(1), 151-174.

Norman, A. J., & Keys, P. R. (1992). Organization Development in public social services—The irresistible force meets the immovable object. *Administration in Social Work, 16*(3, 4), 147-165.

Northrup, H. R. (1984). The rise and demise of PATCO. *Industrial and Labor Relations Review, 37*(2), 167-184.

Occupational Safety and Health Act. (1970). http://www.osha.gov/pls/oshaweb/owasrch.search_form?p_doc_type=OSHACT&p_toc_level=0&p_keyvalue=

Occupational Safety and Health Administration. (1994). *Indoor air quality—59:15968-16039.* http://www.osha.gov/pls/oshaweb/owadisp.show_document?p_table=FEDERAL_REGISTER&p_id=13369

Occupational Safety and Health Administration. (1997, July 25). *Regulations (Standards—29 CFR), Railroad facilities—1917.17.* http://www.osha.gov/pls/oshaweb/owadisp.show_document?p_table=STANDARDS&p_id=10359

Occupational Safety and Health Administration. (2001). *Occupational injury and illness recording and reporting requirements.* http://www.osha.gov/pls/oshaweb/owadisp.show_document?p_table=FEDERAL_REGISTER&p_id=16312

Occupational Safety and Health Administration (2002). *eTool: Scaffolding.* http://www.osha.gov/SLTC/etools/scaffolding/index.html

Occupational Safety and Health Administration. (2004, December). *OSHA facts—December 2004.* http://www.osha.gov/as/opa/oshafacts.html

Occupational Safety and Health Administration. (2004, April). *OSHA fact sheet: Voluntary protection programs.* http://www.osha.gov/OshDoc/data_General_Facts/factsheet-vpp.pdf

Occupational Safety and Health Administration. (2005, August 24). *3M Company in Brookings recognized by OSHA for excellence in occupational safety and health.* OSHA Regional News Release, Region 8. http://www.osha.gov/pls/oshaweb/owadisp.show_document?p_table=NEWS_RELEASES&p_id=11549

Occupational Safety and Health Administration. (2007). *Logging eTool: Chain saw.* http://www.osha.gov/SLTC/substanceabuse/index.html

Occupational Safety and Health Administration. (n.d.). *OSHA forms for recording work-related injuries and illnesses.* http://www.osha.gov/recordkeeping/new-osha300form1-1-04.pdf

Office of Strategic Services. (1948). *Assessment of men: Selection of personnel for the Office of Strategic Services.* New York: Rinehart.

O'Leary, B. J., & Weathington, B. L. (2006). Beyond the business case for diversity in organizations. *Employee Responsibilities and Rights Journal, 18*(4), 283-292.

Omachonu, V. K., & Ross, J. E. (1994). *Principles of total quality.* Delray Beach, FL: St. Lucie.

Ones, D. S., Viswesvaran, C., & Schmidt, F. L. (1993). Comprehensive meta-analysis of integrity test validities: Findings and implications for personnel selection and theories of job performance. *Journal of Applied Psychology, 78*(4), 679-703.

O*Net. (n.d.). *Occupational Information Network.* http://online.onetcenter.org/.

O'Rourke, M. (2004). The costs of overtime. *Risk Management, 51*(3), 44-45.

Orpen, C. (1994). The effects of organizational and individual career management on career success. *International Journal of Manpower, 15*(1), 27-37.

Overman, S. (1999). Splitting hairs. *HRMagazine, 44*(8), 42-48.

Palmer, C. (1978). Dog catchers: A descriptive study. *Qualitative Sociology, 1*(1), 79-107.

Paluck, E. L. (2006). Diversity training and intergroup contact: A call to Action Research. *Journal of Social Issues, 62*(3), 577-595.

Paquet, R., Gaétan, I., & Bergeron, J. (2000). Does Interest-Based Bargaining (IBB) really make a difference in collective bargaining outcomes? *Negotiation Journal, 16*(3), 281-296.

Parry, S. B. (1996). Measuring training's ROI. *Training & Development, 50*(5), 72-77.

Parsons, H. M. (1974). What happened at Hawthorne? *Science, 183*(4128), 922-932.

Pascale, R. T. (1985). The paradox of "corporate culture": Reconciling ourselves to socialization. *California Management Review, 27*(2), 26-41.

Paterson, D. G. (1923). The Scott Company Graphic Rating Scale. *Journal of Personnel Research, 1*(8), 361-376.

Pearson, J. I. (1997). Harassment: Risk management tools. *Risk Management, 44*(1), 25-28.

Peck, D. (2007). High-yield reference checking: Adding new value to the hiring equation. *Employment Relations Today, 33*(4), 51-57.

Peelle, H. E., III. (2006). Appreciative Inquiry and Creative Problem Solving in cross-functional teams. *Journal of Applied Behavioral Science, 42*(4), 447-467.

Peirce, E. R., Smolinski, C. A., & Rosen, B. (1998). Why sexual harassment complaints fall on deaf ears. *Academy of Management Executive, 12*(3), 41-54.

Peltonen, T. (1993). Managerial career patterns in transnational corporations: An organizational capability approach. *European Management Journal, 11*(2), 248-257.

Pendry, L. F., Driscoll, D. M., & Field, C. T. (2007). Diversity training: Putting theory into practice. *Journal of Occupational and Organizational Psychology, 80*(1), 27-50.

Pension Benefit Guaranty Corporation. (2007). http://www.pbgc.gov/

Persinger, M. A., Cooke, W. J., & Janes, J. T. (1978). No evidence for relationship between biorhythms and industrial accidents. *Perceptual and Motor Skills, 46*(2), 423-426.

Peter, L. J., & Hull, R. (1969). *The Peter Principle.* New York: William Morrow.

Peters, K. (2006, May/June). The four stages of management education. *BizEd,* 36-40.

Peterson, N. G., Mumford, M. D., Borman, W. C., Jeanneret, P. R., Fleishman, E. A., Levin, K. Y., et al. (2001). Understanding work using the Occupational Information Network (O*NET): Implications for practice and research. *Personnel Psychology, 54*(2), 451-492.

Phillips, J. J. (1996). ROI: The search for best practices. *Training & Development, 50*(2), 42-47.

Phillips, J., & Phillips, P. (2006). Return on Investment measures success. *Industrial Management, 48*(2), 18-23.

Phillips, J. M. (1998). Effects of realistic job previews on multiple organizational outcomes: A meta-analysis. *Academy of Management Journal, 41*(6), 673-690.

Pickerill, J. M., Jackson, R. A., & Newman, M. A. (2006). Changing perceptions of sexual harassment in the federal workforce, 1987-1994. *Law & Policy, 28*(3), 368-394.

Pickett, L. (2003). Transforming the annual fiasco. *Industrial and Commercial Training, 35*(6/7), 237-240.

Pierce, F. D. (2002). Applying systems thinking to safety. *Professional Safety, 47*(6), 49-52.

Pierson, D. A., Koziara, K. S., & Johannesson, R. E. (1983). Equal pay for jobs of comparable worth: A quantified job content approach. *Public Personnel Management, 12*(4), 445-460.

Piturro, M. (1999). Alternatives to downsizing. *Management Review, 88*(9), 37-41.

Plimpton, G. (1966). *Paper lion.* New York: Harper & Row.

Pointer, T. A., & Kleiner, B. H. (1997). Developments concerning accommodation of wheelchair users within the workplace in accordance to the Americans with Disabilities Act. *Equal Opportunities International, 16*(6/7), 44-49.

Polson, J. M. (2002). The PEO phenomenon: Co-employment at work. *Employee Relations Law Journal, 27*(4), 7-25.

Pomeroy, A. (2006). Earlier coaching pays dividends now and in the future. *HRMagazine, 51*(9), 16.

Porras, J. L., & Robertson, P. J. (1992). Organization development: Theory, practice and research. In M. D. Dunnette & L. M. Hough (Eds.), *Handbook of industrial and organizational psychology* (Vol. 3, 2nd ed., pp. 719-822). Palo Alto, CA: Consulting Psychologist.

Porter, G., & Tansky, J. W. (1999). Expatriate success may depend on a "learning orientation": Considerations for selection and training. *Human Resource Management, 38*(1), 47-60.

Powell, G. N. (1984). Effects of job attributes and recruiting practices on applicant decisions: A comparison. *Personnel Psychology, 37*(4), 721-732.

Powell, G. N., & Butterfield, D. A. (1994). Investigating the "glass ceiling" phenomenon: An empirical study of actual promotions to top management. *Academy of Management Journal, 37*(1), 68-86.

Powell, G. N., Butterfield, D. A., & Parent, J. D. (2002). Gender and managerial stereotypes: Have times changed? *Journal of Management, 28*(2), 177-193.

Powers, R. (2002). Ensuring global consistency: The case for job leveling. *Benefits & Compensation International, 31*(8), 14-16, 18-19.

Premack, S. L., & Wanous, J. P. (1985). A meta-analysis of realistic job preview experiments. *Journal of Applied Psychology, 70*(4), 706-719.

Price Waterhouse v. Hopkins, 490 U.S. 228 (1989).

Pucik, V. (1988). Strategic alliances, organizational learning, and competitive advantage: The HRM agenda. *Human Resource Management, 27*(1), 77-93.

Pulakos, E. D., Borman, W. C., & Hough, L. M. (1988). Test validation for scientific understanding: Two demonstrations of an approach to studying predictor-criterion linkages. *Personnel Psychology, 41*(4), 703-716.

Pulakos, E. D., Schmitt, N., Whitney, D., & Smith, M. (1996). Individual differences in interviewer ratings: The impact of standardization, consensus discussion, and sampling error on the validity of a structured interview. *Personnel Psychology, 49*(1), 85-102.

Pulakos, E. D., White, L. A., Oppler, S. H., & Borman, W. C. (1989). Examination of race and sex effects on performance ratings. *Journal of Applied Psychology, 74*(5), 770-780.

Pynes, J. E. (1995). The ADEA and its exemptions on the mandatory retirement provisions for firefighters. *Public Personnel Administration, 15*(2), 34-45.

Quinn, R. W., & Brockbank, W. (2006). The development of strategic human resource professionals at BAE systems. *Human Resource Management, 45*(3), 477-494.

Ramlall, S. J. (2006). HR competencies and their relationship to organizational practices. *Performance Improvement, 45*(5), 32-43.

Rarick, C., & Baxter, G. (1984). Behaviorally anchored rating scales (BARS): An effective performance appraisal approach. *S.A.M. Advanced Management Journal, 51*, 36-39.

Rau, B. L., & Adams, G. A. (2005). Attracting retirees to apply: Desired organizational characteristics of bridge employment. *Journal of Organizational Behavior, 26*(6), 649-660.

Rau, B. L., & Hyland, M. M. (2002). Role conflict and flexible work arrangements: The effects on applicant attraction. *Personnel Psychology, 55*(1), 111-136.

Rawson, A. J. (1944). Accident proneness. *Psychosomatic Medicine, 6*, 88-94.

Ray, R., & Schmitt, J. (2007). *No-vacation nation.* Washington, DC: Center for Economic and Policy Research.

Rayburn, J. M., & Rayburn, L. G. (1999). Smart alternatives to downsizing. *Competitiveness Review, 9*(2), 49-57.

Reed, J., & Vakola, M. (2006). What role can a training needs analysis play in organisational change? *Journal of Organizational Change Management, 19*(3), 393-407.

Rees, D. I. (1993). The effect of unionization on faculty salaries and compensation: Estimates from the 1980's. *Journal of Labor Research, 14*(4), 399-422.

Rees, D. I. (1994). Does unionization increase faculty retention? *Industrial Relations, 33*(3), 297-321.

Reese, V. (2005). Maximizing your retention and productivity with on-boarding. *Employment Relations Today, 31*(4), 23-29.

Rehder, R. R., & Smith, M. M. (1986). NUMMI: Teamwork in action. *New Management, 4*(2), 47-49.

Reynolds-Fisher, S., & White, M. (2000). Downsizing in a learning organization: Are there hidden costs? *Academy of Management Review, 25*(1), 244-251.

Richman, J. A., Flaherty, J. A., & Johnson, T. P. (1999). Sexual harassment and generalized workplace abuse among university employees: Prevalence and mental health correlates. *American Journal of Public Health, 89*(3), 358-363.

Rimmer, J. H., Riley, B., Wang, E., & Rauworth, A. (2005). Accessibility of health clubs for people with mobility disabilities and visual impairments. *American Journal of Public Health, 95*(11), 2022-2028.

Rinefort, F. C., & Van Fleet, D. D. (2000). The United States safety movement and Howard Pyle. *Journal of Management History, 6*(3), 127-137.

Ritt, M. (Director), Asseyev, T., & Rose, A. (Producers). (1990). *Norma Rae* [Motion picture]. Farmington Hills, MI: CBS/Fox Video.

Rizzo, E., Guerra, D., & Pitocchelli, J. (2006, January/February). A pocket guide to negotiating your small-college contract. *Academe, 92*(1), 42-45.

Roberson, L., Kulik, C. T., & Pepper, M. B. (2001). Designing effective diversity training: Influence of group composition and trainee experience. *Journal of Organizational Behavior, 22*(8), 871-885.

Roberson, L., Kulik, C. T., & Pepper, M. B. (2003). Using needs assessment to resolve controversies in diversity training design. *Group & Organization Management, 28*(1), 148-174.

Roberts, B. (2002). System addresses "applicant" dilemma. *HR Magazine, 47*(9), 111-119.

Roberts, S. (2004). Patient deaths prompt close look at hospital employment practices. *Business Insurance, 38*(3), 3-5.

Robinson, S., Kraatz, M. S., & Rousseau, D. M. (1994). Changing obligations and the psychological contract: A longitudinal study. *Academy of Management Journal, 37*(1), 137-152.

Robinson, T. L. (1992). Revisiting the original management primer: Defending a great productivity innovator. *Industrial Management, 34*(1), 19-20.

Robinson v. Jacksonville Shipyards, Inc., 760 F.Supp 1486 (U.S. District Court for the Middle District of Florida, Jacksonville Division, 1991).

Roethlisberger, F. J., & Dickson, W. J. (1934). *Studies in industrial research: Technical vs. social organization in an industrial plant.* Cambridge, MA: Harvard University, Graduate School of Business.

Rollag, K., Parise, S., & Cross, R. (2005). Getting new hires up to speed quickly. *MIT Sloan Management Review, 46*(2), 35-41.

Rollins, T. (1994). Turning employee survey results into high-impact business improvements. *Employment Relations Today, 21*(1), 35-44.

Romans, J. (2006). Developing high-potential talent at Hughes Supply. *Strategic HR Review, 5*(3), 32-35.

Rosinger, G., Myers, L. B., Levy, G. W., Loar, M., Mohrman, S. A., & Stock, J. R (1982). Development of a behaviorally based performance appraisal system. *Personnel Psychology, 35*, 75-88.

Rousseau, D. M. (1990). New hire perceptions of their own and their employer's obligations: A study of psychological contracts. *Journal of Organizational Behavior, 11*(5), 389-409.

Rowland, H. (2007). Organizational development: The new buzz word. *Strategic Direction, 23*(1), 3-4.

Ruiz, G. (2007). Careerbuilder buys northern European sites. *Workforce Management, 86*(7), 12.

Ruona, W. E. A., & Gibson, S. K. (2004). The making of twenty-first-century HR: An analysis of the convergence of HRM, HRD, and OD. *Human Resource Management, 43*(1), 49-66.

Rupp, D. E., Gibbons, A. M., Baldwin, A. M., & Snyder, L. A., Spain, S. M., Sang, E. W., et al. (2006). An initial validation of developmental assessment centers as accurate assessments and effective training interventions. *Psychological Manager Journal, 9*(2), 171-200.

Rush, C., & Barclay, L. (1995). Executive search: Recruiting a recruiter. *Public Management, 77*(7), 20-22.

Ryan, A. M., Horvath, M., & Kriska, S. D. (2005). The role of recruiting source informativeness and organizational perceptions in decisions to apply. *International Journal of Selection and Assessment, 13*(4), 235-249.

Rynes, S. L. (1991). Recruitment, job choice, and post-hire consequences: A call for new research directions. In M. Dunnette & L. Hough (Eds.), *Handbook of industrial/organizational psychology* (Vol. 2, pp. 399-444). Palo Alto, CA: Consulting Psychologists Press.

Rynes, S. L., & Miller, H. E. (1983). Recruiter and job influences on candidates for employment. *Journal of Applied Psychology, 68*(1), 147-154.

Sadri, G., & Lees, B. (2001). Developing corporate culture as a competitive advantage. *Journal of Management Development, 20*(9/10), 853-859.

Sahdev, K. (2004). Revisiting the survivor syndrome: The role of leadership in implementing downsizing. *European Journal of Work and Organizational Psychology, 13*(2), 165-196.

Saks, A. M., & Ashforth, B. E. (1996). Proactive socialization and behavioral self-management. *Journal of Vocational Behavior, 48*(3), 301-323.

Saks, A. M., Uggerslev, K. L, & Fassina, N. E. (2007). Socialization tactics and newcomer adjustment: A meta-analytic review and test of a model. *Journal of Vocational Behavior, 70*(3), 413-446.

Salgado, J. F. (2003). Predicting job performance using FFM and non-FFM personality measures. *Journal of Occupational and Organizational Psychology, 76*(3), 323-346.

Saltzman, G. M. (2000). *Union organizing and the law: Part-time faculty and graduate teaching assistants* (NEA 2000 Almanac of Higher Education, 2000, 43-55). http://www2.nea.org/he/healma2k/images/a00p43.pdf

Saltzstein, A. L., Ting, Y., & Saltzstein, G. H. (2001). Work-family balance and job satisfaction: The impact of family-friendly policies on attitudes of federal government employees. *Public Administration Review, 61*(4), 452-467.

Sammer, J. (2005). An uncertain future for defined-benefit plans. *Business Finance, 11*(12), 43-45.

Schaaf, R. (2005). From "sick" care to "health" care: Controlling costs through employee wellness. *Employee Benefit Plan Review, 60*(2), 10-11.

Schaefer, M. E., Massey, F. A., & Hermanson, R. H. (1979). The Peter Principle revisited: An economic perspective. *Human Resource Management, 18*(4), 1-5.

Schmidt, F. L., & Hunter, J. E. (1977). Development of a general solution to the problem of validity generalization. *Journal of Applied Psychology, 62*(5), 529-540.

Schmidt, F. L., & Hunter, J. E. (2003). History, development, evolution, and impact of validity generalization and meta-analysis methods, 1975-2001. In K. R. Murphy (Ed.), *Validity generalization: A critical review* (pp. 31-65). Mahwah, NJ: Lawrence Erlbaum.

Schmidt, F. L., & Rader, M. (1999). Exploring the boundary conditions for interview validity: Meta-analytic validity findings for a new interview type. *Personnel Psychology, 52*(2), 445-464.

Schneider, B., & Konz, A. M. (1989). Strategic job analysis. *Human Resource Management, 28*(1), 51-63.

Schneider, K. T., Swan, S., & Fitzgerald, L. F. (1997). Job-related and psychological effects of sexual harassment in the workplace: Empirical evidence from two organizations. *Journal of Applied Psychology, 82*(3), 401-415.

Schor, S. M., Sims, R. R., & Dennehy, R. F. (1996). Power and diversity: Sensitizing yourself and others through self-reflection and storytelling. *Journal of Management Education, 20* (2), 242-256.

Schuler, R. S., & Rogovsky, N. (1998). Understanding compensation practice variations across firms: The impact of national culture. *Journal of International Business Studies, 29*(1), 159-177.

Schulz, E. R., & Tanguay, D. M. (2006). Merit pay in a public higher education institution: Questions of impact and attitudes. *Public Personnel Management, 35*(1), 71-88.

Schuster, M., & Rhodes, S. (1985). The impact of overtime work on industrial accident rates. *Industrial Relations, 24*(2), 234-246.

Segal, J. A. (2006). Time is on their side. *HR Magazine, 51*(2), 129-133.

Seligman, D. (1973). How equal opportunity turned into employment quotas. *Fortune, 87*(3), 160-168.

Senge, P. M. (1990). *The fifth discipline: The art and practice of the learning organization.* New York: Doubleday/Currency.

Settoon, R. P., & Adkins, C. L. (1997). Newcomer socialization: The role of supervisors, coworkers, friends and family members. *Journal of Business and Psychology, 11*(4), 112-124.

Shapiro, D. M., & Stelcner, M. (1997). Language and earnings in Quebec: Trends over twenty years. *Canadian Public Policy, 23*(2), 115-140.

Shaw, J. D., Gupta, N., & Delery, J. E. (2005). Alternative conceptualizations of the relationship between voluntary turnover and organizational performance. *Academy of Management Journal, 48*(1), 50-68.

Shelgren, D. (2004). Why HR outsourcing continues to expand. *Employment Relations Today, 31*(2), 47-53.

Shin, Y. (2004). A person-environment fit model for virtual organizations. *Journal of management, 30*(5), 725-743.

Shipper, F., & Manz, C. C. (1992). Employee self-management without formally designated teams: An alternative road to empowerment. *Organizational Dynamics, 20*(3), 48-61.

Shostak, A. B. (2006). Finding meaning in labor's "perfect storm": Lessons from the 1981 PATCO strike. *Employee Responsibilities and Rights Journal, 18*(3), 223-229.

Shulman, B., & Chiang, G. (2007). When to use an executive search firm and how to get the most out of the relationship. *Employment Relations Today, 34*(1), 13-19.

Siddique, C. M. (2004). Job analysis: A strategic human resource management practice. *International Journal of Human Resource Management, 15*(1), 219-244.

Silvestro, R. (2002). Dispelling the modern myth: Employee satisfaction and loyalty drive service profitability. *International Journal of Operations & Production Management, 22*(1), 30-49.

Simeon, R., & Fujiu, K. (2000). Cross-cultural adjustment strategies of Japanese spouses in Silicon Valley. *Employee Relations, 22*(6), 594-611.

Simon, H. A. (1979). Rational decision making in business organizations. *American Economic Review, 69*(4), 493-513.

Sinclair, U. (1988). *The jungle.* Urbana: University of Illinois Press.

Singh, P., & Finn, D. (2003). The effects of information technology on recruitment. *Journal of Labor Research, 24*(3), 395-408.

Singh, P., Zinni, D. M., & MacLennan, A. F. (2006). Graduate student unions in the United States. *Journal of Labor Research, 27*(1), 55-73.

Siniscalco, G. (1981). Affirmative Action Plan for the XYZ Company. *EEO Today, 8*(1), 73-90.

Skonberg, J., Notestine, K., & Sud, N. (2006, October 5). United States: Sharing compensation or benefit information between competitors may violate antitrust laws. *Mondaq Business Briefing*, 1-5.

Smith, A. (1976). *An inquiry into the nature and causes of the wealth of nations* (R. H. Campbell & A. S. Skinner, Eds.). Oxford, UK: Clarendon. (Original work published 1776)

Smith, C. (2005). Finding the "right people" just got easier. *Franchising World, 37*(11), 46-48.

Smith, P. C., & Kendall, L. M. (1963). Retranslation of expectations: An approach to the construction of unambiguous anchors for rating scales. *Journal of Applied Psychology, 47*(2), 149-155.

Snee, R. D. (1995). Listening to the voice of the employee. *Quality Progress, 28*(1), 91-95.

Snell, A. (2006). Researching onboarding best practice. *Strategic HR Review, 5*(6), 32-35.

Snyder, W., & Cummings, T. (1998). Organizational learning disorders: Conceptual model and intervention hypotheses. *Human Relations, 51*(7), 873-895.

Solomon, C. M. (1995). Global compensation: Learn the ABCs. *Personnel Journal, 74*(7), 70-76.

Sosnin, B. (2007). Filling spots at the top. *HR Magazine, 52*(10), 71-74.

Soutar, G. N., & Weaver, J. R. (1984). Biorhythm and the incidence of industrial accidents. *Journal of Safety Research, 14*(4), 167-172.

Spigener, J. (1995). Behavior-based safety training. *Occupational Hazards, 57*(9), 63-65.

Sproule, C. F., & Berkley, S. (2001). The selection of entry-level corrections officers: Pennsylvania research. *Public Personnel Management, 30*(3), 377-418.

Stahl, G. K., & Cerdin, J. (2004). Global careers in French and German multinational corporations. *Journal of Management Development, 23*(9), 885-902.

Stahl, G. K., Miller, E. L., & Tung, R. L. (2002). Toward the boundaryless career: A closer look at the expatriate career concept and the perceived implications of an international assignment. *Journal of World Business, 37*(3), 216-227.

Stamoulis, D. T., & Hauenstein, M. A. (1993). Rater training and rating accuracy: Training for dimensional accuracy versus training for ratee differentiation. *Journal of Applied Psychology, 78*(6), 994-1003.

Staudohar, P. D. (2005). The hockey lockout of 2004-05. *Monthly Labor Review, 128*(12), 23-29.

Stein, M. A. (2000). Labor markets, rationality, and workers with disabilities. *Berkeley Journal of Employment and Labor Law, 21*, 314-335.

Stein, E. J., Kruger, K. F., & Siegal, P. W. (1996). The role of human resources in supporting reengineering. *Health Care Supervisor, 15*(2), 8-16.

Stiffler, M. A. (2006). Incentive compensation management: making pay-for-performance a reality. *Performance Improvement, 45*(1), 25-30.

Stimpson, J. (2004). Recruiting via the web. *Practical Accountant, 37*(1), 26-30.

Stringer, D. M., Remick, H., Salisbury, J., & Ginorio, A. B. (1990). The power and reasons behind sexual harassment: An employer's guide to solutions. *Public Personnel Management, 19*(1), 43-52.

Stroh, L. K., & Caligiuri, P. M. (1998). Strategic human resources: A new source for competitive advantage in the global arena. *International Journal of Human Resource Management, 9*(1), 1-17.

Sundstrom, E., McIntyre, M., Halfhill, T., & Richards, H. (2000). Work groups: From the Hawthorne studies to work teams of the 1990s and beyond. *Group Dynamics: Theory, Research, and Practice, 4*(1), 44-67.

Sunoo, B. P. (1998). Top-10 ways employees disguise drug abuse. *Workforce, 77*(5), 16.

Sutton, R. I., & Louis, M. R. (1987). How selecting and socializing newcomers influences insiders. *Human Resources Management, 26*(3), 347-361.

Taghaboni-Dutta, F., & Velthouse, B. (2006). RFID technology is revolutionary: Who should be involved in this game of tag? *Academy of Management Perspectives, 20*(4), 65-78.

Tahan, S., & Kleiner, B. H. (2001). New developments concerning giving employment references. *Management Research News, 24*(3/4), 94-96.

Takeuchi, R., Tesluk, P. E., Yun, S., & Lepak, D. P. (2005). An integrative view of international experience. *Academy of Management Journal, 48*(1), 85-100.

Takeuchi, R., Yun, S., & Russell, J. E. A. (2002). Antecedents and consequences of the perceived adjustment of Japanese expatriates in the USA. *International Journal of Human Resource Management, 13*(8), 1224-1244.

Tan, C. S., & Salomone, P. R. (1994). Understanding career plateauing: Implications for counseling. *Career Development Quarterly, 42*(4), 291-302.

Tang, T. S., Hernandez, E. J., & Adams, B. S. (2004). "Learning by teaching": A peer-teaching model for diversity training in medical school. *Teaching and Learning in Medicine, 16*(1), 60-63.

Taylor, F. W. (1911). *The principles of scientific management*. New York: Harper & Bros.

Templer, K. J., Tay, C., & Chandrasekar, N. A. (2006). Motivational cultural intelligence, realistic job preview, realistic living conditions preview, and cross-cultural adjustment. *Group & Organization Management, 31*(1), 154.

Tett, R. P., Jackson, D. N., & Rothstein, M. (1991). Personality measures as predictors of job performance: A meta-analytic review. *Personnel Psychology, 44*(4), 703-742.

Thakor, M. V., & Joshi, A. W. (2005). Motivating salesperson customer orientation: Insights from the Job Characteristics Model. *Journal of Business Research, 58*(5), 584-592.

Thomas, K. M., & Wise, P. G. (1999). Organizational attractiveness and individual differences: Are diverse applicants attracted by different factors? *Journal of Business and Psychology, 13*(3), 375-390.

Thoms, P., Pinto, J. K., Parente, D. H., & Druskat, V. U. (2002). Adaptation to self-managing work teams. *Small Group Research, 33*(1), 3-31.

Thoresen, C. J., Bradley, J. C., Bliese, P. D., & Thoresen, J. D. (2004). The Big Five personality traits and individual job performance growth trajectories in maintenance and transitional job stages. *Journal of Applied Psychology, 89*(5), 835-853.

Thorsteinson, T. J., Palmer, E. M., Wulif, C., & Anderson, A. (2004). Too good to be true? Using realism to enhance applicant attraction. *Journal of Business & Psychology, 19*(1), 125-137.

Tilly, C. (1991). Reasons for the continuing growth of part-time employment. *Monthly Labor Review, 114*(3), 10-18.

Toland, M. (2005). A multilevel factor analysis of students' evaluations of teaching. *Educational and Psychological Measurement, 65*(2), 272-296.

Tomlinson, F., & Egan, S. (2002). Organizational sensemaking in a culturally diverse setting: Limits to the 'valuing diversity' discourse. *Management Learning, 33*(1), 79-97.

Tornow, W. (1976). The development of a managerial job taxonomy—a system for describing, classifying, and evaluating executive positions. *Journal of Applied Psychology, 61*(4), 410-418.

Torraco. R. J. (2005). Word design theory: A review and critique with implications for human resource development. *Human Resource Development Quarterly, 16*(1), 85-109.

Toyota Motor Manufacturing, Kentucky, Inc. v. Williams, 534 U.S. 184 (Supreme Court of the United States, 2002).

Traynor, T. L., & Fichtenbaum, R. H. (1997). The impact of post-PATCO labor relations on U.S. union wages. *Eastern Economic Journal, 23*(1), 61-72.

Tremblay, M., & Roger, A. (2004). Career plateauing reactions: The moderating role of job scope, role ambiguity and participation among Canadian managers. *International Journal of Human Resource Management, 15*(6), 996-1017.

Treven, S. (2006). Human resources management in the global environment. *Journal of American Academy of Business, Cambridge, 8*(1), 120-125.

Triandis, H. C. (2003). The future of workforce diversity in international organisations: A commentary. *Applied Psychology: An International Review, 52*(3), 486-495.

Troy, M. (2004). The writing on the wall reads RFID. *DSN Retailing Today, 43*(2), 36, 60, 66.

Tsui, A. S., & Gutek, B. A. (1984). A role set analysis of gender differences in performance, affective relationships, and career success of industrial middle managers. *Academy of Management Journal, 27*(3), 619-635.

Tuckman, B. W., & Jensen, A. C. (1977). Stages of small-group development revisited. *Group & Organization Studies, 2*(4), 419-427.

Tung, R. L. (1981). Selection and training of personnel for overseas assignments. *Columbia Journal of World Business, 16*(1), 21-25.

Tung, R. L. (1982). Selection and training procedures of U.S., European, and Japanese multinationals. *California Management Review, 25*(1), 57-71.

Tung, R. L. (1983). Selection and training procedures of U.S., European, and Japanese multinationals. *California Management Review, 25*(1), 57-71.

Tung, R. L. (1987). Expatriate assignments: Enhancing success and minimizing failure. *Academy of Management Executive, 1*(2), 117-126.

Tung, R. L. (2001). A contingency framework of selection and training of expatriates revisited. *Human Resources Management Review, 8*(1), 23-37.
Turban, D. B., & Dougherty, T. W. (1992). Influences of campus recruiting on applicant attraction to firms. *Academy of Management Journal, 35*(4), 739-765.
Turban, D. B., Eyring, A. R., & Campion, J. E. (1993). Job attributes: Preferences compared with reasons given for accepting and rejecting job offers. *Journal of Occupational and Organizational Psychology, 66*(1), 71-81.
Turban, D. B., & Keon, T. L. (1993). Organizational attractiveness: An interactionist perspective. *Journal of Applied Psychology, 78*(2), 184-193.
Tyler, K. (2006). Retaining repatriates. *HR Magazine, 51*(3), 97-102.
Ulrich, D. (1997). *Human resource champions: The next agenda for adding value and delivering results.* Boston: Harvard Business School Press.
Ulrich, D., Brockbank, W., Yeung, A. K., & Lake, D. G. (1995). Human resource competencies: An empirical assessment. *Human Resource Management, 34*(4), 473-495.
Umble, M., & Whitten, B. J. (1977). The significant dimensions of teaching behavior and their relative importance for instructor evaluations. *Educational and Psychological Measurement, 37*(4), 1023-1030.
Underwood, E. (1994). Disney charts course to sail into cruises. *Brandweek, 35*(6), 1, 6.
United Steelworkers of America v. Weber, 443 U.S. 193 (Supreme Court of the United States, 1979).
University of California Regents v. Bakke, 438 U.S. 265 (U.S. Supreme Court, 1978).
U.S. Census. (2000). Table DP-1: Profile of general demographic characteristics. http://censtats.census.gov/data/US/01000.pdf
U.S. Census. (2006). Table 2: Labor force status—work disability status of civilians 16 to 74 Years Old, by educational attainment and sex. http://www.census.gov/hhes/www/disability/cps/cps206.xls
U.S. Department of Labor. (1991). *Dictionary of occupational titles.* www.oalj.dol.gov/libdot.htm
U.S. Department of Labor. (2004). *Sample Affirmative Action Plan.* http://www.dol.gov/esa/ofccp/regs/compliance/pdf/sampleaap.pdf
U.S. Department of Labor. (2005, October 7). *Obligation to solicit race and gender data for agency enforcement purposes; Final rule. 41 CFR Part 60-1.* http://www.dol.gov/esa/regs/fedreg/final/2005020176.pdf
U.S. Department of Labor. (2006). *Strategic plan: Fiscal years 2006-2011.* http://www.dol.gov/_sec/stratplan/strat_plan_2006-2011.pdf
U.S. Department of Labor. (n.d.). *Compliance assistance, wages and hours worked: Overtime.* http://www.dol.gov/compliance/topics/wages-overtime-pay.htm
U.S. Equal Employment Opportunity Commission. (1978). *Uniform guidelines on employee selection procedures.* http://www.access.gpo.gov/nara/cfr/waisidx_03/29cfr1607_03.html
U.S. Equal Employment Opportunity Commission. (1979). Affirmative Action appropriate under Title VII of the Civil Rights Act of 1964, as Amended. http://www.access.gpo.gov/nara/cfr/waisidx_03/29cfr1608_03.html
U.S. Equal Employment Opportunity Commission. (1999, March 1). *Small employers and reasonable accommodation.* http://www.eeoc.gov/facts/accommodation.html

U.S. Equal Employment Opportunity Commission. (2005). *The ADA: Your responsibilities as an employer.* http://www.eeoc.gov/facts/ada17.html

U.S. Equal Employment Opportunity Commission. (2006, January). *EEO-1 report, instruction booklet.* http://www.eeoc.gov/eeo1/instruction_rev_2006.pdf

U.S. Equal Employment Opportunity Commission. (2006, May 9). *Title VII/ADEA pre-employment inquiries.* http://www.eeoc.gov/foia/letters/2006/titlevii_adea_preemployment_inquiries.html

U.S. Equal Employment Opportunity Commission. (2007, May 17). *Disability discrimination.* http://www.eeoc.gov/types/ada.html

U.S. Equal Employment Opportunity Commission. (2007). *EEO surveys.* http://www.eeoc.gov/employers/surveys.html

U.S. Equal Employment Opportunity Commission. (2008). *Sexual harassment charges EEOC & FEPAs Combined: FY 1997–FY 2007.* http://www.eeoc.gov/stats/harass.html

U.S. General Accounting Office. (1990, January). *Persons with disabilities: Reports on costs of accommodations. GAO/IiRD-9044BR.* http://archive.gao.gov/d27t7/140318.pdf

Usry, M. L., & White, M. (2000). Multicultural awareness in small businesses. *Business Forum, 25*(1-2), 10-13.

Usselman, S. W. (1984). Air brakes for freight trains: Technological innovation in the American railroad industry 1869-1900. *Business History Review, 58*(1), 30-50.

van der Hek, H., & Plomp, H. N. (1997). Occupational stress management programmes: A practical overview of published effect studies. *Occupational Medicine, 47*(3), 133-141.

Van der Zee, K. I., Bakker, A. B., & Bakker, P. (2002). Why are structured interviews so rarely used in personnel selection? *Journal of Applied Psychology, 87*(1), 176-184.

Van Iddekinge, C. H., Sager, C. E., Burnfield, J. L., & Heffner, T. S. (2006). The variability of criterion-related validity estimates among interviewers and interview panels. *International Journal of Selection and Assessment, 14*(3), 193-205.

Varma, S., & Collins, B. M. (2007). On ramp to success at Network Appliance. *T + D, 61*(7), 59-61.

Vasilash, G. S. (1995). Chrysler New Castle: How to go from near extinction to world class. *Production, 107*(1), 56-59.

Veiga, J. F. (1981). Plateaued versus nonplateaued managers: Career patterns, attitudes, and path potential. *Academy of Management Journal, 24*(3), 566-578.

Veres, J. G., III, Lahey, M. A., & Buckly, R. (1987). A practical rationale for using multi-method job analysis. *Public Personnel Management, 16*(2), 153-157.

Vickers, M. H., & Parris, M. A. (2007). "Your job no longer exists!": From experiences of alienation to expectations of resilience—A phenomenological study. *Employee Responsibilities and Rights Journal, 19*(2), 113-125.

Victor, B., Boynton, A., & Stephens-Jahng, T. (2000). The effective design of work under Total Quality Management. *Organization Science, 11*(1), 102-117.

Vinchur, A. J., Schippman, J. S., Switzer, F. S., III., & Roth, P. L. (1998). A meta-analytic review of predictors of job performance for salespeople. *Journal of Applied Psychology, 83*(4), 586-597.

Vodanovich, S. J., & Lowe, R. H. (1992). They ought to know better: The incidence and correlates of inappropriate application blank inquiries. *Public Personnel Management, 21*(3), 363-370.

Von Bergen, C. W., Soper, B., & Foster, T. (2002). Unintended negative effects of diversity management. *Public Personnel Management, 31*(2), 239-251.

Waldman, J. D., Kelly, F., Arora, S., & Smith, H. L. (2004). The shocking cost of turnover in health care. *Health Care Management Review, 29*(1), 2-7.

Wallace, J. C., Tye, M. G., & Vodanovich, S. J. (2000). Applying for jobs online: Examining the legality of Internet-based application forms. *Public Personnel Management, 29*(4), 497-504.

Walters, D. (2000). Employee representation on health and safety and European Works Councils. *Industrial Relations Journal, 31*(5), 416-436.

Wanek, J. E., Sackett, P. R., Ones, D. S., & Deniz, S. (2003). Towards an understanding of integrity test similarities and differences: An item-level analysis of seven tests. *Personnel Psychology, 56*(4), 873-894.

Wang, Y., & Kleiner, B. H. (2005). Defining employee dishonesty. *Management Research News, 28*(2/3), 11-22.

Wanous, J. P. (1973). Effects of a realistic job preview on job acceptance, job attitudes, and job survival. *Journal of Applied Psychology, 58*(3), 327-332.

Watad, M., & Ospina, S. (1999). Integrated managerial training: A program for strategic management development. *Public Personnel Management, 28*(2), 185-196.

Weisner, W. H., & Cronshaw, S. F. (1988). A meta-analytic investigation of the impact of interview format and degree of structure on the validity of the employment interview. *Journal of Occupational Psychology, 61*(4), 275-290.

Welch, D. E., Welch, L. S., & Worm, V. (2007). The international business traveler: A neglected but strategic human resource. *International Journal of Human Resource Management, 18*(2), 173-184.

Wells, S. J. (2001). Is the ADA working? *HR Magazine, 46*(4), 38-46.

Wells, S. J. (2003). Slow times for executive recruiting. *HR Magazine, 48*(4), 61-68.

Wendt, A. C., & Slonaker, W. M. (2002). Sexual harassment and retaliation: A double-edged sword. *S.A.M. Advanced Management Journal, 67*(4), 49-57.

Whicker, L. M., & Andrews, K. M. (2004). HRM in the knowledge economy: Realising the potential. *Asia Pacific Journal of Human Resources, 42*(2), 156-165.

Wiesner, W. H., & Cronshaw, S. F. (1988). A meta-analytic investigation of the impact of interview format and degree of structure on the validity of the employment interview. *Journal of Occupational Psychology, 61*(4), 275-290.

Wiley, C. (1992). Recruitment research revisited: Effective recruiting methods according to employment outcomes. *Journal of Applied Business Research, 8*(2), 74-79.

Wiley, J. W., Brooks, S. M., & Lundby, K. M. (2006). Put your employees on the other side of the microscope. *Human Resource Planning, 29*(2), 15-21.

Wilkinson, A. (2005). Downsizing, rightsizing or dumbsizing? Quality, human resources and the management of sustainability. *Total Quality Management, 16*(8/9), 1079-1088.

Williams, C. R., Labig, C. E., Jr., & Stone, T. H. (1993). Recruitment sources and posthire outcomes for job applicants and new hires: A test of two hypotheses. *Journal of Applied Psychology, 78*(2), 163-172.

Winstein, K. J., & Golden, D. (2007, April 27). MIT admissions dean lied on resume in 1979, quits. *Wall Street Journal*, p. B1.

Witlin, S. J., & Sloane, J. (2003). The Supreme Court's recent Affirmative Action decisions may provide some guidance for the workplace. *Employment Relations Today, 30*(3), 85-90.

Woehr, D. J. (2003). The construct-related validity of assessment center ratings: A review and meta-analysis of the role of methodological factors. *Journal of Management, 29*(2), 231-258.

Woehr, D. J., & Huffcutt, A. I. (1994). Rater training for performance appraisal: A quantitative review. *Journal of Occupational and Organizational Psychology, 67*, 189-205.

Wojcik, J. (1998). PEOs don't eliminate employer's risks. *Business Insurance, 32*(19), 21.

Wolcott, J. H., McMeekin, R. B., Burgin, R. E., & Yanowitch, R. E. (1977). Correlation of general aviation accidents with biorhythm theory. *Human Factors, 19*(3), 283-293.

Wong-MingJi, D. J., & Millette, W. R. (2002). Dealing with the dynamic duo of innovation and inertia: The "In-" theory of organizational change. *Organizational Development Journal, 20*(1), 36-52.

Woodruff, C. (2006). Coaching: A powerful catalyst for transforming performance. *Training & Development Methods, 20*(2), 401-406.

Woodward, N. H. (2006). Make the most of team building. *HR Magazine, 51*(9), 72-76.

Worley, C. G., & Lawler, E. E., III. (2006). Designing organizations that are built to change. *MIT Sloan Management Review, 48*(1), 19-26.

Worman, D. (2005, May 17). Is there a business case for diversity? *Personnel Today*, pp. 27-28.

Woska, W. J. (2007). Legal issues for HR professionals: Reference checking/background investigations. *Public Personnel Management, 36*(1), 79-89.

Wouk, M., & Cardenas, E. L. (2003, October 14). Resume claims ensnare Duchane; Politicians demand resignation of Sterling Heights manager who cited nonexistent U-M degree. *Detroit News.*

Wright, P. M., Lichtenfels, P. A., & Pursell, E. D. (1989). The structured interview: Additional studies and a meta-analysis. *Journal of Occupational Psychology, 62*(3), 191-199.

Wright, T. (1999). Systems Thinking and systems practice: Working in the Fifth Dimension. *Systemic Practice and Action Research, 12*(6), 607-631.

Wyld, D. C. (1997). Recruit@internet.com: The Internet and the future of corporate recruiting. *Equal Opportunities International, 16*(2), 15-24.

Yamazaki, Y., & Kayes, D. C. (2007). Expatriate learning: Exploring how Japanese managers adapt in the United States. *International Journal of Human Resource Management, 18*(8), 1373-1395.

Yeo, R. K. (2005). Revisiting the roots of the learning organization: A synthesis of the learning organization literature. *The Learning Organization, 12*(4), 368-382.

York, K. M. (2002). Disparate results in adverse impact tests: The 4/5ths Rule and the chi square test. *Public Personnel Management, 31*(2), 253-262.

York, K. M., Strubler, D. C., & Smith, E. M. (2005). A comparison of two methods for scoring an In-Basket exercise. *Public Personnel Management, 34*(3), 271-282.

Zachary, M. (2002). Supreme Court clarifies ADA manual task guidelines. *Supervision, 63*(4), 22-25.

Zackrison, R. E. (2003). Some reasons why consulting interventions fail. *Organization Development Journal, 21*(1), 72-74.

Zaugg, R. J., & Thom, N. (2003). Excellence through implicit competencies: Human resource management—organizational development—knowledge creation. *Journal of Change Management, 3*(3), 199-211.

Zubrin, R. (1996). *The case for Mars.* New York: Free Press.

Index

About the Author

Kenneth M. York received his PhD in industrial and organizational psychology from Bowling Green State University, and is a professor of management in the School of Business Administration, Oakland University, in Rochester, Michigan. His research interests are in applied research problems in human resources management and the creation of experiential learning exercises for the development of management skills. He teaches courses in organizational behavior, human resources management, and motivation, and has consulted in equal employment opportunity cases. Recent research projects have examined enterprise systems training, satisfaction with union representation, group decision making, alternate scoring methods for an in-basket exercise, evaluation of a client- and consultant-based management education program, an exploratory study of the Team Characteristics Model, competitive intelligence processes in the health care industry, and the impact of Total Quality Management methods on the financial success of a firm. His research has been published in *Journal of Operations Management*, *International Journal of Business Information Systems*, *Journal of Collective Negotiations*, *Public Personnel Management*, *Organizational Behavior and Human Decision Processes*, *Journal of the Academy of Business Education*, *Journal of Education for Business*, *Journal of Management Education*, *Small Group Research*, and *Academy of Management Journal*.